KB212987

Theodao (Theology of Dao) II:
Advancing K-Theology in the Anthropocene

**Theodao (Theology of Dao) II:**
**Advancing K-Theology in the Anthropocene**

First published on May 16, 2025

| | |
|---|---|
| Author | Heup Young KIM |
| Publisher | Young Ho Kim |
| Published by | Dong-yeon Press |
| Registration | No. 1-1383 (June 12, 1992) |
| Address | 163-3 World Cup-ro, Mapo-gu, Seoul, South Korea |
| Phone | +82-2-335-2630 |
| Fax | +82-2-335-2640 |
| Email | yh4321@gmail.com |
| Instagram | https://instagram.com/dony-yeon-press |

ISBN 978-89-6447-084-8  93200 (pbk.)
ISBN 978-89-6447-085-5  93200 (e-book)

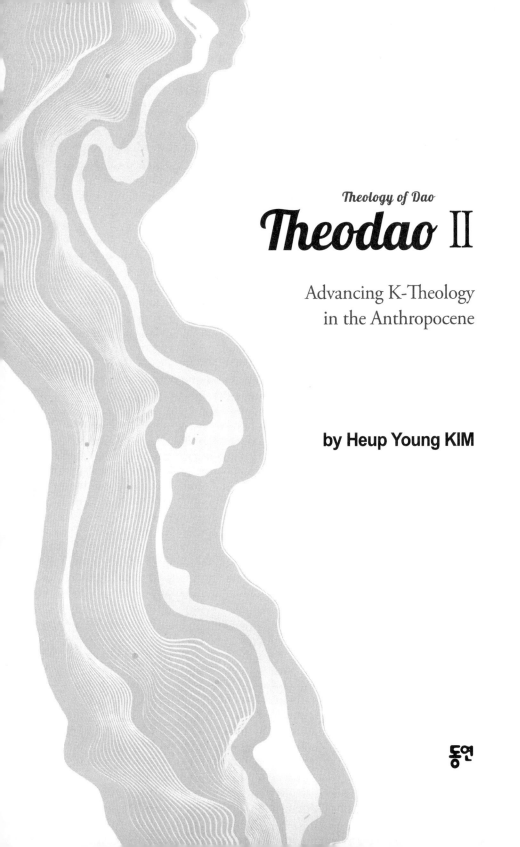

*Theology of Dao*

# *Theodao* II

## Advancing K-Theology
## in the Anthropocene

### by Heup Young KIM

동연

To those the servants of Christ
and stewards of God's mysteries,
required to be trustworthy
(1 Cor 4:1-2)


그리스도의 일꾼이요
하나님의 비밀을 맡은 이들과
충성을 소명으로 받은 이들에게
(고전 4:1-2)

# Preface

In an era marked by unprecedented ecological upheaval, rapid technological advancement, and a growing awareness of cultural plurality, theology is compelled to respond with renewed vigor and creativity. This book, *Theodao (Theology of Dao) II: Advancing K-Theology in the Anthropocene*, continues my journey of exploring the intersections of Eastern and Western thought, particularly through the lens of Theodao (Theology of Dao)—an integration of theology with Confucian and Daoian Wisdom.

This volume is a collection of essays written after my retirement, building upon the foundations laid in my previous work, *Theology of Dao* (Orbis Books, 2017). While that book contains essential content on Theodao, the essays included here are new explorations that extend the dialogue into fresh territories. Notably, the contents from *Theology of Dao* are intentionally excluded to focus on these new contributions.

Most of the essays in this collection were penned before the advent of large language models like ChatGPT. They represent a period of reflection and scholarship unmediated by artificial intelligence, capturing thoughts and analyses formed through traditional research and contemplative practices. This temporal context adds a unique dimension to the work, situating it at the cusp of significant technological shifts that are themselves subjects of theological inquiry within these pages.

## Purpose and Scope

This volume is organized into four thematic parts, each addressing the critical concerns of our time through the integrative lens of Theodao and Korean Theology (K-Theology):

### Part 1: Ecodao in an Age of Ecological Crisis

This part addresses the urgent ecological crisis facing our world. By integrating ecological consciousness from Daoism, Confucianism, and Christian theology, it proposes Ecodao—an ecological theology that emphasizes harmony between humanity and nature. The chapters explore the anthropocosmic vision of East Asian thought, the concept of Dao as a guiding principle for ecological theology and offer a Theodaoian perspective on creation.

### Part 2: Technodao in an Age of Transhumanism and Artificial Intelligence

Delving into the complex implications of technological advancements, this part introduces Technodao as an ethical framework. It critically examines the promises and perils of transhumanism and artificial intelligence, drawing upon East Asian wisdom to offer nuanced perspectives. The chapters challenge the transhumanist pursuit of immortality, explore contrasting visions of human advancement between transhumanism and Confucianism, propose a new humanism responsive to the AI age, and integrate East Asian wisdom into AI ethics.

### Part 3: Theodao in a Global Polyphonic Age of Decolonization

This part expands the discourse to a global context, addressing the impact of Western theological colonialism and advocating for the decolonization of theological thought. It emphasizes the necessity of embracing diverse epistemologies and fostering interreligious dialogue. The chapters reflect on developing Theodao through Confucian-Christian dialogue, explore Dao as a hermeneutical lens for biblical interpretation, and delve into Theodaoian epistemology in the global age of decolonization.

Part 4: Korean Cosmic Spirituality and K-Theology

Focusing on Korean spiritual disciplines and theological thought, this part introduces the works of Korean theologians like Dasŏk Ryu Yŏngmo and Kim Yong-bok. It highlights their contributions to a trans-cosmic and trans-religious spirituality that offers profound insights into contemporary faith practice. The chapters provide introductions to their thought, translations and commentaries on their works, and explore the revival of Minjung Theology in the technological era.

The Appendix: Theodao in Critical Making — Retrieved

This part includes earlier works that lay the groundwork for the themes discussed in the main sections. These essays bridge science and religion, explore hospitality in the Asian context, and critically engage with theological figures like Paul Tillich and movements like Boston Confucianism.

Acknowledgments

I am deeply grateful to the numerous scholars, colleagues, and institutions that have supported my work over the years. Special thanks to President Young-ho Kim and the editors of Dongyeon Publishing. Their collaboration has been invaluable in bringing this collection together.

### Intended Audience

This book is intended for theologians, philosophers, scholars of religion, seminarians, and anyone interested in the intersection of Eastern and Western thought. It aims to be accessible to readers from diverse backgrounds while offering profound insights into complex theological issues.

### A Journey of Discovery

Compiling this volume has been a journey of reflection and discovery. Revisiting these essays allowed me to recognize the threads that weave through my work—a commitment to integrating ecological consciousness, technological ethics, spiritual depth, and cultural diversity into a coherent theological vision.

This collection intentionally focuses on advancing the conversation beyond previously established ideas by excluding the contents from *Theology of Dao* (2017). It seeks to explore new dimensions of Theodao in response to the evolving challenges of the Anthropocene.

### A Temporal Context

Writing these essays before the emergence of advanced AI language models like ChatGPT adds a layer of historical context to this work. The perspectives offered herein are rooted in a time when human scholarship was less influenced by artificial intelligence, a factor particularly relevant given the discussions on technology and transhumanism in Part 2. This temporal positioning provides a contrast between the human contemplative process and the burgeoning influence of AI on thought and communication.

### Invitation to Dialogue

I invite you, the reader, to join me in this exploration. Let us engage in a dialogue that transcends boundaries, challenges assumptions, and seeks wisdom from all corners of human experience. Together, we can envision and enact a theology attuned to the rhythms of the Earth, the complexities of technology, and the rich tapestry of global cultures.

In the face of global challenges, I believe theology must be dynamic, inclusive, and responsive. By engaging with the wisdom of Confucianism, Daoism, and Korean theology, we can enrich global theological discourse and contribute to a more compassionate and sustainable world.

Heup Young KIM
Seoul, November 3, 2024

# Contents

## PART III
## Theodao in a Global Polyphonic Age of Decolonization

## PART IV
## Korean Cosmic Spirituality and K-Theology

# APPENDIX
## Theodao in Critical Making—Retrieved

# Introduction:
# Overviews of Parts and Chapters

**PART ONE: Ecodao in an Age of Ecological Crisis**

The first part of this book, "Ecodao in an Age of Ecological Crisis," addresses one of the most urgent issues of our time: the current ecological crisis. Through the lens of Theodao—an integration of Christian theology with Daoian and Confucian thought—this section explores the profound relationship between humanity and nature, emphasizing the imperative for ecological consciousness and sustainable living.

CHAPTER One: "Theodao: Integrating Ecological Consciousness in Daoism, Confucianism, and Christian Theology"

This chapter lays the foundation for the exploration of Ecodao. It examines how the anthropocosmic vision inherent in East Asian thought—with its emphasis on the interconnectedness of Heaven, Earth, and Humanity—offers a more holistic and balanced perspective compared to the often-anthropocentric worldview prevalent in Western thought. The chapter advocates for a paradigm shift in Christian theology by highlighting the shortcomings of a human-cen-

tered approach. It proposes integrating Daoist and Confucian principles to foster a deeper understanding of ecological issues and to promote a more sustainable relationship with the natural world.

CHAPTER Two: "Ecodao: An Ecological Theology of Dao"

Building upon the groundwork laid in the previous chapter, this
chapter delves deeper into the concept of Dao as a guiding principle
for ecological theology. It introduces Ecodao, a new paradigm that
leverages Dao's inherent ecological ontology, cosmology, and spirituality to construct a theology that is both life-affirming and environmentally conscious. The chapter explores the concept of the
Great Ultimate (Taiji) as an onto-cosmology emphasizing the complementarity of opposites (yin and yang) and the interconnectedness of all beings. It also highlights the significance of $qi$ (ki/chi)
as the metacosmic energy flowing through all living things, connecting them in a web of interdependence. By embracing these concepts, the chapter outlines a framework for an ecological theology
deeply rooted in nature's rhythms and cycles.

CHAPTER Three: "Creation and Dao: A Theodaoian Perspective"

This chapter examines the Daoian view of cosmogony and its
implications for the Christian doctrine of creation. It explores the
concept of non-being (wu) as the origin of all things, emphasizing
that creation emerges from an unmanifested source. The chapter
discusses the complementary nature of chaos (hundun) and cosmos, suggesting that disorder and order are intrinsically linked in
the unfolding of the universe. It also introduces the preferential option for yin, highlighting the paradoxical power of weakness, empti-

ness, and receptivity. By challenging traditional Christian understandings of creation that often prioritize being over non-being and
cosmos over chaos, the chapter invites a re-evaluation of the role
of emptiness, the importance of interconnectedness, and the dynamic interplay of yin and yang in the universe.

## Summary

Collectively, these three chapters offer a comprehensive introduction to the concept of Ecodao and its potential to address
the ecological crisis. They challenge traditional theological and philosophical perspectives by proposing a new framework for understanding the relationship between humanity and nature—one that
is grounded in the wisdom of East Asian traditions. By integrating
Daoian and Confucian insights with Christian theology, this section
underscores the urgent need for ecological consciousness. It offers
innovative pathways toward a more sustainable and harmonious
coexistence with the natural world, emphasizing that true ecological
balance can be achieved by embracing interconnectedness, complementarity, and the intrinsic value of all forms of life.

## PART II: Technodao in an Age of Transhumanism and Artificial Intelligence

The second part of this book, "Technodao in an Age of Transhumanism and Artificial Intelligence," delves into the complex and
rapidly evolving realm of technology, exploring its profound implications for the future of humanity. Through the integrative lens
of Theodao, this section critically examines the promises and perils

of transhumanism and artificial intelligence(AI), offering a nuanced perspective enriched by the wisdom of Daoism and Confucianism.

CHAPTER Four: "Death and Immortality: Biological and K-Religious Reflections on Transhumanism"

This chapter challenges the transhumanist pursuit of immortality, arguing that it is scientifically unfounded and overlooks the essential role of death in the cycle of life. It examines the biological processes of aging and dying, highlighting their evolutionary significance and their integration within East Asian religious thought. By critiquing the transhumanist desire to conquer death, the chapter emphasizes the importance of accepting mortality and embracing the inter-connectedness of life and death as fundamental to the human experience.

CHAPTER Five: "Advancing Humanity: Artificial Intelligence, Trans- humanism, and Confucianism"

Here, the contrasting visions of human advancement offered by transhumanism and Confucianism are explored. While trans-humanism seeks to enhance human capabilities through technology—aiming for superintelligence and immortality—Confucianism focuses on the cultivation of virtue and wisdom through self-improvement and moral development. This chapter critically examines the transhumanist pursuit of technological enhancement, cautioning against its potential dangers and unintended consequences. It advocates for a more balanced approach that integrates technological advancements with ethical considerations and the cultivation of human values rooted in Confucian thought.

CHAPTER Six: "New Humanism in the Age of Artificial Intelligence: A Theodaoian Reflection"

This chapter proposes a new humanism that responds to the challenges and opportunities presented by the AI age. It critiques the technocratic paradigm that prioritizes technological advancement at the expense of environmental sustainability and moral responsibility. By examining the nuances of post-humanism and transhumanism, the chapter highlights their limitations and advocates for a more inclusive humanism. Drawing upon Theodao, it emphasizes the interconnectedness of all life and the necessity of fostering harmony between humanity and nature amidst technological progress.

CHAPTER Seven: "Integrating East Asian Wisdom in AI Ethics: A Theodaoian Critique of the 'Encountering AI' Document"

This chapter explores the integration of East Asian wisdom into AI ethics, offering a cross-cultural critique of the "Encountering AI" document. It highlights the limitations of Western ethical frameworks that often prioritize individual rights and regulatory control, advocating instead of a Theodaoian approach that emphasizes relational personhood, virtue ethics, and ecological harmony. By providing practical case studies, the chapter demonstrates how these principles can be applied to contemporary challenges in AI development, promoting a more holistic and responsible approach to technological innovation.

Summary

Collectively, these four chapters provide a comprehensive analysis of the ethical and philosophical implications of transhumanism and AI. By integrating the wisdom of East Asian traditions with the urgent concerns of our technological age, this section challenges us to rethink our relationship with technology. It advocates for a more balanced and harmonious approach that fosters human flourishing, ecological sustainability, and the cultivation of virtue. The chapters urge a reorientation of technological development in alignment with Theodaoian principles, emphasizing that true advancement lies not merely in technological prowess but in the ethical and spiritual growth of humanity.

## PART III: Theodao in a Global Polyphonic Age of Decolonization

The third part of this book, "Theodao in a Global Polyphonic Age of Decolonization," expands the discourse to a global context, addressing the impact of Western theological colonialism on Korea and other East Asian nations. It advocates for the decolonization of theological thought and the recognition of diverse epistemologies. Through the lens of Theodao, this section explores how integrating East Asian wisdom traditions can contribute to a more inclusive and polyphonic global theological discourse, particularly in addressing the challenges of the Anthropocene era.

CHAPTER Eight: "Theodao Through Confucian-Christian Dialogue: Addressing Theological Challenges in the Anthropocene" This chapter reflects on the author's journey in developing Theodao through dialogues between Confucianism and Christianity. It summarizes key dialogues between theologians such as Karl Barth and Confucian philosopher Wang Yang-ming, and between John

Calvin and Korean Neo-Confucian Yi T'oegye, highlighting the profound resemblances between these seemingly disparate traditions. Challenging the either-or perspective prevalent in Western theologies of religions, the chapter advocates for the legitimacy of dual religious belonging. It argues that East Asian theology should adopt a thematic approach, integrating the Christian faith with the Confucian milieu to address the theological challenges posed by AI and transhumanism in the Anthropocene.

CHAPTER Nine: "Biblical Readings on a Theology of Dao"

This chapter explores the concept of Dao as a hermeneutical lens for interpreting the Bible, particularly for Koreans and East Asians. It posits that Dao, embodying the unity of knowing and acting, is a more appropriate root metaphor for theology than the historically dominant Logos. The chapter examines how the concept of Dao has been utilized in Korean biblical interpretation throughout history, highlighting the works of indigenous Korean Christian thinkers. It suggests several approaches for constructing a Korean biblical hermeneutics of Dao, emphasizing the importance of contextual literacy, hermeneutics of retrieval, and multiple textual hermeneutics. By doing so, it seeks to bridge the gap between Eastern philosophies and Christian theology, fostering a more culturally resonant theological understanding.

CHAPTER Ten: "Theodaoian Epistemology in the Global Age of Decolonization"

This chapter delves into the concept of Theodaoian epistemology, which seeks to decolonize knowledge and integrate indigenous Korean and East Asian epistemologies into contemporary theological discourse. It examines the impact of theological colonialism on Korea, highlighting how indigenous knowledge systems have been marginalized or erased. The chapter introduces metaphors such as Ugeumchi (small fish swimming upstream) to represent resilience and the reawakening of suppressed knowledge. It discusses the significance of *Qi* (*Ki*) epistemology and Taiji (*T'aeguk*) —the Great Ultimate—in promoting a holistic and interconnected worldview. Additionally, it explores the feminine epistemology of Dao, emphasizing the power of return and the subversive wisdom of nature. By integrating these concepts, the chapter advocates for a more inclusive and diverse theological epistemology that challenges Western hegemony.

### Summary

Collectively, these three chapters provide a comprehensive exploration of Theodao's potential to contribute to a global polyphonic age of decolonization. They challenge the dominance of Western theological thought, advocating for the recognition and integration of diverse epistemologies and indigenous knowledge systems. By drawing upon the rich wisdom of East Asian traditions, this section offers a unique and valuable perspective on the theological and philosophical challenges of our times, especially in addressing the complexities of the Anthropocene. The chapters encourage a shift toward a more inclusive, dialogical, and holistic approach to theology that honors the multiplicity of human experiences and cultural contexts.

## PART IV: Korean Cosmic Spirituality and K-Theology

The final part, "Korean Cosmic Spirituality and K-Theology," delves into the rich and often overlooked traditions of Korean spirituality, exploring their potential contributions to global theological discourse. This section examines the works of two prominent Korean thinkers, Dasŏk Ryu Yŏngmo and Kim Yong-bok, highlighting their unique insights into the interconnectedness of life, the importance of ecological consciousness, and the challenges posed by the Anthropocene era.

CHAPTER Eleven: "Introducing Dasŏk Ryu Yŏngmo's Korean Spiritual Disciplines and His Poem 'Being a Christian'"
This chapter offers an introduction to the life and thought of Dasŏk Ryu Yŏngmo, a significant yet understudied Korean Christian thinker. It explores Dasŏk's integration of indigenous Korean spiritual resources from Confucian, Daoist, and Buddhist traditions to contextualize Christianity within a multi-religious Korean context. The chapter examines Dasŏk's concept of "playing rituals in harmony with the emptiness together," highlighting his unique approach to Christian spirituality. It also analyzes his poem "Being a Christian," which encapsulates his synthesis of various spiritual traditions and his emphasis on living in harmony with the cosmos.

CHAPTER Twelve: "Dasŏk Ryu Yŏngmo's Korean Trans-Cosmic and Trans-Religious Spirituality: A Translation and Commentary on 'Spiritual Hiking'"
This chapter provides an original translation and commentary

on Dasŏk's prayer "Spiritual Hiking." It delves into his spiritual principle of "playing rituals in harmony with the emptiness together,"
emphasizing its trans-cosmic and trans-religious dimensions. The
chapter examines how Dasŏk integrates East Asian spiritual practices with Christian themes, offering insights into his understanding
of the interconnectedness of life, the significance of breath and body
in spiritual cultivation, and the pursuit of harmony between humanity and the cosmos. By analyzing "Spiritual Hiking," the chapter illuminates Dasŏk's vision of a spirituality that transcends religious
boundaries and resonates with universal human experiences.

CHAPTER Thirteen: "Reviving Minjung Theology in the
Technological Era: Kim Yong-bok's Seontopian Zoesophia in
Dialogue with Theodao"

This chapter explores Kim Yong-bok's final reflections on
Minjung Theology, a prominent Korean theological movement that
emerged in the 1970s. It examines Kim's concepts of Seontopia (an
East Asian Utopia) and Zoesophia (Wisdom of Life), highlighting
their potential to address the challenges posed by the burgeoning
evolution of artificial intelligence and the Anthropocene era. The
chapter investigates the interconnectedness between Minjung
Theology and Theodao, advocating for the integration of indigenous Korean and East Asian spiritual resources to foster a more
holistic and life-affirming theological paradigm. It emphasizes the
relevance of Kim's thought in navigating the ethical and existential
dilemmas of the technological age.

## Summary

Collectively, these three chapters offer a comprehensive exploration of Korean cosmic spirituality and its potential contributions to global theological discourse. They highlight the unique insights of Korean thinkers who have navigated the complexities of multiple religious traditions, offering nuanced perspectives on the interconnectedness of life, the importance of ecological consciousness, and the challenges posed by the Anthropocene era. By drawing upon the rich spiritual heritage of Korea, this section contributes valuable insights to the ongoing dialogue between East Asian and Western thought, advocating for a more inclusive and polyphonic global theological discourse. It underscores the significance of integrating indigenous spiritual traditions in addressing contemporary global challenges and enriching the collective understanding of spirituality and theology.

## APPENDIX: Theodao in Critical Making — Retrieved

This appendix presents a collection of reflections and critical engagement essays that further illuminate the concept of Theodao and its implications for various facets of human life and thought. These essays delve into specific dialogues and critiques, offering insights into the ongoing process of constructing and refining a theological framework that integrates the wisdom of East Asian traditions with the challenges of the contemporary world.

Appendix One: "The Sciences and the Religions: Some Preliminary East Asian Reflections on Christian Theology of Nature"

This essay examines the relationship between science and religion, critiquing the prevalent Western-centric approach and advocating for a more inclusive dialogue that incorporates perspectives from non-Christian religions, particularly those of East Asia. It challenges the metaphor of "building bridges" between science and religion, arguing that such a notion can obscure the deep, intrinsic connections between these realms in East Asian thought. By exploring the harmonious interplay between scientific inquiry and spiritual understanding inherent in traditions like Daoism and Confucianism, the essay calls for a re-envisioned Christian theology of nature that is open to intercultural insights and acknowledges the interconnectedness of all things.

Appendix Two: "Embracing and Embodying God's Hospitality Today in Asia"

This essay explores the concept of hospitality as a central theme in Christian theology within an Asian context. It challenges traditional understandings of hospitality by calling for a more inclusive and self-critical approach that recognizes the diversity of Asian cultures and religions. Emphasizing the importance of repentance and self-emptying (kenosis) as prerequisites for genuine hospitality, the essay draws upon the example of Jesus Christ and the insights of Asian theologians. It advocates for a hospitality practice that transcends mere tolerance, fostering deep mutual understanding and solidarity among different faiths and cultures. The essay underscores the need for the Christian community to embody God's hospitality by engaging authentically with the religious "other" in a spirit of humility and openness.

Appendix Three: "Paul Tillich, Boston Confucianism, Theology of Religions: A Short Reflection from the Perspective of Theodao"

In this essay, the author critically engages with the theology of Paul Tillich and the contemporary movement known as Boston Confucianism. It examines Tillich's understanding of the Dao and his concept of ultimate concern, questioning whether these notions fully capture the depth and complexity of East Asian thought. The essay critiques the limitations of Boston Confucianism, particularly its potential for Sinocentrism and its neglect of Confucian thought's practical, lived dimensions. Offering a Theodaoian perspective, it highlights the need for a more nuanced and authentic engagement with East Asian philosophies in the theology of religions. The essay calls for a dialogue that respects the integrity of each tradition, moving beyond superficial comparisons to explore deeper resonances and divergences.

Summary

Collectively, these three essays provide a rich tapestry of critical reflections and constructive engagements that contribute to the on-going development of Theodao. They challenge traditional theological paradigms by advocating for a more inclusive and polyphonic discourse that integrates the wisdom of East Asian traditions with the pressing issues of the contemporary world. By critically examining themes such as the relationship between science and religion, the practice of hospitality, and theological engagement

with East Asian philosophies, and theological, the appendix enriches the broader conversation initiated in the main sections of the
book. It underscores the importance of intercultural dialogue and
the integration of diverse epistemologies in crafting a theology that
is responsive to the complexities of the modern age.

These essays not only deepen the understanding of Theodao but
also exemplify the dynamic process of theological reflection that
is open to continual revision and growth. They invite readers to
consider how integrating East Asian wisdom can offer fresh insights
and alternative pathways for addressing global challenges, fostering
a theology that is both contextually grounded and universally
relevant.

## PART I

# Ecodao
# in an Age of Ecological Crisis

# *Theodao* Integrating Ecological Consciousness in Daoism, Confucianism, and Christian Theology

## Abstract

Contemporary theologies have widely discussed ecological issues. From an East Asian theological perspective, however, it is questionable whether they, including ecofeminists, can fully go beyond their inherited habits of Greek dualism and 'either-or' way of thinking (either anthropocentrism or cosmocentricism), which may be a root cause for all these problems. Christian theology may need a major paradigm shift in fundamental worldview (cosmology), hermeneutics, and theological root-metaphor. This chapter proposes three East Asian alternatives, in and through dialogue with East Asian religions, such as Confucianism and Daoism. 1) Cosmology: Theanthropocosmic vision (an East Asian triadic worldview in organismic unity of Heaven, Earth, and Humanity), in the relational paradigm of the Great Ultimate (*Tai-ji*) in the 'both-and' way of thinking (yin-yang). 2) New Hermeneutical key: Pneumato-socio-cosmic biography of the exploited life (in discernment of *ki* [*qi*]). 3) New theology: Theo-dao (changing the theological root-metaphor from two dominant Western logos and praxis to the life-affirming East Asian Dao).

## Introduction

Ecology is, without doubt, a most important issue for contemporary global Christianity. About half a century ago, Lynn White criticized Christianity as the "historical root" of the ecological crisis because it endorsed human domination over nature.[1] This criticism motivated theologians and religious scholars to reexamine the exclusive attitude of Christianity in the interaction with the natural world and to explore alternate wisdom and "new models of ecological wholeness and reciprocity" in other religious traditions.[2] The series editors of *Religions of the World and Ecology*,[3] wrote "[W]e are currently making macro phase change of the life systems of the planet with microphase wisdom. Clearly, we need to expand and deepen the wisdom base for human intervention with nature and other humans."

In a subsequent conference on 'Christianity and Ecology',[4] most

---

1 Lynn White, Jr., "The Historical Roots of Our Ecological Crisis," *Science* 155 (1967): 1203–7.

2 Mary Evelyn Tucker and John Grim, ed. *Worldviews and Ecology: Religion, Philosophy, and the Environment* (Maryknoll, NY: Orbis, 1994).

3 Mary Evelyn Tucker and John Grim, "Series Foreword," in *Christianity and Ecology: Seeking the Well-Being of Earth and Humans,* ed., Dieter T. Hessel and Rosemary Radford Ruether (Cambridge, MA: Harvard University Press, 2000), ix–xxv.

4 The conference was held at the Harvard University Center for the Study of World Religions,

Western participants (including, e.g., Elizabeth Johnson, Sallie McFague, Mark Wallace) agreed that three theological revisions are necessary to construct a proper Christian theology in this age of ecological crisis: a shift of the fundamental vision from anthropocentrism to cosmo- or earth-centrism, a revision of theological metaphors and symbols, and a shift of the focus from orthodoxy and christology to orthopraxis and pneumatology. Nevertheless, theological discourses afterward do not seem to successfully achieve these apposite revisions, conceivably due to the ingrained habits of Western thought.

As Gordon Kaufman pointed out, they seem not to overcome sufficiently the aged habit of anthropomorphism, personifying God in human form, and the modern habit of reductionism in the Enlightenment mentality, reducing everything in human cognition and reasoning.[5] Anthropomorphism and reductionism would be root-causes for bringing about ecological crises. By anthropomorphism Western Christianity lost Earth, by reductionism lost Heaven, and so lost Creation. Reductionism as the basis for modern sciences produced modern static worldviews such as the Newtonian. However, discoveries by contemporary sciences disclose that the universe is neither so much reducible as emergent, nor so much fixed as ever evolving and creative. This vindicates the argument that modern, Western cosmologies based on anthropocentric, reductionist, and static worldviews are scientifically inaccurate.[6]

---

Cambridge, MA, USA, April 16–19, 1998. See *Christianity and Ecology: Seeking the Well-Being of Earth and Humans.*

5 Gordon D. Kaufman, "Response to Elizabeth A. Johnson," in *Christianity and Ecology: Seeking the Well-Being of Earth and Humans,* ed. Dieter T. Hessel and Rosemary Radford Ruether (Cambridge, MA: Harvard University Press, 2000), 224–31.

East Asian traditions are not so much addicted to a narcissistic attachment to the human body but more interested in keeping harmony with nature such as mountains, waters, and trees (compare Greek sculptures with East Asian landscapes). Grounded on the harmony and symbiosis of humanity with nature, East Asian thought is particularly eco-friendly and life-affirming. Tucker and Grim stated that "The East Asian traditions of Confucianism and Taoism remain, in certain ways, some of the most life-affirming in the spectrum of world religions."[7] Furthermore, contemporary sciences continue to suggest that East Asian holistic cosmologies are more accurate than reductionist worldviews of the modern West. The universe is rather interdependent (relational) than independent (essential), circular than linear, flexible than static, and diverse than uniform. Correspondingly, Fritjof Capra, the author of *The Tao of Physics*, proposed interdependence, recycling, partnership, flexibility, and diversity as five basic principles of ecology.[8] In dialogue with East Asian traditions and liberation (minjung) theology, this chapter will suggest East Asian alternatives with respect to the three revisions for a proper Christian theology in an age of ecological crisis: theanthropocosmic vision (cosmology), theo-dao (theology of dao), and pneumato-sociocosmic narratives of the exploited life (pneumatology of *ki* [氣; *qi*]).[9]

---

6 Stuart A. Kauffman, *Reinventing the Sacred: A New View of Science, Reason, and Religion* (New York: Basic Books, 2008).

7 Tucker and Grim, "Series Foreword," xxiv.

8 Fritjof Capra, *The Web of Life: A New Scientific Understanding of Living Systems* (New York: Doubleday, 1996).

9 Ki, a Korean romanization of *qi* (ch'i), is a key East Asian notion similar to the Greek word

## Theanthropocosmic Vision: a New but Ancient Cosmology

Theanthropocosmic vision (God, Humanity, and Cosmos in communion) is a fitting cosmology for Christianity in an age of ecology and science. Tucker and Grim state, "If [western] religions have traditionally concentrated on divine-human and human-human relations, the challenge is that they now explore more fully divine-human-earth relations."[10] Influenced by the tradition of salvation history and modern historical consciousness, Christianity became anthropocentric and history-centered. For the last five hundred years, Earth, nature, and the cosmos "got lost" in Christian theology with an exclusive focus on God and the human self, as Elizabeth Johnson elaborated.[11] The ecological disaster awakened Western theologians to realize the devastating results of "such amnesia about the cosmic world" and become eager to find creation in the Christian tradition.

The loss of creation or amnesia about Earth is a modern phenomenon that had not happened for the first fifteen hundred years of Christianity. The Bible respects the religious value of Earth. The Jewish scriptures speak of an Earth filled with the glory of God. The Christian scriptures are obviously Earth-affirming, as expressed in the notions of incarnation, resurrection of the body, eucharistic

---

*pneuma.* It has various meanings, such as energy, vital force, material force, and breath. This chapter Romanizes this word mainly as *ki* due to contextual considerations.

10 Tucker and Grim, "Series Foreword," xxiv.

11 Elizabeth A. Johnson, "Losing and Finding Creation in the Christian Tradition," in *Christianity and Ecology,* 4-9.

sharing, and eschatological hope. Early and medieval theologies dealt with humanity in association with the natural world as the common creation of God. "God-world-humanity: these form a metaphysical trinity." And "cosmology, anthropology, and theology of God formed a harmonious unity," as in the thought of Hildegard of Bingen, Bonaventure, and Aquinas. Hence, the theanthropocosmic vision is in fact nothing new but was an ancient cosmology for Christianity.

Nevertheless, both Catholic and Protestant theologies "focused on God and human self, leaving the natural world to the side."[12] The Reformation's doctrines of Christ alone, faith alone, grace alone, and scripture alone gave Protestant and, subsequently, Catholic theology "an intensively anthropocentric turn." "The center of gravity shifts to the human subject." However, the thought of reformers such as John Calvin was affirmative toward nature, regarding nature as the inscribed locus of Divine glory. The anti-nature views of modern science, philosophy, and history accelerated this shift.[13] The Cartesian idea of the self and the Kantian turn to the subject divorced the human person (the internal, active subject) from the natural world (the external, passive object). The modern emphasis on history reinforced this division. History was viewed as actual events in linear time and regarded as the locus of God's salvific work, whereas nature (in cyclical time) was seen as the realm of paganism. Most twentieth-century theologies did not take creation seriously, including existentialist theology, neo-orthodoxy, political theology, and

---

12 Ibid, 6, 8.
13 Ibid, 9.

early liberation theologies.

Finally, the ecological crisis has awakened Western Christians "to incorporate the natural world as part or even the center of their work." Geocentric, unchanging, hierarchical medieval cosmology and a deterministic, mechanistic modern worldview are inaccurate views. Rather, the natural world discovered by contemporary science is "surprisingly dynamic, organic, self-organizing, indeterminate, chancy, boundless, and open to the unknown." Furthermore, the "rape of the earth" has a close link with "male hierarchy over women and nature," that is "violent sexual conquest of women, and of virgin forest." Accordingly, Johnson argued for an ecofeminist approach: "To be truly effective, therefore, conversion to the earth needs to cut through the knot of misogynist prejudice and shift from the worldview of patriarchal hierarchy to a holistic worldview of relationships and mutual community."[14]

Ecofeminist theology is an important theological movement with legitimate correctives to Western theologies. However, from an East Asian perspective, it is still questionable whether ecofeminist theology sufficiently transcends the ingrained habit of an 'either-or' way of thinking (anthropocentrism vs. cosmocentrism) or monistic dualism (not unrelated to essentialism, substantialism, and reductionism, though ecofeminist theology tries to avoid them). By monistic dualism, one cannot achieve a genuine holistic, mutual, and reciprocal mode of relationship. The theanthropocosmic vision presupposes an entirely different paradigm that is 'both-and', pluralistic (triadic) and concentric.

---

14 Ibid, 11, 13, 17.

According to Raymond Panikkar, the history of world religions presents three great religious visions; namely, ancient cosmocentrism, medieval theocentrism, and modern historico-anthropocentrism.[15] All of these three are inaccurate, one-sided, reductionist views (monocentrism) of reality. God, humans, and the cosmos constitute three inseparable and concentric axes of the one reality. Early and medieval theologies maintained this theanthropocosmic or cosmo-theandric vision. Moreover, the genius of the doctrine of the Trinity lies in the capacity that enables the articulation of the pluralistic and concentric reality of the Triune Godhead beyond Greek monistic dualism. Nevertheless, the ingrained Western habit of 'either-or' dividing would be problematic, selecting God, Earth, humans, or nature. True humanity can be realized only through the right relationship with Heaven (God) and Earth (cosmos). A theanthropocosmic vision refers to this triadic communion of God, the cosmos, and humans, the ontologically indivisible reality.

Since the beginning, East Asians have believed in the triadic reality of Heaven, Earth, and Humanity, by calling it the Trinity (三才) or the Triune Ultimate (三極). The ideographic structure of the Korean language prominently embodies this triadic vision. It also appears saliently in the trigrams and the hexagrams of *Yìjīng*, a foundation of East Asian thought.[16] A Confucian scholar suggested that East Asians "might see God the Son as the ideal human, God the

---

15 Raimundo Panikkar, *The Cosmotheandric Experience: Emerging Religious Consciousness* (Maryknoll, NY: Orbis, 1993).

16 Hellmut Wilhelm, *Heaven, Earth, and Man in the Book of Changes* (Seattle: University of Washington Press, 1977).

Father would be Heaven (the creative spirit), and God the Holy Spirit the earth (the receptive co-spirit), or agent of the world which testifies to the accomplishment of the divinity."[17]

Furthermore, in East Asian Christianity, the theohistorical vision of Christianity has encountered the anthropocosmic vision of East Asian religions (Neo-Confucianism). Simply, anthropocosmic vision refers to the Confucian idea of the unity of Heaven and humanity (天人合一), whereas theohistorical vision refers to the Christian view of salvation history (God in history). This encounter leads to a fusion of hermeneutical horizons to form a the-anthropo-cosmic vision.[18] In East Asian Christianity, Christian theology, East Asian religions, and ecology meet. Thematizing this fusion of hermeneutical horizons may bring forth a new paradigm of theology, anthropology, and cosmology in an age of ecology and science. Christian theology presents a thoughtful view on God (Heaven, the Father), East Asian religions offer a profound wisdom on humanity and life (the Son), and ecology (Natural Sciences) submits the most updated knowledge on the Earth (the Holy Spirit). Thereupon, Christian theology, East Asian religions, and ecology constitute a triadic polarity that entail a Triune Great Ultimate (三太極). A theanthropocosmic paradigm of Christian theology can be constructed with these three great resources in a Triune Great Ultimate. These relations may be

---

17 Chung-ying Cheng, "The Trinity of Cosmology, Ecology, and Ethics in the Confucian Personhood," in *Confucianism and Ecology: The Interrelation of Heaven, Earth, and Humans,* ed. Mary Evelyn Tucker and John Berthrong (Cambridge, MA: Harvard University Press, 1998), 211–36.

18 Heup Young Kim, *Wang Yang-ming and Karl Barth: A Confucian-Christian Dialogue* (Lanham, MD: University Press of America, 1996), 176-78, 183-84.

illustrated as follows:

| Christian Theology | Theos | Heaven | Ki (Pneuma) | Father | Emancipation |
|---|---|---|---|---|---|
| East Asian Religions | Anthropos | Human (Life) | Society | Son | Dialogue |
| Ecology (Natural Sciences) | Cosmos | Earth | Cosmos | Holy Spirit | Ecology |

*Triune Great Ultimate of Theology*

*of Dao Theanthropocosmic Vision*      *Pneumatosociocosmic Narratives*

## Theo-dao (Theology of Dao): a New Paradigm of Asian Theology

Theology of Dao (Theo-dao) refers to a new paradigm of Christian theology in the theanthropocosmic vision, constructed in dialogue with East Asian religions. It searches for the thean-thropocosmic Dao, the Way of the Triune Great Ultimate where the Heavenly way (天道), the human way (人道), and the earthly way (地道) are in communion. It seeks the way to embody the trinity of theology, life, and ecology, in and through interreligious and in-terdisciplinary dialogues among Christianity, East Asian religions, and natural sciences. It is a theology of learning how to participate in this holistic trajectory of theanthropocosmic Dao.

The dominant root-metaphor of Christian theology for the last two millennia has been 'logos.' However, it was rooted in the Greek hierarchical dualism and further reduced to technical reason by modernism. Logos has become an inappropriate root-metaphor for

Christian theology. Dao could be a more appropriate root-metaphor
for theology in this ecological age. For dao is not only 'the most
life affirming' but also more biblical. Jesus said, "I am the way, truth,
and life" (Jn 14:6a). Jesus identified himself not so much as the incarnate logos as the ultimate way (dao) of life toward God (Jn 14:6b).
Moreover, the first name for Christianity in the New Testament was
*hodos* (way) in Greek, translated as 'dao' in the Korean Bible (Acts
9:2; 19:9; 22:4; 24:14, 22).

The term theo-dao was coined to contrast with the traditional
theo-logy (logos) and its modern alternative, theo-praxis (praxis).[19]
As its Chinese character (道) consists of two ideographs, meaning
'head' (首 being) and 'vehicle' (辶 becoming), dao means both the
source of being (logos) and the way of becoming (praxis). It denotes
the being in becoming or the logos in transformative praxis. Dao
does not refer to an option of either-or, but embraces the whole
of both-and. It does not force one to stay at the crossroads of logos
(being) and praxis (becoming) but actualizes one to participate in
a dynamic movement to be united in the cosmic track. The dao as
the ultimate way and reality embodies the transformative praxis of
the theanthropocosmic trajectory of life in the unity of knowing and
acting (知行合一).

If theo-logy is a perspective from above, and if theo-praxis is that
from below, then theo-dao is a perspective from an entirely different
dimension, theanthropocosmic intersubjectivity. Theodao as a theology of life is neither logos-centric (knowledge) nor praxis-centric

---

19 Heup Young Kim, *Christ and the Tao* (Hong Kong: Christian Conference of Asia, 2003),
135-254.

(action), but dao-centric (so to speak, *sophia* in action). Theodao can be reduced neither to an ortho-doxy (a right doctrine of the church) nor to an ortho-praxis (a right practice in history), but embraces holistically the right way of life (ortho-dao), the transformative wisdom of living in a theanthropocosmic trajectory. What theodao pursues is neither only a metaphysical debate for church doctrines nor exclusively an ideological conscientization for social action, but a holistic way of life. Its key issue is whether it is in the right way to participate in the loving process of theanthropocosmic reconciliation and sanctification.

If orthodoxy emphasizes faith and orthopraxis underscores hope, orthodao focuses on love (1 Cor 13:13). If the traditional theology (theo-logos) focuses on the epistemology of faith and the modern theo-praxis (liberation theology) focuses on the eschatology of hope, the cardinal theme of theo-dao is the pneumatology of love. If the classical definition of theology is *faith-seeking-understanding* (*fides quaerens intellectum*) and if that of theopraxis is the hope-seeking-action, theodao takes the definition of the *love-seeking-dao* (way). If theology (God-talk) focuses on the right understanding of the Christian doctrines and if theopraxis (God- walk) on the right practice of the Christian ideologies, theodao (God-live) searches for the way and wisdom of Christian life.

The actual teachings of Jesus in the Gospels were not so much an orthodox doctrine, a philosophical theology, a manual of orthopraxis, or an ideology of social revolution, but the dao of life and living. Jesus Christ cannot be divided between the historical Jesus (theopraxis) and the kerygmatic Christ (theologos). In fact, the fusion of hermeneutical horizons toward a theodao in a theanthropocosmic vision appeared as soon as Christianity landed on the Neo-Confucian soil of Korea. The first Korean Catholic theologian Yi Pyŏk (1754-1786) conceived Christ as the crossroad of the Heavenly Dao and the human dao, that is, neither Christo-logos nor Christo-praxis, but Christo-dao.[20] Christodao comprehends Jesus Christ as both the dao of crucifixion (i.e., the way of theanthropocosmic reconciliation) and the dao of resurrection (the way of theanthropocosmic sanctification).

Ryu Yŏngmo (1890-1981), a seminal Korean Christian thinker, envisioned the cosmogonic Christ from a deepest heart of the East Asian hermeneutical universe of dao. He believed that, in Christ, the Non-Ultimate (無極; *Wú jí*) and the Great Ultimate (太極; *Tài jí*) become united. In Neo-Confucianism, this unity denotes the ultimate complementary and paradoxical opposites of the ineffable Vacuity (the Non-Ultimate) and the Cosmogony (the Great Ultimate).[21] From the vantage point of this supreme cosmogonic paradox, Ryu understood "the cross as both the Non-Ultimate and the Great Ultimate... Jesus is the one who manifested the ultimate in Asian cosmology. Through the sacrifice of himself, he achieved genuine humanity (仁; *rén*). That is to say, by offering himself as a sacrifice, he saved the human race and opened the kingdom of God for humanity."[22]

---

20 Ibid, 153-82; Jean Sang Ri, *Confucius et Jésus Christ: La Première Théologie Chrétienne en Corée d'Après l'Oeuvre de Yi Piek Lettre Confucéen 1754-1786* (Paris: Éditions Beauchesne, 1979).

21 Wing-tsit Chan, trans., *A Source Book in Chinese Philosophy* (Princeton, NJ: Princeton University Press, 1963).

22 Heung-ho Kim, "Ryu Yŏngmo's View of Christianity from the Asian Perspective," in *Dasŏk Ryu Yŏngmo,* ed. Park Young-ho (Seoul: The Sungchun Institution, 1994), 299.

Further, Ryu articulated the cross as "the blood of the flower" through which the Son reveals the glory of the Father and the Father the glory of the Son. Seeing the blossom of this flower of Jesus (at the cross), he envisioned the glorious blossom of the cosmos (cosmogony). He thought, "[T]he cross is a rush into the cosmic trajectory, resurrection is a participation in the revolution of the cosmic trajectory, and lighting up the world is the judgment sitting in the right-hand side of God."[23] Accordingly, the Crucifixion and the Resurrection of Jesus Christ do not refer to a narrow story about God's saving work exclusively for a species of *homosapiens* in a linear history on a tiny planet of the solar system, Earth. Rather, these events signify a grand narrative of theanthropocosmic drama that Jesus, true humanity, has successfully penetrated into the cosmic trajectory to achieve the cosmotheandric union, lightening up the entire universe, and thus becoming the christic dao of true life (cf. Col 1:16-7, Jn 1:3).

Furthermore, Ryu conceived the Crucifixion and the Resurrection as the events that make the Being in Non-Being. Western christologies, preoccupied by being (substantialism), neglect this dimension of non-being. In fact, the core of christology is in this paradoxical mystery of creating the being (resurrection) from the non-being (crucifixion), which is God's cosmogonic principle (*creatio ex nihilo*). From this vantage point, he formulated a fascinating Korean apophatic christodao. Jesus is the One who "Is" in spite of "Is-Not," that is to say, "Being-in-Non-Being (*Ŏpshi-gyeshin nim*)." Whereas we are those of non-being-in-being, He is the One of Being-in-Non-Being. Whereas we are the "forms" that are "none

---

23 Ibid.

other than emptiness" (*Heart Sutra*), He is the "emptiness" that is "none other than form."[24] Christian theology needs to embody this cosmogonic principle of being-in-non-being in order to be ecological and life-affirming. Here is the significance of the medieval traditions of negative theology (*via negativa*) and *kenosis* (emptiness).

*Dàodéjīng* describes dao with basically feminine metaphors such as "mother of all things," "the root," "the ground" (of Being), "the uncarved block" (the original nature), or "the mystical female." This feminine vision is based on Lǎozǐ's principle of "reversal." Lǎozǐ always put the preferential option to the strategy of *yin* (weak, soft, small, empty) rather than *yang* (strong, hard, big, full), as Graham asserted.[25] This *yin* principle of reversal is closely connected with the principle of return. "Attain complete vacuity, maintain steadfast quietude. All things come into being, and I see thereby their return. All things flourish, but each one returns to its destiny. To return to destiny is called the eternal (Dao). To know the eternal is called enlightenment."[26] The principle of reversal and radical return entails the spirituality of dao with the paradoxical power of weakness and emptiness.

24 Heung-ho Kim, *Jesori* (Seoul: Pungman, 1985).

25 A. C. Graham, *Disputers of the Tao: Philosophical Argument in Ancient China* (La Salle, IL: Open Court, 1989), 223.

26 Wing-tsit Chan, trans., *A Source Book in Chinese Philosophy* (Princeton, NJ: Princeton University Press, 1963), 147.

## Pneumatosociocosmic Narratives of the Exploited Life: a New Pneumatology of *Ki*

The spirituality of dao can strengthen Christianity in this age of ecological crisis. The yin principle of reversal and radical return with the paradoxical power of weakness and emptiness can empower Christianity to resist merciless processes of genocide, biocide, and ecocide. In fact, this yin principle is in accordance with the life-act of Jesus. The life-saving mystery of His resurrection entails a Christian principle of radical return (the victory of life over the power of death). His crucifixion on the cross denotes a Christian principle of reversal with the paradoxical power of weakness and emptiness (cf. Isa 53:5, Lk 6:20f, 1 Cor 1:18). And the yin strategy resonates with the biblical 'preferential option for the poor', a famous idiom of liberation theology. However, the preferential option is related not only to the poor, women, and minjung (the oppressed people), but is extended to the wounded ecosystem as a whole, including endangered species.

Minjung theology argued that the social biography (the under-side history) of minjung is a more authentic historical point of reference for theological reflection than doctrinal discourses (the official history) superimposed by the Church in its orientation of Western rationality.[27] This was an important proposal for Asian theology to realize minjung as the subject of history, correcting traditional theology, primarily based on autobiographical (psychological) or church

---

27 Yong-bok Kim, "Theology and the Social Biography of Minjung," *CTC Bulletin* 5:3–6:1 (1984–1985): 66–78.

(official) narratives. Nevertheless, its exclusive focus on the political history of God and subsequently on anthropocentric history hinders Asian theology's embrace of the full profundities of Asian religious and ecological thoughts. Asian theology need also include underside histories of whole life systems on Earth. It needs to thematize sociocosmic (both social and cosmic) narratives of the exploited life, to be a creative crossover between both the social biography of minjung and the East Asian anthropocosmic vision.

By embodying the spirituality of reversal and return, theology can execute sociocosmic transformative praxis (i.e., the Dao), healing wounded mother Earth. In Christian faith, this spirituality implies a pneumatology empowered by the paradoxical power of the cross with the eschatological hope of resurrection. The East Asian notion of *ki* (氣) is very helpful to articulate this pneumatology. Rephrasing, Christianity needs to focus on sociocosmic narratives of the exploited life in spiritual communion with ki.

Kim Chi Ha,[28] a Korean Catholic poet, presented an insightful parable, "the Ugŭmch'i Phenomenon," to illuminate this *ki* spirituality.[29] To heal his sickness from the long period of imprisonment by the military dictatorship, he retired to a small city. The once pristine stream in front of his house was now hopelessly polluted by industrial waste. However, when it rained, the rain swept out the wastes, and he was surprised to see many small fish swimming upstream against the flood of water! Thus he puzzled, how could such feeble fish swim upward against such a turbulent flow?

---

28 Chi-ha Kim, *Saengmyŏng* [Life] (Seoul: Sol, 1992), 188-92.

29 For a complete English translation, see Heup Young Kim, *Christ and the Tao,* 138-42.

Through meditation, he realized that such a thing could happen by the work of *ki*. When the primordial *ki* of a feeble fish becomes united with that of water, it can swim against even a mighty turbulent flood. Furthermore, as *ki*, "energy," always consists of *yin* and *yang*, the *ki* of water also moves in both directions of *yin* and *yang*. From the exuberant palpitation of the primordial *ki* of many fish in union with the *yin* movement of the water, he discovered the key to understanding the mystery of the Ugŭmch'i War[30] in which the feeble minjung—several hundred thousands of Korean peasants—fought vigorously against Japanese troops armed with powerful mechanized weapons. Their collective *ki* inspired and empowered the minjung to participate courageously in the movement and to be united with the primordial *ki*, in the same manner as the feeble fish that swim vigorously upstream against the formidable flood to be in union with the *yin* movement of the water. The fierce palpitation of the minjung against the turbulent flood of historical demons is in fact a great cosmic movement united with the *yin-yang* movement of ki. He called it the ugŭmch'i phenomenon.

The first realization in this parable was an ecological insight that nature (rain) has a self-saving power to bring forth life in a fateful environment (the polluted water). He saw a hope for life in this spiritually fragmented and ecologically destructive world spawned by developmental ideology. A more important realization, however, was that from the dao world he found the clue to transcending historical dualism and the real source of the life energy which out-

---

30 The last and fiercest battle during the second uprising of the Tonghak Peasant Revolution broke out on the Ugŭmch'i Hill of Gongju, Korea, in December 1894.

pours such a vigorous vitality to the feeble fish and the minjung in Ugŭmch'i. This marked a turning point for his thought as he formulated a creative Korean hermeneutics of suspicion from the perspective of *han*, "the suppressed, amassed and condensed experience of oppression."[31] He argued that minjung must be free from the vicious circle of *han*-riddenness to resolve their *han*. This inspired Korean theologians to formulate minjung theology, and some even argued that a main task of theologians is to become priests of han to motivate and participate in the movement of *hanpuri* (a collective action to release *han*) of minjung, including women.

Finally, he returned to the old Dao world. This implies a paradigm shift in his thought from a Korean version of the dualistic mode of contradiction (*han*) to the East Asian correlative mode of complementary opposites (*yin-yang*). The shift involves his enlightenment to the true source of the tremendously life-empowering force manifested by the feeble fish in the turbulent flood and the multitude of minjung in the Ugŭmch'i War. The key to revealing the mystery of the ugŭmch'i phenomenon is the notion of *ki*, very similar to *pneuma*. *Ki* is not so much dualistic and analytic as holistic and embracing. It is both the source and the medium of empowerment. This insight enables substantiation of a theology of life in the East Asian theanthropocosmic vision with a pneumatology of *ki*. The new horizon in the unity of Heaven (God), Earth (the cosmos), and Humanity can be further extended through the spirit (*ki, pneuma*), namely, "a pneumatoanthropocosmic vision."[32] This pneumatoan-

---

31 Nam-dong Suh, "Towards a Theology of Han," in *Minjung Theology: People as the Subjects of History* (Maryknoll, NY: Orbis, 1981), 65.

thropocosmic vision can cultivate a symbiosis of the life network through the communication of *ki* that fosters the human race's relationship with other lives more holistically.

The ugŭmch'i phenomenon is an example of the sociocosmic narratives of the exploited life, metaphorically telling the story of the two exploited lives, the feeble fish in the turbulent stream and the multitude of minjung in the Ugŭmch'i War. In addition, *ki* as both spirit and matter offers a clue to the mystery of incarnation. While the birth story of Jesus refers to the pneumatoanthropocosmic vision *par excellence*, the passion narratives of Christ tell the sociocosmic biography of the exploited life *par excellence*. Jesus Christ as the theanthropocosmic Dao entails the life-breathing *pneumato-sociocosmic trajectory* of the primordial (holy) *ki*.

Finally, the theology of dao as a new paradigm of theology of life invites Christians to participate in re-habilitating the exploited life, including not only minjung and women but also endangered life systems and polluted nature, by the outpouring power of *ki*. As the ugŭmch'i phenomenon illuminates, it requires the spirituality of dao that empowers the principle of radical return and reversal with the paradoxical power of weakness and emptiness. Thus, a primary task of theology of dao as a new paradigm of Christian theology is to re-habilitate our planetary and cosmic habitats, i.e., 'our' home (*oikos*) in the universe, with the re-visioning of the true communion among God, humanity (life), and Earth (cosmos) and by the outpouring power of the cosmic Spirit, the holy *ki*.

The theology of dao as a new theology of life based on a proper

---

32 Heup Young Kim, *Christ and the Tao,* 142-48.

cosmology and ecology in and through dialogue with East Asian religions and minjung theology demands not just an inter-Christian or an inter-religious dialogue, but also a theanthropocosmic communion to embody the transformative praxis in the pneumatosociocosmic trajectory, the Dao, by the outpouring power of the holy *ki*. This notion of *ki* is well supported by contemporary sciences, as it "bears the most striking resemblance to the concept of quantum field in modern physics."[33] Therefore, a trialogue among Christianity, Asian religions, and natural sciences is an important theme for Asian and global Christianity in the years to come.[34]

---

[33] Fritjof Capra, *The Tao of Physics: An Exploration of the Parallels Between Modern Physics and Eastern Mysticism,* 2nd ed. (Boulder, CO: Shambhala, 1983), 212.

[34] Heup Young Kim, "Asian Christianity: Toward a Trilogue of Humility: Sciences, Theologies, and Asian Religions," in *Why the Science and Religion Dialogue Matters: Voices from the International Society for Science and Religion,* ed. Fraser Watts and Kevin Dutton (West Conshohocken, PA: Templeton Press, 2006), 121–33.

CHAPTER TWO

# Eco-Dao:
# An Ecological Theology of Dao

Abstract

This chapter in "Eco-Dao" redefines Dao as an ecological root-metaphor, positioning it as an alternative to Western dualistic theology. Through the integration of knowing (logos) and acting (praxis), Dao facilitates a holistic understanding of existence that aligns with ecological balance. Drawing from Confucian and Daoian traditions, it presents an "anthropocosmic" vision that sees humanity as inherently interconnected with the cosmos, advocating a shift from anthropocentrism to a more inclusive humanism. Dao's cosmology, symbolized by the yin-yang dynamic, is explored as a model for unity-in-diversity, encouraging harmony with natural systems. The chapter also introduces *ki*/qi as a metaphysical energy fostering ecological and social solidarity. By engaging with breathing practices and the concept of "reversal," Eco-Dao emphasizes a body-centered spirituality, challenging technocentric paradigms. This perspective aligns with Pope Francis's "*Laudato si'*," advocating for an integrated approach to ecological and social justice.

# Dao (道; Way)[1] as Ecological Root-Metaphor

Dao is an overarching concept for East Asian thought. With its adoption as the root-metaphor, I have proposed that the theology of dao (namely, theo-dao) is a proper paradigm in this age to think towards a 'theology without walls' or 'trans-religious theology'.[2] Theo-dao aims to surmount the chronic dualism of contemporary Christian theologies between the paradigm of traditional theo-logos (classical and inculuturationalist theologies) and its modern alternative, theo-praxis (liberationist theologies). As its Chinese character consists of two ideographs, meaning 'head' (knowing) and 'vehicle' (acting), dao connotes holistically both the source of knowing (logos) and the way of acting (praxis) in unity; that is to say, the logos in transformative praxis or the praxis in transformative logos. Hence, dao, a holistic root-metaphor, does not force one to choose between either logos or praxis, but embraces the whole of 'both-and' to enable a person to participate in a dynamic movement to be united in the cosmic track. The dao, also meaning ultimate reality, embodies the transformative praxis of the cosmic trajectory of life in the unity of knowing and acting.

---

1 As the widely used root-metaphor of all classical East Asian religions including Confucianism, Daoism, and Buddhism, dao is an inclusive and polysemous term. For example, Herbert Fingarette defined: "[D]ao is a Way, a path, a road, and by common metaphorical extension it becomes in ancient China the right Way of life, the Way of governing, the ideal Way of human existence, the Way of the Cosmos, the generative-normative Way (Pattern, path, course) of existence as such" (*Confucius—The Secular as Sacred* [New York: Harper & Row, 1972], 19).

2 See Heup Young Kim, *A Theology of Dao* (Maryknoll, NY: Orbis Books, 2017); especially, "God as the Dao: Toward a Theology of Dao (Theodao)," 14-33.

Logos, the dominant root-metaphor of Christian theology for the last two millennia, is rooted in the Greek hierarchical dualism and further reduced to technical reason by the influence of modernism. Thus, it has become an inappropriate root-metaphor for ecological theology. Instead, I argue that dao is a more proper root-metaphor for the theology of ecology and life. First of all, dao is "the most life affirming" root-metaphor.[3] Further, as homologous to *hodos* in the biblical Greek, it is a more biblical term than logos. Jesus said, "I am the way [*hodos*], truth, and life" (Jn 14:6a); that is say, the ultimate way (dao) of life. Jesus did not identify himself as the incarnate logos but rather as the dao toward God (Jn 14:6b). Furthermore, the original title for Christianity was hodos which was translated as "dao" in the Korean Bible (Acts 9:2; 19:9; 22:4; 24:14, 22).

At the core of Daoian thought is to return or act according to nature as it is (無爲自然). Neo-Confucianism also adopted this thought emphatically. In Chinese characters, nature means "*self-so*," "spontaneity" or "naturalness," i.e., "the effective modality of the system that informs the actions of the agents that compose it."[4] In other words, *nature* in East Asian thought is the primary "self-so" (natural) manifestation of the dao (the Way). Dao is an ideal root-metaphor

---

3 In the series forward of Religions of the World and Ecology, Mary Everlyn Tucker and John A. Grim stated, "The East Asian traditions of Confucianism and Taoism remain, in certain ways, some of the most life-affirming in the spectrum of world religions." "Series Forward," in *Christianity and Ecology: Seeking the Well Being of Earth and Humans*, ed. Dieter T. Hessel and Rosemary Radford Ruether [Cambridge, MA: Harvard University Press, 2000], xxvi.

4 Michael C. Kalton, "Asian Religious Tradition and Natural Science: Potentials, Present and Future," unpublished paper, the CTNS Korea Religion & Science Workshop, Seoul, January 18-22, 2002.

for ecology, because its ontology, cosmology, and spirituality per se are precisely ecological. For this reason, I propose to make use of dao as the root-metaphor for an apposite paradigm of ecological theology; namely, eco-dao.[5] Furthermore, the "onto-cosmology" of dao (the Great Ultimate) entails profoundly "a sense of cosmo-genesis" (or cosmogony) which Thomas Berry and Brian Swim advocated with their prophecy of the eco-zoic era.[6]

## The Great Ultimate(太極; *T'aegŭk/Tài jì*)[7] as Onto-Cosmology

An axiomatic view of Confucianism is the "anthropocosmic vision" that affirms the "mutual dependence and organic unity" of Heaven and humanity.[8] *The Doctrine of the Mean*, one of the Confucian Four Books, states, "What Heaven imparts to man is called human nature. To follow our nature is called the Way (Dao). Cultivating the Way is called education."[9] This anthropocosmic vision sees that

---

5 See Heup Young Kim, "Eco-Dao: Life, Ecology, and Theodao," in *A Theology of Dao*, 204-222; also, idem, "Theodao: Integrating Ecological Consciousness in Daoism, Confucianism, and Christian Theology," in The Wiley Blackwell Companion to Religion and Ecology, ed. John Hart (Oxford: John Wiley & Sons, Ltd, 2017), 104-14.

6 Brian Swimme & Thomas Berry, *The Universe Story: From the Primordial Flaring Forth to the Ecozoic Era—A Celebration of the Unfolding of Cosmos* (New York: HarperCollins Publishers, 1992), 2-3, 66-68. In formulation of Christo-dao, I had used the cosmogonic nature of dao (see Kim, A Theology of Dao, 40-43).

7 Romanizations of the Great Ultimate (太極): T'aegŭk (Korean); Tàijí (Pinyin), T'ai-chi (Wade-Giles).

8 Tu Wei-ming, *Centrality and Commonality: An Essay on Confucian Religiousness* (Albany, NY: State University of New York Press, 1989), 107.

humanity (anthropology) is inseparable from Heaven (cosmology) and conceived as its microcosm. Hence, East Asian anthropology is cosmocentric in contrast to the anthropocentric approach to cosmology prevalent in the West.[10]

This anthropocosmic view presents "inclusive humanism" which Confucian scholar Cheng Chung-ying sharply distinguishes with the "exclusive humanism" dominant in the West since Descartes' dualistic rationalism. Whereas exclusive humanism "exalts the human species, placing it in a position of mastery of and domination over the universe," inclusive humanism "stresses the coordinating powers of humanity as the very reason for its existence." Cheng contested that "humanism in the modern West is nothing more than a secular will for power or a striving for domination, with rationalistic science at its disposal... Humanism in this exclusive sense is a disguise for the individualistic entrepreneurship of modern man armed with science and technology as tools of conquest and devastation." In contrast, he argued that the inclusive humanism rooted in Confucianism "focuses on the human person as an agency of both self-transformation and transformation of reality at large. As the self-transformation of a person is rooted in reality and the transformation of reality is rooted in the person, there is no dichotomy or bifurcation between the human and reality."[11]

---

9 Wing-tsit Chan, trans., *A Source Book in Chinese Philosophy* (Princeton, NJ: Princeton University Press, 1963), 98.

10 Jung Young Lee, *The Trinity in Asian Perspective* (Nashville, TN: Abingdon Press, 1996), 18.

11 Cheng Chung-ying, "The Trinity of Cosmology, Ecology, and Ethics in the Confucian Personhood," in *Confucianism and Ecology: The Interrelation of Heaven, Earth, and*

Over against the essentialist and exclusivist view of the human
person, inclusive humanism stresses the "between-ness" or "among-
ness" of the person. (The Chinese character for the human being
人間 connotes in-between-ness). In inclusive humanism, a person
is not so much a static substance (an isolated ego) as a network
of relationships in constant change (*Yi* 易).[12] This relational vision
of being in continual change is called "onto-cosmology."[13] This
Confucian/Daoian (Neo-Confucian) onto-cosmology is basically
related to the notion of the Great Ultimate. In *An Explanation of the
Diagram of the Great Ultimate*, Zhou Dunyi (1017-1073) stated:

> The Ultimate of Non-being and also the Great Ultimate! The Great
> Ultimate through movement generates yang. When its activity reaches
> its limit, it becomes tranquil. Through tranquility the Great Ultimate gen-
> erates yin. When tranquility reaches its limit, activity begins again. So
> movement and tranquility alternate and become the root of each other,
> giving rise to the distinction of yin and yang, and the two modes are
> thus established.[14]

---

*Humans*, ed. Mary Evelyn Tucker and John Berthrong (Cambridge, MA: Harvard
University Press, 1998), 213-215. The recent encyclical on ecology seems to be in agreement with this critical analysis on the "exclusive humanism" prevailed in the West and
East Asian "inclusive humanism". See "Laudato si' of the Holy Father Francis on Care
for Our Common Home" (24 May 2015): 115, 141; http://w2.vatican.va/con-
tent/francesco/en/encyclicals/documents/papa-francesco_20150524_enciclica-lau
dato-si.html (accessed April 30, 2017).

12 This key Confucian/Daoian notion is presented in the Book of Changes, one of the
Five Confucian Classics. Richard Wilhelm and Cary F. Baynes, trans., *The I Ching or
Book of Changes*, 3rd edn. (Princeton, NJ: Princeton University Press, 1967).

13 Cheng, "The Trinity," 216.

14 Chan, *A Source Book*, 463.

The Great Ultimate, symbolized by a circle enclosing yin and yang, denotes the complementarity of opposites. The circle signifies "an inexhaustible source of creativity, which is one and un-differentiated," and the dynamic process of yin-yang interaction is "always ready to be differentiated into concrete and individual things." It is "the constant fountainhead amidst all things and pro-vides the integrative and purposive unity of any type or any in-dividual token while, at the same time, it also serves as the impetus for the diversity of things as types of tokens."[15] The Great Ultimate so conceived entails precisely a cosmogony (or cosmogenesis) of the dao in the continual process of unity in multiplicity or diversity in unity.

This Neo-Confucian onto-cosmology is also pertinent to Daoism, as Laozi states:

[D]ao produced the One.

The One produced the two.

The two produced the three.

And the three produced the ten thousand things.

The ten thousand things carry the yin and embrace the yang, and through the blending of the material force [ki/qi] they achieve harmony.[16]

This statement refers to the dynamic creative process of dao in the metaphorical symbolism of the Great Ultimate. It produces the

---

15 Cheng, "The Trinity," 219.

16 Daodejing: 42. Chan, A Source Book, 160-61. Romanizations of material force, vital energy, or meta-cosmic energy (氣): ki (Korean); qi (Pinyin); ch'i (Wade-Giles).

One, the Two (yin-yang), and the Three (offspring of yin-yang). "The whole is both absolute and relative, it is both one (singularity) and two (plurality) at the same time."[17] The creativity of dao is the cosmogenetic (or cosmogonic) process of the Great Ultimate through the dynamic yin-yang interaction and always in the process of change. It stipulates the dialogical paradigm of harmony and equilibrium in East Asian thought, in contrast to the dialectical paradigm of strife and conflict in Western thought. The Great Ultimate "signifies both a process and world qua the totality of things in which there is a profound equilibrium from the beginning and a pervasive accord or harmony among all things at any time."[18] In this regard, the Great Ultimate is a prototype of "the cosmogenetic principle" which Berry and Swimme try to articulate; "*differentiation, autopoiesis,* and *communion* throughout time and space and at every level of reality."[19]

Inclusive humanism rooted in this onto-cosmology of dao developed a vision of 'cosmic togetherness' in an organismic unity with Heaven, Earth, and the myriad things. In *the Western Inscription*, Zhang Zai (1022-1077) beautifully expressed it thusly:

> Heaven is my father and Earth is my mother, and even such a small creature as I finds an intimate place in their midst. Therefore, that which fills the universe I regard as my body and that which directs the universe I consider as my nature. All people are my brothers and sisters, and

---

17 Lee, *The Trinity*, 30.

18 Cheng, "The Trinity," 291.

19 Swimme & Berry, *The Universe Story*, 71. For the cosmogenetic principle, see ibid, 70-79.

all things are my companions.[20]

Wang Yang-ming (1472-1529) further expanded this ecodaoian
vision in his doctrine of the Oneness of All Things:

> The great man regards Heaven, Earth, and the myriad things as one
> body. He regards the world as one family and the country as one person.
> As to those who make a cleavage between objects and distinguish be-
> tween the self and others, they are small men. That the great man can
> regard Heaven, Earth, and the myriad things as one body is not because
> he deliberately wants to do so, but because it is the natural humane
> nature of his mind that he does so. Forming one body with Heaven,
> Earth, and the myriad things is not only true of the great man. Even
> the mind of the small man is no different. Only he himself makes it
> small.[21]

---

20 Chan, *A Source Book*, 497. This Neo-Confucian view of cosmic family resembles with
the hymn of St. Francis cited in the Laudato si, 87. "Praised be you, my Lord, with all
your creatures, especially Sir Brother Sun, who is the day and through whom you give
us light. And he is beautiful and radiant with great splendour; and bears a likeness of
you, Most High. Praised be you, my Lord, through Sister Moon and the stars, in heaven
you formed them clear and precious and beautiful. Praised be you, my Lord, through
Brother Wind, and through the air, cloudy and serene, and every kind of weather through
whom you give sustenance to your creatures. Praised be you, my Lord, through Sister
Water, who is very useful and humble and precious and chaste. Praised be you, my
Lord, through Brother Fire, through whom you light the night, and he is beautiful and
playful and robust and strong".

21 Chan Wing-tsit, trans., *Instructions for Practical Living and Other Neo-Confucian
Writings* (New York: Columbia University Press, 1963), 272. Also, see Heup Young
Kim, *Wang Yang-ming and Karl Barth: A Confucian-Christian Dialogue* (Lamham,
MD: University Press of America, 1996), 42-46.

Here, the universe is depicted as a cosmic triune family, and a human being is depicted as a cosmic person and a member of the cosmic Trinity.[22] From this vantage point, Cheng suggested a Confucian-Christian idea of the Trinity: "[W]e might see God the Son as the ideal human, God the Father would be heaven (the creative spirit), and God the Holy Spirit the earth (the receptive co-spirit), or agent of the world which testifies to the accomplishment of the divinity."[23]

## *Ki/Qi* (氣)[24] as Metacosmic Energy

As in the cited passage of Laozi, *ki/qi* is regarded as the medium and the source of force to enable unification and harmony among all creations through interaction of yin and yang. For this reason, Mary Evelyn Tucker argued that the philosophy of *ki/qi* has profound potentialities as an ecological cosmology.[25] However, *ki/qi* is not just a philosophical or metaphysical notion but also, more im-

---

22 Cf., a cosmic "Trinitarian key," addressed in the Laudato si', 239.

23 Cheng, "The Trinity," 225.

24 *Ki* (in Chinese, qì [ch'i]) is a term very similar to pneuma and translated variously such as material force, ether, energy, vital force, vital power, psychophysical energy, or spirit. Etymologically, however, it means breath, wind, and air, similar to ruach (in Hebrew) and pneuma (in Greek). The Great Ultimate views that it consists of two forms of movement, the yin (negative or female) and the yang (positive or male) that form a unity of complementary opposites. In this chapter, I use this term with its Korean/Chinese romanizations (*ki/qì*), but sometimes translate as metacosmic energy.

25 Mary Evelyn Tucker, "The Philosophy as an Ecological Cosmology," in *Confucianism and Ecology*, ed. Tucker and Berthrong, 187-207.

portantly, a physically materializing and ubiquitously — embodying reality. However, it is difficult for the analytically and scientifically oriented modern mind to know and realize it. It requires purifying one's mind (*kenosis* or self-emptying) to experience its subtle movements and covert reality through psychosomatic practices, which sometimes requires rigorously ascetic disciplines, such as meditation, contemplation, yoga, and East Asian martial arts (most of all, proper breathing exercises are crucial).

Zhuangzi had Confucius saying: "Make your will one! Don't listen with your ears, listen with your mind. No, don't listen with your mind, but listen with your spirit [*ki/qi*]. Listening stops with the ears, the mind stops with recognition, but spirit is empty and waits on all things. The Way [dao] gathers in emptiness alone. Emptiness is the fasting of the mind."[26] This passage stipulates three ways of knowing toward the enlightenment of dao, namely: (1) objective, (2) intuitive, and (3) spiritual. The first way of knowing (epistemic) is based on an objective (scientific) observation through sensory organs such as ("ears" and eyes). The second one refers to an intuitive perception through the operation of the "mind" (psychic) which, though more advanced than the first epistemic one, still remains within the limit of a penultimate recognition. The final one is the right path to attain the enlightenment of dao by a spiritual realization of *ki/qi*, the metacosmic energy, in and through the human body. This accurate way can surpass flaws and limitations of the objective and the intuitive knowing. However, it needs a rig-

---

26 Translation from Burton Watson, trans,, *The Complete Works Of Chuang Tzu* (New York & London: Columbia University Press, 1968), 58.

orous discipline of self-cultivation and self-empting to attain emptiness or vacuity ("the fasting of mind"), which is the precondition
to realize the movement of *ki/qi*.

Thus, ecodao as a new ecological theology underscores the realization of *ki/qi*. However, it is not easy for the modern people to
recognize *ki/qi*. For its subtle and apophatic movement is beyond
cognitive knowing and verbal expressions but needs to be realized
in and through bodily experiences (even beyond intuition), particularly through breathing. This point is crucial in this technocratic
era, not only in danger of a total destruction of ecosystems, but also
challenged by the movement of transhumanism that advocates the
maximum use of science and technology to end up or upgrade the
species of homo sapiens to the post-human by substituting the problematic bio-body with a superman-like machine body.[27] In this regard, the distinction of Thomas Berry between "the Technozoic"
and "the Ecozoic" is insightful and significant.[28]

---

27 See Heup Young Kim, "Techno-Dao: Transhumanism Debates (Cyborg, Sage, and Saint),"
   in *A Theology of Dao*, 238-259; also idem, "Cyborg, Sage, and Saint: Transhumanism as Seen
   from an East Asian Theological Setting," in Religion and Transhumanism: the Unknown
   Future of Human Enhancement, ed. Calvin Mercer and Tracy J. Trothen (Santa Barbara,
   CA: Praeger, 2015), 97-114. Transhumanism in this chapter mainly refers to this kind of
   technocratic movement towards a cybernectic post-human, distinguished from posthumanism which has a variety of meanings.

28 Swimme & Berry said, "This future will be worked out in the tension between those
   committed to the Technozoic, a future of increased exploitation of Earth as resource,
   all for the benefit of human, and those committed to the Ecozoic, a new mode of human-Earth relations, one where the well-being of the entire Earth community is the primary concern" (*The Universe Story*, 15). In fact, this cannot be said as "a new mode,"
   but return to "the old, original mode of human-Earth relations", of course with far advanced knowledge of science.

The Reformation accelerated "an intensively anthropocentric turn" of Christian theology[29] and dissociated the anthropocosmic unity implicit in the medieval Christianity, and the Industrial Revolution promoted the use of modern science to massively exploit the body of the Earth. Furthermore, transhumanists are now contriving a revolution for an extinction of the human body, preaching a technozoic gospel for an omnipotent and eternal post-human without death and diseases. However, the significance of breathing lies in the fact cybernetic post-human with machine bodies cannot breathe. Their source of energy is not a metacosmic and life-giving energy like *ki/qi*, which is psycho-physical (spirit and matter) and interpenetrating (in and out) phenomenon, but an electrico-chemically working machine, like batteries (cf., *Matrix*). Hence, I argue that a spirituality of body and breathing in theory and praxis (ecodao) is what is imperative to move in the Ecozoic and resist against the Technozoic. The movie *Star Wars* is prophetic here, with a visionary slogan of Jedi knights like Yoda (a messianic daoist warrior): "May the Force [*ki/qi*] be with you."

## Breathing as Spirituality

In fact, a simple way to experience and realize the *ki/qi* is to feel and discern its movement through the practice of breathing in and

---

29 Elizabeth A. Johson, "Losing and Finding Creation in the Christian Tradition," in *Christianity and Ecology*, ed. Hessel and Ruether, 3-21. Also see Kim, "Theodao," 105-107.

out. Zhuangzi said, "All things that have consciousness depend upon breath [息]. But if they do not get their fill of breath, it is not the fault of Heaven. Heaven opens up the passages and supplies them day and night without stopping. But man, on the contrary, blocks up." The Book of Changes states that "the successive alteration of one yin and one yang is called the Dao [一陰一陽之謂道]..."[30] This symbolic statement has profound philosophical implications and has produced manifold interpretations in the history of East Asian thought. Simply speaking, however, using the metaphors of yin and yang and dao, it figuratively describes the phenomenology of breathing; the way a life is sustained by a successively, alternating movement of inhalation (yin: breathing air and *ki/qi* in) and exhalation (yang: breathing air and *ki/qi* out). Another important point is that the term *ki/qi* connotes not only the meta cosmic energy but also air in the sky, as air in the Chinese character literary means the '*ki/qi* in the emptiness.'

In the process of breathing, when inspiration reaches its limit, it alternates with the expiration, and vice versa. In the diagram of the Great Ultimate, therefore, there is an eye (a small circle of yang) inside the yin, and another eye (a small circle of yin) inside the yang. They symbolize the "inness" (inclusion) of yang "in" the yin and of yin "in" the yang, or the existence of "the inner connecting principle" between yin and yang (when yin reaches its limit, it becomes yang, and vice versa). This insight of the inness or the inner connecting principle in yin and yang resembles the notion of *perichoresis* (coinherence) in the Christian doctrine of the Trinity, such as when

---

30 Cf. Wilhelm, *The I Ching*, 297.

as Jesus says, "Believe me that I am in the Father and the Father is *in* me" (Jn 14:11). Breathing is not just a process of the inhalation of fresh air with oxygen and the exhalation of used air, but also, more importantly, a bodily embodiment of *ki/qi* in the process of this yin-yang alternation. Through the breathing of *ki/qi*, humans sustain life in communion and communication with that of the universe. "The [*ki/qi*] involved in human breathing is the [*ki/qi*] of universe... Heaven (or Nature) and humans are basically not two."[31] Hence, *ki/qi*, life-giving meta-cosmic energy, and breathing (often mutually interchangeable terms) have profound spiritual implications for ecodao. This is similar to the passage in Genesis, which states that "the Lord God formed man from the dust of the ground, and breathed into his nostrils the breath [ki in the Korean Bible] of life, and the man became a living being" (Gen. 2:7 NRSV).

The spirituality grounded on the onto-cosmology of the Great Ultimate and the kenotic dao does not imply an abstract metaphysical cosmology or an individually isolated ascetic discipline. On the contrary, the spirituality of *ki/qi* (breathing) entails the concrete trajectory of the revolutionary and subversive life force. As the divine breath (*sum*) initiated the creation of cosmos and inspired humans to life, it is a cosmogonic (or cosmogenetic) life-giving force (*ki/qi*) that can make all things alive. A clue to understanding the mystery of the hidden but dynamic metacosmic power of the dao is the principle of "reversal" and the power of radical return.[32] In

---

31 Lo Ch'in-shun, *Knowledge Painfully Acquired*, trans., Irene Bloom (New York: Columbia Press, 1987), 161-162.

32 Kim, *A Theology of Dao*, 40-43.

the Christian Bible, Jesus also speaks of the principle of reversal: "Blessed are you that are hungry now, for you will be filled... Woe to you who are full now, for you will be hungry" (Lk. 21: 25); "Whoever wants to be first must be last of all" (Mk 9:35); or "For those who want to save their life will lose it, and those who lose their life for my sake will find it" (Mt. 16:25). A vivid metaphor of dao's radical power of return is a feeble fish's jumping up against the mighty downstream in order to return to its origin.[33] Another reversal/return metaphor in the *Daodejing* can be found in the gendered nature of yin and yang. *Daodejing* describes dao with basically feminine metaphors such as "mother of all things" and "the mystical female." This feminine vision is based on Laozi's principle of "reversal." Laozi gave a preferential option to the strategy of *yin* (weak, soft, small, empty) rather than *yang* (strong, hard, big, full).[34] This *yin* principle of reversal is closely connected with the principle of return. The principle of reversal and radical return entails the spirituality of dao with the paradoxical power of weakness and emptiness.

Ecodao embodied with this East Asian spirituality of dao can strengthen ecological theology, extending it beyond Christian resources. The spirituality of dao with the *yin* principle of reversal and radical return with the paradoxical power of weakness and emptiness could empower resistance to merciless processes of genocide, biocide, and ecocide. In fact, this *yin* principle is in accordance

---

33 Ibid, 18-23, 138-144.

34 A. C. Graham, *Disputers of the Tao: Philosophical Argument in Ancient China* (La Salle, IL: Open Court, 1989), 223.

with the life-act of Jesus. The life-saving mystery of his resurrection entails a Christian principle of radical return (the victory of life over the power of death). His crucifixion on the cross denotes a Christian principle of reversal with the paradoxical power of weakness and emptiness (cf. Isa. 53:5, Lk. 6:20-21, 1 Cor. 1:18). And the yin strategy resonates with the biblical 'preferential option for the poor', a famous idiom of liberation theology. However, the preferential option should be extended to the wounded ecosystem as a whole, including endangered species, in addition to minjung (the poor, women, the oppressed, and the underprivileged).

## Ki-Socio-Cosmic Biography of the Exploited Life as a Hermeneutical Key

Korean minjung theologian Kim Yong-bock argued that the social biography (the underside history) of minjung is a more authentic historical point of reference for theological reflection than doctrinal discourses (the official history) superimposed by the Church in the orientation of Western rationality.[35] This was important for Asian theology. The recognition of minjung as the subject of history rectified traditional theologies that tended to regard minjung as the object of mission and control. Nevertheless, its exclusive focus is on the political history of God, and such an anthropocentric history hinders to make full use of the depths of Asian religious and eco-

---

35 Kim Yong-bock, "Theology and the Social Biography of Minjung," *CTC Bulletin* 5:3-6:1 (1984-1985): 66-78.

logical thoughts. East Asian theology should also include the under-side histories of life systems on Earth, expanding its hermeneutical horizon beyond the historico-social to the socio-cosmic (both social and cosmic). It requires a fusion of horizons (or "a new synthesis") between the sociobiography of minjung and the anthropocosmic vision so as to construct a sociocosmic biography (story, narrative) of exploited life.[36] Then, an important task of ecodao is to monitor and articulate such a sociocosmic narrative of the exploited life en-compassing not only the oppressed people but also the other sen-tient beings and the insentient things in the whole ecosystem under the exploitation of industrial-capitalist imperialism and scien-tific-technocratic fundamentalism.

East Asian anthropocosmic visions entails a symbiosis of the life network through the metacosmic communion and interpenetration of *ki/qi*, which I call a *ki*-anthropocosmic vision. This vision (*symbiosis*) cultivates more suitable human relationships with other lives and things in the cosmos than both societas (by contract) and communi-tas (by fellowship [koinonia]) which are still anthropocentric. However, ecodao should not halt at a romantic hermeneutics of retrieval but instead employ a critical hermeneutics of suspicion (e.g., why is it that East Asians who inherited beautifully ecological traditions now live in the most polluted regions in the world?).[37] Ecodao needs to focus on a *sociocosmic biography of the exploited life*

---

36 Cf. Laudato si', 112, 121.

37 Heup Young Kim, "Response to Peter K. H. Lee," in *Christianity and Ecology: Seeking the Well-Being of Earth and Humans*, ed. Dieter T. Hessel and Rosemary R. Ruether (Cambridge, MA: Harvard University Press, 2000), 357-361.

as a hermeneutical key and attempt to find a way to rejuvenate the broken sociocosmic network of exploited life by the communicative and transformative force of *ki/qi*. This meta cosmic energy is salvific, both emancipatory and reconciliatory. By embodying the *ki/qi* spirituality of reversal and return, ecodao finds a way to implement a sociocosmic transformative praxis (the dao) to heal and revitalize the wounded Mother Earth. This *ki*-sociocosmic (or pneumato-sociocosmic) narrative resonates with the consummate Christian story of Jesus Christ, pneumatologically empowered by the paradoxical power of the cross (reversal) with an eschatological hope for resurrection (return).

Pain is a way for the sentient body to send an urgent sign and message to an ignorant consciousness to make it aware of possible physical problems such as the coming danger of diseases. For this reason, ecodao pays close attention to the sociocosmic biography of the exploited life to hear signs and messages of pain from the body of Mother Earth. In his doctrine of oneness of all things, Wang Yang-ming ecologically expanded "the sense of commiseration," the first of the Confucian "four beginnings" to be a bona fide human being:[38]

> Therefore, when he sees a child about to fall into a well, he cannot help a feeling of alarm and commiseration. This shows that his humanity [*rén*] forms one body with the child. It may be objected that the child belongs to the same species. Again, when he observes the pitiful cries

---

38 Michael C. Kalton, trans., *To Become a Sage: The Ten Diagrams on Sage Learning by Yi T'oegye* (New York: Columbia University Press, 1988), 120-125.

and frightened appearance of birds and animals about to be slaughtered, he cannot help feeling an "inability to bear" their suffering. This shows that his humanity forms one body with birds and animals. It may be objected that birds and animals are sentient beings as he is. But when he sees plants broken and destroyed, he cannot help a feeling of pity. This shows that his humanity forms one body with plants. It may be said that plants are living things as he is. Yet, even when he sees tiles and stones shattered and crushed, he cannot help a feeling of regret. This shows that his humanity forms one body with tiles and stones. This means that even the mind of the small man necessarily has the humanity that forms one body with all. Such a mind is rooted in his Heaven-endowed nature, and is naturally intelligent, clear, and not beclouded."[39]

## Ecodao and *Laudato si*

The recent encyclical of Pope Francis on ecology "*Laudato si*" is impressively resonant with the views of ecodao in various ways. First of all, the proposal for "integral ecology" is in favor of the eco-daoian project I have outlined here, making genuine dialogues with and utilizing our own religious and wisdom traditions beyond the wall of traditional Christianity. The emphasis on "cultural ecology" is remarkable.[40] This point is particularly significant for developing

---

39 Chan Wing-tsit, trans., *Instructions for Practical Living and Other Neo-Confucian Writings by Wang Yang-ming* (New York: Columbia University Press, 1963), 272.

40 Laudato si', 143.

and developed countries in the Global South where the logic of development is still strong and robust and where in many cases ecological destructions are creating greater dysfunctions with accompanying destructions of local religious and cultural traditions, which are irreversible in most cases. The document states:

> Rather, there is a need to incorporate the history, culture and architecture of each place, thus preserving its original identity. Ecology, then, also involves protecting the cultural treasures of humanity in the broadest sense. More specifically, it calls for greater attention to local cultures when studying environmental problems... Culture is more than what we have inherited from the past; it is also, and above all, a living, dynamic and participatory present reality, which cannot be excluded as we rethink the relationship between human beings and the environment.[41]

It The document makes an imperative claim that ecology should be built in the context of "the constant and active involvement of local people within their proper culture." Furthermore, it asserts rightfully, "Nor can the notion of the quality of life be imposed from without, for quality of life must be understood within the world of symbols and customs proper to each human group."[42]

Secondly, the emphasis of the universal interconnectedness resonates with the East Asian theanthropocosmic (and ontocosmological) vision in the communicative unity of God, Earth, and

---

41 Ibid.

42 Ibid, 144. Cf., Heup Young Kim, "Owning Up to Our Own Metaphors: A Christian Journey in the Confucian Stronghold," in *A Theology of Dao*, 3-13.

Humanity. "The creation accounts in the book of Genesis contain, in their own symbolic and narrative language... suggest that human life is grounded in three fundamental and closely intertwined relationships: with God, with our neighbor and with the earth itself."[43] As already noted, St. Francis' ecological vision of a cosmic family has many echoes of the Neo-Confucian vision as in the cited passage from the *Western Inscription*: "Everything is related, and we human beings are united as brothers and sisters on a wonderful pilgrimage, woven together by the love God has for each of his creatures and which also unites us in fond affection with brother sun, sister moon, brother river and mother earth".[44] The ecodaoian suggestion for a sociocosmic biography of the exploited life is relevant to the encyclical's points on the issues of biodiversity, global warming, desertification, etc. The "new synthesis" of ecology and social justice issues (liberation theology) is in accord with the ecodaoian fusion of anthropocosmic vision and minjung theology: "Hence, every ecological approach needs to incorporate a social perspective which takes into account the fundamental rights of the poor and the underprivileged."[45]

Thirdly, the critique of "unhealthy dualism" is in consonance with the theodaoian criticism of the "either-or" mentality in the Western thought.[46] The claim of the inseparability of spirit and body is a core claim of theodao and ecodao; "the life of the spirit is not dis-

---

43 Laudato si': 68. Cf. also ibid, 70, 240.

44 Ibid, 68.

45 Ibid, 93.

46 Ibid, 98.

sociated from the body or from nature or from worldly realities, but lived in and with them, in communion with all that surrounds us."[47] At this juncture, it is worth remembering that Christianity with the doctrine of the Trinity (both one and three) and Christology (both divine and human) already had overcome Greek dualism (either one or three; either divine or human). Further, the critique of modern anthropocentrism is honest and consistent with that of theodao. "Modern anthropocentrism has paradoxically ended up prizing technical thought over reality, since the technological mind sees nature as an insensate order, as a cold body of facts, as a mere 'given', as an object of utility, as raw material to be hammered into useful shape; it views the cosmos similarly as a mere 'space' into which objects can be thrown with complete indifference'."[48] Furthermore, the encyclical asserts, "We no longer speak of sustainable development apart from intergenerational solidarity".[49] The intergenerational solidarity has particularly significant implications vis-à-vis the challenge of transhumanism which attempts to impose "a tyranny of the present over the future" and over the past as well.[50]

Fourthly, the focus on humanism is a breakthrough in Christian theology. It is consistent with the theodaoian criticism of "exclusive humanism" developed under the influence of modern individualism, and it seems to endorse the theodaoian proposal for "inclusive humanism" based on the Neo-Confucian theanthropocosmic vision.

---

47 Ibid, 216.

48 Ibid, 115.

49 Ibid, 159.

50 Brent Waters, "Flesh Made Data: The Posthuman Project in Light of the Incarnation," in *Religion and Transhumanism*, ed. Mercer and Trothen, 297-301.

"We urgently need a humanism capable of bringing together the different fields of knowledge, including economics, in the service of a more integral and integrating vision."[51] The appeal for an integral ecology highlighting human ecology sounds almost like a Neo-Confucian statement. The document states that; "an integral ecology calls for openness to categories which transcend the language of mathematics and biology, and take us to the heart of what it is to be human."[52] Moreover, the encyclical underlines the exercise of a concrete spirituality, such as ascetic practices, calling for "ecological [interior] conversion" by rejecting "self-interested pragmatism."[53] This aligns with an ecodaoian interest in self-cultivation, self-empting, spiritual discipline of *ki/qi.*

Fifthly, the view of the Trinity as "a web of relationship" converges with the theodaoian view of the Trinity.[54] The encyclical asserts that, "The Franciscan saint teaches us that *each creature bears in itself a specifically Trinitarian structure,* so real that it could be readily contemplated if only the human gaze were not so partial, dark and fragile. In this way, he points out to us the challenge of trying to read reality in a Trinitarian key."(239) In a similar Trinitarian key, a Neo-Confucian scholar suggested a new synthesis based on the onto-cosmology of the dao and the Great Ultimate:

If Heaven embodies the spirit of incessant creativity and the develop-

---

51 Laudato si', ibid, 141.

52 Ibid, 11.

53 Ibid, 215-217.

54 Ibid, 240.

ment of life and Earth the everlasting receptivity and consistence of love, then the human must embody their combination in a harmonious fusion and should apply both in appropriate measure in thought, emotion, and conduct. Heaven is a symbol of the cosmology of creativity and development; Earth is a symbol of an ecology of the combination of the two, this producing the ethics of integration and fulfillment of values. Hence, we see in the Confucian sage the trinity of Heaven, Earth, and human that embodies the unity of cosmology, ecology, and ethics. It is important to see that the unity of the three is based on and unified in the onto-cosmology of the Tao and *t'ai-chi* [the Great Ultimate].[55]

Finally, the encyclical presents a hint for Christian theology of the body in which ecodao has a special interest: "Christianity does not reject matter. Rather, bodiliness is considered in all its value in the liturgical act, whereby the human body is disclosed in its inner nature as a temple of the Holy Spirit and is united with the Lord Jesus, who himself took a body for the world's salvation."[56]

Thus, ecodao and *Laudato si'* share many common points that enable mutually constructive and fruitful dialogues. Especially I would like to highlight the spirituality of breathing and the insight and reality of *ki/qi*, a recuperating and outpouring metacosmic energy with the *yin* principle of reversal and return. In and through a constructive dialogue (or new synthesis) with the Orthodox tradition of Jesus Prayer and the liberation theology' insight of a preferential option for the poor respectably, for example, those ecodaoian

---

55 Cheng, "The Trinity," 224-225.
56 Laudato si', 235.

perspectives could help develop a more concrete ecological theology and spirituality of incarnation (body) for an ecozoic period. These only some examples for which ecodao can make substantial contributions to ecological discourses in the years to come, anticipating and foretelling the Return of the Dao (of Jesus Christ):

> Attain complete vacuity, maintain steadfast quietude.
>
> All things come into being, and I see thereby their return.
>
> All things flourish, but each one returns to its root.
>
> This return to its root means tranquility.
>
> It is called returning to its destiny.
>
> To return to destiny is called the eternal ([d]ao).
>
> To know the eternal is called enlightenment.
>
> He who knows the eternal is all-embracing.
>
> Being all-embracing, ... he is one with Nature.
>
> Being one with Nature, he is in accord with [d]ao.[57]

---

57 Daodejing: 16. Chan, *A Source Book*, 147.

CHAPTER THREE

# Creation and Dao:
# A Theodaoian Perspective

Abstract

Like the *logos* (word, speech, reason) in Western theology, the
*Dao* (the Way) is the overarching concept in East Asian religious
thinking, such as expressed in Confucianism and Daoism. This led
to the construction of theo-dao, an East Asian contextual theology
that adopts the Dao root-metaphor, as Western theologies (theo-
logos) do with the *logos*. The Daoian view of cosmogony is profoundly similar in structure to the Christian doctrine of creation, but
with some subtle differences in content. On the one hand, the
Christian doctrine underscores the yang dimension of creation, such
as, most notably, the ontology of being, duality, the cosmos, and
theo-historical aspects. On the other hand, the Daoian view focuses
on the yin dimension, such as the meontology of nothingness,
wholeness in duality, chaos, and the anthropo-cosmic aspect
(cosmic/ecological being-in-togetherness). However, these two
views no longer need to be seen as contradictory but rather can
be viewed as complementary, via completing the complementary

opposites of the yang (theo-logos) and the yin (theo-dao) dimensions of creation. Discoveries from the natural sciences may further explain this holistic understanding of the universe. Hence, a theodaoian contribution invites Christian theology to recover the disregarded path of yin (Dao) by positively engaging in a trialogue with East Asian religions and natural sciences, and reappreciating the traditions of apophatic spirituality and negative theology.

## Introduction

Like the *logos* (word, speech, reason) in Western theology, the *Dao* (the Way) is the overarching concept in East Asian religious thinking, such as expressed in Confucianism and Daoism. Unlike other theistic world religions, Confucianism and Daoism arise from a sapiential paradigm centered around Dao's thoughts and spirituality. Furthermore, they have views on the creation (precisely, cosmogony) of the universe akin to the Christian doctrine of creation, but with different nuances. This chapter discusses the challenges and complementary measures that the Daoian view of cosmogony can contribute to a Christian doctrine of creation. First, it introduces Confucianism and Daoism as the third paradigm of world religions, considering Western scholarship's interpretations of Dao. It presents *theo-dao* (a theology of Dao) as an East Asian contextual theology that adopts the Dao as its root-metaphor, like Western theologies (theo-logos) have done with *logos*. It then explicates early Daoist and Neo-Confucian thoughts on creation, examines their challenges and alternative insights to the traditional Christian doctrine of creation, highlighting the following topics: meontology of nothingness, complementary opposites (the Great Ultimate), primordiality of chaos, preferential option for yin, and humanity as cosmic/ecological being-in-togetherness.

## Confucianism/Daoism: Third Great Paradigm of World Religions

Although long neglected by the dominant dipolar view of world religions, Confucianism and Daoism, broad and complex religio-cultural traditions with a history longer than Christianity by about five centuries, represent a distinctive feature of East Asian religious culture. More precisely, Neo-Confucianism, a reformed Confucianism in synthesis with Daoism, is recognized as "the common background of the peoples of East Asia' and 'the most plausible rationale" in attempting to understand the attitude of 'the inward-looking civilization of East Asia';[1] namely, Korea, China, Japan, Taiwan, Vietnam, and Singapore. Tu Wei-ming states: "East Asians may profess themselves to be Shintoists, Taoists, Buddhists, Muslims, or Christians, but by announcing their religious affiliations seldom do they cease to be Confucians."[2]

Accordingly, Hans Küng made a helpful correction to the geog-

---

1 Wm. Theodore de Bary, *East Asian Civilizations: A Dialogue in Five Stages* (Cambridge: Harvard University Press, 1989), 44.

2 Tu Wei-ming, *Confucianism in a Historical Perspective* (Singapore: The Institute of East Asian Philosophies, 1989), 3.

raphy of world religions. Instead of the generally accepted dipolar view of Middle Eastern (West Asian) and Indian (Middle Asian) religions, he argued for a tripolar view that includes East Asian religions such as Confucianism and Daoism. He claimed that Confucianism and Daoism consist as the third great paradigm of world religions ('a third independent religious river system') of East Asian origin and sapiential character, comparable to the other two great religious paradigms.[3] In contrast, the first great paradigm (Judaism, Christianity, and Islam) is of West Asian (Semitic) origin and prophetic character, and the second paradigm (Hinduism, Buddhism, Jainism, etc.) is of Middle Asian origin and mystical character.

## Dao (Tao)[4]

Like the logos in Western thought, the Dao (usually meaning 'the Way') is a central concept in East Asian (traditionally, Neo-Confucian) countries.[5] It is a holistic notion with multiple meanings that are hard to define, that are challenging to modern people accustomed to analytical and critical thinking. Although many misunderstand that Dao is only related to Daoism, Dao is an all-embracing umbrella

---

3 Hans Küng and Julia Ching, *Christianity and Chinese Religions*, trans. Peter Beyer (New York: Doubleday, 1989), xi-xv.

4 Generally, its character (道) is romanizedRomanised as 'Dao' (Pinyin) or 'Tao' (Wade-Giles). For Chinese characters in what follows, I basically follow the Pinyin romanization system, but also use romanizations according to Korean pronunciation for some terms special in the Korean context, such as T'aegŭk (太極 Taiji; the Great Ultimate).

5 Although Dao is an all-embracing term in East Asian thought, what follows arises primarily from Korean Daoist and Neo-Confucian contexts.

concept that other religions in East Asia widely use — the Dao of Confucianism, the Dao of Buddhism, and the Dao of Christianity are among such uses.

Among Western scholars, Herbert Fingarette and C. S. Lewis have presented valuable definitions of Dao in English. On the one hand, Fingarette defined the Dao in a Confucian way, interpreting Confucius's *Analects*: "Tao [Dao] is a Way, a path, a road, and by common metaphorical extension it becomes in ancient China the right Way of life, the Way of governing, the ideal Way of human existence, the Way of the Cosmos, the generative-normative Way (Pattern, path, course) of existence as such."[6] Conversely, Lewis presented a more ontological understanding in a Daoist way:

> The *Tao*, which others may call Natural Law or Traditional Morality or the First Principles of Practical Reason or the First Platitudes, is not one among a series of possible systems of value. It is the sole source of all value judgements. If it is rejected, all value is rejected. If any value is retained, it is retained. The effort to refute it and raise a new system of value in its place is self-contradictory. There has never been, and never will be, a radically new judgement of value in the history of the world. What purport to be new systems or... ideologies... all consist of fragments from the *Tao* itself, arbitrarily wrenched from their context in the whole and then swollen to madness in their isolation, yet still owing to the *Tao* and to it alone such validity as they possess.[7]

---

6 Herbert Fingarette, *Confucius — The Secular as Sacred* (New York: Harper & Row, 1972), 19.

7 C. S. Lewis, *The Abolition of Man: Or, Reflections on Education with Special Reference to the Teaching of English in the Upper Forms of Schools* (New York: Macmillan, 1947),

Lewis's thought has attracted attention under challenges from transhumanism that urge the maximum use of science and technology to engineer human enhancement and evolution to the next stage of *homo sapiens* — the post-human.[8] However, such movements utilizing radical biohacking were anticipated even at the beginning of the twentieth century. In the 1940s, Lewis had already foreseen the danger of such arising scientism, emboldened by an Enlightenment mentality. In response to this particular challenge, Lewis proposed a turn to the thought of Dao rather than that of Western Christianity.

## Theo-dao: An East Asian Contextual Theology

As a 28th-generation descendant of a Korean Confucian family converted to Christianity, I have engaged in Confucian- Christian dialogue since undertaking doctoral studies. The first study defended the thesis that 'in the light of Wang Yang-ming (1472-1529) and Karl Barth (1886-1968), Neo-Confucian self-cultivation and Christian sanctification are thickly resemblant views of a common issue — how to be fully human'. It also showed that both of them used the Dao mode of theology; namely, "in search for the Tao of a new cosmic humanity."[9] This led to the formulation of *theo-dao* (a theology of Dao) by applying the Dao as theology's root-metaphor.

---

28-29.

8 Heup Young Kim (Hŭb-yŏng Kim), *A Theology of Dao* (Maryknoll: Orbis Books, 2017), 238-259.

9 Heup Young Kim, *Wang Yang-ming and Karl Barth: A Confucian-Christian Dialogue* (Lanham: University Press of America, 1996), 175-188.

It represented a way of owning up to one's own metaphors.[10] If theo-logy (*theo-logos*) entails the relationship between 'God and *logos*', theo-dao does likewise between 'God and Dao'. Since its character (道) consists of two parts, the head (首) and movement (辶), Dao, etymologically, means the unity of knowing and acting (知行合一). It converges with Barth's insistence on the unity of theology (knowing) and ethics (acting). The dualism between *logos* (word) and praxis (deed) is a central problem in Western theologies inherited from dualistic Greek thought, and subsequently promotes a dilemma in contemporary global theology between theo-logos (classical theologies) and theo-praxis (liberationist theologies). Therefore, I advocated a constructive theology of Dao (theo-dao) as a third paradigm for advancing global theology by overcoming this persistent dualism.[11]

Put simply, both theo-logos and theo-praxis are related to the substantialist-essentialist and either-or (either *logos* or praxis) mode of Western thinking. Theo-logos is doctrinal (knowledge-oriented), while theo-praxis is ideological (action-oriented). By contrast, the Dao, referring to the unity of knowing and acting, transcends the dualism of logos and praxis. To summarize in terms of the three cardinal virtues in 1 Corinthians 13: faith is for theo-logos (a faith-seeking-understanding, focusing on ortho-doxy, on right doctrine for the church), hope is for theo-praxis (a hope-seeking-action, focusing on ortho-praxis, the right action for the reign of God), and love is for theo-dao (a love-seeking-dao, focusing on ortho-dao,

---

10 Kim, *A Theology of Dao*, 3-13.

11 Ibid, 14-33.

the right way/wisdom of life).[12]

Furthermore, the term Dao is more biblical (at least for christology), as it is homologous to biblical Greek term *hodos* ('way, road, highway' as a place; 'way, journey' as an action; 'way of life, way of acting, conduct;' 'the whole way of life').[13] Jesus never identified himself as the *logos* but rather as the *hodos*, saying, "I am the way, and the truth, and the life" (Jn 14.6). Although John used the term *logos* (the Word) in John 1.1, it does not refer to its logos-centric reductions but rather has a closer connotation to the Hebrew term *dabar*, which underlines action. Although both terms express 'the Word', *dabar* focuses more on the deed (wisdom), whereas *logos* places the focus on reason (knowledge and order).[14] By using *logos* as the root-metaphor, Western theology became doctrinal, intellectual, and theoretical, overlooking the importance of praxis (deed and action), a hermeneutical root cause for the rise of lib-

---

12 The three theological paradigms with the three root metaphors can be compared as following:

| Root metaphor | Theology | Christology | Metaphor | Character | Objective |
|---|---|---|---|---|---|
| logos | theo-logy | christo-logy | faith | understanding (doctrine) | orthodoxy |
| praxis | theo-praxis | christo-praxis | hope | action (ideology) | orthopraxis |
| dao | theo-dao | christo-dao | love | living (way of life) | orthodao |

13 William F. Arndt and F. Wilbur Gingrich, *A Greek-English Lexicon of the New Testament and Other Early Christian Literature: A Translation and Adaptation of the Fourth Revised and Augmented Edition of Walter Bauer's 'Griechisch-Deutsches Wörterbuch zu den Schriften des Neuen Testaments und der übrigen urchristlichen Literatur',* 2nd ed. (Chicago: The University of Chicago Press, 1979), 553-55.

14 George R. Beasley-Murray, *John, Word Biblical Commentary,* vol. 36 (Waco: Word Books, 1982), 9.

eration theologies (theo-praxis). Even in John 1.1, hence, Dao, with the meaning of the unity of knowledge and action, could be said more appropriate than is the term *logos*.

## Daoian[15] Creation: Cosmogony

Theology divides the creation narratives in two stages, the first creation (*creatio prima*) and the second creation (*creatio secunda*). The first creation refers to Genesis 1.1-2, whereas the second designates the further specific creation, including humans. The first creation depicts the creation of heaven and earth from nothing, the situation described as formless and void (תֹהוּ וָבֹהוּ, tōhū wā-bōhū) and marked by darkness or obscurity (חֹשֶׁךְ, wǝḥōšek) over the face of the deep (פְּנֵי תְהוֹם, al-pǝnê tǝhôm), and by the activity of a wind or spirit or breath (רוּחַ wǝrûaḥ) from God. Hence, the *creatio prima* entails four important themes comparable to the Daoian cosmogony — creation from nothing (*creatio ex nihilo*), chaos before forming the cosmos, the duality of light and darkness (heaven and earth), and the mysterious work of *ruach* (breath, wind, spirit).

The first chapter of *Dàodéjīng*, a Chinese text traditionally credited to the sixth century BCE sage Lao Tzu, states: "Non-being is the origin of Heaven and Earth; Being is the mother of all things."[16] Another

---

15 This chapter uses 'Daoian' as a term distinct from 'Daoist'. 'Daoian' is an adjective and refers to the dao as a general East Asian (and Korean) concept beyond Daoism, while 'Daoist' is related to Daoism, especially as a structural religion.

16 Wing-Tsit Chan, *A Source Book in Chinese Philosophy* (Princeton: Princeton University Press, 1963), 139.

ancient Chinese text, *Zhuangzi*, dated from around 476-221 BCE, also states: "In the Great Beginning, there was non-being; there was no being, no name. Out of it arose one, but it had no form. Things got hold of it and came to life, but it had no form."[17] Thus, the first tenet of the Daoian vision of creation is analogous to the Christian notion of creation from nothing (*creatio ex nihilo*), although the notion of nothing (non-being) has some different subtle nuances (see the following session). The Daoian cosmogony also has a similar structure to the creation account in Genesis (especially the *creatio prima*). Dao is the origin of all things which are produced by three steps. *Dàodéjīng* explains it in terms of a trinitarian process of one, two, and three. First, Dao produced One. Second, the one produced Two (duality such as light and darkness). Third, the two produced Three, and the three continuously produce myriad things by interacting yin and yang via the material force (氣).[18]

> Tao produced the One. The One produced the two.
>
> The two produced the three. And the three produced the ten thousand things.
>
> The ten thousand things carry the yin and embrace the yang,
>
> and through the blending of the material force (*ch'i*) they achieve harmony.[19]

---

17 Chuang Tzu, *The Complete Works of Chuang Tzu*, trans. Burton Watson (New York: Columbia University Press, 1968), 131.

18 The material force has various meanings such as vital force, breath, and meta-cosmic energy, which are parallel to the Hebrew ruach (wind, breath, spirit) and the Greek pneuma (wind, breath, spirit). Its romanizations are also various; ch'i in the Wade-Gile system, qì in Pinyin, and *ki* in Korean.

Although the structure is similar to Genesis 1, there are also some critical differences. The Daoian cosmogony is not based on the view of linear time like an arrow flowing straight to the end of time (*eschaton*), as in Christianity. Rather, the Daoian view understands that the universe's generation is continuously produced by the continual interaction of yin and yang, analogous to men and women combining to produce children. With bio-cosmic imageries, 'cosmogony' is a more appropriate term than is 'creation'. The Daoian cosmogony presents some crucial insights on themes often neglected in the Christian doctrine of creation. What follows will focus on these themes.

## Meontology of Nothingness

Daoian cosmogony unequivocally views non-being as more primordial than is being. The opening chapter of *Dàodéjīng* states:

The Tao (Way) that can be told of is not the eternal Tao;

The name that can be named is not the eternal name.

Non-being is the origin of Heaven and Earth; Being is the mother of all things.

Therefore, let there always be non-being so we may see their subtlety.

And let there always be being so we may see their manifestation.[20]

---

19 Chan, *A Source Book*, 160.

20 Ibid, 139.

Although the Christian doctrine of *creatio ex nihilo* endorses the primordiality of nothingness, it does so primarily in the service of an ontology of being rather than of non-being. Western theological ontologies tend to disregard non-being, or consider it only as a negative dialectic to being, which inevitably entails a conflict (rather than harmony) paradigm when the necessity for change (or becoming) occurs. For example, early Tillichian theology dealt with non-being, but it was with reservation, or, more likely, as a negative or inferior antithesis (finitude or the estrangement) of being.[21] Thus, Tillich also claimed the Protestant principle as "eternal and a permanent criterion of everything temporal."[22] It would be a Tillichian way of justifying Protestant theology's ontological weakness that denies the ontological possibility of change to insist on his static and essentialist ontology of being. In this regard, David Chai offers a helpful comparative study between Tillich and Zhuangzi:

> Herein is where Zhuangzi's meontology surpasses Tillich's *ex nihilo* hybrid. Unlike Tillich, Zhuangzi does not 'weaponize' non-being by turning it into the ultimate threat facing being; on the contrary, he takes non-being to be the root and mutual partner of being. In this way, the world is nourished, not harmed, by non-being, living freely and without despondency.[23]

---

21 Paul Tillich, *Systematic Theology*, vol .1 (Chicago: The University of Chicago Press, 1973), 186-203.

22 Paul Tillich, *The Protestant Era*, trans. James Luther Adams (Chicago: The University of Chicago Press, 1948), xii.

23 David Chai, "Paul Tillich, Zhuangzi, and the Creation Role of Nonbeing," *Philosophy East & West* 69, no. 2 (2019), 352.

As *Dàodéjīng* has it: "All things come from being. And being comes from non-being... The Tao is hidden and nameless. Yet it is Tao alone that skillfully provides for all and brings them to perfection."[24] The notion of the ineffable Dao as the non-being parallels that of the 'supraessential Trinity' in Eastern apophatic theology. Reminiscent of the opening lines of the *Dàodéjīng*, John of Damascus states: "The Deity being incomprehensible is also assuredly nameless. Therefore, since we know not His essence, let us not seek for a name for his essence."[25] In their points of contact, Eastern apophatic theology and East Asian theology of the Dao (theo-dao) have a valuable contribution to make to the development of a truly global theology.[26]

## Complementary Opposites

*Dàodéjīng* also equates non-being ontologically with being: "The two are the same. But after they are produced, they have different names. They both may be called deep and profound. Deeper and more profound. The door of all subtleties!"[27] Neo-Confucianism further validates that non-being and being form one as yin and yang to compose the Daoian onto-cosmology of the Great Ultimate (太極).

---

24 Chan, *A Source Book*, 160.

25 John of Damascus, *On the Orthodox Faith*, 1.12. Cited in Thomas Hopko, "Apophatic Theology and the Naming of God in Eastern Orthodox Tradition," in *Speaking the Christian God: The Holy Trinity and the Challenges of Feminism*, ed. Alvin F. Kimel, Jr. (Leominster/Grand Rapids: Gracewing/Wm. B. Eerdmans, 1992), 157.

26 For a discussion on Dao and the Trinity, see Kim, *A Theology of Dao*, 57-74.

27 Chan, *A Source Book*, 139.

It reaffirms the primordiality of the Non-being (無極) as the foundation of the Great Ultimate.[28] Zhou Dunyi (1017-1073) summarized the complementary paradox of opposites in *An Explanation of the Diagram of the Great Ultimate*:

> The Ultimate of Non-being and also the Great Ultimate! The Great Ultimate through movement generates yang. When its activity reaches its limit, it becomes tranquil. Through tranquility the Great Ultimate generates yin. When tranquility reaches its limit, activity begins again. So movement and tranquility alternate and become the root of each other, giving rise to the distinction of yin and yang, and the two modes are thus established.[29]

The Great Ultimate is symbolized by a circle enclosing yin and yang, denoting the complementary opposites. The circle signifies 'an inexhaustible source of creativity, which is one and undifferentiated', and the dynamic process of yin-yang interaction is 'always ready to be differentiated into concrete and individual things'. It is "the constant fountainhead amidst all things and provides the integrative and purposive unity of any type or any individual token while, at the same time, it also serves as the impetus for the diversity of things as types of tokens."[30] Furthermore, the yin-yang mode of thinking

---

28 Romanizations of Non-being (無極) include Mugŭk (Korean), Wú jí (Pinyin), and Wu chi (Wade-Giles). Romanizations of the Great Ultimate (太極) include T'aegŭk (Korean), Tài jí (Pinyin), and T'ai-chi (Wade-Giles).

29 Chan, *A Source Book*, 463.

30 Chung-Ying Cheng, "The Trinity of Cosmology, Ecology, and Ethics in the Confucian Personhood," in *Confucianism and Ecology: The Interrelation of Heaven, Earth, and*

entails *the ontology of change,* compared with the ontology of substance so dominant in the West. In fact, the yin-yang relationship
characterizes continuous change, change that is primary to ontic
being or substance. Change is "the matrix of all that was, is, and
shall be. It is the ground of all being and becoming."[31] In this onto-cosmology of the Great Ultimate, change is not a function of being, as Western ontologies generally assumes. On the contrary,
change is the ultimate itself, whereas being or substance is a penultimate manifestation of change.

Moreover, in the yin-yang relationship, the two opposites are
not in conflict but rather complement each other to attain harmony
and equilibrium. In Western models of conflict, one must choose
one of the two alternatives and eliminate the other ('either-or'). In
the East Asian model of harmony, the two opposites are complementary and belong to each other ('both-and'). So, Wilfred Cantwell
Smith: "We in the West presume that an intelligent man must choose
either this or that... [But] In all ultimate matters, truth lies not in an
either-or, but in a both-and."[32]

By applying a Daoian thought of the Great Ultimate, theo-dao
can overcome Western christologies's impasse due to the inherited
dualism between divinity and humanity. Theo-dao can articulate
Christ as the ultimate Dao (Christo-dao) by a both-and and nei-

*Humans,* ed. Mary Evelyn Tucker and John Berthrong (Cambridge: Harvard University Press, 1998), 219.

31 Jung Young Lee, *The Theology of Change: A Christian Concept of God in an Eastern Perspective* (Maryknoll: Orbis Books, 1979), 20.

32 Wilfred Cantwell Smith, *The Faith of Other Men* (New York: New American Library, 1963), 72.

ther-nor mode of thinking. The Nicene-Chalcedonian formula's genius lies in articulating the ultimate and cosmogonic nature of Christ in such a way that presses beyond the Greek dualistic framework. The Nicene Creed (325) adopted the both-and mode to articulate Christ as both *vere Deus* and *vere homo*. The Chalcedonian formula (451) used the neither-nor mode to express that the two natures in Christ are neither confused, changed, divided, nor separated. In terms of theo-dao, the fourth-century Christians intuitively had perceived the cosmogonic nature of Christ as the supreme paradox of the Great Ultimate (total affirmation of the both-and) and the Non-being (total negation of the neither-nor).[33] This theodaoian mode of paradoxical thought also appeared in creative early Christian theologians such as Gregory of Nyssa (c. 335-395) and Dionysius the Areopagite (fl. 500), in Christian mystics such as Francis of Assisi (c. 1182-1226), Meister Eckhart (c. 1260-1328), and Julian of Norwich (1343-after 1416), and is explicitly formulated by Nicholas of Cusa (1401-1464) in the principle of *coincidentia oppositorum*.[34]

Ryu Yŏngmo (1890-1981), a Korean Christian-Daoian thinker, formulated the cosmogonic Christ from the heart of the East Asian hermeneutical universe of Dao. Zhou Dunyi's explanation of the Great Ultimate denotes the ultimate complementary and paradoxical opposites of the ineffably vacuous Non-being and the cos-

---

33 On Christo-dao, see Kim, *A Theology of Dao*, 34-56, 147-68.

34 For an introduction to Nicholas of Cusa, Karl Jaspers, *The Great Philosophers: The Original Thinkers*, trans. Ralph Manheim (New York: Harcourt, Brace & World, Inc., 1966), 116-272.

mogonic Being (the Great Ultimate). From the vantage point of this supreme paradox of Dao, Ryu 'understood the cross as both the Ultimate of Non-being and the Great Ultimate... Jesus is the One who manifested the ultimate in Asian cosmology. Through the sacrifice of himself, he achieved genuine humanity (*rén*). By offering himself as a sacrifice, he saved humans and opened the kingdom of God for humanity'.[35] Moreover, he presented a unique Korean apophatic Christo-dao. Jesus is the One who 'Is' despite the 'Is-Not'. In other words, whereas human persons are those of 'non-being-in-being', Jesus is the One of 'Being-in-Non-Being' (*Ŏpshi-gye-shin nim)*'. Whereas human persons are the 'forms' that are 'none other than emptiness' (空即是色), Jesus is the 'emptiness' that is 'none other than form' (色即是空).[36]

## The Primordiality of Chaos

Genesis 1.2 bears witness to a chaotic situation before the creation of the cosmos, with terms like 'formless' (tōhū), 'void' (wā-bōhū), 'darkness' (wǝḥōšek), and 'the deep' (tǝhôm). Likewise, *Dàodéjīng* also describes the state of precosmic chaos (混沌):

We look at it and do not see it; Its name is The Invisible.
We listen to it and do not hear it; Its name is The Inaudible.

---

35 Kim Heung-ho, "Ryu Yŏngmo's View of Christianity from the Asian Perspective," in *Dasŏk Ryu Yŏngmo*, ed. Park Young-ho (Seoul: Sungchun Institution, 1994), 299.

36 Kim Heung-ho, *Jesori* (Seoul: Pungman, 1985), 68. On Ryu Yŏngmo's concept of Christo-dao, see Kim, *A Theology of Dao*, 147-68.

We touch it and do not find it; Its name is The Subtle (formless).

These three cannot be further inquired into, and hence merge into one.

Going up high, it is not bright, and coming down low, it is not dark.

Infinite and boundless, it cannot be given any name; It reverts to nothingness.

This is called shape without shape, Form (*hsiang*) without object.

It is the Vague and Elusive.

Meet it and you will not see its back.

Hold on to the Tao of old in order to master the things of the present.

From this one may know the primeval beginning [of the universe].

This is called the bond of Tao.[37]

In this way, *Dàodéjīng* emphasizes the primordiality of chaos, prioritizing subtlety over manifestation. Although Genesis explicitly states it, Western theologies have not paid much attention to the importance of chaos in creation. The natural sciences continuously uncover unseen places and elements of the universe, such as dark matter and dark energy, and reveal the significance of chaos.[38] *Dàodéjīng* insists that this chaotic primeval beginning should be taken seriously. Everything is ready in this state of chaos. *Dàodéjīng* argues that, though it is undifferentiated, nothing has been achieved, but everything has already been completed; namely, 'Something Chaotic and Yet Complete':[39]

---

37 Chan, *A Source Book*, 146.

38 Fritjof Capra, *The Tao of Physics: An Exploration of the Parallels Between Modern Physics and Eastern Mysticism*, 5th ed. (Boston: Shambhala, 2010).

39 N. J. Girardot, *Myth and Meaning in Early Taoism: The Theme of Chaos (hun-tun)* (Berkeley: University of California Press, 1983), 49-56.

There was something undifferentiated [chaotic] and yet complete,

Which existed before the creation of heaven and earth.

Soundless and formless, it depends on nothing and does not change.

It operates everywhere and is free from danger.

It may be considered the mother of the universe.

I do not know its name; I call it Tao.

If forced to give it a name, I shall call it Great.

Now being great means functioning everywhere.

Functioning everywhere means far-reaching.

Being far-reaching means to returning to the original point.[40]


## The Preferential Option for Yin

*Dàodéjīng* describes Dao with basically feminine metaphors such as 'mother of all things', 'the root', 'the ground' (of Being), 'the un-carved block' (the original nature), or 'mysterious female':

The spirit of valley never dies.

This is called the mysterious female [or mother].

The gateway [or womb] of the mysterious female [mother]

Is called the root of Heaven and Earth.

Dimly visible, it seems as if it were there,

Yet use will never drain it.[41]

---

40 Chan, *A Source Book*, 152.

41 Lao Tzu, *Tao Te Ching,* trans., D. C. Lau (Harmondsworth: Penguin Books, 1963), 62.

As such, *Dàodéjīng* places a priority on the female and on weakness rather than on the male and on strength. A. C. Graham argued that *Dàodéjīng* always puts the preferential option to yin rather than yang in the series of complementary oppositions.[42] This reversal principle is a clue to understanding the mystery of the Dao's hidden but unquenchable power. Jesus occasionally spoke of a similar principle of reversal: "Blessed are you that are hungry now, for you will be filled... Woe to you who are full now, for you will be hungry" (Lk. 6.21, 25). Also, Saint Paul said: "Whenever I am weak, then I am strong" (2 Cor. 12.10). The paradoxical power of weakness and emptiness entails the Daoian principle of *wú wéi* (無爲; non-action action). Bede Griffiths (1907-1993), a Benedictine monk who lived for many years in Indian ashrams, reflected thus on the implications of *Dàodéjīng* to Western religion:

> The most typical concept in the *Tao Te Ching* is that of *wu wei*, that is 'actionless activity'. It is a state of passivity, of 'non-action', but a passivity that is totally active, in the sense of receptivity. This is the essence of the feminine. The woman is made to be passive in relation to the man, to receive the seed which makes her fertile. But this passivity is an active

---

42 See Angus C. Graham, *Disputers of the Tao: Philosophical Argument in Ancient China* (Chicago: Open Court, 1989), 223.

| Yang | Yin | Yang | Yin |
|------|-----|------|-----|
| something | nothing | before | behind |
| doing something | doing nothing | moving | still |
| knowledge | ignorance | big | small |
| male | female | strong | weak |
| full | empty | hard | soft |
| above | below | straight | bent |

passivity, a receptivity which is dynamic and creative, from which all life and fruitfulness, all live and communion, grow. The world today needs to recover this sense of feminine power, which is complementary to the masculine and without which man becomes dominating, sterile and destructive. But this means that western religion must come to recognize the feminine aspect of God. This leads to *the paradox of the value of emptiness*. 'We make pots of clay', it is said, 'but it is the empty space in them which makes them useful. We make a wheel with many spokes joined in a hub, but it is the empty space in the hub which makes the wheel go round. We make houses of brick and wood, but it is the empty spaces in the doors and windows that make them habitable'. This again is the value of 'non-action', what Gandhi called *ahimsa*.[43]

## Humanity as Cosmic/Ecological Being-In-Togetherness

While Genesis 1.27 states that God created human beings in the image of God (*imago Dei*), the Confucian scripture *Doctrine of the Mean*, or *Zhongyong*, also declares: "What Heaven (T'ien, Nature) imparts to [hu]man is called human nature. To follow our nature is called the Way (Tao). Cultivating the Way is called education."[44] Therefore, Christianity and Confucianism have similarities in understanding ontological humanity; *imago Dei* and Heavenly endowment,

---

43 Bede Griffiths, *Universal Wisdom: A Journey Through the Sacred Wisdom of the World* (San Francisco: HarperCollins, 1994), 27.

44 Chan, *A Source Book*, 98.

respectably. Furthermore, the Confucian notion of *rén* (仁, benevolence) and Barth's understanding of the *imago Dei* show many points of convergence. The cardinal Confucian virtue, *rén*, implies benevolent co-humanity, as its etymology denotes two people. Likewise, Barth also interpreted the creation of two humans according to God's image as 'joyful *Mitmenschlichkeit*' (co-humanity).[45] Hence, both Barth and Neo-Confucianism arrived at the same conclusion that the ontological definition of humanity is benevolent or joyful co-humanity, being-with-others, or being-in-togetherness.[46]

Confucianism and Christianity (or at least that of Barth's type) share a congruent understanding of what it means to be human. To be human means to realize a radical being-in-togetherness in one's total unity of body and soul. Being a Confucian or a Christian means being radically human; that is, being co-human. Although this congruence establishes a material point of convergence, it also shows differences due to their divergent visions (anthropo-cosmic vs. theo-historical).[47] Whereas Confucianism extended the notion of togetherness to the cosmic dimension, Christianity focused on the meaning of co-humanity to the historical situation. In this encounter, the Christian historical consciousness challenges Confucianism to move beyond an innocent dream of anthropo-cosmic vision. Conversely, the Confucian understanding of the human as a cosmic being-in-togetherness challenges Christian theology to move be-

---

45 Karl Barth, *Church Dogmatics III.2*, trans. Harold Knight, Geoffrey W. Bromiley, J. K. S. Reid, and R. H. Fuller (Edinburgh: T&T Clark, 1960), 265.

46 For comparison of *ren* and *imago Dei*, see Kim, *Wang Yang-ming and Karl Barth*, 43-46, 86-90, 158-60.

47 Kim, *Wang Yang-ming and Karl Barth*, 175-78.

yond the modern inclinations of anthropocentric, anthropomorphic, and history-centred understandings, which, not a few would argue, share responsibility for the present ecological crisis.[48]

Zhang Zai (1022-1077) brilliantly expressed Neo-Confucian ecological thought in terms of the Confucian Trinity — Heaven, Earth, and Humanity:

> Heaven is my father and Earth is my mother, and even such a small creature as I finds an intimate place in their midst. Therefore, that which fills the universe I regard as my body and that which directs the universe I consider as my nature. All people are my brothers and sisters, and all things are my companions.[49]

## Conclusion

The Daoian view of cosmogony can provide the Christian doctrine of creation with significant challenges and complementary insights. First, although Western theologies advocate for the doctrine of *creatio ex nihilo*, such tend to denigrate non-being in favour of being. An invitation and challenge arising from theological engagement with Daoian thought may be that Christian theology could take much more seriously the primordiality of nothingness and the ontology of non-being. This could be made possible by reinterpret-

---

48 For an example for Daoian ecological theology (eco-dao), see Kim, A *Theology of Dao*, 204-22.

49 Chan, *A Source Book*, 497.

ing apophatic spirituality and negative theology traditions through dialogue with Daoian insights of cosmogony and natural sciences; namely, a trialogue between Christian theology, East Asian religions, and the natural sciences.[50]

Second, new scientific discoveries related to chaos theory, dark matter, and dark energy call forth more developed understandings of chaos in the creation and a revision of a longstanding commitment to unsustainable dualism, such that defines the chaos as evil and the cosmos as good. Daoian views of cosmogony and the Great Ultimate yin-yang theory offer an alternative solution to overcome this dualism, and in ways that might avoid some of the pitfalls typically associated with its Manichean and other expressions. For them, chaos and cosmos are not in conflicted relationships like good and evil but are rather complementary opposites like two sides of a coin. Furthermore, the developments of physics and mathematics since the time of Einstein evoke a theological paradigm shift to the both-and paradigm from the old either-or paradigm that divides non-being and being, chaos and cosmos, day and night, spirit and flesh, male and female, humanity and nature, etc. The early Christians solved this problem through developing wholistic doctrines of the Trinity (both one and three) and of Christ (true divinity and true humanity). Unfortunately, the deep-seated dualisms that remain characteristic of Western approaches to theology have largely ignored these significant breakthroughs of the early Christian faith, especially through the doctrines of Triune God and Christ (both God and human).

------------

50 On the possibility of such a trialogue, see Kim, *A Theology of Dao*, 189-203.

Third, Western Protestant theologies have tended to neglect the significance of the body and ecosystem by predominantly focusing on the salvation of the individual soul. Human beings were created when God breathed into the human body which was called forth from the earth. The creation of humanity in the image of the Trinity denotes co-humanity (*Mitmenschlichkeit*) and being-in-togetherness, parallel to *rén*, the cardinal virtue of Confucianism. In dialogue with Daoian insights of cosmogony and the Neo-Confucian anthropo-cosmic vision, Christian theology can further develop the doctrine of creation and eco-theologies with more updated and comprehensive views of the universe and creation, liberated from the persistent dualism of 'either-or'.

These are some examples that theo-dao could contribute to the Christian doctrine of creation to move global theology forward, beyond the limits of theo-logos. However, theo-logos and theo-dao no longer need to be seen as conflicting but rather as complementary, like the the yang and the yin dimensions of creation and cosmogony. On the one hand, the Christian doctrine of creation underscores the yang dimension of creation, such as the ontology of being, duality, the cosmos, and its theo-historical aspect. On the other hand, the Daoian view focuses on the yin dimension, the meontology of nothingness, wholeness in duality, chaos, and the anthropo-cosmic aspects (humanity as cosmic/ecological being-in-togetherness). The continuous discoveries of natural sciences may further explain this holistic understanding of the universe.

Hence, Christian theology should recover the long-overlooked path of yin by effectively engaging in a trialogue with East Asian religions (Dao) and natural sciences, reappreciating the traditions of apophatic spirituality and negative theology. For this, Bede Griffiths had proposed a macro-paradigm shift.

> This may sound paradoxical and unreal, but for centuries now the western world has been following the path of yang — of the masculine, active, aggressive, rational, scientific mind — and has subsequently brought the world near destruction. It is time now to recover the path of yin — the way of the feminine, passive, patient, intuitive, and poetic mind. This is the path, the way, which the Tao Te Ching sets before us.[51]

---

51 Griffiths, *Universal Wisdom*, 27-28.

## PART II

# Technodao
# in an Age of Transhumanism and
# Artificial Intelligence

CHAPTER FOUR

# Death and Immortality: Biological and K-Religious Reflections on Transhumanism

## Abstract

This chapter critically examines the transhumanist pursuit of digital immortality by contrasting it with biological and East Asian perspectives on death. The chapter argues that transhumanist immortality is scientifically unsound, as life inherently involves a cyclical integration of life and death. Exploring the biological concepts of cellular senescence and evolutionary development, it reveals death as a vital evolutionary process for sustaining complex life. East Asian religious thought complements this view, treating death as integral to life's transformative process rather than as an adversary to conquer. Concepts from Neo-Confucianism and Buddhism support the idea that death allows for the cyclical renewal and evolution of life, underscoring a communal and intergenerational continuity. Ultimately, the chapter critiques transhumanism for its narrow focus on individual immortality, emphasizing the importance of accepting death as essential for personal and communal growth.

## Introduction

To be blessed in death, one must learn to live.

To be blessed in life, one must learn to die.[1]

In March 2016, a historical Go match between AlphaGo, an up-dated Artificial Intelligence (AI) developed by Google's DeepMind unit, and Sedol Lee, a Korean Go grandmaster, took place in Seoul, and AlphaGo handily won by 4:1.[2] Most people in Korea and East Asia reacted to AI's triumphant victory with fear and intimidation, rather than with joy and inspiration. This victory emphasizes the achievements made by human technologies and the subsequent possibilities of AI's conquest over humans and digitalization of humanity. Today, AI is on every corner of Korean society. For the past several decades, Korea has spearheaded the frontier of information technology fields with conscious efforts to make information technology its national industrial base. Given this historical push, we predict that transhumanism will soon gain popularity and propagate quickly in Korea. Moreover, the appearance of a

---

1 Philippe Ariès, *The Hour of Our Death* (Oxford: Oxford University Press, 1981), 300.

2 See Christof Koch, "How the Computer Beat the Go Master," *Scientific American* (March 19, 2016), http://www.scientificamerican.com/article/how-the-computer-beat-the-go-master/?WT.mc_id=SA_WR_20160323. For an East Asian reflection on this event, see Heup Young Kim, "AlphaGgo's Victory over Korean Go-master Showcases Western vs. Neo-Confucian Values," *Sightings*, the University of Chicago Divinity School Martin Marty Center (June 23, 2016), https://divinity.uchicago.edu/sightings/ alphagos-victory-over-korean-go-master-showcases-western-vs-neo-confucian-values. Go, a popular game in East Asia like *Chess* in the West, is? "an abstract strategy board game for two players in which the aim is to surround more territory than the opponent;" for more on Go, see https://en.wikipedia.org/wiki/Go_(game).

Transhumanist Party' candidate in the US presidential election could encourage some attention to transhumanism. A provocative slogan of this candidate, "Let's make Americans immortal," would worry even more those who are convinced that transhumanism is one of "the most dangerous ideas" that the West has ever produced.[3]

This chapter will argue that the transhumanist notion of immortality is scientifically invalid, because immortality inherently requires a cyclic integration of life and death. Our day-to-day operating paradigm is predicated upon a dualistic distinction between life and death. However, contemporary life science does not adequately support this binary thinking. Life and death are two sides of a single coin. This chapter aims to shed new light on a biological notion of death and its implications for the concept of digital immortality, in dialogue with East Asian religious (and theological) thought.

## 1. A Biological Appraisal of Death

Although immortality has been a culturally and linguistically prominent symbolic term, it is ambiguous and often causes confusion because of its semantic breadth. This chapter focuses on the transhumanist general program to eliminate death. Digital immortality, technically termed "whole brain emulation" is commonly referred to as mind-uploading. It is a key transhumanist strategy.

---

3 Brett McGinness, "Zoltan Istvan 2016: Let's Make Americans Immortal," *Reno Gazette-Journal* (June 14, 2016), http://www.rgj.com/story/news/politics/2016/06/ 15/ zoltan-istvan-2016-lets-make-americans-immortal/85909236. Francis Fukuyama, "The World's Most Dangerous Ideas: Transhumanism," *Foreign Policy* 144 (2009): 42-43.

Digital immortality is the hypothetical concept of a personal mind living eternally in durable artificial hardware. It is one example of the transhumanist attempt to defeat death. Anders Sandberg and Nick Bostrom believe it would enable "back-up copies and digital immortality" by basically modeling the function of the human brain.[4] Many transhumanists easily accept that digital immortality can be realized in the near future partially through the development of a sophisticated AI like AlphaGo.

Digital immortality presents serious scientific and conceptual challenges. As noted in the ongoing debate about weak versus strong AI, there are a huge number of unresolved questions and problems. In addition, digital immortality entails an intellectual leap from the functioning of intelligence to an ontological status of immortality, i.e., continuing and maintaining life without death. A proper assessment of mMind uploading, along with other transhumanist anti-death programs, necessitate a reflection on scientific theories in order to probe the notions of death and immortality.[5]

*Definitions of Life and Death*

Tibor Gánti, an unrecognized Hungarian biochemist during the

---

4 Anders Sandberg and Nick Bostrom, *Whole Brain Emulation, A Road Map* (Oxford: Oxford University, 2008), http://www.fhi.ox.ac.uk/wp-content/uploads/brain-emulation-roadmap-report1.pdf.

5 Calvin Mercer has provided some of the most thoroughgoing Christian theological assessments of whole brain emulation. See, e.g., "Whole Brain Emulation Requires Enhanced Theology, and a 'Handmaiden'," *Theology and Science* 13/2 (April 2015): 175-186; "Bodies and Persons: Theological Reflections on Transhumanism," *Dialog: A Journal of Theology* 54/1 (March 2015): 27-33.

communist regime, has suggested the following classification of the world: 1) the living, 2) the potentially living but not dead (i.e., resting seeds), 3) the dead (it has lived earlier but has lost the capacity of living) and the non-living (it does not live, never was alive, and is not going to live).[6] Discriminating the living from the non-living is a seemingly easy and familiar task. However, it is notoriously difficult to precisely define life. All entities are essentially composed of the same atoms that are not themselves alive. But in what way do the living and the non-living differ?[7] What transforms the chemistry of the non-living to the biology of the living? Life can be defined with a long list of operational features, such as homeostasis, metabolism, growth, reproduction, adaptation, and evolution. There seems to be an enormous gap between our scientific knowledge and the unifying laws of life. Is life the extremely well-coordinated collective behavior of non-living matter driven by certain environmental conditions? Is there a continuum between the living and the non-living? How about the connection between cognition and life? These questions remain insufficiently answered.[8] It is almost embarrassing to realize our fundamental failure to grasp what exactly distinguishes life from death. A novel and interdisciplinary field of "systems biology," based on an anti-reductionistic approach and systems theory, addresses and investigates the properties of life from a holistic perspective.[9]

---

6 Tibor Gánti, *The Principles of Life* (New York: Oxford University Press, 2003), 1-10.

7 See Rodney Brooks, "The Relationship between Matter and Life," *Nature* 409 (2001): 409-411; and Rasmussen Steenet, et. al., "Transitions from Nonliving to Living Matter," *Science* 3 (2004): 963-65.

8 Mark Bedau, "Four Puzzles about Life," *Artificial Life* 4 (1998), 125.

An alternative approach is to try to define death. Death is one of the most obvious and profound human experiences. Someday we will die. Despite our familiarity with death, however, death itself seldom has been the independent subject of scientific inquiry, largely because the phenomenon of death is regarded as an irreversible end-result of many different causes. Given the lack of scientific discourse on death, how can we derive any reasonable meaning of death through scientific lens without personal biases? The scientific approach to death can be understood as having two different dimensions, namely, the death of a physical existence and the death of a conscious existence. The former denotes an objective approach, which can be pursued by examining the evolutionary history of life and death on earth. The latter signifies a subjective approach for which understanding the human brain is necessary, leading us to the seemingly intractable mind-body problem. This next section will first examine death from an evolutionary perspective and then touch upon the special property of the brain in relation to human subjective death.

*Evolutionary History of Death*

Is death inevitable? Quite contrary to the common-sense human experience, biology tells us that death is not the universal fate of all living organisms. The smallest unit of life is a single cell, which

---

9 See Fred C. Boogerd, et. al., "Towards Philosophical Foundations of Systems Biology: Iintroduction," in *Systems Biology: Philosophical Foundation*, ed. Fred C. Boogerd, et. al. (Amsterdam: Elsevier, 2007), 3-19.

provides life as a scientific subject. Unicellular (single-celled) organisms, like bacteria and amoebae, can divide into two newborn cells without resulting in a death of either entity. Genes, molecules, and various structures are replicated into two new organisms, and this process can continue indefinitely as long as energy and an adequate environment are provided. Single-celled bacteria have been the major form of life for the first two billion years of life history on earth . What is the secret of the biological immortality of cells? Surprisingly, the answer to this question is simple. It is the cell's capacity to divide. Any cell, including human germ cells and cancer cells capable of division and proliferation, is potentially immortal.[10]

A major jump in the evolution of life occurred one billion years ago when multicellular organisms arose from unicellular organisms. Multicellular organisms are not a mere collection of identical cells; instead, they consist of many different cells, tissues, organs, and parts of the body. A multicellular organism has to undergo the processes of development, cell differentiation, morphogenesis, and growth. During the entire life of a multicellular organism, each cell must shift its main mission from vigorous multiplication to a cooperative orchestration in order to build the whole organism. The ability to proliferate must be under tight control and regulation by genes inside the cells.

At this point, death appears for the first time on the stage of the evolutionary history and starts to play a leading role in the history of life. During early development, cell death is particularly important

---

10 Herman Denis and Jean-Claude Lacroix, "The Dichotomy between Germ Line and Somatic Line, and the Origin of Cell Mortality," *Trends in Genetics* 9(1) (1993): 7-11.

in shaping the body and forming different organs. For example, before birth, a human fetus has web or paddle-like hands with connective tissues between fingers. As development proceeds, these unnecessary connective tissues disappear as their cells undergo the process of death, freeing the individual fingers. This process of cell death is called "apoptosis," meaning that cells die in a programmed manner executed by active gene operation, not by accident or trauma.[11] The apoptotic cell death is a crucial component in normal development.

During the adulthood of an organism, after its full growth, multicellular organisms contain two fundamentally different cell types, germ cells and somatic cells. Germ cells are considered to be immortal because they create generation after generation through sexual reproduction. Somatic cells are the remaining cells that form all the tissues, organs, and other body parts. Somatic cells are categorized into two groups: fully differentiated somatic cells that cannot divide and stem cells that divide. The stem cells in a differentiated tissue allow it to renew damaged somatic cells, repair the local function, and regenerate tissue. However, unlike unicellular organisms, these stem cells cannot divide indefinitely.[12] They have a limited capacity to proliferate, and they lose the ability for cell division after a certain number of divisions. For example, a fibroblast can only reach a maximum of 50 cell divisions, even in an ideal culture medium. This

---

11 Cinthya Assuncao Guimaraes and Rafael Linden, "Programmed Cell Death: Apoptosis and Alternative Death Styles," *European Journal of Biochemistry* 271 (2004): 1638-50.

12 Michael B. Schultz and David A. Sinclair, "When Stem Cells Grow Old: Phenotypes and Mechanisms of Stem Cell Aging," *Development* 143 (2016): 3-14.

phenomenon is called "cellular senescence."[13] Why is stem cell division limited? Cellular senescence is believed to have intended purposes and consequences. If stem cells are allowed to have an unlimited capacity for division, the overproduction of cells may well disrupt the fine integration of the tissue circuitry. It is now clear that cellular senescence is a crucial anticancer mechanism. In multicellular organisms, a dark flip side of cellular immortality is the development of uncontrollable cell proliferation, e.g., cancer.[14]

Since aging is by far the leading cause of death in modern society, the most relevant scientific inquiry into death can be framed as a question of aging. Why do we age?[15] We usually take aging for granted. Aging is easily regarded as "wear and tear" occurring in our body after many years of usage. This is the "cumulative damage theory of aging."[16] There are many ways in which the natural process of living damages our cells and body. One example is the production of reactive oxygen species, often referred to with the acronym ROS. ROS is an inevitable consequence of inhalation of oxygen during respiration. ROS causes damage and mutation in DNA, and dysfunction of energy generation. Another example is the accumulation of by-products of cellular metabolism. Alzheimer's dementia is most

---

13 Francis Rodier and Judith Campisi, "Four Faces of Cellular Senescence," *Journal of Cell Biology* 192 (2011): 547-56.

14 Sui Huang, "On the Intrinsic Inevitability of Cancer: From Foetal to Fatal Attraction," *Seminars in Cancer Biology* 21 (2011): 183-99.

15 Thomas B. L. Kirkwood and Steven N. Austad, "Why Do We Age?," *Nature* 408 (2000): 233-38.

16 Dazhong Yin and Keji Chen, "The Essential Mechanisms of Aging: Irreparable Damage Accumulation of Biochemical Side-reactions," *Experimental Gerontology* 40 (2005): 455-65.

likely due to deposition of non-degradable abnormal beta-amyloid protein resulting in neuronal death and brain atrophy. However, this "wear and tear" theory of aging is being discredited as the sole cause of death.[17] The modern "programmed theory of aging"[18] argues that aging is not a result of a random and stochastic process occurring over a long period of time, but rather it is driven on purpose by genetically regulated processes. The fact that all multicellular species have their own fixed lifespans supports this notion that there are genetic programs that determine when an organism will age and die.

The programmed aging and subsequent death at the organism level makes sense. A way to bypass the accumulation of damaged DNA and toxic products in multicellular organisms is to make a new organism through reproduction so that it can start fresh again with new cells. Reproduction is a much more efficient and robust way of sustaining life than repair and maintenance of a pre-existing old organism that has accumulated many errors and troubles. In some species, reproduction facilitates death. For example, salmons die quickly after they finish spawning. One could argue that death is a necessary component in the cycle of multicellular lives. Programmed aging theories argue that aging is ultimately a pre-programmed

---

17 Some extreme proponents such as Aubrey de Grey assert that aging is entirely explained by the accumulated damage theory and therefore aging can be totally reversible and human lifespan can be extended indefinitely by biomedical technology. However, this notion is not endorsed by the mainstream academic community. See Warner et al., "Science Fact and the SENS Agenda: What can We Reasonably Expect from Ageing Research?," *EMBO Reports* 6 (2005): 1006-8.

18 Lucas S. Trindade, et. al., "A Novel Classification System for Evolutionary Aging Theories," *Frontiers in Genetics* 4 (2013): 1-8.

process that purposely causes deterioration and death in order to obtain an evolutionary benefit achieved by limiting lifespan.

## Brain Death

The death of homo-sapiens in the twenty first century is much more complicated than it is with more simple organisms, warranting the reconceptualization of our fundamental concept of death. From a strict biological point of view, we humans die because our cells die. With the advent of multicellular organisms, the nature of an organism, especially a human, can no longer be defined in terms of cellular function alone. As the human body consists of many different cells and various organs with different vulnerabilities, the definition of human death has become a very important practical issue, particularly the identification of the time of critical irreversibility, in medical practice as well as in legal fields. Until the late 1960s, human death was defined and accepted only when the cardinal signs of human life, such as heartbeat and respiration, completely ceased to function. However, advances in medical sciences and technologies have made life support for cardio-respiratory function in patients with severe irreversible brain damage possible. Thus, the irreversible loss of entire brain functions has become accepted as the legal definition of death throughout the world.[19]

What makes the brain so special? How can we position the human brain in a scientific understanding of death? The human brain is

19 Michael A. de Georgia, "History of Brain Death as Death: 1968 to the Present," *Journal of Critical Care* 29 (2014): 673-78.

a hugely complex system.[20] It is estimated that the human brain has at least 100 billion neurons and 100 trillion synapses. The "mystery" of the brain lies in its collective mode of operation, not in the features of individual nerve cells. Complex systems are typically made up of a very large number of constituent entities that interact with each other and also with their environment. Some complex systems are categorized as "complex adaptive systems." which exhibit behaviors like self-organization, emergence, learning, adaptive behavior, and even evolution.[21] It is now believed that the brain is this sort of system, in which mental states, such as consciousness, emotion, and memory, emerge from the interaction among multiple physical and functional levels.[22] The irreversible loss of emergence in the brain is regarded as the death of personhood.

The complexity of the human organism means that physicians confront very difficult situations at the hospital bedside.[23] For example, what would you do with a brain-dead pregnant woman whose uterus is functioning perfectly to gestate a fetus? How would you persuade the parents to agree to remove a respirator from a brain-dead child who otherwise is growing and developing? These questions clearly reveal that the definition of human death as brain

---

20 Wolf Singer, "Understanding the Brain," *EMBO Reports* 8 (2007): 516-19.

21 Roy J. Eidelson, "Complex Adaptive Systems in the Behavioral and Social Sciences," *Review of General Psychology* 1 (1997): 42-71; and Gerard Weisbuch, "The Complex Adaptive Systems Approach to Biology," *Evolution and Cognition* 5 (1999): 1-11.

22 Daniells S. Bassett and Michael S. Gazzaniga, "Understanding Complexity in the Human Brain," *Trends in Cognitive Sciences* 15 (2011): 200-9.

23 Samuel H. LiPuma and Joseph P. DeMarco, "Reviving Brain Death: A Functionalist View," *Bioethical Inquiry* 10 (2013): 383-92.

death is a cultural construct and formed by general social agreement, rather than biological fact. The brain, understood narrowly as one body organ, is not the sole determinant of human life. The human mind is not only connected to the brain but also the body in general. It seems that many transhumanists hold to an outdated notion that mind and body are separable entities. However, this simplistic notion ignores the complex relationship between the brain and the body. In a scale of complexity, the brain would be at a higher level than the rest of the body. But that does not mean that the information at the level of the brain completely vanishes after brain death. David Keirsey, a complexity scientist, insightfully said that "the process of death is not as complete as it implies. Even in 'death', something remains of the original entity. Some parts of the entity still remain, and those remaining parts will interact with the surrounding environment at a lower level of complexity. The potential diversity of the lower level of complexity increases with death. Thus, death is a form of information feedback between levels of complexity."[24] This information feedback system between different levels of complexities could be applied to the relation between the brain and the body. The brain is organically intertwined with the rest of the body, and there is constant information exchange between brain and body throughout life; even after death, the information at the level of the brain does not vanish but transforms into a lower level of life and gets integrated back with the rest of the system. In other words, with regard to the human brain and its relationship to the

---

24 David M. Keirsey, "Toward the Physics of 'Death'," in *Unifying Themes in Complex Systems*, ed. Yaneer Bar-Yam (Cambridge: Perseus Books, 2000), 306.

rest of the body, interpenetrating levels of complexities cannot be explained by the dualistic distinction between mind and body, and death and life.

*Interim Summary*

Our examination of the hierarchical levels of single cell, multi-cellular organism, and brain has demonstrated that death cannot be separated from life. Rather, death must be understood as inter-penetrating multilayered and multifaceted phenomena. Death is far more subtle and profound than common conceptualizations allow. Mortality is not an inescapable fate of cells. Death was designed during the later phase of evolution to produce complex multicellular organisms, including homo sapiens. The limited human lifespan is a trade-off between aging and cancer. Death is a crucial compo-nent for the uninterrupted flourishing of life on earth. However, this conclusion does not address the entire problem of death. Brain death, as the death of personhood and cessation of subjective con-scious experiences, poses an existential challenge. We do not know the ultimate fate of our consciousness following brain death, in part because we do not know what consciousness is and how it is related to the material brain.

Despite this qualification, our scientific reflection reveals that death is a dynamic evolutionary process rather than an irreversible perishment. While death remains elusive, it clearly plays a crucial role in shaping the larger picture of the universe. Death is not the process of destroying life, but rather it is "directly linked to the proc-ess of emergence of meaningful information."[25] So death and immortality co-exist in our cells, body, brain, eco-system, and even in the entire universe. Thus, the transhumanist pursuit for digital immortality, or any program bypassing death, is flawed, since death and life are an integrated whole.

## 2. An East Asian Religious Reflection

A leading transhumanist, Simon Young, declared, "Bio-fatalism will increasingly be replaced by techno-can-do-ism—the belief in the power of the new technology to free us from the limitations of our bodies and minds... In the twenty-first century, the belief in the Fall of Man will be replaced by the belief in his inevitable transcendence—through Superbiology."[26] He also boldly proclaimed, "Let us cast aside cowardice and seize the torch of Prometheus with both hands."[27] As we have seen, however, recent developments in biology and brain science do not support this Promethean courage of transhumanists. Instead, they demonstrate that it is not well-grounded in science. The future of 'Systems Biology' seems to be more convincing than Young's 'Superbiology'. Furthermore, transhumanists do not appreciate the values of death and mortality, treating them as "enemies to be conquered or as brute objects ranged

---

25 Luc Jaeger, "A Biochemical Perspectives on the Origin of Life and Death," in *The Role of Death in Life*, ed. John Behr and Conor Cunningham (Eugene, OR: Wipf and Stock Publisher, 2015), 28.

26 Simon Young, *Designer Evolution: A Transhumanist Manifesto* (Amherst, NY: Prometheus Books, 2006), 20.

27 Young, *Designer Evolution*, 40.

over and against us—as aliens, monsters, as victims."[28] Ray Kurzweil, the present director of Google's Deep Mind Program, once announced, "Our mortality will be in our hands."[29] However, East Asian religious thought refutes this transhumanist attitude toward death, while supporting the biological appraisal with some strikingly converging points.

## Life and Death Co-exist as Part of the Whole

East Asian religions in general reject the transhumanist conception of death as an enemy or a monster (like a tyrant dragon),[30] but endorse the biological observation that assumes death is a part of life.

They resist the division between life and death. Buddhism strongly rejects this dualism, arguing that both life and death are ontologically unreal and illusory. Both death and life are unreal. Thus, there need no distinction between the two. There is no death, if there is no life. Life and death are dependently co-arising (*pratītyasamutpāda*). The problem occurs when one thinks about them as divided and contradictory. Ultimately, there is neither death nor life,; and practically, they are not different (生死一如) as they are two indivisible as-

---

28 Mary Midgle, *Science as Salvation: A Modern Myth and Its Meaning* (London, UK: Routledge, 1992), 74.

29 Ray Kurzweil, *The Singularity Is Now* (New York: Viking Press, 2005), 9.

30 See Nick Bostrom, "The Fate of the Dragon Tyrant," *Journal of Medical Ethics* 31 (2005): 273-277. Unlike its popular maleficent images in the West, East Asians traditionally view the dragon as an auspicious and benevolent symbolic being that brings happiness and fortune.

pects of one co-arising reality. In Buddhism, therefore, "death does not signify an abandonment of life but aims its completion."[31]

Neo-Confucianism, too, conceives death as a part of life. More precisely, life and death exists as a whole in complementary opposition, as in the relationship between yin and yang in the Great Ultimate (*Taiji*).[32] As we have noted earlier, biologically, life and death are two sides of the same coin (yin and yang) that comprise the integrated whole (*Taiji*). We live by breathing, continually repeating the processes of exhalation and inhalation. Breathing, as key for sustaining life, analogically denotes the fact that life itself is continuity (inspiration, life) in discontinuity (expiration, death). It is interesting that exhalation comes before inhalation in the Chinese character for breathing (呼吸). *Yijing* (*Changes*), an important book in the Confucian canon, states that one yin and one yang form the dao of life (一陰一陽謂之道). So, congruence with the biological observation, East Asian religious thoughts in general denies the transhumanist dualistic assumption that life and death are two different entities, events, or realities.

## *Death is Critical to Our Transformation*

In accord with the biological observation that death "a dynamic

---

31 Jin-hong Chung, "Our Traditional Understanding of Death and Today's Tasks," in *Sammgwa Jukeumeui Inmunhak* (*Life and Death: a Study of Humanities*), ed. Jae-gap Park (Seoul: Seoktap Publications, 2012), 68.

32 For this discussion, see Heup Young Kim, "The Tao in Confucianism and Taoism; Trinity in East Asian Perspective," in *The Cambridge Companion to the Trinity*, ed. Peter C. Phan (Cambridge, UK: Cambridge University Press, 2011), 296-98.

evolutionary process," East Asian religions view death as an opportunity, to grow, into a higher stage of life (sometimes understood as returning to the original state of life). The present human existential situation is not of the goal of true humanity,; death is the way to purify one's self to attain true humanity through self-transformation. The self-cultivation emphasis in Neo-Confucianism underscores the discontinuity of habits polluted with selfish human desires and cultivating selfhood for the recovery of the original benevolent humanity.[33] Through its notion of *samsara* (the cycle of birth and death), Buddhism strongly encourages the perception of death as an opportunity for a transformation into an elevated being.

East Asian religions often illustrate this process with the imagery of transformation from cocoon to butterfly. A cocoon should cast off its shell in order to be transformed into a butterfly. Death is like this natural process. To attain a true selfhood, i.e., the great person, one should rid oneself of concupiscence, sin, *karma*, and human desires (私慾) that contaminate the existential self (小我). This process of purification, albeit with a different name (e.g., justification, sanctification, self-cultivation, awakening, or nirvana) is found in many religions.

Present existential humanity is far from perfect, indeed, it is troublesome, and so it must be subject to rigorous scrutiny and self-examinations through various ways of self-cultivation and sanctification, such as self-denial (無我), meditation, and prayer.[34] Thus, from

33 For a comparative study between Christian sanctification and Neo-Confucian self-cultivation, see Heup Young Kim, *Wang Yang-ming and Karl Barth: a Confucian-Christian Dialogue* (Lanham, MD: University Press of America, 1996).

an East Asian religious perspective, it is dangerous for an uncultivated, imperfect person or group of people to perpetuate life
without the necessary self-examination and self-transformation.
From this vantage point, the transhumanist proposal for immortality
is one of the most dangerous ideas ever generated. The transhumanist goal can be seen as the immortalization of selfish desires
and the will to power, which is similar to the way that cancer cells
analogically function at the cellular level (cf., the biological anti-can-
cer mechanism of apoptosis and *cellular senescence*).

## *Death Contributes to Our Role in Stories Larger than Ourselves*

East Asian religions agree with the biological approach that the
locus of human evolution, advancement, or emergence is not limited to an individual person living at a specific time and space, but
rather is expanded to wider spatiotemporal horizons, and relationships of species, family, clan, group, nation, and world. In this regard, Brent Waters made significant criticism based on "natality,"
a term coined by Hannah Arendt.[35] Clearly, birth and death are two
distinguishable aspects of he human condition. The biological sciences shows that reproduction is an efficient mechanism in the larger

---

34 For the Christian-Confucian way of humanization in comparison with transhumanism,
see Heup Young Kim, "Cyborg, Sage, and Saint: Transhumanism seen from an East Asian
Theological Setting," in *Religion and Transhumanism: the Unknown Future of
Human Enhancement*, eds. Calvin Mercer and Tracy J. Trothen (Praeger, 2015),
97-114.

35 Brent Waters, "Flesh Made Data: The Posthuman Project in Light of the Incarnation,"
in *Religion and Transhumanism*, 292.

picture of human evolution, but it requires death. Transhumanists, however, do not speak about offspring, but, rather, focusing on personal immortality. Waters rightly said,

"This disdain for generational interdependency discloses both the lynchpin of the posthuman project and the reason why it is a perilous enterprise... Through its futuristic rhetoric, post-human discourse amplifies, exemplifies, and justifies one of the most pervasive late modern illusions—namely, that of an impervious individual autonomy and its resulting narcissism... Despite their futuristic rhetoric, posthumanists are merely attempting to impose a tyranny of the present over the future."[36]

From the East Asian perspective, Waters' brilliant evaluation can be supplemented by the critical domain of intergenerational relationship;, namely, ancestry. In fact, posthumanists are imposing "a tyranny of the present" not only on the future but also on the past. Neo-Confucianism, in particular, emphasizes this dimension and profoundly incorporates it in the ritual of ancestor veneration or worship. In ancestor veneration rituals the dead meet the living. Through the ritual, the dead return to and participate in the communal life of the living, and at the same time, the living shares the life of the dead. In this way, ancestors become immortal in the life of their descendants. Ancestor veneration entails rituals where East Asians create space to transcend their personal mortality and establish collective immortality of their familial community and lineage.

---

36 Waters, "Flesh Made Data," 297-301.

Whereas transhumanists strive for a personal immortality, East Asians pursue a communal immortality by means of revitalizing the intergenerational relatedness among the dead, the living, and the unborn. Resisting the propensity of human hubris to impose a tyranny of the present over the future or the past, East Asians pursue a transtemporal unity and a harmonious and holistic co-existence of the past, the present, and the future in the community. We see this, for example, in the Confucian notion of immortality. The Confucian very definition of humanity is not an autonomous individual or an isolated ego, but, rather, a being-in-togetherness or being-in-relationship (仁).

## Conclusion

Digital and other versions of transhumanist Iimmortality are misnamed and scientifically invalid, because immortality paradoxically requires the very process of death to be integrated in life if life is to be sustained. The biological sciences show that death plays a critical role in the life of single cells, multicellular organisms, and human brains. Life and death cannot be separated,; they are two sides of a single coin. Life viewed holistically is the process of a complex system, sustaining its status by means of self-organization and emergence.[37] Life moves through a constant cycle of birth, development, regeneration, and death. Overall, ranging from single

---

37 Fulvio Mazzocchi, "Complexity in Biology. Exceeding the Limits of Reductionism and Determinism Using Complexity Theory," *EMBO Reports* 9 (2008): 10-14.

cells to entire biological systems, the scientific appraisal of death suggests that the process of death is pivotal in producing novelty, creativity, and life in the universe.

East Asian religions in general support this scientific observation (which is also basically consistent with theology). First, they agree that death is not an enemy to conquer but an essential part of authentic life. Life and death are not two different entities, events, or realities, but, rather, compose an integrated whole in the same manner as yin and yang function in *Taiji*. Further, death is an opportunity, to grow, into a higher stage of life. The present human condition is not true humanity; death is the ultimate way to purify one's self to accomplish or recover true humanity. The transhumanist idea about immortality is dangerous, because that idea can be the expression of technological hubris in the service of an imperfect human will to power and hegemony, analogically the same as cancer cells at the cellular level. Furthermore, the locus of human evolution, advancement, or emergence is not limited to an individual person, but is enlarged in the ever-expanding horizons of spatial-temporal and communal relatedness. A critical error in the transhumanist vision for immortality lies in the tyranny of the present over the past and the future by denying linkage to wider and bigger ancestral, evolutionary, planetary, and cosmic stories.

So, death is not only an integral part of life, but it is also a gracious gift that enables a life to grow into its higher reaches. Mortality is the presupposition of an elevated life and eventual immortality. We need to celebrate what Dowd and Barlow call "the gifts of death:"

Without the death of stars, there would be no planets and no life. Without the death of creatures, there would be no evolution... Without the death of neurons, wisdom and creativity would not blossom... Without the death of old ways of thinking, there would be no room for the new. Without death, there would be no ancestors. Without death, time would not be precious.[38]

38 Michael Dowd and Connie Barlow, "A Scientific Honoring of Death," *Metanexus* (July 15, 2012), http://metanexus.net/blog. http://metanexus.net/blog/scientific-honoring- death?utm_source=2012.07.17.+Honoring+Death&utm_campaign=2012.07.17. &utm_medium=email.

CHAPTER FIVE

# Advancing Humanity:
# Artificial Intelligence, Transhumanism,
# Confucianism, and Theo-Dao

## Challenges of Artificial Intelligence and Transhumanism

The victory of Artificial Intelligence (AI) AlphaGo over a Korean Go-Master Lee Sedol (March 2016) was enough to shock the Korean and East Asian public.[1] For it is believed that playing Go, unlike Chess, needs much more than logical thinking but also requires human intuition, which is a dimension even the most developed computer would be unable to access. Nonetheless, an AI developed by DeepMind, based in London, undoubtedly crushed this confidence. It is a revelation to the world that by deep learning, a machine can now learn on its own and push the level of intelligence beyond humans, namely, superintelligence. In East Asia, this shocking news was not limited to a machine-to-human confrontation but also led

---

1 Heup Young Kim, "Alphgo's Victory Over Korea Go-Master Showcases Western vs. Neo-Confucian Values," *Sightings*, June 23, 2016, https://divinity.uchicago.edu/sightings/alphagos-victory-over-korean-go-master-showcases-western-vs-neo-confucian-values.

some people to regard it as a showdown between the West and the East. AlphaGo has been further developed to AlphaGo Zero and AlphaZero, which beat all of the Go masters in East Asia, demonstrating that there was no longer any human equal.

Google's parent company, Alphabet Inc., acquired DeepMind in 2014. However, Google's AI ethics board had remained "one of the biggest mysteries in tech, with both Google and DeepMind refusing to reveal who sits on it."[2] Moreover, the suspicion was amplified when it was revealed that the person in charge of such areas was Ray Kurzweil, who aggressively promoted the transhumanist movement, claiming the idea of 'technological singularity.' He said:

[W]hen artificial intelligence becomes powerful enough to program better versions of itself. If it happens, such an explosion of digital intelligence will quickly surpass human comprehension and, depending on who you ask, either lead to a Terminatoresque apocalypse or fuse with the human brain, bringing our species to new intellectual heights."[3]

There have been warnings from scientists and engineers about the dangers of AI. Elon Musk, the founder of Tesla, viewed it as "summoning the demon," envisaging "an immortal dictator from which we can never escape."[4] The late Stephen Hawking said,

---

2 Sam Shead, "The biggest mystery in AI right now is the ethics board that Google set up after buying DeepMind," *Business Insider*, Mar 26, 2016, https://www.businessinsider.com/google-ai-ethics-board-remains-a-mystery-2016-3.

3 Sean Kane, "How a pianist became the world's most famous futurist," Business Insider, March 19, 2016, https://www.businessinsider.com/how-ray-kurzweil-became-famous-2016-3.

"Artificial intelligence could spell the end of the human race."[5] Even at the beginning of computer invention, Alan Turing (1951) predicted that machines would "outstrip our feeble powers" and "take control." Moreover, Irving Good (1965) foretold:

> Let an ultraintelligent machine be defined as a machine that can far surpass all the intellectual activities of any man however clever. Since the design of machines is one of these intellectual activities, an ultraintelligent machine could design even better machines; there would then unquestionably be an 'intelligence explosion', and the intelligence of man would be left far behind. *Thus, the first ultraintelligent machine is the last invention that man need ever make, provided that the machine is docile enough to tell us how to keep it under control.*[6]

Henry Kissinger, former US Secretary of State, also expressed extreme concern about the danger of AI and said, "AI could mean

---

4 Matt McFarland, "Elon Musk: 'With artificial intelligence we are summoning the demon'," *Washington Post*, Oct 24, 2014, https://www.washingtonpost.com/news/innovations/wp/2014/10/24/elon-musk-with-artificial-intelligence-we-are-summoning-the-demon/?noredirect=on&utm_term=.6eb0773904ae. Also Peter Holley, "Elon Musk's nightmarish warning: AI could become 'an immortal dictator from which we would never escape'," *Washington Post*, April 6, 2018, https://www.washingtonpost.com/news/innovations/wp/2018/04/06/elon-musks-nightmarish-warning-ai-could-become-an-immortal-dictator-from-which-we-would-never-escape/?utm_term=.6b513c62cf52.

5 Rory Cellian-Jones, "Stephen Hawking warns artificial intelligence could end mankind," *BBC News*, Dec 2, 2014, https://www.bbc.com/news/technology-30290540.

6 I. J. Good, "Speculations Concerning the First Ultraintelligent Machine," Archived 28 November 2011 at the Wayback Machine (HTML), *Advances in Computers* vol. 6 (1965). Italics are mine.

the end of human history." AI may accomplish unintended results because it does not understand context. Even if AI reaches intended goals, it will be unable to explain the rationale for its conclusions. In addition, "in achieving intended goals, AI may change human thought processes and human values" and could invent something like AlphaGod.[7] Of course, this is not just a purely historical, intellectual prediction. However, as a US politician, Kissinger was concerned about the possibility of geopolitical dangers from China when fully militarized with AI weapons, which could evoke a clash of techno-civilizations between East and West.[8] However, Kissinger admitted that the rise of AI is rooted in the Enlightenment and that the West is unprepared, as he titled the article.

Yuval Noah Harari further predicted the end of *homo sapiens*.[9] Harari broke the history of *homo sapiens* down into four periods; (1) the Cognitive Revolution (c. 70,000 BCE, when Sapiens evolved imagination), (2) the Agricultural Revolution (c. 12,000 BCE, the development of farming), (3) the unification of humankind (the gradual consolidation of human political organizations towards one global empire), and (4) The Scientific Revolution (c. 1500 CE, the emergence of objective science). He concluded that by considering how current technology moves into genetic editing, amortality, and

---

7 Henry Kissinger, "How the Enlightenment Ends: Philosophically, intellectually—in every way—human society is unprepared for the rise of artificial intelligence," *The Atlantic*, June, 2018, https://www.theatlantic.com/magazine/archive/ 2018/06/henry-kissinger-ai-could-mean-the-end-of-human-history/559124.

8 Tom Upchurch, "How China could beat the West in the deadly race for AI weapons," *Wired*, Aug 8, 2018, https://www.wired.co.uk/article/artificial-intelligence-weapons-warfare-project-maven-google-china.

9 Yuval Noah Harari, *Sapiens: A Brief History of Humankind* (New York: Harper, 2011).

non-organic life, it might soon end the species of *homo sapiens* and create new, godlike species. Harari argued that since organisms are algorithms, *homo sapiens* as such may not be dominant in a universe where *dataism* becomes the paradigm. Furthermore, as techno-logical developments have threatened the continued ability of humans to give meaning to their lives, the replacement of humankind with a super-human or *homo deus* (human god) endowed with su-pernatural abilities such as superintelligence and immortality:

> Success breeds ambition, and our recent achievements are now pushing humankind to set itself even more daring goals. Having secured un-precedented levels of prosperity, health and harmony, and given our past record and our current values, humanity's next targets are likely to be immortality, happiness and divinity. Having reduced mortality from starvation, disease and violence, we will now aim to overcome old age and even death itself. Having saved people from abject misery, we will now aim to upgrade humans into gods, and turn *Homo sapiens* into *Homo deus*.[10]

Thus, transhumanism challenges 'advancing humanity' to max-imum enhancement by using cutting-edge science and technology to achieve its posthuman goal, entering into the next stage of human evolution with superintelligence. In this chapter, I will investigate as a theologian how Confucianism, as arguably the world's longest living sapiential tradition, can respond to this challenge of trans-

---

10 Yuval Noah Harari, *Homo Deus: A Brief History of Tomorrow* (New York: Harper, 2017), 20-21.

humanism with the exponential development of AI technology.

Although both transhumanism and Confucianism pursue the advancement of humanity, their goals and methods are profoundly different. While transhumanism advocates external means of science and technology for human evolutionary progress, Confucianism promotes internal means of learning and self-cultivation for the full flowering of our natures.

This chapter consists of four sections. The first two sections briefly describe the basic insights of transhumanism and the Confucian view of the *telos* of humanity and our path to reach this goal. The third section compares and contrasts these two proposals for advancing humanity. The last section adds a brief theological reflection on the challenges of artificial intelligence and transhumanism from an East Asian (Confucian) Christian viewpoint.

## 1. Transhumanism: Advancing Humanity via Manufacturing Superintelligence

We are the analog prelude to the digital main event.[11]

Nick Bostrom defined transhumanism as "the intellectual and cultural movement that affirms the possibility and desirability of fundamentally improving the human condition through applied reason, especially by developing and making widely available technologies to eliminate aging and to greatly enhance human in-

---

11 Tad Friends, "Superior Intelligence," *The New Yorker*, May 14, 2018.

tellectual, physical, and psychological capacities."[12] Bostrom insisted that transhumanism is "an extension of humanism." However, humanism here means first and foremost an individual matter, as "transhumanism places a high value on autonomy: the ability and right of individuals to plan and choose their own lives." Furthermore, Bostrom emphasized, "just as we use rational means to improve the human condition and the external world, we can also use such means to improve ourselves, the human organism. In doing so, we are not limited to traditional humanistic methods, such as education and cultural development. We can also use technological means that will eventually enable us to move beyond what some would think of as 'human.'"[13] However, it is unclear what the enhanced and advanced humanity in transhumanism really means, except naming the state as 'posthuman'. In this perspective, 'transhuman' refers to a "transitional human" or "the earliest manifestation of new evolutionary being" in "an intermediary form between the human and the posthuman."[14]

### Posthuman

'Posthuman' is a hypothetical term still in construction. Bostrom identified posthumans as "possible future beings whose basic capacities so radically exceed those of present humans as to be no

---

12 Nick Bostrom, "Introduction — the Transhumanism FAQ: a General Introduction," in *Transhumanism and the Body: the World Religions Speak*, edited by Calvin Mercer and Derek F. Maher (New York, NY: Palgrave Macmillan, 2014), 1. ed.

13 Ibid, 1-2.

14 Ibid, 4.

longer unambiguously human by our current standards." However, we seem to be stuck in the dream-phase: "Posthuman persons... yearn to reach intellectual heights as far above any human genius... to be resistant to disease and impervious to aging; to have unlimited youth and vigor." Bostrom stresses human beings' longing "to exercise control over their own desires, moods, and mental states; to be able to avoid feeling tired, hateful, or irritated about petty things; to have an increased capacity for pleasure, love, artistic appreciation, and serenity; to experience novel states of consciousness that current human brains cannot access." However, none of this implies that these states are to be reached through internal self-cultivation of the mind (e.g. via a Confucianesque blocking of selfish desires), but rather by external means such as medicines and technologies: "The changes required to make us posthuman are too profound to be achievable by merely altering some aspect of psychological theory or the way we think about ourselves. Radical modifications to our brains and bodies are needed." Transhumanism focuses more on the functionally cognitive side: "Posthumans could be completely synthetic artificial intelligence, or they could be enhanced uploads, or they could... jettison their bodies altogether and live as information patterns on vast superfast computer networks."[15]

*Superintelligence*

A central goal for advancing humanity in transhumanism is to acquire *superintelligence*. Bostrom, famous for his book Superintelli-

---

15 Ibid, 3-4.

gence,[16] described a superintelligent intellect as "one that has the capacity to radically outperform the best human brains in practically every field, including scientific creativity, general wisdom, and social skills." Bostrom goes on to distinguish between weak and strong superintelligences: whereas a weak superintelligence refers to a humanesque intellect operating "at an accelerated clock speed, such as by uploading it to a fast computer," a strong superintelligence designates "an intellect that is not only faster than a human brain but also smarter, in a qualitative sense." Creating superintelligences "may the last invention that humans will ever need to make, since superintelligences could themselves take care of further scientific and technological development. They would do so more effectively than humans. Biological humanity would no longer be the smartest life form on the block." Affirming the Mind Uploading and Whole Brain Emulation (WBE), Bostrom stated:

> Many transhumanists would like to become superintelligent themselves. This is obviously a long-term and uncertain goal, but it might be achievable either through uploading and subsequent enhancement or through the gradual augmentation of our biological brains, by means of future nootropics (cognitive enhancement drugs), cognitive techniques, IT tools (e.g., wearable computer, smart agents, information filtering systems, visualization software, etc.), neural-computer interfaces, or brain implants.[17]

---

16 Nick Bostrom, *Superintelligence: Paths, Dangers, Strategies* (Oxford: Oxford University Press, 2014).

17 Bostrom, "Introduction," 7-9.

## *Immortality*

Another foremost goal is to extend the lifespan radically in order to achieve a high degree of freedom from aging and death. Bostrom declared, "Ideally everybody should have the right to choose when and how to die—or not to die." Rejecting a traditional prejudice that natural is good, he argued, "Changing nature for the better is a noble and glorious thing for humans to do."[18] Moreover, whether "something is natural or not is irrelevant to whether it is good or desirable." Thus, 'deathism' and death apologists that admit "dying of old age is a fine thing" are "dangerous, indeed fatal, since they teach hopelessness and encourage passivity. ... The transhumanist position on the ethics of death is crystal clear: death should be voluntary. This means that everybody should be free to extend their lives and to arrange for cryonic suspension of their deanimated bodies. It also means that voluntary euthanasia, under conditions of informed consent, is a basic human right."[19] Furthermore, a transhumanist scientist said, "Immortality is mathematical, not mystical."[20]

## *Uploading*

As a paramount means of expediting posthumanity, transhumanism proposes 'uploading' (or whole brain emulation), a

---

18 Ibid, 12.

19 Ibid, 14-15.

20 Raffi Khatchadourian, "The Doomsday Invention: Will artificial intelligence bring us utopia or destruction?" *The New Yorker* (Nov. 23, 2015), 67.

"process of transferring intellect from a biological brain to a computer."[21] Bostrom summarized its advantages:

— Uploads would not be subject to biological senescence.
— Back-up copies of uploads could be created regularly so that you could be rebooted if something bad happened. (Thus, your life-span could potentially be as long as the universe.)
— You could potentially live much more economically as an upload since you wouldn't need physical food, housing, transportation, etc.
— If you were running on a fast computer, you would think faster than in a biological implementation... You would thus get to experience more subjective time, and live more, during any given day.
— You could travel at the speed of light as an information pattern, which could be convenient in a future age of large-scale space settlements.
— Radical cognitive enhancements would likely be easier to implement in an upload than in an organic brain.[22]

## 2. Confucianism: Advancing Humanity via Self-Cultivating the Mind-and-Heart

What Heaven imparts to humanity is called human nature.
To follow our nature is called the Way [Dao 道].
Cultivating the Way is called education.[23]

---

21 Bostrom, "Introduction," 9.

22 Ibid, 41.

23 Chan Wing-tsit, trans., *A Source Book in Chinese Philosophy* (Princeton: Princeton

Advanced or enhanced humanity is an immodest phrase for
Confucianism, which regards reverence and humility as the foundation of virtuous living.[24] Nevertheless, Confucianism cherishes ex-
plicit notions about the advancement of humanity beyond its current
existential status, as its most important project is to attain ideal personhood, namely, a profound person, great person, or Sage. Hence,
Confucianism is also called Sage Learning. Similar to Christian theology, Confucian anthropology consists of a threefold structure: original humanity (the mind of Dao 道心), existential humanity (the human mind 人心), and the restoration of original humanity (via
self-cultivation 修身).[25]

### Original Humanity: Tiān mìng 天命

*The Doctrine of the Mean* states: "What Heaven imparts to man [*Tiān
mìng*] is called human nature."[26] Just as the doctrine of imago Dei
is the center of Christian theological anthropology, the teaching of

---

University Press, 1963), 98.

24 Like Christianity, Confucianism which has a longer history consists in diverse schools.
For the sake of comparison, however, this short paper does not deal with those complex
subjects, nor make a distinction between Confucianism and Neo-Confucianism. It focuses on the Neo-Confucian understanding of T'oegye Yi Hwang (1501-1570), a seminal
figure in the history of Korean (and East Asian) Confucianism. For an introduction to
his life and thought, see Michael C. Kalton, trans., *To Become a Sage: The Ten Diagrams
on Sage Learning by Yi T'oegye* (New York: Columbia University Press, 1988).

25 For more on this subject, see Heup Young Kim, "Imago Dei and Tian ming: John Calvin
Meets Yi T'ogye," *A Theology of Dao* (Maryknoll, NY: Orbis Books, 2017), 115-146. Also,
idem, *Wang Yang-ming and Karl Barth: a Confucian-Christian Dialogue* (Lanham,
MD: University Press of America, 1996).

26 Chan, *A Source Book*, 98.

*Tiān mìng* is the heart of Confucian anthropology. It explicitly states that humanity is relational, and inseparably intertwined with its transcendent ontological ground. Confucianism presupposes that, as a heavenly endowment, human nature—original humanity (*xìng* 性)—was perfect. This flawless condition includes four "constant characteristics" of the Dao of Heaven, namely, origination, flourishing, benefitting, and firmness (元亨利貞).[27]

The school of *xìnglǐ* (性理學), to which Korean Neo-Confucianism faithfully attached, identified original humanity with the meta-cosmic principle of *li* (理). Since Heavenly endowment is identified with *li*, humanity is viewed in unity with Heaven through the same *li*. In correspondence to the four constant characteristics of the Dao of Heaven, Confucianism designates four attributes of original humanity as benevolence (*rén* 仁), righteousness (*yì* 義), propriety (*lǐ* 禮), and wisdom (*zhī* 智). Although *rén*, the cardinal virtue of Confucianism, is generally translated as benevolence, its etymological meaning is co-humanity (literally, two humans) or being-in-togetherness.[28] Thus, mutuality and reciprocity is a consistent principle of Confucianism. Through the endowment-relation, a person could participate in the principle of Heaven, and in this context, advancing humanity means recovering the whole human nature in accordance with the original meta-cosmic principle.

---

27 See Kalton, *To Become a Sage*, 66-69, 143-49.

28 Karl Barth also interpreted *imago Dei in this way*, based on Gen. 1:28. See Kim, *Wang Yang-ming and Karl Barth*, 43-46, 86-90, 158-60.

### Existential Humanity: The Human Mind

Confucians typically argue that the *locus* of the human relationship with the transcendent lies not in the mind alone, differentiated
from the body, but rather in the mind-and-heart, a psychosomatic
totality. This mind-and-heart (*xīn* 心) is a unique East Asian notion
that transcends body-and-soul dualism. As the master of the self,
the mind-and-heart is the nucleus of humanity; cultivating a
mind-and-heart that is sensible and vulnerable in real-life situations
was a central challenge of Korean Neo-Confucianism.[29] To explain
this ambiguity, Neo-Confucianism made subtle distinctions between the mind of Dao and the human mind, principle (*lǐ*) and material force (or meta-cosmic energy; *qì* 氣), and original humanity (*xìng*
性) and feelings (*qíng* 情).

In the unity with the body, the mind-and-heart functions freely
in the universe with no limitation of time and space. However, this
(ontological) capacity can be disturbed after it has been aroused
(existentially). The substance (*tǐ* 體) of the mind-and-heart before
it is aroused is called original humanity, and its function (*yòng* 用)
after arousal is recognized as feelings.[30] Feelings issue from the substance of original humanity in the mind-and-heart.[31] Since the
mind-and-heart is also a unity of *lǐ* and *qì*, these feelings consist of
two kinds. The first exposes the *lǐ* of original humanity in the form
of the so-called "four beginnings"; namely, commiseration (惻隱),

---

29 See Kalton, *To Become Sage*, 9-19.

30 For the relationship of *tǐ* (subject) and *yòng* (function), see ibid, 211-12.

31 For this view, see ibid, 119-21.

modesty and deference (辭讓), shame and dislike (羞惡), and approving and disapproving (是非). The second, in which the physical disposition perturbs the *li* of original humanity, consists of seven feelings; namely, joy, anger, grief, fear, love, hate, and desire (喜怒哀懼愛惡慾).

The polarity of the human mind and the mind of Dao is essential because it entails the foundation of human morality and the practice of self-cultivation. Whereas the human mind issues from the form of material force, the mind of Dao is based on the natural endowment, though they are mutually interrelated rather than clearly divided. While the human mind consists in the impartiality of one's body, the mind of Dao reveals the Mandate of Heaven. The former can be in unity with the latter only after hearing the mandate of the latter. Since sages also possess human minds, we must distinguish between pre- and post-sagely states.

### *Restoration of Original Humanity:*
### *Self-Cultivation (Advancing Humanity)*

The basic methodology of sage learning is 'dwelling in mindfulness (敬 *kyŏng* [*jing*])' and the 'investigating the principle (*li*)' (居敬窮理). 'Investigating the principle' means to know and perceive *li* in everything and every event in one's life. *The Great Learning* suggests a specific method to investigate the principle of things, i.e., the 'investigation of things' (格物) and the 'extension of knowledge' (致知). The investigation of things is a process of learning in which, by investigating *li* in-depth, the mind-and-heart grows to attain knowledge.

*Kyŏng* (敬), as the center of self-cultivation, is the nucleus in which the mind-and-heart is regulated and converged. The idea of "focusing on one thing without departing from it" bespeaks of the state when the mind-and-heart is so concentrated and attentive as to be fully mindful. In the polarity of the mind of Dao and the human mind, Yi T'oegye (1501-1570) summed up the Neo-Confucian method of self-cultivation in terms of the 'blocking of human desires and preservation of the Heavenly principle' (去人慾 存天理): "All the matters that are involved in blocking human desires should be categorized on the side of the human mind, and all that pertains to preserving the principle of Heaven should be categorized on the side of the mind of the [D]ao."[32] The purpose of *kyŏng* lies in attaining harmoniously corresponding relationships with other people and Heaven in the practice of everyday life. This learning leads us finally to obtain sagehood in the (anthropocosmic) unity of Heaven and humanity, transcending the polarity of the mind of Dao and the human mind. From the Confucian perspective, humans are not expansive conquerors of the universe but interdependent co-spectators who witness the glorious cosmic drama of Dao, and ecological gatekeepers who harmonize Heaven's gracious trajectory in this anthropocosmic theatre.

---

32 Kalton, *To Become a Sage*, 169.

## 3. Advancing Humanity in Confucianism and Transhumanism: To Become a Sage or a Cyborg?

*Advanced Humanity*

Both Confucianism and transhumanism envision advanced humanity, but their goals and means are very different. Confucianism clearly specifies it as the ideal person, a complete embodiment of the mind of Dao (ontological morality), with a full recovery of original humanity as the heavenly endowment (benevolence, righteousness, propriety, wisdom) through self-cultivation. However, it is unclear what transhumanists visualize as advanced humanity, except that they seek to functionally push beyond humans' biological limitations, including aging and death, by using science and technology aggressively. The very label "posthuman" or "transhuman" suggests a desire to become a powerful, quasi-immortal being with super-intelligence who can govern even the entire universe. In short, whereas Confucianism pursues humanity's advancement via the self-cultivation of virtue and morality (sagehood), transhumanism chases the utmost enhancement of human capability in terms of intelligence and power via maximum use of science and technology (cyborghood).

The ultimate goal of the posthuman vision seems to acquire an omnipresence, omniscience, and omnipotence parallel to divine attributes in traditional Christian theologies. The final objective of transhumanism seems to be little more than 'playing God' in a Judeo-Christian sense. Thus, the directions of human advancement proposed by Confucianism and transhumanism would seem to be

entirely opposed: whereas Confucianism aims at a profoundly virtuous human person through the cultivation of the mind-and-heart
to recover the originary ontological state of humanity, transhumanism aims at a powerful post-humanity with superintelligences
making daring mechanical and digital transformations (such as
mind-uploading into supercomputers) in the expectation of the
coming singularity of techno-divinization (*apotheosis*). In a nutshell,
while the Confucian project is to return to the original humanity
as endowed by Heaven (the ultimate ground of being), the transhuman project is to break the biological bondage of the present, fragile
human condition to drive further evolution with radical scientific
and technological interventions.

## *Existential Humanity*

From a Confucian point of view, transhumanism exhibits a very
naïve anthropology, particularly in analyzing existential humanity
and the human mind. Among transhumanist discourses, it is hard
to find profound concerns on ambiguous and susceptible human
desires - what Christian theology calls concupiscence (and what
Confucianism identifies as selfish desires in the human mind).
Taking the mind-and-heart as a primary locus of self-cultivation,
Confucianism rigorously investigates the complex dynamics of the
human mind concerning desire and will, associated with delicate
human feelings, not to mention the complicated relationship of li
with *qi* that can disturb the existential mind away from the mind
of Dao to become dysfunctional. However, transhumanism does
not take seriously such ambiguities and vulnerabilities of the human

mind but understands the mind functionally as a mere intelligence reducible to an information pattern.

Confucianism's human mind (more precisely, the mind-and-heart) is foreign to Western thought under the dominant legacy of mind-and-body dualism. This subject was especially a central theme of Korean Neo-Confucianism. The existential human mind-and-heart is exceedingly vulnerable to selfish desires and so subject to serious scrutiny in real everyday life situations. Transhumanism may regard "the mind as immaculate-code, the body as inefficient hardware—able to accommodate limited hacks but probably destined for replacement."[33] From a Confucian point of view, however, a techno-logically engineered enhancement and mechanical transformation of humanity without rigorous self-cultivation not only reflects naïve ignorance about the dark side of humanity but also a most perilous idea (of a 'small person' with an uncultivated mind) that could bring fatal disasters upon the world.

*Advancing Humanity*

The transhumanist method for advancing humanity is essentially technological, the hope of a posthuman transformation to super-intelligence. Transhumanism offers no clear notion that the culti-vation of the mind is a precondition to pursuing the advancement of humanity as in Confucianism, but rather displays unbridled con-fidence that external means of medical and technical engineering of intelligence can accomplish it. For Confucianism, however, in-

---

33 Khatchadourian, "The Doomsday Invention," 68.

telligence is only one attribute of humanity, and a highly ambiguous and dangerous one at that. It should be carefully examined and regulated by the right mind (正心) and the righteous will (誠意) under the frame of reference of the Confucian prime virtue of benevolence (*ren*). Moreover, knowing and reasoning in Confucianism do not refer only to functional intelligence (or mathematical reasoning), but rather to wisdom, an awakened and holistic knowing following the mind of Dao, capable of prudent judgment and with profound spiritual dimensions. Confucian wisdom does not mean merely an epistemic intelligence (or information) but ontological knowledge of the unity of the transcendent ground of being.

In transhumanism, it is hard to find an ontological ground for human advancement beyond a techno-version of the Enlightenment's optimistic belief in historical progress and the power of autonomous reason. However, human experience in the modern era since the Enlightenment, which include global warfare and ecological destruction, suggests that historical progress is mixed at best, and that the power of human reason is easily manipulated for the sake of evil purposes. Tu Wei-ming reviewed the Enlightenment mentality in the following terms:

> [T]he Enlightenment mentality, fueled by the Faustian drive to explore, to know, to conquer, and to subdue, persisted as the reigning ideology of the modern West... However, a realistic appraisal of the Enlightenment mentality reveals many faces of the modern West incongruent with the image of 'the Age of Reason.' In the context of modern Western hegemonic discourse, progress may entail inequality, reason, self-interest, and individual greed.[34]

Furthermore, 20th-century history unveiled the dreadful reality of a structural, industrial evil that is much more ruthless and formidable than anything before it, perhaps even foretelling that the *eschaton* of the human race is near! Both Confucianism and these historical experiences caution that the transhumanist hope for a singularity of techno-human transcendence entails a naïve understanding of human realities. Lacking an acute awareness of the complexities of human evil and the potential structural wickednesses of industrial civilization, transhumanism could even be "one of the most dangerous ideas the West has ever produced."[35]

Confucianism sees a human being as a network of relationships that should be expanded in ever-widening circles of relatedness, from self, through family and society, to the world. If an essential gateway to the posthuman goal for transhumanism is artificial intelligence, the gateway to authentic human self-realization for Confucians is filial piety, which is the root of reverence and humility more generally and a recipe for achieving peace in the world through harmonious human relationships. Ancestor veneration is hence an indispensable part of Confucian practice of filial piety, the very foundational beginning of moral life. With an excessive reliance on individual autonomy, from this perspective, transhumanism does violate a "tyranny of presence," forgetting both descendants (the future) and ancestors (the past) and ignoring collective identities that entail

---

34 See Tu Wei-ming, "Beyond the Enlightenment Mentality," in *Confucianism and Ecology: The Interrelation of Heaven, Earth, and Humans,* ed. Mary Evelyn Tucker and John Berthrong (Cambridge: Harvard University Press, 1998), 4.

35 Francis Fukuyama, "The world's most dangerous ideas: transhumanism," *Foreign Policy* 144 (2009): 42-43.

collective immortality rather than individual amortality.[36] While transhumanism is highly individualistic (as autonomy is a supreme value), Confucianism is meticulously communal in its pursuit of benevolent co-human living in propriety (as the family is the concrete starting point of such co-creation, and genealogy is essential as a documented historical proof of such collective living).

Whereas transhumanism sees the human body as a regrettably imperfect object susceptible to further development by advanced science and technologies, Confucianism regards it as an inseparable part of the human self (mind-and-heart) on its path to becoming fully human. Confucianism obliges us to preserve our bodies as precious givens from Heaven, passed down through our ancestors, whereas transhumanism advocates engineering and manipulation as if of defective hardware. In sum, ideal human beings in Confucianism are prudent 'players' or moral agents (sages) who humbly participate in the anthropocosmic drama of the Dao, while posthumans in the transhumanist vision are technical 'managers', cold conquerors who control this planet and conquer the universe, possibly to ending up as the lonely *homo deus*.

## Conclusion

Although advancing humanity is a central theme of Confucianism and transhumanism, their goals and methods differ. Confucianism

---

36 Brent Waters, "Flesh Made Data: The Posthuman Project in Light of the Incarnation," in *Religion and Transhumanism: The Unknown Future of Human Enhancement*, ed,, Calvin Mercer and Tracy J. Trothen (Santa Barbara, CA: Praeger, 2014), 297-301.

seeks to recover ontological human goodness by cultivating the mind-and-heart via education (sage learning): Transhumanism wants to transcend natural human limitations to achieve posthuman superintelligence through the radical adoption of science and technology. Although transhumanists argue that their position is "an extension of humanism," it denotes an "exclusive humanism," which Cheng Chung-ying criticized as the root cause of all crises arising from the West since the Enlightenment. Whereas exclusive humanism "exalts the human species, placing it in a position of mastery of and domination over the universe" (a conquest paradigm), Confucianism advocates an "inclusive humanism" that "stresses the coordinating powers of humanity as the very reason for its existence" (a harmony paradigm). As Cheng argues,

[H]umanism in the modern West is nothing more than a secular will for power or a striving for domination, with rationalistic science at its disposal. In fact, the fascination with power leads to a Faustian trade-off of knowledge and power (pleasure and self-glorification) for value and truth, a trade-off which can lead to the final destruction of the meaning of the human self and human freedom... Humanism in this exclusive sense is a disguise for the individualistic entrepreneurship of modern man armed with science and technology as tools of conquest and devastation.[37]

---

37 Cheng Chung-ying, "The Trinity of Cosmology, Ecology, and Ethics in the Confucian Personhood," in *Confucianism and Ecology: The Interrelation of Heaven, Earth, and Humans*, ed. Mary Evelyn Tucker and John Berthrong (Cambridge, MA: Harvard University Press, 1998), 213-14.

Perhaps transhumanism is simply the most radical descendant, the logical endpoint of this exclusive humanism and Enlightenment mentality. The fundamental issue is "what it means to be human after all." Bostrom argues that "the important thing is not to be human but to be humane."[38] From a Confucian point of view, however, it is meaningless to be functionally humane (*yòng*) without being a particular person (as a subject [*ti*]) in a specific context, struggling with seemingly ambiguous and unintelligible realities and so always in search of the Dao through the cultivation of original virtues (benevolence, righteousness, propriety, and wisdom), the preservation of mindfulness (*kyŏng*), and the blocking of selfish desires.

## 4. A Brief Theological Reflection: Toward Techno-dao and Theo-dao (Theology of Dao)

A serious theological issue amid the challenges of AI technology and transhumanism is the rise of AI religion. A recent article in Forbes dramatically titled "AI vs. God: Who Stays And Who Leaves?"[39] If "one goal of transhumanism is to make humans more godlike, another is to create a new kind of God altogether." Some people in Silicon Valley are already moving in the latter direction by founding a church to worship an AI god. Anthony Levandowski, a former

---

38 Bostrom, "Introduction," 13.

39 Kate Levchuk, "AI vs. God: Who stays And Who Leaves?" *Forbes*, Aug 6, 2018, https://www.forbes.com/sites/cognitiveworld/2018/08/05/ai-vs-god-who-stays-and-who-leaves/#49b0b78e2713.

executive of Google and Uber executive, said about an idea of the "Way of Future" church.

— The "Way of the Future" church will have its own gospel called "The Manual," public worship ceremonies, and probably a physical place of worship.

— The idea behind his religion is that one day — "not next week or next year" — sufficiently advanced artificial intelligence will be smarter than humans, and will effectively become a god.

— "Part of it being smarter than us means it will decide how it evolves, but at least we can decide how we act around it," Levandowski told Wired. "I would love for the machine to see us as its beloved elders that it respects and takes care of. We would want this intelligence to say, 'Humans should still have rights, even though I'm in charge.'"[40]

So comes an AI religion with a superintelligent God, "When Silicon Valley Gets Religion."[41] This realization would be not only for those in Silicon Valley but also for so-called Christian transhumanists. The theology of a superintelligent God is a predictable consequence in the historical trajectory of theo-logos. Western theology has used logos as its dominant root-metaphor and critical concept, incorporat-

---

40 Kif Leswing, "Ex-Google executive Anthony Levandowski is founding a church where people worship an artificial intelligence god," *Business Insider*, Nov 16, 2017, https://www.businessinsider.com.au/anthony-levandowski-way-of-the-future-church-where-people-worship-ai-god-2017-11.

41 Galen Beebe and Zachary Davis, "When Silicon Valley gets religion — and vice versa," *Boston Globe*, Nov 7, 2018, https://www.bostonglobe.com/ideas/2018/11/07/when-silicon-valley-gets-religion-and-vice-versa/L5xOYtgwd4VImwcj52YxtK/story.html.

ing Greek philosophy which idolized the mind (intelligence) by separating it from the body (emotion). Overstressing the salvation of the individual soul, the Reformation deepened this reductionist view of humanity by strengthening individualism. The Enlightenment further intensified the focus on autonomous intelligence, neglecting the wholeness of humanity with its bodies and emotions. Coupled with cyberspace and virtual reality, the invention of superintelligent artificial intelligence could be an accomplishment of the Platonian ultimate vision, the purely intellectual dimension of logos.[42] Furthermore, a traditional belief in an omniscient, omnipresent, omnipotent God comes into crisis with the advent of a superintelligent AI who knows everything (dataism), acts everywhere, and has much more powerful intelligence.

Theologically, artificial intelligence ultimately reveals the limit of the logos theology that pursues the intelligent knowledge of God (defined as *fides quaerens intellectum*) in terms of propositional doctrines and highly metaphysical discourses. The theo-logos that has dominated the world for centuries under a Western aegis now faces an acute crisis. The challenges of AI and transhumanism may imply not only 'the end of human history' but also 'the end of theo-logos.' Indeed, Christian theology needs a macro-paradigm shift, that is to say, from a theology of intelligence (knowledge) to a theology of wisdom (virtues). In other words, *from theo-logos to theo-dao.*

As an East Asian theologian, I also view transhumanism as one of "the most dangerous ideas" the West has ever produced.[43] As

---

42 See Michael Heim, *The Metaphysics of Virtual Reality* (Oxford: Oxford University Press, 1994).

I have said elsewhere,

> while it presents rosy scenarios and science fiction fantasies, trans-
> humanism, from the eyes of a theologian based in the realistic global sit-
> uation in Asia, does not seem to go much beyond the wild dreams and
> armchair imaginations of futurist techno-enthusiasts in the first world.
> Technology is fascinating and offers promise to humanity. However, his-
> tory shows that strong, technologically advanced countries are more inter-
> ested in using newly acquired advantages to maintain their hegemonies
> and strengthen their supremacies, rather than to help the human race as
> a whole. The situation of the real world we live in is and will be much
> more complicated than the virtual realities which techno-visionaries in
> the first world have imagined with their techno-hypes and digital fanta-
> sies expressed in science fiction films such as *Star Trek, Star Wars, The
> Matrix,* and *Avatar.*[44]

Instead of *techno-logy,* I coined the term *techno-dao,* observing the
powerful appearance of artificial intelligence.[45] I believe that we
somehow have to develop AI in association with human values,
neither based on exclusive humanism nor entirely on intelligence,
but somewhat based on inclusive humanism and wisdom (not just
smart and fast but rather wise and virtuous; namely, 'Virtuous AI').

43 Francis Fukuyama, "The world's most dangerous ideas: transhumanism," *Foreign Policy*
144 (2009): 42-43.

44 Heup Young Kim, "Cyborg, Sage, and Saint: Transhumanism as Seen from an East Asian
Theological Setting," in *Religion and Transhumanism,* ed. Mercer and Trothen, 101.

45 See Kim, "Alphgo's Victory;" and Heup Young Kim, *A Theology of Dao* (Maryknoll:
Orbis Books, 2017), 238-59.

This will require a radical revision of our thinking, and in particular a shift in our attitudes to AI, namely from a *techno-logy* based on the Western logos paradigm (in pursuit of supreme intelligence) to a *techno-dao* based on the East Asian Dao paradigm (in pursuit of the Way of life and the Wisdom of humanity).

Some AI luminaries in the West are also espousing such developments. Tim Cook, Apple's CEO, has said that "for artificial intelligence to be truly smart, it must respect human values, including privacy. If we get this wrong, the dangers are profound... We can achieve both great artificial intelligence and great privacy standards. It's not only a possibility, it is a responsibility. In the pursuit of artificial intelligence, we should not sacrifice the humanity, creativity, and ingenuity that define our human intelligence."[46] The late Stephen Hawking put the problem in similar terms:

Presumably, [ordinary people] will die out, or become unimportant. Instead, there will be a race of self-designing beings who are improving at an ever-increasing rate... Our future is a race between the growing power of our technology and the wisdom with which we use it. Let's make sure that wisdom wins.[47]

Recently, the European Commission pronounced AI Ethics Guidelines, suggesting terms such as "Trustworthy AI," "Ethical AI,"

---

46 Isobel Asher Hamilton, "Apple CEO Tim Cook has warned that the 'dangers are profound' if AI falls into the wrong hands," *Business Insider* (Oct 24, 2018).

47 Michael Cook, "Stephen Hawking, transhumanist," *BioEdge*, Oct 21, 2018, https://www.bioedge.org/bioethics/stephen-hawking-transhumanist/12863.

and "Human-centric AI."[48] Stanford University also established the Institute for Human-Centered Artificial Intelligence. However, such work is still very much being conducted under the framework of the Enlightenment mentality. Terms such as "human-centric AI" are problematic since they convey anthropocentrism (and exclusive humanism), which postmodernism and ecological consciousness have tried to overcome. Western theology and thought reach a dead-lock from the breakdown of the ontology of humanity and the loss of *bona fide* humanism due to an inherited theocentrism and its rigid anthropocentric dualism. The wisdom of Confucianism, humanity's longest-running sapiential tradition, could help us to overcome this dilemma.

In the face of superintelligent AI (AGI) and transhumanism, an urgent challenge for Christian theology is hence to liberate global theology from the dominant theologies of logos (theo-logos), cen-tered on intelligence (knowledge) due to its inherited Greek in-telligence-centered dualism which the Reformation and the Enlightenment further deepened. The reality of AI reveals the limits of theo-logos and calls for new theological alternatives. Instead of theo-logos, I have been proposing *theo-dao* (a theology of Dao) as a new paradigm of Christian theology in an anthropogenic age of science and technology. In and through an active *trialogue* (religion-and-science dialogue + interreligious dialogue) among the Sciences (including applied sciences and engineering), Christian Theology,

---

48 European Commission, "Communication from the Commission to the European Parliament, the Council, the European Economic and Social Committee and the Committee of the Regions: 'Building Trust in Human-Centric Artificial intelligence'," Brussels, April 8, 2019.

and East Asian Religions (Confucianism and Daoism), theo-dao will provide a viable alternative paradigm for global theology in an era of artificial intelligence. This will entail a macro-paradigm shift that may include the following substantial changes.[49]

- Logos → Hodos (Way, Dao): Biblical (Jn 14:6; cf. John 1:1 *Dabar* vs. Logos)
- Knowledge → Wisdom
- Intelligence → Way of Life
- Essence (Analysis) → Whole (Virtues)
- Conflict (相剋) → Harmony (Sangsaeng 相生)
- Domination (Positive Golden Rule) → Reciprocity (Negative Golden Rule)
- Exclusive Humanism → Inclusive Humanism
- Either-or → Both-and Paradigm
- Theocentric vs. Anthropocentric → Theanthropocosmic Vision
- Theo-Logos (Theo+Logos) vs. Theo-Praxis (Theo+Praxis) → Theo-Dao (Theo+Dao)
- Techno-logy (AI + Logos) → Techno-dao (AI + Dao)

---

49 See Kim, *A Theology of Dao*. For trialogue, see ibid, 189-203.

# CHAPTER SIX

# New Humanism in the Age of Artificial Intelligence: A Theo-Daoian Reflection

## Abstract

This chapter explores humanism in the contemporary context where artificial intelligence (AI) is reshaping every facet of human life. It employs the unique lens of Theo-Dao, an East Asian Contextual Theology deeply rooted in Daoian and Confucian wisdom. The paper juxtaposes enduring humanistic values derived from Confucianism, emphasizing virtues such as benevolence (ren), righteousness (yi), propriety (li), wisdom (zhi), and trustworthiness (xin), against the backdrop of the Enlightenment's rationality-driven modern humanism. It engages with Pope Francis's critique of the technocratic paradigm in *Laudato Si'*, scrutinizing the contemporary era's tendency to prioritize technological advancement at the expense of the environment and morality.

Furthermore, it investigates the nuances of posthumanism, highlighting its emergent critique amidst the global ecological crisis and its anti-humanistic tendencies within the realm of transhumanism.

Through a Confucian critique, the work proposes an inclusive humanism that transcends the limitations of its modern counterpart's exclusivity. It advocates for a paradigm of harmony that encapsulates human virtues, cosmogonic relationality (Taiji), and an interrelated the-anthropo-cosmic (triadic) wholeness (Dao).

By weaving together Theo-Daoian insights, including the Daoian thought of non-intentional, supra-apophatic spirituality, the study champions a recalibration of humanism in the age of AI. It posits a forward-thinking anthropology that not only incorporates technological advancements but also profoundly reconnects with the Earth and its myriad inhabitants through a lens of mutual respect and interdependence. This work aims to contribute a pivotal perspective to the dialogue on technology and ethics, advocating for a future where technology enhances, rather than eclipses, the human spirit and its virtuous potential.

## Introduction

In the 21st century's rapidly evolving landscape, artificial intelligence (AI) has emerged as a transformative force, reshaping industries, societal structures, and individual lives at an unprecedented speed and scale. From automating routine tasks to pioneering new frontiers in healthcare, education, and environmental conservation, AI's influence permeates every facet of contemporary life, heralding a new era of innovation and challenge. However, as this technological revolution unfolds, it also raises profound questions about the nature of humanism, ethics, and the very essence of human agency in a world increasingly mediated by machine intelligence.[1]

It is within this context that "New Humanism at the Time of Artificial Intelligence: A Theo-Daoian Reflection" seeks to explore and articulate a vision of humanism that is both responsive to and reflective of the unique challenges and opportunities presented by the age of AI. This exploration is anchored in the intriguing insights of Theo-Dao (Theology of Dao), a theological paradigm that emerges from the confluence of Daoism and Confucianism, two of East Asia's most enduring and influential systems of thought.[2] These traditions offer a reservoir of wisdom (Dao) focused on harmony, balance, and the ethical cultivation of self and society, providing a timely counterpoint to the prevailing narratives of technological determinism and the mechanization of human life.[3]

Theo-Dao, with its emphasis on Dao (interconnected whole), Taiji (relational harmony), and wuwei (non-intentional action), offers a framework for understanding and engaging with the world that transcends the binary oppositions of human and machine, nature and technology.[4] At its core, it advocates for a holistic vision

---

1 Nick Bostrom, *Superintelligence: Paths, Dangers, Strategies* (Oxford: Oxford University Press, 2014).

2 Heup Young Kim, *A Theology of Dao* (Maryknoll: Orbis Books, 2017).

3 As a widely used root metaphor in all classical East Asian religions—including Confucianism, Daoism, and Buddhism—Dao [Tao] (the Way, *do* in Korean) is a highly inclusive term with various meanings. For example, "[D]ao is a way, a path, a road, and by common metaphorical extension, it becomes in ancient China the right way of life, the way of governing, the ideal way of human existence, the way of the cosmos, the generative-normative way (pattern, path, course) of existence as such" (Herbert Fingarette, *Confucius: The Secular as Sacred*, New York: Harper & Row, 1972, 19). However, for the sake of discussion, this paper adopts a narrower definition, focusing on the concept of the "interconnected whole."

of human existence, one that recognizes the mutual dependencies between humans and their environments, both natural and constructed. By drawing on the virtues espoused by Confucianism —ren (benevolence), yi (righteousness), li (ritual propriety), zhi (wisdom), and xin (faithfulness)—alongside the Daoian appreciation for the fluid and dynamic nature of reality, Theo-Dao provides a robust foundation for reimagining humanism in an era dominated by digital technologies.

As we venture deeper into the age of artificial intelligence, the need for a new humanism—a Theo-Daoian reflection—becomes ever more pressing. This paper aims to chart a course through the complexities of modern technological society, advocating for a model of humanism that not only embraces the transformative potential of AI but also reaffirms the fundamental values and virtues that sustain a just and flourishing human community.

## 1. Critique of the Technocratic Paradigm

In his encyclical *Laudato Si'*, Pope Francis offers a powerful critique of the technocratic paradigm that has come to dominate contemporary society.[5] This paradigm, characterized by an unrelenting faith in technological progress and an instrumental view of nature,

---

4 Roger T. Ames and David L. Hall, *Dao De Jing: A Philosophical Translation* (New York: Ballantine Books, 2003).

5 Pope Francis, *Laudato Si': On Care for Our Common Home* (Vatican City: Libreria Editrice Vaticana, 2015).

places a premium on efficiency, productivity, and economic growth, often at the expense of environmental sustainability and ethical responsibilities. Pope Francis warns of the inherent dangers in a worldview that positions technological advancement as the ultimate solution to all human problems, neglecting the deeper ethical, social, and spiritual dimensions of human existence.

The technocratic paradigm assumes that technological power can and should be used to control and manipulate the natural world, transforming it into a resource for human consumption and convenience. This utilitarian approach not only leads to widespread environmental degradation but also fosters a societal model in which human relationships and ethical considerations are increasingly mediated by technological systems. The encyclical highlights how this paradigm encourages a culture of disposability, where both material goods and human lives are valued only insofar as they contribute to economic productivity or technological efficiency.

Pope Francis's critique is not an outright rejection of technology but rather a call for a critical reassessment of how it is developed and used. He advocates for an "integral ecology" that acknowledges the interdependence of all living beings and respects the intrinsic value of the natural world. This perspective challenges the technocratic paradigm by insisting that technological advancement should not come at the expense of environmental health or moral integrity but rather be aligned with principles of justice, sustainability, and the common good.[6]

---

6 Celia Deane-Drummond, "Theological Ethics for a Technological Age," *Theology and Science* 17, no. 1 (2019): 89-102.

In today's society, the prioritization of technological advancement over environmental and moral considerations is evident in
various areas, ranging from the relentless exploitation of natural
resources to the deployment of AI and big data in ways that threaten
privacy and human dignity. The technocratic paradigm often masks
the potential harms of unchecked technological progress, promoting an illusion of neutrality that conceals the embedded values and
interests driving technological development.[7]

### Theo-Daoian Resonance: A Holistic Ethical Vision

Pope Francis's critique resonates profoundly with the insights
of Theo-Dao, which also challenges the technocratic paradigm by
advocating for a more harmonious and integrated approach to technology and nature. Eco-Dao, an ecological extension of Theo-Dao,
emphasizes the interconnectedness of all things and the need for
human actions to align with the natural rhythms of the universe.[8]
This perspective mirrors Francis's call for an "integral ecology" and
offers a deeper spiritual and ethical foundation for recalibrating our
relationship with technology.

In Daoian thought, wuwei (non-coercive action) encourages living in accordance with the natural flow of life, rather than attempting
to control or dominate it. Similarly, Taiji (the balance of yin and

---

7 Langdon Winner, *Autonomous Technology: Technics-out-of-Control as a Theme in
Political Thought* (Cambridge, MA: MIT Press, 1977).

8 Heup Young Kim, "Eco-Dao: An Ecological Theology of Dao," in *The Bloomsbury
Handbook of Religion and Nature: The Elements*, ed. Laura Hobgood and Whitney
Bauman (London: Bloomsbury Academic, 2018), 99-108.

yang) emphasizes the importance of dynamic equilibrium, where harmony is achieved through the balance of opposing forces, not through exploitation or domination. These Daoian principles align with Francis's warning against the unchecked use of technology to control nature and commodify human life. Instead, they call for an approach to technology that fosters balance, respect, and mutual enhancement between humanity, technology, and nature.

Moreover, the Confucian virtues, such as benevolence, righteousness, wisdom, and trustworthiness, further reinforce the idea that technology must serve the collective well-being, not just economic gain. A Theo-Daoian vision insists that technology should enhance human flourishing while respecting the intrinsic value of all life forms. This ethical vision not only addresses the shortcomings of the technocratic paradigm but also provides a more holistic framework for integrating technological advancement with ecological stewardship and moral integrity.

### A Path Forward: Reimagining Humanism in the Age of AI

Pope Francis's critique, when viewed through the lens of Theo-Dao, invites us to envision a path forward that embraces technological innovation without sacrificing ethical principles or environmental responsibilities. This alternative path is one in which technology, rather than being a tool for domination, becomes a means of enhancing harmony, both within society and with the natural world.

The shortcomings of the technocratic paradigm underscore the urgent need to rethink our relationship with technology and its role in shaping the future. By integrating the insights of Theo-Dao, we can cultivate a humanism that is not only compatible with technological advancement but also deeply rooted in a commitment to environmental stewardship, relational harmony, and ethical integrity. This recalibrated humanism would prioritize balance, interconnectedness, and respect for the intrinsic value of all beings, ensuring that technology serves the common good rather than perpetuating environmental degradation or social injustice.

In conclusion, both Pope Francis and Theo-Dao challenge us to rethink the way we approach technological progress. Their shared critique highlights the importance of aligning technological development with ethical and ecological principles, fostering a future in which technology supports rather than undermines the well-being of all life on Earth. Through this integrated, holistic vision, we can move beyond the limitations of the technocratic paradigm and toward a more balanced and harmonious relationship between humanity, technology, and the natural world.

## 2. Post-humanism and Transhumanism: Critique and the Call for Inclusive Humanism

In contemporary discourse on the future of humanity, post-humanism and transhumanism emerge as two influential yet distinct philosophical movements that challenge traditional humanism in light of technological advancements and ecological crises. Despite their innovative approaches, both remain largely rooted in exclusive humanism, an Enlightenment mentality that continues to frame humanity's relationship with technology and nature in ways that diverge significantly from the Confucian inclusive humanism of East Asia. A celebrated contemporary Confucian humanist, Tu Wei-ming, critiques the Enlightenment mentality, stating:

> [T]he Enlightenment mentality, fueled by the Faustian drive to explore, to know, to conquer, and to subdue, persisted as the reigning ideology of the modern West... However, a realistic appraisal of the Enlightenment mentality reveals many faces of the modern West incongruent with the image of 'the Age of Reason.' In the context of modern Western hegemonic discourse, progress may entail inequality, reason, self-interest, and individual greed.[9]

Post-humanism critically examines classical humanism's anthropocentric assumptions, questioning the sustainability of human dominance over nature, especially amid global ecological crises. It advocates for decentering humans in ethical and philosophical frameworks, urging consideration of the rights and intrinsic value of non-human entities and the environment. Post-humanism argues that environmental degradation and species extinction are direct consequences of an outdated humanism that prioritizes human desires over the well-being of other life forms. By emphasizing interconnectedness among all life, post-humanism calls for an ethical rethinking of humanity's place in the natural world.[10]

---

9 See Tu Wei-ming, "Beyond the Enlightenment Mentality," in *Confucianism and Ecology: The Interrelation of Heaven, Earth, and Humans*, ed. Mary Evelyn Tucker and John Berthrong (Cambridge: Harvard University Press, 1998), 4.

However, despite its critique of anthropocentrism, post-humanism remains tied to the Enlightenment's exclusive humanism, which seeks to correct humanity's flawed dominance over nature by advocating for a reimagined role for humans within ecological systems. This remains grounded in the individualistic and rationalistic paradigms of the Enlightenment, often neglecting the relational, virtue-based approaches to humanism seen in Confucian thought.

Transhumanism, on the other hand, presents a more techno-optimistic vision, championing the use of technology to enhance human physical and cognitive abilities, ultimately transcending the limitations of the human body and lifespan.[11] Transhumanists advocate for the use of biotechnology, AI, and cybernetics to achieve a post-human future where humans evolve into a new species or co-exist with advanced AI entities.[12] While this vision emphasizes human progress through technological enhancement, it often inherits the Enlightenment's quest for mastery over both human nature and the environment.[13]

Despite its optimism, transhumanism shares with post-humanism the limitations of Enlightenment-based exclusive humanism. The relentless pursuit of enhancement and perfection risks devalu-

---

10 Rosi Braidotti, *The Posthuman* (Cambridge: Polity Press, 2013).

11 Nick Bostrom, "A History of Transhumanist Thought," *Journal of Evolution and Technology* 14:1 (2005): 1-25.

12 Katherine Hayles, *How We Became Posthuman: Virtual Bodies in Cybernetics, Literature, and Informatics* (Chicago: University of Chicago Press, 1999).

13 Heup Young Kim, "Cyborg, Sage, and Saint: Transhumanism as Seen from an East Asian Theological Setting," in *Religion and Transhumanism: The Unknown Future of Human Enhancement*, ed. Calvin Mercer and Tracy J. Trothen (Santa Barbara, CA: Praeger, 2014), 97-114.

ing the inherent worth of unenhanced human life and overlooks
the richness of human diversity and imperfection. Moreover, the
transhumanist emphasis on surpassing human limitations perpetuates the Enlightenment focus on individual achievement, often at
the expense of communal well-being and ecological harmony.[14]

### The Need for Confucian Inclusive Humanism

Both post-humanism and transhumanism highlight the need for
a new paradigm of humanism that responds to the ethical and ecological challenges of the modern life. However, this new humanism
must go beyond the limits of Enlightenment-based exclusive humanism and embrace a more inclusive humanism that recognizes
the interconnectedness of all life and the intrinsic value of nature,
as seen in East Asian philosophical traditions.

Confucian inclusive humanism offers a robust alternative. Rooted
in the relational and virtue-based framework of Confucian thought,
this approach emphasizes the cultivation of virtues (benevolence,
righteousness, propriety, wisdom, trustworthiness) in shaping human relationships with both society and the natural world. Rather
than focusing on the mastery of nature or the enhancement of individual capabilities, Confucian humanism stresses the importance
of harmony between humans and the cosmos. It seeks balance, not

---

14 Heup Young Kim, "Perfecting Humanity in Confucianism and Transhumanism," in
   *Religious Transhumanism and Its Critics,* ed. Arvin Gouw, Brian Patrick Green, and
   Ted Peters (Lanham, MD: Lexington Books, 2022), 101-112; J. Sandel, The Case Against
   Perfection: Ethics in the Age of Genetic Engineering (Cambridge, MA: Harvard University
   Press, 2007).

domination, and promotes a holistic vision where the flourishing of individuals is intimately tied to the flourishing of communities and ecosystems.

An inclusive humanism informed by Confucian principles would embrace the post-humanist call for a broader ethical framework that includes non-human entities and the environment. It acknowledges the deep interconnections between humans, society, and the natural world, fostering a sense of mutual responsibility. Simultaneously, it would critically engage with transhumanist aspirations, ensuring that technological advancements serve to enhance human well-being and freedom without compromising ethical principles or exacerbating social inequalities. In this vision, technology is not an end in itself but a means to foster harmony and balance in the world.

*A Path Forward: Inclusive Humanism for the 21st Century*

The need for inclusive humanism is clear: it must address the critiques raised by both post-humanism and transhumanism while moving beyond the Enlightenment's exclusive humanism. Confucian inclusive humanism offers a path that celebrates human diversity, protects the environment, and harnesses technological advancements for the collective good. By fostering a relational and virtue-based approach, this framework respects the dignity of all forms of life and recognizes the profound responsibilities that come with our technological capabilities.

Incorporating the insights of Confucian inclusive humanism, we can envision a future that embraces technological innovation while remaining deeply attuned to the ethical, social, and ecological dimensions of human life. This inclusive humanism offers not only a critique of the limitations of traditional Western humanism but also a guiding framework for navigating the complex ethical landscapes of the 21st century, ensuring that humanity's pursuit of progress aligns with the broader good of all living beings and the planet itself.

## Confucian Critique of Modern Exclusive Humanism

Confucianism, as an East Asian tradition, views individual flourishing within the context of relationships—whether with other people, society, or the natural world. In contrast, modern exclusive humanism often prioritizes individual autonomy and rationality, sometimes at the expense of these broader relational contexts. From a Confucian perspective, this approach risks fostering detachment from communal and environmental responsibilities, leading to social fragmentation and ecological neglect. The Confucian critique emphasizes the interdependence of all aspects of life, asserting that true human flourishing cannot be achieved through individualism alone, but through the cultivation of virtue and harmony in all relationships.

Another Chinese-American Confucian scholar offers a sharp critique of modern Western humanism. Cheng states:

In this sense, humanism in the modern West is nothing more than a secular will for power or a striving for domination, with rationalistic science at its disposal. In fact, the fascination with power leads to a Faustian trade-off of knowledge and power (pleasure and self-glorification) for value and truth, a trade-off which can lead to the final de-

struction of the meaning of the human self and human freedom...
Humanism in this exclusive sense is a disguise for the individualistic
entrepreneurship of modern man armed with science and technology
as tools of conquest and devastation.[15]

## *Proposal for an Inclusive Humanism*

Building on this critique, Confucianism proposes an inclusive
humanism that integrates key Confucian virtues (benevolence,
righteousness, propriety, trustworthiness) with a cosmogonic sense
of relationality.[16] This inclusive humanism advocates for a holistic
view of human existence, where personal and social ethics are inseparable from the cosmic order. It recognizes that human beings
are not isolated entities but part of a vast, interconnected cosmos,
with responsibilities that extend beyond the self to include the community and the natural environment.

## *The-anthropo-cosmic Wholeness*

The concept of the-anthropo-cosmic wholeness further eluci-
dates this inclusive humanism. It suggests a seamless integration

---

15 Cheng Chung-ying, "The Trinity of Cosmology, Ecology, and Ethics in the Confucian
Personhood," in *Confucianism and Ecology: The Interrelation of Heaven, Earth, and
Humans*, ed. Mary Evelyn Tucker and John Berthrong (Cambridge, MA: Harvard
University Press, 1998), 213-14.

16 Tu Wei-Ming, *Humanity and Self-Cultivation: Essays in Confucian Thought* (Berkeley:
Asian Humanities Press, 1979); "A Confucian Perspective on Human Rights," in *The East
Asian Challenge for Human Rights*, ed. Joanne R. Bauer and Daniel A. Bell (Cambridge:
Cambridge University Press, 1999), 238-68.

of the divine (theo), the human (anthropo), and the cosmic, underscoring the Confucian view of a universe where human actions are
deeply entwined with cosmic principles.[17] This wholeness implies
that ethical living and human flourishing are contingent upon acknowledging and acting in accordance with these interconnected
realms.[18] By aligning human endeavors with the broader rhythms
and patterns of the cosmos, inclusive humanism fosters a sense of
unity and purpose that transcends individualistic pursuits.

In summary, the Confucian critique of modern exclusive humanism, coupled with the proposal for an inclusive humanism rooted
in Confucian virtues and the-anthropo-cosmic wholeness, offers
a rich, relational framework for understanding and addressing the
ethical challenges of our time. By embracing this inclusive humanism, we can cultivate a society that values communal well-being
and environmental stewardship as essential components of human
flourishing.

## 3. Theo-Daoian Insights and the Recalibration of Humanism

The recalibration of humanism in our rapidly evolving, technol-

---

17 Heup Young Kim, "Theo-dao: Integrating Ecological Consciousness in Daoism,
   Confucianism, and Christian Theology," in *The Wiley Blackwell Companion to Religion
   and Ecology*, ed. John Hart (Oxford: Wiley Blackwell, 2017), 104-14.

18 Tu Wei-Ming, "The Continuity of Being: Chinese Visions of Nature," in *Nature in Asian
   Traditions of Thought: Essays in Environmental Philosophy*, ed. J. Baird Callicott and
   Roger T. Ames (Albany: State University of New York Press, 1989), 67-79.

ogy-driven era necessitates a profound reevaluation of philosophical underpinnings. Theo-Daoian insights, rich with understandings of the nature of existence, action, harmony, and virtue, provide a comprehensive framework for re-envisioning humanism that aligns with the complexities of modernity, particularly in the age of artificial intelligence.

## Dao: The Way of Interconnected Whole

The concept of Dao emphasizes interconnectedness and fluidity, suggesting that the best path is always the one that flows naturally with the universe's rhythms.[19] In terms of humanism recalibrated for an AI-driven world, Dao encourages us to design technology that complements and integrates into human societal and ecological networks, enhancing rather than overriding or simplifying complex human and natural systems.

## Taiji:[20] The Principle of Dynamic Balance (Yin-Yang)

Taiji (the supreme ultimate) refers to the fundamental principle

---

19 David Loy, *Nonduality: A Study in Comparative Philosophy* (New Haven: Yale University Press, 1988).

20 Within the realms of Daoian and Neo-Confucian thought, Taiji (*Taegŭk* in Korean) signifies the dynamic equilibrium of yin (receptive, feminine) and yang (active, masculine) energies. This philosophical stance transcends Western dualistic epistemology, which often positions binaries in opposition. Taiji offers a holistic perspective, viewing opposites as complementary components within a cohesive whole. This framework encourages a reinterpretation of conflicts and dichotomies as opportunities to achieve deeper harmony and balance across various dimensions of existence.

of dynamic balance and relational harmony within the cosmos. It embodies the interaction of yin and yang, asserting that true harmony is achieved not through dominance or submission, but through the perpetual balancing of opposing forces.[21] In the application of AI, the principle of Taiji encourages technologies that balance human needs with ethical considerations, fostering systems that enhance societal equilibrium rather than create disruption.

### *Wuwei:[22] Non-Intentional, Supra-Apophatic Spirituality*

At the heart of Daoian thought is wuwei, often translated as non-action or effortless action. Far from advocating passivity, wuwei represents a type of action that is perfectly aligned with the natural flow of life. It is a form of engagement that is spontaneous and in harmony with the environment, emphasizing responsiveness over force.[23] In the context of AI, wuwei suggests a model of technology use that is intuitive and enhances human capabilities without disrupting natural human rhythms.

---

21 Robin R. Wang, *Yinyang: The Way of Heaven and Earth in Chinese Thought and Culture* (Cambridge: Cambridge University Press, 2012).

22 Within the *Daodejing*, the concept of wuwei embodies a state of dynamic and creative passivity aligned with the feminine principle of receptivity. Griffiths highlights wuwei as a crucial counterpoint to dominant masculine tendencies in Western religion, emphasizing that true strength lies not in forceful manipulation but in aligning oneself with the natural flow of the universe—a flow orchestrated by the dynamic interplay of yin and yang (Bede Griffiths, *Universal Wisdom. A Journey Through the Sacred Wisdom of the World* (San Francisco: HarperCollins, 1994), 27.

23 Edward Slingerland, *Effortless Action: Wu-wei as Conceptual Metaphor and Spiritual Ideal in Early China* (Oxford: Oxford University Press, 2007).

*Confucian Virtues: Foundations for Virtuous AI*

Integrating Confucian virtues (ren, yi, li, zhi, xin) into the fabric of AI development and deployment can recalibrate humanism to foster more ethical interactions between humans and machines.[24] Each virtue offers a dimension of ethical consideration:

— Ren (benevolence) calls for AI to be developed with compassion and empathy, prioritizing human welfare in all decisions.
— Yi (righteousness) emphasizes the importance of justice and fairness, ensuring that AI systems do not perpetuate biases but rather mitigate them.
— Li (propriety) stresses the importance of appropriate behavior and the observance of social rituals, suggesting that AI should enhance human social interactions without replacing them.
— Zhi (wisdom) demands wisdom in the use of AI, advocating for thoughtful and prudent decision-making that considers long-term impacts.
— Xin (trustworthiness) promotes trustworthiness and integrity, which are essential in building and maintaining trust in AI technologies.

*Conclusion*

The insights of Theo-Dao, particularly through the concepts of Dao, Taiji, Wuwei, and the Confucian virtues, provide a powerful

---

24 Bryan W. Van Norden, "Ren and Li in the Analects," *Philosophy East and West* 45, no. 3 (1995): 313-39.

framework for rethinking humanism in the age of AI. By embracing these insights, we can move toward a model of humanism that not only incorporates advanced technologies but also enhances the ethical, social, and spiritual dimensions of human life. This recalibration encourages a future where technology supports our deepest human values, fostering a world where AI enhances rather than eclipses the human spirit.[25]

### Forward-thinking Anthropology

In an era where technological advancements unfold at an unprecedented pace, there arises a critical need for a forward-thinking anthropology that not only embraces these innovations but also seeks to harmonize them with the fundamental principles of human existence and ecological stewardship.[26] This proposed anthropology advocates for a deep, integrative approach to technology, one that transcends utilitarian applications and addresses the broader implications of our technological entanglements for society, culture, and the environment.

---

25 For further epistemological insights, see Heup Young Kim, "Theodaoian Epistemology in a Global Age of Decolonization," *Intercultural Theology/ZMiss*, 2024:2.

26 Bruno Latour, *We Have Never Been Modern* (Cambridge, MA: Harvard University Press, 1993).

## 4. Embracing Technological Advancements Through Techno-Dao

A forward-thinking anthropology recognizes the transformative potential of technology to enhance human life in myriad ways, from improving health and extending lifespans to facilitating global communication and access to information. However, it also calls for a critical assessment of how these technologies are designed, implemented, and integrated into daily life. Rather than uncritically accepting technological advancements as inherently positive, this perspective encourages a nuanced understanding of technology's role in shaping human values, relationships, and societal structures.[27]

This is where the concept of Techno-Dao becomes essential. As an extension of Theo-Dao, Techno-Dao integrates the principles of Daoian and Confucian wisdom into the ethical development and use of technology. It emphasizes that technological progress should not be disconnected from the natural, social, and spiritual dimensions of life. Techno-Dao advocates for the creation of technologies that work in harmony with the natural world, human nature, and the broader cosmic order, ensuring that innovation serves the holistic well-being of humanity and the planet.

### Techno-Dao and Ethical Technology

Techno-Dao challenges the conventional technocratic approach

---

27 Sherry Turkle, *Alone Together: Why We Expect More from Technology and Less from Each Other* (New York: Basic Books, 2011).

that prioritizes efficiency and productivity, often at the expense of inclusivity, equity, and sustainability. It calls for an ethical framework for technological development that aligns with these values, ensuring that technology serves to amplify human capacities without diminishing the richness of human experience or exacerbating social inequalities. Drawing on the Daoian concept of Dao—effortless action in harmony with the natural world—Techno-Dao advocates for innovations that are not only technologically advanced but also aligned with the rhythms, needs, and complexities of both the Earth and its inhabitants.

Technologies rooted in Dao emphasize responsiveness over force. They operate seamlessly within existing natural and social systems, supporting balance rather than disruption. This approach envisions technology not as a dominating force but as a subtle tool that enhances human and ecological flourishing without imposing artificial constraints or creating new hierarchies.

## *Techno-Dao's Role in Addressing Global Challenges*

Techno-Dao also addresses some of the most pressing global challenges, such as environmental degradation and social inequality. In recognizing that technology has the potential to either deepen these crises or help solve them, Techno-Dao advocates for innovations that prioritize ecological stewardship and social justice. By integrating the principles of Taiji (relational dynamics) and wu-wei (natural harmony) and the Confucian five virtues (benevolence, justice, propriety, wisdom, trustworthiness), Techno-Dao promotes the development of technologies that benefit the many rather

Chapter Six _ New Humanism in the Age of Artificial Intelligence 181

than the few, while also respecting the integrity of the planet.

In this way, Techno-Dao extends beyond traditional notions of ethical technology by embedding it within a broader, holistic worldview. It recognizes that technological innovation, when aligned with nature and moral principles, can foster a future where humanity and technology coexist in balance, serving the common good and preserving the Earth's ecosystems.

## *Reconnecting with the Earth and Its Inhabitants*

Central to a forward-thinking anthropology is the imperative to reconnect with the Earth and its myriad inhabitants through mutual respect and interdependence. In the face of environmental degradation and climate change, there is an urgent need to recalibrate our relationship with the natural world, moving from exploitation and domination to stewardship and care.[28] This requires a profound reevaluation of our values and practices, including the ways in which we employ technology.

By drawing on the insights of Theo-Dao, particularly its emphasis on interconnectedness and relational harmony, this anthropology seeks to foster a deeper sense of belonging to the Earth community. It champions technologies and practices that respect the integrity of ecosystems, promote biodiversity, and sustain the life-supporting systems of the planet. Moreover, it advocates for a relational ethic that recognizes the intrinsic value of all beings—human and non-human alike—and seeks to cultivate relationships based on empathy,

---

28 Aldo Leopold, *A Sand County Almanac* (New York: Oxford University Press, 1949).

compassion, and solidarity.[29]

## Conclusion

"New Humanism at the Time of Artificial Intelligence: A
Theo-Daoian Reflection" invites us to fundamentally rethink our
relationship with technology and reimagine the possibilities of humanism in the 21st century. By integrating Christian theology and
East Asian wisdom of Daoism and Confucianism with contemporary
technological advancements, Theo-Dao offers a pathway to a future
where technology and humanity can coexist in harmony. This coexistence must be guided by a deep commitment to ethical principles,
mutual respect, and the collective pursuit of a flourishing world.

This work not only critiques the technocratic paradigm, which
prioritizes efficiency and control at the expense of moral and ecological integrity, but also addresses the limitations of post-humanism and transhumanism—philosophical movements that, despite
their critiques of classical humanism, remain rooted in the exclusive,
Enlightenment-based drive for mastery and individual enhancement.
By contrast, the Theo-Daoian perspective aligns with a more inclusive
humanism, one that recognizes the interconnectedness of all life
and fosters a balanced relationship between humans, technology,
and the natural world.

Through the integration of Techno-Dao, this reflection provides
a practical and philosophical roadmap for navigating the complex-

---

29 Val Plumwood, *Feminism and the Mastery of Nature* (London: Routledge, 1993).

ities of the AI age. It emphasizes that technological advancements should not merely push the boundaries of human ability or efficiency, but should also serve to enhance the ethical, social, and ecological dimensions of human life. Daoian insights such as Dao (The-anthopo-cosmic wholeness), Taiji (dynamic balance), Wuwei (effortless action), and Confucian virtues such as ren (benevolence), yi (righteousness), li (propriety), zhi (wisdom), xin (trustworthiness) provide a framework for ensuring that technology is developed and used in ways that align with the deeper principles of harmony and justice.

Ultimately, this recalibrated humanism calls for a future in which technology enhances—rather than diminishes—the human spirit. It urges us to use technology not as a tool for domination or exploitation, but as a means of fostering greater harmony within ourselves, with each other, and with the planet. By embracing the insights of Theo-Dao, we can ensure that technological progress contributes to a world where humanity thrives in balance with nature, grounded in the *inclusive humanism* that respects the dignity and value of all life.

CHAPTER SEVEN

# Integrating East Asian Wisdom in AI Ethics: A Theodaoian Critique of the "Encountering AI" Document

## Abstract

This paper explores the integration of Theodaoian and Techno-daoian principles into AI ethics, offering a cross-cultural critique of the *Encountering AI* document. While Western frameworks for AI ethics often prioritize individual rights and regulatory control, Theodaoian ethics emphasize relational personhood, virtue ethics, and ecological harmony. Technodao extends these principles to the technological realm, advocating for the development of AI systems that foster social cohesion, sustainability, and moral cultivation. Through real-world case studies in healthcare, environmental monitoring, education, and corporate governance, this paper demonstrates how these principles can be practically applied to address contemporary challenges in AI development. By engaging with potential counterarguments and highlighting the importance of a pluralistic, cross-cultural ethical framework, the paper proposes a path forward for AI ethics that prioritizes relational well-being, fairness, and ecological responsibility.

## Introduction

*Artificial intelligence (AI)* presents both exciting possibilities and profound ethical challenges. The rapid development of AI technologies has spurred debates over their societal impact, prompting the need for robust ethical frameworks that guide their development and deployment. While existing AI ethics are largely dominated by Western individualistic frameworks—focusing on rights, fairness, and regulation—there is a growing recognition of the need for a more holistic, cross-cultural approach.[1] Recent research points to a global convergence around five core ethical principles for AI: transparency, justice and fairness, non-maleficence, responsibility, and privacy.[2] However, interpretations of these principles differ across cultures.[3] This paper proposes the integration of Theodaoian and Technodaoian principles—rooted in East Asian wisdom—into AI ethics.

Theodao represents the integration of Confucian, Daoian, and

---

1 Anna Jobin, Marcello Ienca, and Effy Vayena, "The Global Landscape of AI Ethics Guidelines," *Nature Machine Intelligence* 1, no. 9 (2019): 389–99, https://doi.org/10.1038/s42256-019-0088-2.

2 Luciano Floridi and Josh Cowls, "A Unified Framework of Five Principles for AI in Society," *Harvard Data Science Review* 1, no. 1 (2019), https://doi.org/10.1162/99608f92.8cd550d1.

3 Mariarosaria Taddeo and Luciano Floridi, "Regulate Artificial Intelligence to Avert Cyber Arms Race," *Nature* 556, no. 7701 (2018): 296–98, https://doi.org/10.1038/d41586-018-04602-6.

Christian theological perspectives, with a focus on relational personhood, virtue ethics, and harmony with nature.[4] Technodao, an
extension of Theodao, applies these principles specifically to the
development of technology, advocating for AI systems that promote
community well-being, environmental sustainability, and moral
cultivation.[5]

This interdisciplinary approach aims to enrich the global discourse on AI ethics by offering a critique of the *Encountering Artificial
Intelligence: Ethical and Anthropological Investigations* document from
the perspective of Theodaoian ethics.[6] The critique highlights the
limitations of Western ethical frameworks in addressing issues such
as relational personhood, ecological responsibility, and the role of
AI in fostering social harmony. Moreover, this paper provides practical
case studies that demonstrate how Theodaoian and Technodaoian principles can be applied to AI technologies in healthcare, environmental
conservation, education, and corporate settings.

By addressing key counterarguments and challenges, this paper
underscores the importance of adopting a pluralistic ethical framework for AI development—one that not only advances technological innovation but also upholds the dignity of individuals, communities, and the environment.

---

4 Heup Young Kim, *Theology of Dao* (Maryknoll, NY: Orbis, 2017).

5 Heup Young Kim, "Advancing Humanity: Artificial Intelligence, Transhumanism,
Confucianism, and Theo-Dao," in *New Confucianism: Essays in Honor of Tu Weiming,*
ed. Young-Chan Ro, Jonathan Keir, and Peter C. Phan (Lanham, MD: Lexington Books,
2024), 231-50.

6 North American AI Research Group of the Dicastery for Culture and Education of the Holy
See, *Encountering Artificial Intelligence: Ethical and Anthropological Investigations*
(Eugene, OR: Pickwick Publications, 2024).

# 1. Theodao: A Christian Contextual Theology Incorporating Confucianism and Daoism

## *Origin and Purpose of Theodao*

Theodao emerged in response to the need for a theological framework that resonates with East Asian cultural contexts while remaining faithful to Christian doctrines. As articulated in *A Theology of Dao*, Theodao enriches Christian theology by incorporating key insights from Confucianism and Daoism, two major philosophical traditions in East Asia. Importantly, this approach does not advocate for religious syncretism, but rather an engagement with cultural wisdom that deepens the understanding of Christian faith and ethics in a broader, cross-cultural context.

## *Integrating Confucianism and Daoism within a Christian Framework*

Theodao draws several key virtues from Confucianism to enhance Christian ethical thought, blending these values in a way that emphasizes moral integrity, relationality, and responsibility. These virtues include:[7]

— Ren (仁, Benevolence): Confucian *Ren* stresses altruism, empathy, and

---

7 Heup Young Kim, *Wang Yang-ming and Karl Barth: A Confucian-Christian Dialogue* (Lanham, MD: University Press of America, 1996); M. C. Kalton, *To Become a Sage: The Ten Diagrams on Sage Learning by Yi T'oegye* (New York: Columbia University Press, 1988).

humaneness,[8] aligning closely with Christian agape love. In AI ethics, this calls for compassion-driven development of AI technologies that prioritize human well-being and care (Mt. 22:37-39).

— Yi (義, Righteousness): *Yi* reflects moral integrity, justice, and fairness. This virtue corresponds with Christian ethical values, particularly in ensuring that AI systems promote fairness and righteousness in decision-making processes (Mic. 6:8).

— Li (禮, Ritual Propriety): Confucian *Li* underscores the importance of respect, proper conduct, and ritual in community life.[9] This parallels Christian practices of worship and discipline and can suggest that AI technologies should engage respectfully with human dignity and societal norms (Jn. 4:24).

— Zhi (智, Wisdom): *Zhi* emphasizes discernment, understanding, and wisdom in action.[10] In Christian thought, wisdom is also highly valued for ethical decision-making. In the context of AI, this virtue encourages careful consideration of how AI systems are developed and the moral responsibility they entail (Prov. 3:13-18).

— Xin (信, Trustworthiness): *Xin* represents reliability, faithfulness, and trust.[11] This virtue complements Christian values of transparency and accountability, especially in ensuring that AI systems are trustworthy,

---

8 Confucius, *The Analects*, trans. Edward Slingerland (Oxford: Oxford University Press, 2007).

9 Tu Weiming, *Confucian Thought: Selfhood as Creative Transformation* (Albany, NY: State University of New York Press, 1979).

10 Zhu Xi, *Reflections on Things at Hand: The Neo-Confucian Anthology*, trans. Wing-tsit Chan (New York: Columbia University Press, 1990).

11 Roger T. Ames and Henry Rosemont, Jr., *The Analects of Confucius: A Philosophical Translation* (New York: Ballantine Books, 1998); Heup Young Kim, *Christ and the Tao* (Hong Kong: Christian Conference of Asia, 2003).

transparent, and accountable to the communities they serve (Prov. 12:22).

Theodao also incorporates Daoian principles, which further enrich its theological and ethical framework:

— Dao (The Way): In Daoism, *Dao* represents the fundamental way or path of the universe. The Christian equivalent is the Logos, as seen in John 1:1, where Jesus is described as the Word. Theodao applies this concept to AI ethics, suggesting that AI development should align with the natural order and divine will (Jn. 14:6).
— Wuwei (Non-intentional action): *Wuwei* emphasizes humility, non-aggressive action, and surrender to the flow of nature or divine will. In Christian terms, this can be seen as trust in God's plan. For AI development, it advocates for a cautious, mindful approach to innovation, where developers seek to align their actions with ethical principles and a greater purpose (Prov. 3:5-6).
— Taiji (The Great Ultimate): *Taiji* symbolizes harmony and balance in the universe, reflecting the Christian understanding of the Trinity's harmony. This principle suggests that AI systems should promote balance and harmony in society and in humanity's relationship with the natural world (Col. 1:17).

Theodao emphasizes *balance, harmony,* and *ecological consciousness*—values deeply rooted in both Daoism and Confucianism, and aligned with Christian theology. These principles demand that AI development promote sustainability and minimize environmental harm, reflecting humanity's responsibility as stewards of creation

(Gen. 1:26-28). Moreover, Theodao highlights the concept of rela-tional personhood, advocating for AI design that fosters human rela-tionships, strengthens community bonds, and promotes holistic well-being—spiritually, physically, and mentally (1 Cor. 12:12-27; 1 Thess. 5:23).

## *Technodao: Extending Theodao to the Realm of Tech- nology*

Technodao applies the core principles of Theodao to the ethical challenges posed by modern technological developments, partic-ularly in the realm of AI. As technological advancements outpace ethical considerations, Technodao seeks to bridge this gap, provid-ing a culturally grounded and relational perspective on AI ethics.[12] Technodao offers a framework that addresses not only the efficiency of AI systems but also their moral and ecological responsibilities.

Key Technodaoian principles include:

— Harmonious Integration: Technodao advocates for AI development that complements human life and society without disrupting societal val-ues or human dignity. This principle aligns with the Christian call to love and serve others (Mk. 12:31) and the Daoian emphasis on harmony. It supports human-centered AI that prioritizes human well-being, relational dynamics, and flourishing, reflecting broader global concerns about the ethical use of AI.[13]

---

12 Heup Young Kim, "Advancing Humanity."
13 Floridi and Cowls, "A Unified Framework."

— Ethical AI Development: Technodao emphasizes the importance of developing AI systems that respect human rights, promote justice, and meet the highest ethical standards. This includes addressing issues like algorithmic bias, ensuring transparency in AI decision-making, and safeguarding privacy. These concerns reflect the increasing global focus on fairness and transparency in AI ethics.[14]

— Sustainable Progress: A core Technodaoian principle is the integration of environmental sustainability into AI development. The principle of stewardship, rooted in Christian theology (Gen. 1:26-28), calls for responsible management of God's creation. In Technodao, this translates into designing AI systems that minimize their carbon footprints and contribute to a more sustainable technological ecosystem.

— Virtue Cultivation in Technology: Technodao stresses the cultivation of virtues, such as benevolence, righteousness, and trustworthiness, within AI systems and the individuals who design them. This virtue-centered approach reflects the Christian emphasis on moral character (Gal. 5:22-23) and the Confucian goal of cultivating virtues to promote social harmony. In AI, this means ensuring that systems are built to promote ethical behavior and the common good.

Technodao provides a culturally inclusive path to more ethical, responsible AI development by integrating East Asian and Western ethical traditions. It promotes the development of AI systems that are not only effective and efficient but also aligned with ethical principles, contributing to human flourishing, societal harmony, and ecological sustainability.

---

14 Jobin, Ienca, and Vayena, "The Global Landscape."

## 2. Theodaoian and Technodaoian Critique of Key Themes in the "Encountering AI" Document

This section critically examines the Encountering AI document through a combined Theodaoian and Technodaoian lens, addressing key themes such as personhood, consciousness, ethical challenges, and AI's broader societal impact. By integrating theological insights and technological applications, this critique offers a holistic, culturally sensitive approach to AI ethics.

### *AI and the Human Person*

### Relational Personhood

The Theodaoian understanding of personhood emphasizes relationality and interconnectedness, focusing on human relationships with others, the natural world, and the divine. In contrast to the individualistic view often present in Western AI ethics, Theodao advocates for a community-oriented approach where personhood is shaped by social bonds and ecological responsibilities. This challenges the *Encountering AI* document's emphasis on individual autonomy and dignity without considering how AI technologies affect human relationships and communities.

In the *Encountering AI* document, the exploration of personhood acknowledges relationality through Trinitarian theology, suggesting that the human person flourishes in relationships with God and others (p. 70). However, this relational view is primarily theological and lacks a broader application to social structures or ecological interdependencies, which are central to the Theodaoian critique. The document's limited discussion of personhood neglects the wider relational dimensions that include human interconnectedness with the environment—critical in shaping AI systems designed to foster communal well-being.

From a Technodao perspective, AI systems should be designed to enhance, rather than disrupt, social cohesion. Practical applications of Technodaoian principles might involve AI technologies that prioritize social and emotional well-being, ensuring that technology builds, rather than erodes, social bonds. These suggestions go beyond the personhood discussion in *Encountering AI*, which tends to isolate AI ethics within the context of individual dignity, rather than relationally-oriented, community-based ethics (p. 45).

Critique of the Encountering AI Document:

— Individualistic Focus: While the document touches on relational aspects of personhood, it does so mainly within a theological context without addressing broader social and ecological implications of relationality in AI systems (p. 70).

Suggestions for Improvement:

— Expand the discussion on relational personhood to include not only human-to-God relationships but also human-to-human and human-to-environment relationships.
— Consider how AI technologies can be designed to foster social cohesion and communal well-being rather than focusing solely on in-

dividual autonomy.

## *Consciousness and Relationality*

### Relational Consciousness

The Theodaoian perspective views consciousness as inherently relational, emerging from relationships with others and the environment. This contrasts with Western views that often emphasize individual cognitive processes. According to Theodao, true consciousness requires not just cognitive capabilities, but also the capacity to engage in meaningful relationships, experience empathy, and connect with the world.

The *Encountering AI* document discusses consciousness, particularly in its relational and phenomenological dimensions. It asserts that AI systems, while capable of sophisticated behavior, lack the first-person experiential dimension that is intrinsic to human relationality and consciousness (p. 69). This point aligns with the Theodaoian view that AI cannot replicate full relational consciousness. However, the document does not explore the possibility that AI, despite its lack of consciousness, might still play a role in fostering relationships and enhancing social interactions. The Technodao perspective emphasizes the potential for AI systems to support human relationships even if they cannot themselves engage in relational consciousness, suggesting a more practical application that *Encountering AI* omits.

Critique of the *Encountering AI* Document:

— Neglect of Relationality in AI: The document focuses on the limitations of AI in replicating human consciousness, but it does not fully explore how AI might enhance human relationality even without possessing consciousness itself (p. 69).

Suggestions for Improvement:

— Consider the ways in which AI, despite lacking consciousness, could be designed to support human relationality, such as through enhancing empathy, collaboration, and community-building technologies.

*Ethical Challenges and Ecological Impact*

**Virtue Ethics and Ecological Harmony**

The Theodaoian ethical framework is rooted in virtue ethics, emphasizing the cultivation of moral character and relational virtues such as benevolence, righteousness, and trustworthiness.[15] This contrasts with the ethical framework in *Encountering AI*, which largely revolves around rights-based approaches and external regulation. While the document briefly touches on ethical considerations related to AI development, it tends to emphasize external controls like transparency, accountability, and fairness (p. 26). It does not

---

15 Kim, *Wang Yang-ming and Karl Barth;* Kalton, *To Become a Sage.*

fully integrate virtue ethics, which focus on internal moral development, particularly in AI developers and users, as a means to ensure
ethical AI systems.

From a Technodao perspective, AI systems should reflect virtues
such as benevolence and ecological harmony. The *Encountering AI*
document acknowledges the need for environmental responsibility
but offers limited concrete guidelines for embedding sustainability
and ecological balance into AI systems (p. 34). This critique suggests
that a more integrated ethical framework is needed—one that addresses not only the rights of individuals but also the broader responsibilities to the environment and future generations.

Critique of the Encountering AI Document:

— External vs. Internal Ethical Focus: The document emphasizes external
   regulatory measures but does not sufficiently address internal moral
   cultivation, which is central to a virtue-ethics approach (p. 26).
— Limited Ecological Focus: While environmental concerns are acknowledged, there is no thorough framework for sustainable AI development that aligns with Theodaoian principles of ecological harmony
   (p. 34).

Suggestions for Improvement:

— Integrate virtue ethics more fully into the framework, emphasizing
   the cultivation of moral virtues among AI developers and users.
— Provide specific guidelines for the sustainable development of AI
   systems, ensuring that they promote ecological balance and environ-

mental responsibility.

## *AI's Social and Spiritual Impact*

### Community-Centered AI

Both Theodao and Technodao stress the importance of designing AI systems that respect and support social structures. The *Encountering AI* document focuses primarily on individual dignity and rights but lacks a robust discussion of how AI technologies could enhance social cohesion and communal well-being. AI should not only be assessed by its impact on individuals but also by its influence on communities and social structures (p. 161).

From a spiritual perspective, Theodao emphasizes that AI should align with deeper ethical values that support human flourishing in all dimensions—intellectual, moral, and spiritual. The *Encountering AI* document does not fully address how AI technologies might interact with or influence spiritual practices and communities, which are vital considerations from a Theodaoian standpoint (p. 106).

Critique of the Encountering AI Document:

— Lack of Focus on Social Impact: The document does not explore how AI can contribute to or detract from social structures and community well-being (p. 161).

— Inadequate Consideration of Spiritual Life: There is limited discussion of AI's potential impact on spiritual practices and religious communities (p. 106).

Suggestions for Improvement:

— Include a discussion on how AI can be designed to foster social cohesion and support community well-being, in line with Technodaoian principles.
— Expand the ethical framework to consider AI's impact on spiritual practices and religious life, ensuring that AI technologies respect and enhance human spirituality.

# 3. Addressing Challenges and Counterarguments

In this section, potential challenges and counterarguments to integrating Theodaoian and Technodaoian principles into AI ethics are addressed. By engaging with possible objections, this paper aims to refine and strengthen the practical application of these cross-cultural perspectives in AI ethics.

## Challenge: Overemphasis on Relationality and Virtue Ethics

Counterargument: A common critique of Theodaoian and Technodaoian ethics is that these frameworks overemphasize relationality and virtue ethics, which may not be fully compatible with existing legal, regulatory, and rights-based frameworks in AI ethics. Critics might argue that virtue ethics, with its focus on internal moral cultivation, is difficult to apply in global, secular, and pluralistic contexts. Furthermore, a strong emphasis on relational personhood and ecological harmony may be seen as culturally specific and potentially incompatible with the technological priorities of Western AI development.

Response: While Theodaoian and Technodaoian ethics do indeed emphasize relationality and virtue ethics, these frameworks do not reject the importance of rights-based and regulatory approaches. Instead, they complement existing ethical frameworks by filling gaps in areas such as moral cultivation, community well-being, and ecological responsibility. In fact, combining virtue ethics with rule-based systems can strengthen the ethical foundations of AI development.

Practical Implementation:

— Hybrid Ethical Guidelines: AI design principles could require developers to undergo ethics training that emphasizes moral cultivation and community impact assessments alongside technical competence.
— Collaborative Frameworks: Collaborative frameworks between Eastern and Western ethical models can be established to ensure that AI development respects both relational and rights-based ethics. For instance, AI technologies could be assessed not only by how they protect individual rights but also by how they contribute to social cohesion and environmental sustainability.

*Challenge: Practicality of Ecological Concerns in AI Development*

Counterargument: Critics might argue that the Technodaoian focus on ecological harmony could be seen as idealistic and difficult to implement in practical AI development, particularly in a profit-driven technological landscape. Many AI technologies are developed with efficiency, productivity, and innovation in mind, and incorporating environmental sustainability might be seen as a secondary or even incompatible priority.

Response: While ecological harmony may seem challenging to implement, it is becoming increasingly clear that the long-term viability of technology depends on its sustainability. Environmental considerations should not be viewed as burdensome, but rather as essential to the responsible development of AI. In fact, environmentally responsible AI can offer a competitive advantage in a world increasingly focused on sustainability and climate change mitigation.

Practical Steps:

— Green AI Initiatives: AI developers should prioritize energy-efficient algorithms and data processing techniques. Companies can optimize AI models to minimize energy consumption and reduce the environmental footprint of data centers.
— Sustainable AI Certifications: Certifications similar to those used in green building or sustainable agriculture could reward companies that develop eco-friendly technologies. Governments and industries can collaborate to create policies that incentivize the development of AI systems that adhere to ecological standards.

## Challenge: AI's Role in Enhancing Human Relationality

Counterargument: Some may argue that AI, lacking consciousness and relational subjectivity, cannot truly enhance human relationality.

Critics might suggest that AI systems are merely tools, and expecting them to foster social cohesion or improve relational well-being is unrealistic and outside the scope of what AI can achieve.

Response: While AI indeed lacks consciousness, it can still play a significant role in mediating and enhancing human relationships. Theodaoian and Technodaoian ethics do not claim that AI can replace genuine human relationality. Rather, AI can be designed to support human relationships by facilitating collaboration, communication, and empathy.

Practical Applications:

— AI as a Social Facilitator: AI-powered tools such as communication platforms, virtual reality systems, or social robots can strengthen human interactions, particularly in elderly care, education, and mental health support. For example, AI companions can help reduce social isolation, fostering a sense of connection even if the AI itself is not conscious.

— AI in Collaborative Workspaces: AI can facilitate teamwork by analyzing communication patterns and suggesting improvements to group dynamics. These tools are particularly useful in virtual work environments where human relational elements are often diminished.

## Challenge: Cultural Relevance and Global Applicability

Counterargument: Some may argue that Theodaoian and Technodaoian principles, while valuable, are culturally specific and may not be universally applicable—especially in Western contexts where individual autonomy, rights-based approaches, and regulatory mechanisms dominate ethical discussions. Critics might claim that imposing these Eastern perspectives on global AI development could be seen as paternalistic or inappropriate for cultures that prioritize different values.

Response: While Theodaoian and Technodaoian ethics are rooted in East Asian wisdom, they offer universal insights that can enrich global AI ethics discussions. However, it is important to acknowledge that integrating these frameworks into Western, rights-based ethical models is not without significant challenges. Relational personhood and virtue ethics can complement—but not seamlessly replace—individualistic frameworks in Western AI ethics. This calls for a pluralistic dialogue between cultures, respecting the values of each tradition.

Practical Applications:

— Cultural Adaptation: Efforts to integrate Theodaoian and Technodaoian ethics into global AI governance should be culturally adaptive, recognizing that different regions may prioritize different ethical principles. Relational personhood and virtue ethics might be adapted in ways that harmonize with existing rights-based frameworks while fostering communal values.

— Cross-Cultural Ethical Forums: Multilateral forums for AI ethics can bring together representatives from diverse ethical traditions to develop guidelines that reflect both individual rights and relational responsibilities. This dialogue can foster more relevant and effective frameworks across different cultural contexts.

*Challenge: Balancing Regulation with Innovation*

Counterargument: Concerns may arise that the ethical frameworks proposed by Theodao and Technodao, particularly those centered on moral cultivation and relational personhood, could stifle innovation. AI developers might argue that too many ethical restrictions could slow down technological advancements and make it harder for companies to compete in a fast-paced global market.

Response: Ethical considerations do not have to come at the expense of innovation. In fact, the best innovations often emerge from constraints that challenge developers to think more creatively and responsibly. By embedding Theodaoian and Technodaoian principles into the design process, developers can create technologies that are both cutting-edge and socially responsible.

Practical Strategies:

— Ethical by Design Frameworks: Ethical principles, such as those from Theodao, should be integrated into the early stages of AI development. Rather than treating ethics as an afterthought, these frameworks ensure that ethical considerations are embedded into AI technologies from the outset.

— Collaborative Innovation Ecosystems: Governments, corporations, and ethical experts can work together to create an environment that promotes both technological advancement and ethical responsibility. Incentives like grants, awards, and public recognition can encourage companies to innovate ethically.

# 4. Case Studies and Real-World Applications

In this section, we explore how Theodaoian and Technodaoian principles can be applied to real-world AI systems, offering practical examples from sectors such as healthcare, environmental conservation, and social welfare. These case studies demonstrate how cross-cultural ethical frameworks can influence AI development and usage in ways that promote both technological advancement and the common good.

*Case Study: Healthcare AI Supporting Elderly Care*

## Context

The integration of AI technologies into elderly care has gained traction as populations in many countries age rapidly. AI-powered systems—such as virtual companions, healthcare monitoring tools, and assistive robots—offer potential solutions to address the growing needs of older adults while reducing the strain on healthcare systems. However, the use of AI in this context raises ethical concerns around autonomy, dignity, and relational well-being.

## Application of Theodaoian and Technodaoian Principles

From a Theodaoian perspective, elderly care must prioritize relational personhood, ensuring that AI systems do not replace human relationships but rather enhance the ability of caregivers to foster meaningful interactions with elderly patients. In the context of

Technodao, AI tools should be designed to support social engagement and emotional well-being, recognizing that care is not solely about medical interventions but also about nurturing relational bonds.

Real-World Example: AI-powered social robots like *ElliQ* or *PARO* used in elderly care provide companionship to older adults while helping them stay socially and emotionally engaged.[16] These robots do not attempt to replace human caregivers but offer supplementary support to enhance human interactions. ElliQ is designed to foster social engagement and assist in daily activities, while PARO is a therapeutic robot designed to comfort patients through tactile interaction, particularly in dementia care settings.

Practical Takeaways:

— Relational Support Tools: AI systems in elderly care should be designed to facilitate human-to-human interaction rather than focusing solely on automation. For example, AI tools can remind caregivers to check in with patients more frequently, emphasizing human presence and attention.
— Ethics Training for Developers: AI developers in healthcare should be trained to incorporate virtue ethics into the design process, ensuring

16 Sharmishta Shukla, "Meet ElliQ: The Robot Companion for the Elderly," *TechRadar*, February 2021, https://www.techradar.com/news/meet-elliq-the-robot-companion -for-the-elderly; Kazuyoshi Wada and Takanori Shibata, "Living with Seal Robots Its Sociopsychological and Physiological Influences on the Elderly at a Care House," *IEEE Transactions on Robotics* 23, no. 5 (2007): 972–980, https://doi.org/10.1109/TRO .2007.906261.

that systems promote dignity and foster human connections. This aligns with the Technodaoian principle of relational harmony.

## Case Study: Environmental Monitoring and AI for Ecological Balance

### Context

AI technologies are increasingly being used to monitor and address environmental concerns, from wildlife conservation to climate change mitigation. AI systems can help track deforestation, predict weather patterns, and optimize energy usage. However, the environmental impact of AI itself—due to energy-intensive data centers and resource consumption—poses a paradox in sustainability.

### Application of Theodaoian and Technodaoian Principles

Technodaoian ethics emphasize ecological harmony and the responsibility to use technology in a way that aligns with nature. AI systems in environmental applications must, therefore, not only contribute to environmental conservation but also be developed in a way that minimizes their ecological footprint. Theodaoian wisdom calls for AI technologies that foster a sense of interconnectedness with the natural world, reinforcing the idea that humanity and the environment are interdependent.

Real-World Example: AI-based environmental monitoring systems like *Microsoft's AI for Earth* initiative are helping to address biodiversity loss and climate change by analyzing large datasets to identify areas at risk and optimize conservation efforts.[17] This initiative leverages AI to improve our understanding of ecosystems and supports sustainable management of natural resources through innovative technologies such as satellite imagery analysis and species recognition algorithms.

Practical Takeaways:

— **Green AI Practices**: AI developers should adopt green computing techniques, such as energy-efficient algorithms and hardware that minimizes the carbon footprint of AI systems. This aligns with Technodaoian principles of ecological sustainability.
— **Partnerships with Environmental Organizations**: Companies developing AI for environmental monitoring should collaborate with conservation groups to ensure that their systems address real-world ecological needs and promote sustainable practices.

*Case Study: AI in Education and Social Welfare*

**Context**

AI is increasingly utilized in education to personalize learning experiences, assess student progress, and provide resources for underprivileged communities. While these technologies can improve

---

17 Microsoft, "AI for Earth: Empowering People and Organizations to Solve Global Environmental Challenges," Microsoft, 2020, https://www.microsoft.com/en-us/ai /ai-for-earth.

access to education, concerns arise about the potential loss of human connection in teaching, as well as issues related to equity and fairness in AI algorithms that affect marginalized groups.

## Application of Theodaoian and Technodaoian Principles

From a Theodaoian perspective, education is not just about knowledge acquisition but also about the cultivation of moral virtues and relational understanding. AI systems should, therefore, enhance, rather than diminish, the relational aspects of education, ensuring that students remain connected to teachers and peers. The Technodaoian approach emphasizes fairness and inclusivity, urging that AI systems in education be designed to avoid reinforcing biases that disadvantage marginalized communities.

Practical Takeaways:

— **Balanced AI Integration:** AI in education should be used as a tool to supplement, not replace, the relational dynamic between students and teachers. Systems that encourage collaboration and peer-to-peer learning can reinforce the importance of social engagement.

— **Equitable Design Principles:** AI developers should ensure that educational algorithms are designed to mitigate bias and promote access to quality education for all students, regardless of socioeconomic background. This aligns with Technodao's focus on justice and fairness.

*Case Study: AI in Corporate and Workplace Environments*

## Context

In the corporate world, AI technologies are transforming work-places by automating repetitive tasks, enhancing decision-making, and optimizing productivity. However, the widespread adoption of AI in corporate settings also raises concerns about job displace-ment, worker alienation, and ethical oversight in decision-making algorithms.

## Application of Theodaoian and Technodaoian Principles

Theodaoian ethics stress the importance of maintaining human dignity and relational integrity in the workplace. AI should not be seen as a means to replace human workers but rather as a tool that enhances human creativity, collaboration, and well-being. From a Technodao perspective, corporate AI systems should be designed to promote fairness, inclusivity, and transparency, ensuring that all employees benefit from technological advancements.

**Real-World Example:** AI-driven human resources (HR) tools like *HireVue* or *Workday* use algorithms to assess job applicants and man-age employee performance.[18] While these systems can streamline

---

18 Jeffrey Dastin, "Facial Recognition Technology Moves into HR," *Reuters*, November 2018, https://www.reuters.com/article/us-hirevue-facial-recognition -idUSKCN1NK0J1; Sunil Chander, "The Risks of AI-Driven HR Tools: Bias and Transparency," *Harvard Business Review*, December 2020, https://hbr.org/2020/12 /the-risks-of-ai-driven-hr-tools-bias-and-transparency.

human resources processes, they also raise concerns about transparency, bias, and worker dignity. HireVue uses video analysis and AI to assess candidates' facial expressions, tone of voice, and word choice, while Workday employs machine learning to evaluate employee performance and optimize workforce management.

Practical Takeaways:

— Human-Centered AI Tools: Companies should prioritize AI systems that enhance worker well-being and creativity, rather than purely focusing on efficiency and cost reduction. This could involve AI tools that automate mundane tasks while preserving roles that require human ingenuity and collaboration.
— Ethical AI Audits: To ensure fairness and transparency in AI-driven decision-making, corporations should regularly conduct ethical audits of their AI systems. These audits would assess whether AI systems align with principles of justice, fairness, and transparency, as emphasized in Technodaoian ethics.

*Case Study: AI for Public Health and Global Good*

Context

AI technologies are being used to improve public health outcomes, particularly in the areas of disease prevention, diagnostics, and global health monitoring. However, concerns remain regarding data privacy, the ethical use of personal health information, and ensuring equitable access to AI-driven healthcare technologies, especially in underserved communities.

## Application of Theodaoian and Technodaoian Principles

Theodaoian principles emphasize the interconnectedness of human health, well-being, and ethical care practices. Public health AI should prioritize relational aspects of healthcare, focusing on holistic patient care and ethical data use. Technodaoian principles of justice and inclusivity highlight the importance of making AI-driven healthcare accessible to marginalized communities, ensuring that technological advancements do not exacerbate healthcare disparities.

**Real-World Example:** AI-based diagnostic tools like *IBM Watson for Health* or *Google's DeepMind* are being used to diagnose diseases such as cancer and retinal conditions (Ross & Swetlitz, 2017; Vincent, 2018). While these technologies have the potential to improve health outcomes, there is a risk that they could lead to over-reliance on machine diagnostics at the expense of human doctors' relational and ethical judgment. IBM Watson for Health uses AI to analyze medical data and suggest treatment options, while DeepMind has developed AI systems capable of detecting eye diseases from retinal scans.

Practical Takeaways:

— **Human-AI Collaboration in Healthcare:** AI should complement, not replace, human doctors in making ethical decisions that consider patients' emotional and relational needs. This can include AI systems that provide doctors with decision support while still allowing them to exercise clinical judgment.

— **Equitable Access to AI Healthcare**: Public health institutions should ensure that AI-driven healthcare technologies are accessible to underserved populations. This could involve partnerships with non-profit organizations and governments to subsidize AI tools in low-income communities, ensuring fairness and equity in health outcomes.

# Conclusion: Integrating Theodaoian and Technodaoian Ethics in AI Development

In this paper, we have argued for the integration of Theodaoian and Technodaoian principles into the ethical frameworks guiding AI development. As AI technologies continue to influence various aspects of society—from healthcare and education to environmental conservation and corporate governance—there is a growing need for a more comprehensive and cross-cultural approach to AI ethics. By drawing from East Asian wisdom, particularly the relational, virtue-based ethics of Confucianism and Daoism, and integrating it with Christian theological insights, Theodao and Technodao provide a framework that complements existing Western approaches while addressing their limitations.

## The Key Contributions of Theodaoian Ethics

One of the primary contributions of Theodaoian ethics to AI development is its emphasis on *relational personhood*. In contrast to the individualistic focus often found in Western ethical frameworks, Theodaoian ethics highlights the interconnectedness of human beings, their communities, and the environment. Theodao views personhood as inherently relational, suggesting that AI systems should be developed not only to respect individual rights but also to foster social cohesion, community well-being, and ecological harmony. This relational perspective challenges the prevailing focus on autonomy and individual rights in AI ethics, urging us to think more deeply about how AI can strengthen, rather than disrupt, our relationships.

In addition, Theodaoian ethics stresses the importance of *virtue cultivation* as a foundation for ethical behavior, both in humans and in AI systems. This virtue-based approach complements rule-based or outcome-focused ethics by emphasizing moral character and the development of virtuous practices over time. By integrating virtues such as benevolence, righteousness, and wisdom into AI design, Theodaoian ethics offer a way to ensure that AI systems promote not only fairness and justice but also a deeper moral responsibility toward others and the world.

### *Technodao and the Practical Application of Ethical Principles*

Building on the theological foundation of Theodao, Technodao extends these principles into the realm of technology, offering a concrete framework for the ethical design, development, and deployment of AI systems. Technodao advocates for AI systems that are transparent, inclusive, and environmentally sustainable, aligning technological progress with relational, moral, and ecological values.

Through the practical case studies in healthcare, environmental monitoring, education, and corporate settings, we have shown how Theodaoian and Technodaoian principles can be applied to real-world AI systems. For example:

— In healthcare, AI systems like social robots and diagnostic tools can support patient care by fostering relational well-being and human dignity, ensuring that AI enhances rather than replaces human relationships.

— In environmental conservation, AI technologies can be used to monitor ecosystems and address climate change while adhering to principles of ecological harmony and sustainability.

— In education, AI can personalize learning experiences while maintaining the importance of human interaction and collaboration, balancing technological innovation with relational personhood.

— In corporate environments, AI systems can be designed to improve worker well-being and social justice, promoting inclusivity and fairness in workplace settings.

These applications demonstrate that Theodao and Technodao are not abstract theological concepts but practical ethical tools that can help guide AI development in ways that prioritize human flourishing and ecological balance.

## Addressing Challenges and Counterarguments

While the integration of Theodaoian and Technodaoian ethics

into AI development offers substantial benefits, it is not without challenges. Critics may argue that these frameworks overemphasize relationality and virtue ethics, making them difficult to apply in secular, rights-based contexts. Moreover, the practicality of implementing ecological concerns in AI development may be questioned, especially in profit-driven industries. Additionally, some may view these frameworks as culturally specific to East Asia and potentially incompatible with Western ethical traditions.

However, we have addressed these challenges by showing how Theodao and Technodao can complement, rather than replace, existing ethical frameworks. The ethical guidelines proposed in this paper allow for the integration of relational personhood, virtue cultivation, and ecological responsibility into AI design, while respecting global and pluralistic contexts. By fostering cross-cultural dialogue and adopting a pluralistic approach to AI ethics, these frameworks can enrich global conversations on AI governance and promote more inclusive, ethically responsible technologies.

### Toward a Pluralistic AI Future

The future of AI development requires an ethical framework that goes beyond national or cultural boundaries. The integration of Theodaoian and Technodaoian principles into global AI ethics offers an opportunity to create a pluralistic and inclusive ethical framework that reflects the diversity of human values and experiences. This paper has argued that cross-cultural perspectives are essential for addressing the complex challenges posed by AI, including the need for social cohesion, moral cultivation, and ecological sustainability.

By embracing a pluralistic approach that incorporates East Asian wisdom, Western ethics, and other cultural traditions, we can develop AI systems that are not only technologically advanced but also ethically grounded. The global nature of AI development demands that we draw on a wide range of ethical traditions to ensure that AI technologies serve the common good and contribute to a more just and sustainable world.

*Final Reflections: A Path Forward for Ethical AI*

In conclusion, this paper has demonstrated that Theodaoian and Technodaoian ethics provide a comprehensive and practical framework for addressing the ethical challenges posed by AI. By emphasizing relational personhood, virtue ethics, and ecological harmony, these frameworks offer valuable insights for AI development in various sectors. Moreover, by engaging with potential counterarguments and proposing practical solutions, this paper has shown that Theodao and Technodao can be integrated into existing AI governance models to promote socially responsible and ecologically sustainable technologies.

As we move toward a future where AI plays an increasingly significant role in society, it is essential that we adopt ethical frameworks that reflect the full spectrum of human values. The integration of Theodao and Technodao into AI ethics is a crucial step toward creating technologies that not only advance human knowledge but also promote the flourishing of individuals, communities, and the planet. By grounding AI development in relational and ecological ethics, we can ensure that AI technologies genuinely serve the common good, contribute to the well-being of future generations, and honor our shared values.

## PART III

# Theodao in a Global Polyphonic Age of Decolonization

# Theodao Through Confucian-Christian Dialogue: Addressing Theological Challenges in the Anthropocene

## Abstract

This chapter reflects upon the dialogues between Confucianism and Christianity that I have formulated, which have been instrumental in developing a theology of dao (theo-dao). It explores their significance for contemporary and future theological discourse. The paper summarizes two key dialogues: between Karl Barth and Wang Yang-ming, and John Calvin and Yi T'oegye. These discussions prompted a paradigm shift in theology towards a theo-dao perspective, moving beyond the longstanding dualism in Western theology between theo-logos and theo-praxis. The paper challenges the either-or perspective prevalent in Western theologies of religions and in early comparative theological approaches that regard indigenous religions like Confucianism as 'the other.' This viewpoint is deemed unsuitable for East Asian Christians, for whom Confucianism is an integral part of their religio-cultural heritage. Instead, it advocates for the legitimacy of dual religious belonging, embracing a both-and attitude. It argues that East Asian theology should transcend the descriptive-comparative and normative-constructive methods, adopting a themative approach to appropriately contextualize the Christian faith within the Confucian milieu. Lastly, the article posits that theodao, as developed through Confucian-Christian dialogue, offers significant insights into theology and religion in the ecological era of science and technology. This is particularly relevant in addressing the challenges posed by Artificial Intelligence and Transhumanism in the technological age of the Anthropocene.

# 1. Confucian-Christian Encounters

## Confucianism Meets Christianity

The late Wm. Theodore de Bary (1919-2017), a forerunner of East Asian Studies in the West, argued that Confucianism, more precisely Neo-Confucianism, is not only "the common background of the peoples of East Asia," but also "the most plausible rationale" and "the key" to understanding the attitude of "the inward-looking civilization of East Asia." Moreover, he observed that "the expansionist" Westerners in the eighteenth and nineteenth centuries, unfortunately, misunderstood this East Asian inward-looking attitude "as ingrown, self-contented, smug, and isolationist." At the same time, East Asians regarded this Western expansionism as "the very embodiment of uncontrolled aggressiveness—power on the loose, bound to no moral and spiritual center."[1]

As in his insightful observation, there is the sharp contrast reflecting two radically different views embedded in their ways of life between the West and the East;[2] namely, Christianity with its evangelical and missionary zeal versus Confucianism with its belief in the natural transmission of the Dao through the inner power of virtues. Comparing to this misplaced view of the modern West, the precursors of modernity such as Blaise Pascal (1623-1662) and G. W. Leibniz (1646-1716) intimately informed by the school of Matteo Ricci (1552-1610) would have much better comprehensions of Confucianism, at least with much keener awareness of its significance for their Christian faith. Leibniz said, "I am afraid that soon in our relation we are inferior to Chinese so that it will be almost necessary to receive their missionaries to teach us the usage and practice of the natural theology, while we dispatch ours them to teach the usage and the practice of the revealed theology."[3] As Julia Ching (1934-2001) argued, Confucianism itself is "a misnomer" of Western scholarship to designate a typical *East Asian* religio-cultural tradition accumulated with a long and complicated history of development.[4] Now, some scholars contend to substitute the term with "Ruism," according to its original romanization (儒), mainly

1 Wm. Theodore De Bary, *East Asian Civilizations: A Dialogue in Five Stages* (Cambridge: Harvard University Press, 1988), 44.

2 Generally, in religious discussion, the East means India and South East Asia, but they are still the West for us East Asians.

3 "*Novissima Sinica*" [1698-1699], quoted in David Chung, *Syncretism: The Religious Context of Christian Beginnings in Korea* (Albany, NY: State University of New York Press, 2001), 115-16.

4 Julia Ching, *Confucianism and Christianity: A Comparative Study* (Tokyo: Kodansha International, 1977), xv.

because Confucius is not a Christ-like figure.

Along with the rising interest in this East Asian tradition due to
the rapid economic growth of the Neo-Confucian world, notably
such as China, Japan, Korea, Taiwan, Hong Kong, and Singapore,
scholars have attempted to correct the modern misconception of
Confucianism in the West. Chinese scholars in the West, such as
Tu Wei-ming (sometimes called a Confucian theologian or evangel-
ist) and Julia Ching, have made visible contributions in the interpretation of Confucianism for theology in the English-speaking
world. Hans Küng also added Confucianism as "a third independent
religious river system" of sapiential character (i.e., Confucianism
and Daoism). He argued for a tripolar view of World Religions, instead of the predominant dipolar view that contains only two religious river systems; namely, prophetic religions of Middle Eastern
origin (Judaism, Christianity, and Islam) and mystical religions
(Hinduism, Buddhism, etc.) of Indian origin.[5]

North American theologians and scholars such as Robert C.
Neville, Lee Yearly, Mary Evelyn Tucker, Judith Berling, and John
Berthrong became deeply interested in Confucian-Christian dialogue and enthusiastically supported to organize international
Confucian-Christian dialogues; 1988 in Hong Kong, 1991 in Berkeley,
1994 in Boston, and 1998 in Hong Kong.[6] This interest in East Asian
studies brings out an interesting scholarly phenomenon, a significant

---

5 Hans Küng and Julia Ching, *Christianity and Chinese Religions* (New York: Doubleday,
1989), xi-xix.

6 Cf. John Berthrong, *All Under Heaven: Transforming Paradigms in Confucian-Christian
dialogue* (Albany: State University of New York Press, 1994).

shift in the Western (Christianity's) view of Confucianism. There even have appeared communities of Western scholars who, though initially came from a Christian background, became fascinated with Confucianism and went into a scholarly "pilgrimage" in East Asian culture (such as "Boston Confucianism"). After experiences of this pilgrimage in a new vista of East Asian religious traditions, their Western religious views have been seriously challenged and restructured. Furthermore, they began to ask theological questions, what this change means to their Christian faith.[7]

This discovery helped to develop a new genre of Christian theology, namely, *comparative theology*. Comparative theology primarily referred to a theological enterprise of Western scholars who attempt to incorporate new insights acquired from the experiences of new religious vistas. Comparative theologians at the early stage can be divided into two groups by the principal means of comparison, by philosophy (Yearly and Neville) and by text (Francis Clooney). The beginning of comparative theology was, without a doubt, significant development of interreligious dialogue and the theology of religions. Nevertheless, it was not only highly elitist and theoretical but also romantic and speculative. Most of the early comparative theologians in the West learned the other traditions through the literature studies, without sufficient first-hand experiences. Their interpretations of *the other* frequently neglected historical and cultural realities but were often construed with a romantic imagination, wishful thinking, and even manufacturing.[8]

---

7 Cf. Judith A. Berling, *A Pilgrim in Chinese Culture: Negotiating Religious Diversity* (Maryknoll, NY: Orbis Books, 1997), vii-ix.

## Dual Religious Belonging?

Above all, dual religious belonging (citizenship) was a most intricate problem of early comparative theologians with which native (in this case, East Asian) theologians could not comply despite its profound merits. Does this point to the limit where 'wider ecumenism' in Western Christianity can go? Most of the Western theologians, including not only theological inclusivist Hans Küng but also liberal pluralist John Hick, warned not to cross the Rubicon of dual religious citizenship: "one can only center one's religious life wholeheartedly and unambiguously upon one of them... but not more than one at once."9 In dialogue with Ching, classifying dual citizenship in three categories, cultural, ethical, and religious, Küng concluded, "as much as cultural and ethical dual citizenship is possible and ought to be made possible even anew, a religious dual citizenship in the deepest sense of faith should be excluded—by all the great religions." He cautioned, "*Christian inculturation, not dual religious citizenship*, must be the watchword!"10

For East Asian Christians, however, this is indeed an odd watchword. Although exceptionally sympathetic toward the East Asian religious situation, Küng as a most open-minded European theologian in the 20th century, could not transcend an epistemological dualism in the either-or mode of thinking inherited through

---

8 Cf. Lionel M. Jensen, *Manufacturing Confucianism: Chinese Traditions and Universal Civilization* (Durham, NC: Duke University Press, 1998).

9 John Hick, *An Interpretation of Religion: Human Responses to the Transcendent* (New Haven: Yale University Press, 1989), 373.

10 Küng and Ching, *Christianity and Chinese Religions*, 282.

Western theology. He said, "Therefore, even with every cultural and ethical possibility for integration, the truth of every religion extends to a depth that ultimately challenges every person to a yes or no, to an either-or."[11] However, the genius of the Nicene Creed of the Trinity (not *either* one *or* three, but *both* one *and* three) and the Chalcedonian Christology lie in the fact that Church Fathers enable Christian faith to overcome Greek dualism (*either* divinity *or* humanity) to declare Christological dual citizenship (*both* heavenly *and* earthly citizenships). Nevertheless, the Western Church has not fully grasped this wisdom of the Ancient Church, but, turning the clock back, maintained ecclesiastical and epistemological intolerance to *the other*, stuck to an Arian monotheism ("only one!") and a Roman confessional complex ("either-or") acquired by the experiences of martyrdom and persecutions during pre-Constantine periods.

For East Asian Christians, however, dual religious belonging is not so much an epistemological and speculative but a hermeneutical and existential issue. For us, Confucianism is a historical reality, ontologically given as our own (perhaps, by the grace of God's Creation as much as Western theologians admit their own Western traditions). We have no hermeneutical distance to put aside and objectify Confucianism as the status of the other religion.[12] As Tu Wei-ming stated, "East Asians may profess themselves to be Shintoists, Taoists, Buddhists, Muslims, or Christians, but by announcing their religious

---

11 Ibid, 281.

12 See Heup Young Kim, "Multiple Religious Belonging as Hospitality: a Korean Confucian-Christian Perspective," in *Many Yet One? Multiple Religious Belonging*, eds. Peniel J. R. Rufus Rajkumar and Joseph P. Dayan (World Council of Churches, 2016), 75-88.

affiliations seldom do they cease to be Confucians."[13]

As a Korean/East Asian theologian, at this juncture, it may also need to clarify another misnomer, "Confucianism a Chinese religion." Confucianism is not only a Chinese religion, just as Christianity or Buddhism is not only a Palestine or an Indian religion. Further, as Tu argued, it is not China but Korea that was "undoubtedly the most thoroughly Confucianized" country.[14] Likewise, Grayson observed, "[A]lthough Confucianism originated in China, it never had the over-all impact on Chinese society that Neo-Confucianism had on Korea over five hundred years of the last dynasty. In Japan, Confucianism was primarily a concern of the ruling elite and the associated schol-arly class."[15] Moreover, Grayson claimed, "It is only in Korea we find a society in which the predominant political, cultural, and social influ-ences were and are Confucians."[16] Furthermore, this misnomer could carry an undertone of the Sinocentric worldview—a suspi-cious rationale for Chinese imperialism--that is by no means in-nocent in the history of East Asia.

## East Asian (Constructive) Theology (of Religions)

As a Korean Christian theologian raised in a family that has main-tained fully recorded genealogy of its clan's thousand-year history

---

13 Tu Wei-ming, *Confucianism in a Historical Perspective* (Singapore: The Institute of East Asian Philosophies, 1989), 3.

14 Ibid, 35.

15 James H. Grayson, *Korea: the Religious History* (Oxford: Clarendon Press, 1989), 216.

16 James H. Grayson, "The Study of Korean Religions & Their Role in Inter-Religious Dialogue," *Inculturation* 3:4 (1988), 8.

in Confucianism (as one of the 29th generation), I confessed three decades ago:

> The more I study Christian theology, the more I become convinced how deeply Confucianism is embedded in my soul and body, my spirituality. Subtly but powerfully, Confucianism still works inside me, as my native religious language. If theology involves the response of one's total being to God, it also entails a critical wrestling with this embedded Confucian tradition. Doing East Asian theology necessarily involves the study of Confucianism as a theological task.[17]

In this Confucian-Christian encounter, there is no clear-cut distinction for "the other" religion or faith that Western theologians seem to have presupposed based on their European experiences, it is a "both-and" situation rather than an "either-or." Thus East Asian theology of religion (*theologia religionum* [TR]), if you say so, is compelled to agree to dual religious citizenship (or a hyphenated identity, *Confucian-Christian* or *Christian-Confucian*). Accordingly, in this context, "themative" (*intra*-religious and constructive) approach is a more proper attitude that may need to combine both the "descriptive" (comparative and inter-religious) and the "prescriptive" (inter-religious and normative) inquiries. A thematic approach refers to a hermeneutical enterprise to *thematize* a wholistic meaning of Christian faith for a life in a culture and society predominantly shaped by Confucianism. However, it does not denote a false syncre-

---

17 Heup Young Kim, *Wang Yang-ming and Karl Barth: A Confucian-Christian Dialogue* (Lanham and London: University Press of America, 1996), 1.

tism, but an authentic theological engagement in and through one's own religious horizons that give the one better, more relevant, and more proper understandings of Christian faith in one's own context ("owning up to one's own metaphors").[18]

I proposed that East Asian TR consists of two hermeneutical stages; "a descriptive-comparative" and "a normative-constructive."[19] The first stage correlates with the descriptive approach of TR, while the second stage does with the prescriptive approach. For the first descriptive-comparative stage, I suggested a coined term, *confuciology*, a protective and heuristic device to preserve Confucian intra-textualities (narratives), to develop a thickly descriptive interreligious dialogue.[20] For the second normative-constructive stage, the focus shifts to the East Asian Christian Communities that necessitate a normative (or prescriptive) articulation of Christian faith in their given Confucian context.

The following sections illustrate an example of thematizing this East Asian TR. First, it summarizes two Confucian-Christian dialogues I developed, between Wang Yang-ming (a seminal Neo-Confucian thinker in China) and Karl Barth (a most important Christian theologian in the 20th century) and between Yi T'oe-gye (a most crucial Confucian scholar in Korea) and John Calvin (a most influential

---

18 See Heup Young Kim, "Owning Up to One's Own Metaphors: A Christian Journey in the Neo-Confucian Wilderness," *Third Millennium* 4:1 (2001): 31-40.

19 See Kim, *Wang Yang-ming and Karl Barth*, 139-41.

20 Confuciology is coined to designate a term in Confucianism, functionally equivalent [homological]to theology in Christianity: "Analogously as theology refers to a coherent reflection of the Christian faith in a given context, confuciology does that for the Confucian faith" (ibid, 135).

Protestant theologian). Then, it shows an example of East Asian TR, which led to a constructive theology of dao (tao), namely, theo-dao (theo-tao).

## 2. Confucian-Christian Dialogue: Thick Resemblances in Radical Differences

*Wang Yang-ming (1472-1529) Meets Karl Barth (1886- 1968): Self-cultivation and Sanctification*

In the book *Wang Yang-ming and Karl Barth: a Confucian- Christian Dialogue*, I developed the first dialogue, based on the paradigmatic teachings of two seminal thinkers of two traditions There I argued that, if properly understood, the Confucian teaching of self-cultivation and the Christian doctrine of sanctification are *"thickly resemblant views of a common issue, i.e., how to be fully human."*[21] In a nutshell, self-cultivation (a primary tenet of Confucianism) is to realize the true self (良知 liang-chih; liáng zhī) latent in original human nature, while sanctification (a central doctrine of Christianity) is to realize one's true elected nature.

Basically, Confucianism and Christianity are two radically different religious paradigms, emerged from different historical-cultural-social-linguistic backgrounds; generally, human-centered versus God-centered, subjective versus objective, inner versus outer, and so on. These differences appear in the dialogue between

---

21 Kim, *Wang Yang-ming and Karl Barth*, 139.

Wang and Barth. While Barth's theology emphasizes historicality, Wang's confuciology stresses immanence. The Confucian source is the sapiential tradition transmitted through human mind-and-heart (心 *hsin*; *xīn*), whereas the Christian source is the prophetic tradition revealed through the Word of God. The root-paradigms of humanity epitomize their differences. The innate knowledge of the good (*liáng zhī*) is immanent-transcendence, while the *humanitas Christi* (the humanity of Christ) is characterized as *historico-transcendence*. The Confucian vision as an inclusive humanism presents an *anthropocosmic* vision (the unity of humanity and cosmos), while the Christian vision (the salvific Christ event) does a *theo-historical* vision (salvation history). Hence, Confucianism (self-cultivation) is more ontological and cosmic, while Christianity (sanctification) is more existential and historical.

This distinction is saliently revealed in the analysis of evil. Confuciology focuses on reaffirming the primordial unity and ontological goodness, whereas theology analyzes the sinful structure of the existential human condition. This nuance is also apparent in anthropology. Whereas confuciology grasps (仁 *jen*; *rén*) as cosmic togetherness, theology articulates *imago Dei* (the image of God) as historical togetherness. These differences reflect divergent priorities in the movement of radical humanization: self-cultivation first looks at the human inner self and makes an outward move (致良知 *chih liang-chih*; *zhì liáng zhī*), whereas sanctification begins with the historical event and turns to subjectivity (the direction of the Holy Spirit). The Confucian ideal of human being is a profound person, a sincere digger (誠; *ch'eng chéng*), if the Christian model is the disturbed sinner, an obedient hearer/doer to the commandments of

God (*agape*). In the final analysis, these differences can be summarized in two fundamental visions; namely, *the Confucian anthropocosmic vision* versus *the Christian theohistorical vision*.

Despite these fundamental differences, nevertheless, the Confucian-Christian dialogue between Wang and Barth demonstrates thick resemblances in dealing with the common issue of how to be fully human, *radical humanization* (self-cultivation and sanctification). Both of them believe that radical humanity (*liáng zhī* and *humanitas Christi*) is the ultimate ontological reality (the most concrete-universal of true humanity). Both agree that evil arises existentially by dysfunction and denial of this ontological reality. Radical humanity as ontological reality not only illuminates but also has an intrinsic power to remove evil. Radical humanization is a transcendent process of realizing this ontological reality beyond the structure of ambiguous human existential situations; in their terms, identification of subjectivity and ontological reality in mind-and-heart (Wang) and historical self-realization of the ontological connection with Jesus Christ (Barth). In this process, radical humanity endows the concrete spiritual direction through spiritual empowerment.

Further, Wang and Barth present a similar material definition of humanity. Being human means being-in-togetherness, namely, a creative co-humanity (*rén*) according to Confucianism, whereas a joyful *Mitmenschlichkeit* (*imago Dei*), according to Karl Barth. For both of theme, the modern notion of selfhood as an individual ego is incorrect and dangerous. Instead, it is a communal center of the relationship, and thus humanization entails self-transformation as a communal act. The meaning of humanity should be realized through the concrete-universal way of the ever-expanding circles of human relatedness and in the ethico-religious unity of ontological knowledge (being) and ethical action (becoming). In this manner, Wang's confuciology of self-cultivation and Barth's theology of sanctification present remarkably similar concrete-universal ways of radical humanization.

Furthermore, I argued, there are some very valuable implications of this dialogue. It warrants three corresponding modes of thinking, originally Confucian and properly Christian, helpful to deal with serious issues of contemporary theology. Firstly, Confucianism and Christianity converge in *the* rén *mode of thinking*, i.e., "thinking in relationships and communities."[22] This mode would be a proper corrective to modern and contemporary individualism. It demands that the mode of thinking in relationship and community must be expanded to the broadest horizon, beyond boundaries, in solidarity not only with the people of other races, sexes, classes, cultures, and religions but also with nature, in order to actualize the goal of humanity as the cosmic being-in-togetherness. Secondly, Confucianism and Christianity converge in the chéng *mode of thinking*. As *cheng* literally means the accomplishment of the Word, it connotes the unity of logs and praxis, knowing and acting, and theology and ethics. Both Wang and Barth propose the concrete-universal mode of self-transformation as a communal act rooted in the unity of ontological knowledge and ethical practice. It would be also a significant corrective for our divided world. It enables us to overcome difficult polarities such as particularity and universality, diversity and unity,

---

22 Jürgen Moltmann, trans. Margaret Kohl, *The Way of Jesus Christ: Christology in Messianic Dimensions* (San Francisco: HarperSanFrancisco, 1990), 19.

theory and practice, and orthodoxy and orthopraxis.

Finally, Confucianism and Christianity converge in *the* Dao (道 Tao) *mode of thinking*, in the emphasis of the orthopraxis in the communal interrelatedness (*propriety* 禮 and discipleship). Wang and Barth share a claim that radical humanization implies primarily Dao (the Way of Life always in transformation), the transformative praxis of life. In the final analysis, all these modes of thinking refer to earnest participation in search of the Dao (Way) of common humanity, a genuine "dialogical participation" for the "common quest for a new humanism."[23] From this point, I began to develop the paradigm of *theo-dao* (*A Theology of Dao*).[24]

## *John Calvin (1509-1564) Meets Yi T'oegye (1501-1570): Imago Dei and T'ien-ming*

The thick resemblances within radical differences are presented more strikingly in the second dialogue between two of perhaps the most significant thinkers of Korean Christianit.[25] T'oegye Yi Hwang (退溪 李滉) firmly established Korean Neo-Confucianism, and his school of the Way or Dao (道學) had played decisive roles in the history of Korean Confucianism. The Reformed tradition (Presbyterianism), founded by John Calvin, has exceptionally flourished ever since it was introduced into this country. The Korean

---

23 Cf. M. M. Thomas, *Risking Christ For Christ's Sake: Towards an Ecumenical Theology of Pluralism* (Geneva: WCC Publications, 1987).

24 Heup Young Kim, *A Theology of Dao* (Maryknoll, NY: Orbis Books, 2017).

25 For more discussion in detail, see Heup Young Kim, "Imago Dei and T'ien-ming: John Calvin and Yi T'oegye on Humanity," *Ching Feng* 41: 3-4 (1998): 275-308.

Presbyterian Church becomes not only the largest in total membership but also culturally and socially the most active one among all
Christian denominations in Korea. For little more than a century,
she has grown to have the largest membership among all Reformed
churches in the world. In Korea, the Reformed tradition has achieved
perhaps the most successful mission in its entire history. I argued,
thus, that this success was possible because of these astonishing similarities between Korean Confucianism and Reformed Christianity,
as expressed between Calvin's theology and Yi's confuciology.

Ontological Humanity: Both Calvin and Yi believed that human
beings are relational to and inseparably intertwined with the transcendent grounds of being (namely, God and Heaven). The Christian
doctrine of *Imago Dei* and the Confucian notion of *Tiān mìng*
(*T'ien-ming* 天命; Heavenly endowment) manifest these relational
and transcendental anthropologies saliently. Both of them define
humanity as a mirror or a microcosm to image and reflect the glory
and the goodness of the transcendent ground of being. Furthermore,
they are remarkably similar in understanding the attributes of the
goodness endowed in original humanity. On the one hand, Calvin
described them as wisdom, virtue, justice, and holiness; in short,
integrity and rectitude. On the other hand, Yi expressed the attributes of the original nature as benevolence, righteousness, propriety,
and wisdom; in short, sincerity and principle. If idiosyncratic
(vertical) differences between God and Heaven are bracketed, the
(horizontal) understandings of Calvin and Yi on ontological humanity would be almost mutually interchangeable.

Existential Humanity (Fallen Nature and the Human Mind): Calvin
and Yi are similar in perceiving the mind-and-heart as the primary

locus of original humanity. They agreed that the mind-and-heart in reality, however, is so ambivalent and vulnerable that it functions ambiguously against its original goodness. Accordingly, both of them distinguished between original humanity with the original goodness (ontological humanity) and the actual humanity in ambiguity and ambivalence (existential humanity). In theology, it is expressed as a sharp distinction between the original humanity first created by God and the actual humanity after the Fall. In confuciology, it is indicated as a dichotomy between the mind of Dao (道心) and the human mind (人心). Consequently, how to recover and restore the original goodness immanent in the ontological humanity beyond the ambivalent and dualistic nature of existential humanity becomes the primary subject matter for both of them. This primary project of humanization, i.e., learning how to restore true and full humanity, is expressed in the doctrines of sanctification and self-cultivation (sage learning), respectively, in each tradition.

It is true that Calvin defended the doctrine of original sin and rigorously scrutinized the negative reality of corrupted humanity, whereas Yi carefully investigated the phenomena of mind-and-heart. If we look deeper into their thoughts, however, we can find that the differences in their analyses of human reality are not so thick but subtle. Calvin's doctrines of original sin and total depravity should not be understood independently but as corollaries to the doctrines of Grace and Christology.[26] Yi's view of the human mind-and-heart is not so romantic, as much as he experienced four bloody purges among Confucian literati, one of which killed his beloved brother.

---

26 Cf. T. F. Torrance, *Calvin's Doctrine of Man* ( London: Lutterworth Press), 1949.

Moreover, they converge in the comprehension of humanity's existential ambiguities as arising from distortion and perversion of original goodness, rejecting the ontological status of evil.

Restoration of Original Humanity: For both Calvin and Yi, piety (pietas and *jĭng*) is the central concept that permeates throughout their thoughts. For Yi, without doubt, *jĭng* (敬 *ching*) is the cardinal concept of self-cultivation, which involves a personal and corresponding relationship with the Lord of Heaven (上帝 *Shàng dì*). For Calvin, *pietas* is "the shorthand symbol for his whole understanding and practice of Christian faith and life."[27] For both of them, piety includes both fear and love (*mysterium tremendum et fascinas*, according to Rudolf Otto) toward the ultimate ground of being and has doctrinal precedence to knowledge (*doctrina* and *li*).

The overarching methodology of Yi's sage learning is the 'dwelling in the piety and investigating the principle' (居敬窮理). It is not too much to say that, though the object of investigation is different, Calvin holds structurally the same methodology (the classical definition of theology is *fides quaerens intellectum* [faith-seeking-understanding]). Whereas *li* (理 the universal principle) is the object of investigation for Yi's confuciology, Jesus Christ (the Word) is the object of faith for Calvin's theology. Furthermore, they converge in a belief that these objects of investigation are also the transcendent grounds of being, which enable us to attain radical humanity with original goodness. For *li* and Jesus Christ refer to the perfect manifestations of *Tiān mìng* and *imago Dei* respectably. On the one

---

27 Ford Lewis Battles, "True Piety According to Calvin," in *Readings in Calvin's Theology*, ed. Donald K. McKim, (Grand Rapids: Baker Book House Co., 1984), 192-211.

hand, Yi articulated this task as 're-embodying Heaven and pro-
gressing along the Way (Dao).' On the other hand, Calvin explained
it by way of restoring the original image of God through faith in
Christ and walking under the direction of the Holy Spirit. Both of
them congruently argued for piety and righteousness as the inner
and outer means in order to achieve sanctification and self-cultivation respectably.

In a nutshell, sanctification in Christianity is the realization of
Christ (the perfect image of God) through hearing the Word, and
self-cultivation in Confucianism is the embodiment of *T'ien-ming*
through the investigation of *li*. If Christ (the Word) is identified with
*li* (the principle), the structure of humanization in Calvin's theology
and Yi's confuciology will be identical; both of them point to
saint/sage learning, which is the study of Dao (道學).

Ecological Vision (*Pietas* and *Jing*): Calvin and Yi had a similar view
on human's relationship with nature. With the doctrines of the image
of God and the Heavenly endowment, both of them denied the qualitative differences between humanity and nature. In the narrow definition, only humanity can function as the true mirror of their transcendental ground of being. On the broader definition, nevertheless, humans and things are the same as the image of God and
the Heavenly endowed nature. Yi explained their differences in
terms of 'physical disposition.' A human being consists of upright
and transparent *qi* (氣 *ch'i*, material force), whereas things are composed of leaned and opaque *qi*. Hence, the posture of human bodies
is upright (toward Heaven), that of wild animals is horizontal
(parallel to the Earth), and plants grow vertically in a reverse
direction. Calvin also agreed this point, "God made man erect, unlike

the other creatures, that he might know and worship God." Finally, Calvin and Yi converged at a similar vision that the transcendent (God and Heaven), the human, and cosmos are closely interrelated (through the *imago Dei* and the *Tiān mìng*). From this vantage point, Calvin and Yi agreed in advocating a the-anthropo-cosmic vision (the transcendent, human, and nature interrelated). From this vantage point, human beings are not vicious conquers of the universe or the sole independent subjects of history in the linear cosmos, but interdependent co-spectators to witness the glorious cosmic drama of God or ecological keepers to harmonizing the wonderful trajectory of Heaven in the theanthropocosmic theater.

## 3. Christian Theology of Confucianism East Asian Constructive Theology: Toward a Theology of Dao (Theo-dao)

In the second, normative-constructive stage, the focus is placed on Christian theology in this historic collision with Confucianism. Christian communities in East Asia need a wholistic understanding of Christian faith in their own religio-cultural-linguistic matrix (e.g., Confucianism). It is an impelling moment for an East Asian TR to move beyond an a *priori* level. It is a moment of the "beyond dialogue,"[28] to move forward beyond a dialogical moment of either 'Wang Yang-ming and Karl Barth' or 'Calvin and T'oegye.' The main

---

28 John B. Cobb, Jr., *Beyond Dialogue: Towards a Mutual Transformation and Buddhism* (Philadelphia: Fortress Press), 1982.

task of this constructive moment is to construct an a *posteriori* articulation of the normative Christian faith for the communities in the historic fusion of the two great hermeneutical horizons, the two powerful stories of humanity and full humanization. Primarily, this normative-constructive enterprise does not refer to a descriptive study of religious phenomena or an arbitrary deliberation of speculative comparison, but to an imperative *thematization* for these Christian communities to acquire an integrated understanding of Christian faith in their own contexts (so-called as a themative approach). However, again, this enterprise does not imply a naïve, eclectic religious syncretism (cf. Thomas), but "a confessional method" (Niebuhr) in and through "intra-religious dialogue" (Panikkar).[29]

In this stage, the thick resemblances between Confucianism and Christianity furnish the common ground to develop an East Asian Christian TR (Confucianism). The understandings of humanity in their traditional terms of *rén* and *imago Dei* respectively, are homologically and materially congruent, namely, co-humanity, being-in-togetherness, or being for others. East Asian Christians have no difficulty confessing Jesus Christ as the paradigm of humanity that perfects both *rén* and *imago Dei*. In Jesus Christ, they also find a perfect unity for the two root-metaphors (*chéng* and *agape*) of radical humanization for both traditions. Hence, the thick resemblances between Confucianism and Christianity discovered through the dialogues become substantiated in the form of Christology. If East Asian

---

29 Cf. Thomas, M. M., *Risking Christ For Christ's Sake*; H. Richard Niebuhr, *The Meaning of Revelation* (New York: Macmillan, 1962), 41; Raymundo Panikkar, *The Intrareligious Dialogue* (New York: Paulist Press, 1978).

Christians confess Jesus Christ as the ultimate paradigm of sincere humanity (Sage) who has authenticated once and for all the Confucian faith in humanity's intrinsic possibility of self-transcendence, the Confucian story of humanization will become a profound resource to deepening and enriching the reality and meaning of Jesus Christ and theological anthropology. This East Asian understanding of Christianity out of Confucian-Christian experiences introduces some profound insights and new dimensions to Christian theology. The dialogue between Wang and Barth showed that this new paradigm of theology has three important postmodern characteristics; namely, the dao mode of theology (wholistic), the *rén* mode of theology (dialogical), and the *theanthropocosmic* mode of theology (ecological).

Firstly, it entails a *dao* mode of theology (namely, *theo-dao*). The *Dao* of Jesus Christ, explicitly denoting a christology on the way, is a more preferable term than Christology, as the *hodos* (translated as the *dao* originally in Korean and Chinese Bibles) was the original name for Christianity (Acts 9:2; 19:9; 22:4; 24:14, 22). Moltmann argued, "I am no longer trying to think of Christ statistically as one person in two natures or as a historical personality. I am trying to grasp him dynamically [*as the Way*], in the forward movement of God's history with the world."[30] *Christo-dao*, conceiving Jesus Christ as the Dao (transformative praxis) of radial humanization,[31] is an *emancipatory* paradigm to plea the world to move beyond the contra-

---

30 Moltmann, *The Way of Jesus Christ*, xv.

31 Heup Young Kim, "Toward a Christodao: Christ as the Theanthropocosmic Tao," *Studies in Interreligious Dialogue* 10:1 (2000): 1-25.

dictions of scientific and technological civilization such as the surplus masses of people and poverty in the Third World, nuclearism threatened by the nuclear inferno, and ecological disaster. As an alternative paradigm of equilibrium and harmony, it can help to correct contemporary paradigms of domination and expansion.

Further, it introduces a *rén* mode of theology, *dialogical* in the form (Confucian-Christian dialogue) as well as the content (*rén*). Christology itself always has been developed by dialogue: "Christology is never final but always in dialogue."[32] The *rén* mode of theology can overcome the defects of modern, anthropological theologies, because it is not based on the modern anthropology of the isolated ego, but the Confucian anthropology that underscores a person as the center of a relationship. Hence, *christodao* is not a "logy," a metaphysical understanding, of the prototype of the ego, but a *Dao*, a transformative praxis, for a person to attain full humanity (*rén*) accomplished by Christ, co-humanity, being-in-togetherness, being-in-encounter, being-for-others, and life in partnership. Envisioning Jesus, the root-paradigm of humanity (*rén*), as a cosmic, reconciled being-in-togetherness, it expands and empowers the Confucian principle of reciprocity and mutuality to the cosmic dimension. The *rén* mode of theology with humility and modesty can correct the *epistemological immodesty* and *ethical hubris* Christian theology often has committed in history. It would foster a liberation of humanity and nature from the principle of domination and exploitation.[33]

---

32 Robert F. Berkeley and Sarah A. Edwards, *Christology in Dialogue* (Cleveland, OH: Pilgrim Press, 1993), 24-25.

33 Tu Wei-ming, *Centrality and Commonality: An Essay on Confucian Religiousness*

Furthermore, the new paradigm entails a *theanthropocosmic* mode of theology. In this paradigm, the *anthropocosmic* vision of Confucianism fully encounters, collides, and fuses with the *theohistorical* vision of Christianity. These visions move beyond dialogue and are mutually transformed into a *theanthropocosmic* vision. This mode of theology may overcome "the crisis of history" by introducing ecological and cosmic dimensions of Confucian-Christian theanthropocosmic vision.[34] Conceiving Jesus Christ as the ultimate embodiment of the theanthropocosmic Dao, christodao transcends every dualism; knowing and acting, theology and ethics, logos and ethos, orthodoxy and orthopraxis, and so on. Jesus Christ is the Crucified and Risen Cosmic Sage who fully actualized the messianic *Dao* for the eschatological theanthropocosmic equilibrium and harmony, traditionally expressed in terms of new Heaven, new Earth, and new Humanity. In sum, Jesus Christ is the *Dao* of new cosmic humanity. As Moltmann criticized, ancient cosmological, modern anthropological, and contemporary scientific-technological christologies are too narrow and problematic.[35] Hence, christodao that understands Jesus Christ as the *Dao* of new cosmic humanity would be an appropriate a new christological paradigm for the third millennium.[36]

---

(Albany: State University of New York Press, 1989), 102-7.

34 Panikkar, Raymundo, *The Cosmotheandric Experience: Emerging Religious Consciousness* (Maryknoll, NY: Orbis Books, 1993), 108-19.

35 Moltmann, *The Way of Jesus Christ*, 46-72.

36 See Kim, "Toward a Christotao."

## 4. Confucian-Christian Dialogue and Theodao for a Technological Age of Anthropocene

The Confucian-Christian dialogue provided a cornerstone to develop a new paradigm of theology, namely, *theo-dao* (a theology of dao). I also think that it has some significant implications for today's problems and future theology. I would like to end the article with a few comments.

Theodao: First of all, the Confucian-Christian dialogue provided the basis for starting the formulation of theodao. In the dialogue between Wang and Barth, dao was narrowly viewed as a transformative praxis. However, as imprinted by Wang's doctrine of the unity of knowing and acting, it was extended theologically to the unity of theo-logos (doctrine) and theo-praxis (action). I have pointed out that the dilemma of modern theologies, dominated by the Western, is a dualization of their root-metaphors between logos and praxis. Dao whose Chinese character literally means the unity of knowing and acting is a root-metaphor more proper for theological construction than logos and praxis.[37] As we saw in the previous dialogues, Calvin, the founder of Reformed theology, and Barth, a theological giant in the 20th century, can be viewed virtually as theologians of dao rather than of logos who emphasized the doctrine of sanctification. Theologians mostly accept that theology is fundamentally practical theology.

---

37 Kim, *A Theology of Dao*, 14-18.

Ecodao: Secondly, the dialogue between Confucianism and Christianity enabled the construction of a new ecological theology. Mary Evelyn Tucker and John Grim, pioneers in the field of Religion and Ecology through the dialogue of world religions beyond the limits of Christian theology, stated, "The East Asian tradition of Confucianism and Daoism remain, in certain ways, some of the most life-affirming in the spectrum of world religions."[38] That is to say, Confucianism and Daoism are the most eco-friendly traditions, and so dao, the central notion of both traditions, is the most eco-friendly metaphor than other religious metaphors, including logos and praxis. The theanthropocosmic paradigm derived as a result of the Confucian-Christian dialogue would be a worldview that ecological theology has been pursuing. Neo-Confucianism further supports this view with the cosmology of the Great Ultimate (*Taiji*). From this, I coined a new term, 'eco-dao', in contrast with ecology (eco-logos).[39] Ecodao with wholistic, dialogical, theanthropocosmic metaphor of dao will provide more suitable paradigms than ecology and ecological theology in the epoch of Anthropocene.

Trilogue: Thirdly, the Confucian-Christian dialogue helped to cor-

---

38 Mary Evelyn Tucker and John Grim, "Series Foreward," in *Christianity and Ecology: Seeking the Well-Being of Earth and Humans*, eds. Dieter T. Hessel abd Rosemary R. Ruether (Cambridge, MA: Harvard University Press, 2000), xxvi.

39 See Heup Young Kim, "Theodao: Integrating Ecological Consciousness in Daoism, Confucianism, and Christian Theology," in *The Wiley Blackwell Companion to Religion and Ecology*, ed. John Hart (Oxford: Wiley Blackwell, 2017), 104-114; also, "Eco-Dao: an Ecological Theology of Dao," in *The Bloosmbury Handbook of Religion and Nature: The Elements*, eds. Laura Hobgood abd Whitney Bauman (New York, NY: Bloomsbury Academic, 2018), 99-108.

rect the limitations of the dialogue between religion and science, which has become more critical with the advent of the scientific age but been reduced to the dialogue between Christian theology and science. Abrahamic and other theistic religions are challenging to overcome the dualism between supernature and nature and between transcendence and immanence, because of their theocentricism. However, Confucianism, as a sapiential paradigm that does not hold strong dualism between nature and supernature, encompasses both transcendence and immanence in the conception of nature (nature can have an identical character with Heaven) can have a genuine dialogue with the natural science studying nature *per se*. The religion-and-science discourses led by the West, which grew up in the late 20th century, had been *de facto* a dual dialogue between theology and science that lacks participation of other religions and perspectives of interreligious dialogue. Confucian-Christian dialogue can be fruitful means to overcome this deficiency of the dialogue between religion and science, dominated by Christian and other theistic religions, by generating a trialogue that consists of natural science, theology, and East Asian religions (Confucianism and Daoism).[40]

Technodao: Fourth, the dialogue between Confucianism and Christianity can provide clues to critical moral issues of today, facing the advancement of Artificial Intelligence (AI), which could surpass

[40] See Heup Young Kim, "Asian Christianity: Toward a Trilogue of Humility: Sciences, Theologies, and Asian Religions," in *Why the Science and Religion Dialogue Matters: Voices from the International Society for Science and Religion*, eds. Fraser Watts and Kevin Dutton (Philadelphia, PA: Templeton Press, 2006), 121-33.

human intelligence. As transhumanist futurists predict the immediate coming of Singularity, there would be not much time to prepare for the peaceful coexistence between AI and humans. Therefore, how to develop human-centered or ethical AI that can support human humanity and guarantee morality is emerging as a top issue. AI would be a mechanical completion of pure intelligence that has been pursued by Western thought since Plato, and so embedded in the logos theology. At the same time, it also shows its limitation. For it is a reduction of human beings into intelligence, which sustains the prolonged error of Western thought that overlooks human emotion and body. The modern logos theology failed to overcome this fallacy sufficiently. It could allow the idea of cyber or cyborg post-humanity, which would be either without the human body or replacing the biological body with a machine. On the contrary, Christianity believes in the resurrection of the body, and Confucianism places more importance on mind-heart and wisdom than intelligence. Therefore, the Confucian-Christian dialogue can offer the possibility to shift beyond the existing morally irresponsible paradigm of technology (techno+logos) to techno-dao (techno+dao) that secures ontological humanity and morality.[41]

The Dao of Humanity (Anthropodao): Finally, the dialogue between Confucianism and Christianity can provide resources to answer the most prominent theological and religious subject of today, what

---

[41] See Heup Young Kim, "Cyborg, Sage, and Saint: Transhumanism as Seen from an East Asian Theological Setting," in *Religion and Transhumanism: The Unknown Future of Human Enhancement*, Calvin Mercer and Tracy J. T Rothen (Santa Barbara, CA: Praeger, 2014), 97-114.

is humanity after all? Transhumanists argue that transhumanism is a humanism that inherits the spirit of the Enlightenment. However, they aim primarily for superintelligence with attributes of humaneness rather than ontological humanity. Postmodernism has already called for fierce criticisms on Enlightenment humanism, which has defined humans as isolated egos rather than relational beings for anthropocosmic togetherness. From the perspective of Confucian-Christian dialogues we have seen, the modern West is losing the ontology of humanity and authentic humanism by theonomism and excessive individualism. Confucianism is the longest tradition that has developed humanism with a firm belief in the ontology of humanity. The world has yet to find a suitable answer to the fundamental question of what humanity (and human morality) despite the urgent need for preparation is to develop human-centered AI. The Confucian-Christian dialogue could offer some viable understanding of humanity and the way (dao) to sustain humanity in an exponentially developing age of AI, which could terminate it; that is to say, an *anthropodao*.

CHAPTER NINE

# Biblical Readings on a Theology of Dao/Do

Abstract

This chapter highlights that the do (dao/tao, the way), a crucial and common concept in East Asian thought (Confucianism, Daoism, and Buddhism), is a more appropriate interpretative lens for Koreans and East Asians to read the Bible than that of the historically dominant logos of Christian theology. It is useful not only for contextual theology but also for autogenous Korean Christian thought. Further, the do is biblically more appropriate than logos as the root metaphor. Jesus never identified himself as the logos but rather as the hodos, a homologous term to the do. The hermeneutical key of do (dao), which means the unity of knowing and acting, overcomes a dilemma in Western theology, namely, the dichotomy between the conventional theo-logos and the liberational theo-praxis. Here, from the third perspective of theo-dao, the Bible may be read from the interpretative metaphor of do.

## *Do* (도 道 dao/tao, the way)

Like the logos of Western thought, the *do* is the crucial concept in Korea and East Asia (traditionally Neo-Confucian countries). Generally, the Chinese character (道) is romanized as "dao" (Pinyin) or "tao" (Wade-Giles), according to Chinese pronunciation. However, this chapter, in the context of Korean biblical interpretation, uses "*do*" as its romanization in the Korean pronunciation (도). The holistic notion of the polysemic word *do* is challenging to understand for modern people with analytical dispositions. They often misunderstand *do* as only related to Daoism. But other East Asian traditions widely use *do*, including Confucianism, Buddhism, and even Christianity.

Although Westerners, Herbert Fingarette and C. S. Lewis presented helpful English descriptions of *do*. Fingarette defined the *do* in a Confucian way:

> Tao [*Do*] is a Way, a path, a road, and by common metaphorical extension it becomes in ancient China the right Way of life, the Way of governing, the ideal Way of human existence, the Way of the Cosmos, the generative-normative Way (pattern, path, course) of existence as such.[1]

Lewis understood it in a more ontologically Daoian way:

> The *Tao* [*Do*], which others may call Natural Law or Traditional Morality

---

1 Herbert Fingarette, *Confucius— The Secular as Sacred* (New York: Harper & Row, 1972), 19.

or the First Principles of Practical Reason or the First Platitudes, is not one among a series of possible systems of value. It is the sole source of all value judgments. If it is rejected, all value is rejected. If any value is retained, it is retained.[2]

First and foremost, the *do* is inexplicable as God. If it is defined with any intention, hence, it can be idolatrous. *Dàodéjīng* begins with the following saying:

> The Tao (Way) that can be told of is not the eternal Tao;
> The name that can be named is not the eternal name;
> The Nameless is the origin of Heaven and Earth;
> The Named is the mother of all things.[3]

On a similar note, the first biblical commandment also said, "You shall not make yourself an idol, whether in the form of anything that is in heaven above, that is on the earth, or that is in the water under the earth" (Exod. 20:4). These definitions of the *do* will be helpful in understanding and using theologies of the *do*.

---

2 C. S. Lewis, *The Abolition of Man: Reflections on Education with Special Reference to the Teaching of English in the Upper Forms of Schools* (New York: Macmillan, 1947), 28-29.

3 Chan Wing-Tsit, *A Source Book in Chinese Philosophy* (Princeton, NJ: Princeton University Press, 1963), 139.

## Theo-dao (a Theology of *Do*)

The *do* mode of thought has a long history in East Asia and crucially contributed to the development of Korean thought. In Korea, therefore, the Christian faith and biblical interpretation has been characterized through the interpretative lens of *do* and the subsequent *do* mode of theology. Despite the strong sense of *do*, Western missionaries transmitted the logos mode of Christianity that exclusively focuses on Western doctrinal, historical, and intellectual aspects to Korea. Korean Christian leaders, theologians, and scholars uncritically followed in adopting the Western theological education system, while ignoring their contextualities and rejecting their indigenous religious and cultural traditions.

I experienced these educational shortcomings during seminary. And as a twenty-eighth-generation descendant of a Korean Confucian family, after my conversion to Christianity, I wanted to engage these shortcomings. So, I argued for the study of Confucianism as a theological task and engaged in a dialogue between Christianity and Confucianism to produce *Wang Yang-ming and Karl Barth: A Confucian-Christian Dialogue* (1996).[4] This Confucian-Christian dialogue brought out a thesis that "in the light of Wang Yang-ming and Karl Barth, self-cultivation and sanctification are thickly resemblant views of a common issue; how to be fully human, or the Tao [*Do*] of radical humanization." It also showed that not only did Wang Yang-ming (1472-1529), a seminal Confucian scholar, use a *do* mode

---

4 Kim Heup Young, *Wang Yang-Ming and Karl Barth: A Confucian-Christian Dialogue* (Lanham, MD: University Press of America, 1996).

of thought but also did the crucial twentieth-century Christian theologian Karl Barth (1886-1968), who used a *do* mode of theology, namely, "in search for the Tao [*do*] of new cosmic humanity."[5]

Historically, theologies have been developing through continuous paradigm shifts with changes in their relating cultures. Theology is inevitably contextual. However, Western theologies have been divided basically in two macro-paradigms, the classical logos paradigm (theo-logos) and its antithetical liberationist paradigm (theo-praxis). This dichotomy resembles leftovers of the Greek dualism (form and matter, soul and body, theory and practice, etc.). However, God can be reduced neither to logos (Word or doctrines) nor to praxis (Deeds or actions). God cannot be fully grasped with these two Western root-metaphors. God transcends Greek dualisms such as form and matter, body and soul, divinity and humanity, and logos and praxis. Thus, the holistic *do* (dao) articulates God more appropriately than these two Western metaphors. I call this theological paradigm theo-dao (theos + dao), because it is constructed with the root-metaphor of dao (*do*), in contrast to theo-logy (theos + logos) and theo-praxis (theos + praxis).

As it consists of two ideographs, meaning "head" (體, being) and "vehicle" (辶, becoming), *do* (道) entails both the source of being (logos) and the way of becoming (praxis). Thus, *do* can be reduced neither to being nor to becoming. Instead, it is the being in becoming or the logos in transformative praxis. *Do* does not force a person to stay at the crossroad of logos (being) and praxis (becoming), but it actualizes participation in a dynamic movement to unite with the

---

5 Kim, *Wang Yang-Ming and Karl Barth*, 175-88.

trajectory of the truth. The *do* as the ultimate way and reality embodies the transformative praxis of the sociocosmic trajectory of life in the unity of knowing and acting. While theo-logy is the perspective from above and theo-praxis that from below, theo-dao is the perspective from an entirely different dimension, a the-anthropo-cosmic intersubjectivity of God, humanity, and the cosmos.

Theo-dao suggests that Korean and East Asian theology cannot be only logos-centric (knowledge) or only praxis-centric (action); it must be dao-centric (in the unity of knowledge and action). Korean theology as a theo-dao can aim neither only to an ortho-doxy (a right doctrine of the church) nor only to an ortho-praxis (a right practice in history) but should embrace holistically the right way of life (ortho-dao) or the transformative wisdom of living in a the-anthropo-cosmic trajectory. Theo-dao is not just an orthodoxy or only an orthopraxis, but an ortho-dao; namely, it's concerned with whether Christians are in the right way of God as revealed in Jesus Christ and live under the direction of the Holy Spirit. In fact, the Greek word *hodos* (the way, also meaning path, road, route, journey, march, etc.) was the original name for Christianity (Acts 9:2; 19:9; 22:4; 24:14, 22).

Hence, the fundamental issue is whether Christians are correctly participating in the gracious process of theanthropocosmic (theos + anthropos+cosmos) reconciliation and sanctification. In terms of the three cardinal virtues of 1 Corinthians 13, faith is for theo-logos, whose classical definition is a faith-seeking-understanding (*fides quarens intellectum*) that focuses on ortho-doxy. Hope is for theo-praxis, a hope-seeking-action, focusing on ortho-praxis, the right liberating action for the Kingdom of God. Love is for theo-dao, which is a love-seeking-dao, focusing on ortho-dao, the right way/wisdom of life. To summarize, if the primary theme of the traditional theology (theo-logos) is the epistemology of faith, and the theme of modern liberation theology (theo-praxis) is the eschatology of hope, the cardinal theme of the Korean *do* theology (theo-dao) is the pneumatology of love.

## Christo-dao (a Christology of *Do*)

To more fully flesh out a theo-dao, the principles of *do* should be extended to Christology. Applying the *do* mode of thinking, such as the Great Ultimate (太極Taegŭk), theo-dao can construct a Christology of *do* (Christo-dao)[6] that can overcome the enduring impasse of Western Christologies due to the inherited dualism between divinity and humanity. The Confucian/Daoian onto-cosmology of *do* is directly related to *Taegŭk* (the main symbol on the Korean national flag). In *An Explanation of the Diagram of the Great Ultimate*, Zhou Dunyi (1017-1073) states:

> The Ultimate of Non-being and also the Great Ultimate! The Great Ultimate through movement generates *yang*. When its activity reaches its limit, it becomes tranquil. Through tranquility the Great Ultimate generates *yin*. When tranquility reaches its limit, activity begins again. So movement and tranquility alternate and become the root of each other,

---

6 For the Christology of theo-dao (Christodao), see Kim Heup Young, *A Theology of Dao* (Maryknoll, NY: Orbis Books, 2017), 34-56, 147-68.

giving rise to the distinction of *yin* and *yang*, and the two modes are thus established.[7]

*Taegŭk*, symbolized by a circle consisting of *yin* and *yang*, denotes the unity of complementarity of opposites (also, tranquility and activity). By the notion of the Great Ultimate, Christo-dao can articulate the cosmic Christ as the ultimate *do* (Christo-dao) by thinking in terms of both-and (both yin and yang) and neither-nor. The Nicene-Chalcedonian formulas of Christology had already articulated the ultimate and cosmogonic (*do*) nature of Christ beyond the Greek dualistic framework. Christian faith empowered fourth-century Christians to transcend the either-or logic of Greek dualistic thinking. On the one hand, the Nicene Creed (325) used the both-and (complementary opposites) mode to confess Christ as both *vere Deus* and *vere homo*. On the other hand, the Chalcedonian formula (451) utilized the neither-nor mode to express that Christ's two natures are neither confused, changed, divided, nor separated. Thus, the early Church had recognized the *do* nature of Christ as the supreme paradox of the Great Ultimate (total affirmation of the both-and) and the Non-Ultimate (total negation of the neither-nor).

This *do*-mode of paradoxical thought had appeared in early Christian theologians such as Gregory of Nyssa (c. 395) and Dionysius the Areopagite (fl. 500), in Christian mystics such as Francis of Assisi (1182-1226), Meister Eckhart (d. 1327), and Julian of Norwich (b. 1343). Most explicitly, it appears in the principle of *coincidentia oppositorum* formulated by Nicholas of Cusa (1401-1464). However, this

---

7 Chan, *Source Book*, 463.

early church tradition and effort have been suppressed by the dominant Western ways of thinking that epitomized the Enlightenment,
such as scientific historicism and linear progress. Thus, through
theo-dao, I want to revive the suppressed integral view of the early
Church, while connecting it with *do* thinking. In short, with the integral thinking of the *do* as witnessed in the early Church, Christians
can better comprehend the foundation of the Christian faith, the
mystery of the supreme paradox: The Crucifixion and Resurrection
of Jesus Christ.

## *Do* and the Bible

On at least a Christological level, *do* is more biblical than logos
because it is profoundly more homologous to the biblical Greek
term *hodos* ("way, road, highway" as a place; "way, journey" as an
action; "way of life, way of acting, conduct;" "the whole way of life").[8]
In this respect, Jesus never called himself the *logos*, but the *hodos*,
by saying, "I am the way, and the truth, and the life" (Jn. 14:6). A
text that must inevitably be dealt with here is John 1:1, where John
directly uses *logos*. But here, it does not refer to its modern logo-pho-
no-centric reductions but has a closer connotation with the Hebrew
*dabar*, which underlines action. Although both terms express "the

---

8 Walter Bauer et al., *A Greek-English Lexicon of the New Testament and Other Early
   Christian Literature: A Translation and Adaptation of the Fourth Revised and
   Augmented Edition of Walter Bauer's Griechisch-Deutsches Wörterbuch Zu Den
   Schriften Des Neuen Testaments Und Der Übrigen Urchristlichen Literatur*, 2d ed.
   (Chicago: University of Chicago Press, 1979), 553-55.

Word," *dabar* focuses more on the deed (wisdom) and *logos* on reason (knowledge and order).[9] By using *logos* as the central concept, Western theology became doctrinal, intellectual, and theoretical, overlooking the importance of praxis (deed and action), which was a hermeneutical root-cause for the rise of liberation theologies (theo-praxis). Even in the case of John 1:1, hence, *do*, with the meaning of the unity of knowledge and action, seems more appropriate than *logos*, a Johannine interpretation.

In the first Korean translation of "the Gospel according to John" (1882), moreover, John Ross (1842-1915) translated *logos* in John 1:1 as *do*, following the *Wenli* version of the Chinese Bible (dao).[10] Korean Bibles, such as *Korean Revised Version* (KRV, 1961) and *New Korean Revised Version* (NKRV, 1998), continuously translated Jesus's teachings as "the *do* (way)" of the Lord (Acts 18:25, 19:9, 22:4) and "the *do* of the cross" (1 Cor. 1:18). Koreans even called the first Christians "followers of the do" of Jesus Christ (Acts 24:14). From the beginning, the Korean biblical hermeneutical key of *do* has been operative in the translation of Korean Bibles (KRV, NKRV), such as the *do* of God (2 Sam. 22:31; Ps. 18:30; Matt. 22:16; Mark 12:14; Luke 20:21; Acts 18:26), the *do* of the Lord (Ps. 25:4, 51:13, 67:2, 77:13, 86:11, 119:3, 119:15, 119:37; Jer. 32:23, Acts 18:25), and the *do* of Jehovah (Gen. 18:19, Judg. 2:22, 2 Sam. 22:22, 2 Ch 17:6; Ps. 18:21, 138:5, Prov. 10:29; Hosea 14:9). Thus, the *do* mode of Christian

---

9 David Allan Hubbard and Glenn W. Barker, eds., *Word Biblical Commentary* (Waco, TX: Word Books, 1982), 9.

10 John Ross, ed., *The Gospel according to St. John* (Shimyang, Korea: Mungwang Sowon, 1882), 1.

thought (theo-dao) has been operative from the beginning of Christianity in Korea.

## Theo-dao in History

Theo-dao, hence, is justified in at least three ways: contextually, constructively, and biblically. Theo-dao theologies were also visible from the start of the short history of the Korean indigenous theology. Notably, it appeared among autogenous Christian thinkers who were not affected much by the influence of Western missions and theological education. The models of Ryu Yŏng-mo, Lee Jung Young, and Pyŏn Chan-lin are examples of Korean theo-dao theologies that are rather divorced from Western influences.

## Indigenous Scriptures as the Old Testament

Ryu Yŏngmo (1890-1981), who, although being unpopular among mainstream Korean churches, was a forerunner of indigenous intertextual interpretation, multifaith hermeneutics, and comparative theology. He was convinced that "After Confucianism, Buddhism, and Christianity illuminate each other, they also know themselves better."[11] Deeply embedded in East Asian scriptures, Ryu developed a fascinating interpretation of Christian faith in the

---

11 Ryu Yŏngmo, *Seeds' Echo Echoes of Seeds: The Words of Tasŏk Ryu Yŏngmo* (Korean) (Seoul: Hongikje, 1993), 365.

light of East Asian thoughts. All scriptures of East Asian religions, he argues, should be regarded as the Old Testament for Koreans. Accepting the theory that the Old Testament plays a preparatory role for God's plan for the creation and the New Testament fulfills such a plan, he regards Christianity as a New Testament. Thus, for him, the New Testament has completed all the truth revealed in East Asian religious thoughts, so to speak, the East Asian Old Testaments.

Ryu was not as particularly interested in the epistemology of religious pluralism per se; he was more concerned with a constructive hermeneutic of his faith in and through (not out of) the profundities of multiple Korean traditional, indigenous religions. He freely employed scriptural resources of Korean indigenous religions to understand the Christian Bible better and more appropriately in the Korean context. Through more than one millennium with Korean people, the East Asian scriptures of Confucianism, Buddhism, and Daoism have profoundly influenced and been deeply embedded in Korean modes of life and thought. By reading the Bible in and through these indigenous scriptures, he conceived his new faith in Jesus Christ more clearly, intelligibly, and practically.

Using John 14:6, Ryu also conceived Jesus as the *do*, the way of the truth toward life in God. Christ is *the* brightest *way* on which we can walk safely (*the truth*) to attain unity with God (*the life*). It is the way to achieve the goal of Confucianism, the anthropocosmic unity of Heaven and humanity, as *the Doctrine of the Mean* begins with saying, "What Heaven imparts to man is called human nature."[12]

---

12 Chan, *A Source Book*, 95.

Ryu wrote:

> Then, what are "the way (道 *do*), the truth (眞理), and the life (生命)"
> Jesus envisioned? He seems to understand them as follows. The way
> refers to ascending again to Heaven after having descended from
> Heaven to the earth. The truth means walking brightly along the way,
> and life means that the Father and the Son become one as the brightest
> light. The Son of Man came from Heaven and returned to Heaven. There
> is no brighter way than this. Going straight along this way without error
> is the truth. Finally, meeting with God is life. Compare it to the railroad!
> The railroad is the way, the train is the truth, and arrival is life.[13]

Ryu thought that human beings are constantly on the road or
the way until they enter the heavenly kingdom in search of heavenly
nature, which is true human nature. As explaining the path, the route
(*do*), the Bible is the way to Heaven and true human nature, to the
*do* of self-cultivation, and to the recovery of original selfhood in
the process of restoring true humanity.

Furthermore, Ryu conceived that Jesus is ultimately the true "I."
"The way, the truth, and the life," after all, refer to this real "I." Ryu
writes, "The way is eternally coming and eternally going. However,
'I' come and go on the way. If I come and go on the way, I become
the way. Just as a silkworm's cocoon makes thread and as a spider
spins a web, I produce the way."[14] This is an ingenious East Asian
interpretation of Paul's passage, "it is no longer I who live, but it

---

13 Ryu, *Echoes of Seeds*, 167.
14 Ibid, 43-44.

is the Christ who lives in me" (Gal. 2:20). From his East Asian perspective, he concludes that this Pauline passage means that the Christ who lives within a Christian ("me") is the true "I" (true humanity). Then, Neo-Confucian insights on true humanity, such as the mind-and-heart (心), original human nature (性), and the principle (理), can be profoundly resourceful for biblical interpretation and theology. In doing this, Ryu unfolded a thick Confucian (do) interpretation of the Bible.

## Yin-Yang (陰陽) Hermeneutics of Change (易)

Lee Jung Young (1935-1996), a Korean American theologian, formulated his theology with East Asian metaphysics of Change (易). Lee argued for a paradigm shift in theological thinking from both substantialism (being) and process (becoming) to Change (being and becoming). Modern physics, such as Einstein's theory of relativity and the growing field of quantum physics, demonstrated that the ultimate reality is likely both 'being and becoming' (Change). This stands in opposition to an ultimate reality as either 'being' (substance) in Greek metaphysics (Aristotelian logic, Euclidean geometry, and Newtonian physics) or 'becoming' in (Whiteheadian) process metaphysics. Change is related to the Neo-Confucian metaphysics of the Great Ultimate in the complementary opposites of yin and yang. Lee applied it to a theology of Change.

The either-or logic, deeply rooted in Western thought, is often uncritically applied in Western theology and biblical interpretation. However, the either-or option is incomplete, as Wilfred Cantwell

Smith said: "In all ultimate matters, the truth lies not in an either-or, but a both-and."[15] Lee argued, the both-and logic of Change is more theologically accurate (God as the Change): "Change in the *I-Ching* [易經] is certainly beyond categorization. It is simultaneously personal and impersonal, male and female, immanent and transcendent."[16] This total affirmation (both-and), furthermore, is complementary to total negation (neither-nor). The supreme paradox of Change is that the Great Ultimate is the Non-Ultimate (無極而太極). Here, the Great Ultimate signifies the total affirmation and the Non-Ultimate total negation. Change refers to the Great Ultimate, which is the *do* in successive alteration (一陰一陽謂之道). From this vantage point, God, as the Ultimate *Do*, is simultaneously personal and impersonal, male and female, immanent and transcendent. At the same time, God as the Ultimate *Do* is neither personal nor impersonal, neither male nor female, neither immanent nor transcendent. This persists with the Incarnate person of God, Jesus Christ, who is the perfect realization of Change or the Great Ultimate (*yin-yang*), and therefore, Jesus is both personal and impersonal, male and female, and individual and communal.[17]

> In Jesus as the Christ, man and God are in perfect harmony. Jesus' identity does not preclude his humanity but presupposes it, just as *yang* presup-

---

15 Wilfred Cantwell Smith, *Faith of Other Men* (New York: New American Library, 1963), 72.

16 Lee Jung Young, *The Theology of Change: A Christian Concept of God in an Eastern Perspective* (Maryknoll, NY: Orbis Books, 1979), 22.

17 Lee Jung Young, *The Trinity in Asian Perspective* (Nashville, TN: Abingdon, 1996), 78-82.

poses the existence of *yin.* Furthermore, perfect humanity presupposes perfect divinity. In his perfect complementarity of divinity and humanity, or of the change and the changing, he is both perfect man and perfect God. Being the symbol of perfect harmony between the change and the changing, Jesus Christ is the ultimate reality of change and transformation.[18]

Lee's proposal for a theology of change, though it has many brilliant points, is metaphysically positivistic and excessively rhetorical, as if it is making a universal claim for Change as an alternative metaphysics for a new theology. His hermeneutics of retrieval is admirable, but romantic, without applying the necessary hermeneutics of suspicion to his own tradition. His theology is a good model for Asian theo-logos of religions, but not for Asian theo-praxis of liberation, since it lacks a sufficient consideration of historical situations. In a passionate polemic against the Western metaphysics of contradiction, Lee, contrary to his intention, also fell into the trajectory of theo-logos, though he began from a theo-daoian perspective. He forgot that *do,* by definition, cannot be described objectively but only heuristically. The *do,* as the constant change, has no fixed face; its many faces change constantly from context to context and from person to person. Hence, in the dynamic hermeneutics of *do,* the context and the role of an interpreter are mutually constitutive. The *do* hermeneutics requires a creative and holistic engagement consisting of an interpreter (a community of interpretation), the context, and the trajectory of *do.* At the same time, it is a *do* (skill) for

---

18 Lee, *Theology of Change,* 99.

interpreters to discern how they can participate appropriately in the cosmic movement of *Do* (or the Way of God) at any given time.

## The Paths of Do (道脈 *Do-Maek*) in the Bible

If Ryu Yŏngmo and Jung Yong Lee read the Bible in Confucian ways, Pyŏn Ch'an-lin (1934-1985) made a creative interpretation with Daoist imaginations. Daoism here does not refer to the organized Chinese religion but to an ascetic tradition (*Sŏndo*) that transmitted through Korea's long history, such as with the thoughts of Mountain Immortal (*Sinsŏn*) and elegant culture (*Pungryu*). However, his idiosyncratic interpretations are much beyond traditional theological frameworks and so much arguable and subject to careful scrutiny. This treatment is only to introduce a further example of autogenously unique interpretations of the Bible in Korea, withholding my theological view on Pyŏn's thought.

Pyŏn argued that "the Bible is not a document for any particular religion; it is a document of the Great *Do* (大道)." He wrote:

> The authentic path of the Great Do that stretched out in the Bible was the path of *Sŏn* (仙脈). The Bible is a document that hides the mystery of *Sŏn*. The paths of *Do* leading up to Enoch, Melchizedek, Elijah, Moses, and Jesus were undeveloped golden paths until this day. *Sŏn*, the spiritual path of the living person, is a mysterious revelation that cannot be deciphered without East Asian wisdom.[19]

---

19 Pyŏn Ch'al-lin, *The Principles of the Bible*, vol. 1 (Korean) (Seoul, Korea: Han'guk

In this text, Pyŏn believes that the Bible reveals "the paths of *Do*," which have remained elusive to Western theologians and scholars. The core of the Old and New Testaments is cultivating the *do* through *Sŏn*, the development of one's mind-heart field. As the Garden of Eden refers to the symbolic name for a place of cultivating the *do*, the Old Testament recounts diverse methods for cultivating the *do*. In contrast, the New Testament explains the principles of cultivation. Together the entire Bible, for him, shows broadly the two paths of *do*: one for the living and one for the dead. Ordinary humans could only proceed on the path of the dead, as Adam and Eve failed to attain the *do* of the living by eating the unpermitted fruit of good and evil. Instead, they should have eaten the fruit of life that could lead to the paths to eternal life, the paths of the living, which are the central, and still hidden, pillars of the Bible.

> The biblical paths of *do* form the paths of the living, which are the un-developed treasures not yet been discovered. Enoch, Melchizedek, and Elijah were not the dead whose souls only went to Heaven. They ascended without dying and with the complete transformation... The paths of the living refer to the path of *Sŏn*, lively ascending to Heaven. They are the original paths of *do* and the true nature of the living, attaining without death.[20]

Pyŏn considered that the paths of the living represent the historical accounts of attaining the *do* (道通). He used Enoch, Elijah, and

---

Shinhak Yŏn'guso, 2019), 11.

20 Ibid, 67.

Jesus as the representative biblical figures who attained the do. In the Bible, a person can accomplish it in two ways: transformation and resurrection. Enoch and Elijah accomplished it in the path of transformation. But since ordinary people cannot do it by transformation, Jesus developed and perfected the path of resurrection by executing death and raising from the dead. Further, he said, "The paths of the dead are those of blood and flesh, and the paths of the living are born again with the blood of Christ,"[21] Therefore, he explained, Jesus was incarnated into the human body not by a fleshly conception in blood relation but by a spiritual conception (of *do*) with no human father.

As such, Pyŏn's biblical interpretations move beyond traditional hermeneutical horizons by centering on the notion of *do* in an exceedingly allegorical way. However, his uncharacteristic exegesis of the Bible needs careful scrutiny. Korean Biblical scholars and theologians need to carefully review his interpretations in order to analyze his theology systematically.

## Some Suggestions for Constructive Korean Biblical Hermeneutics of *Do*

The discussions of a theology of *Do* may shed some lights on how to conduct a Korean biblical interpretation influenced by the concept of *Do*. First is to pay attention to contextual literacy. Influenced by Western missionaries, theological education in Korea

---

21 Ibid, 64.

has focused on *textual literacy* to "catch up" with Western biblical studies and theology. As a result, Korean theological education has neglected and ignored the studies of their *contextual literacy*, such as Korean and East Asian cultures, religions, concepts, and metaphors. In this context, indigenous Korean Christian thinkers such as Ryu Yŏngmo, Lee Jung Yong, and Pyŏn Ch'an-lin are significant and their work functions as an antidote to Western-dominated Korean theological education.

In the history of Korean Christian thought, for example, in his well-known book, Ryu Tong-sik summarized three figures as representing Korean theological landscape: Park Hyung-ryong (1897-1978, Evangelical Presbyterian), Kim Chae-joon (1901-1987, Ecumenical Presbyterian), and Chung Kyung-ok (1903-1945, Liberal Methodist).[22] Park Hyung-ryong founded the conservative, dogmatic school (presently, Chongshin University), and his Calvinist fundamentalism contributed to two major schisms among Korean Presbyterian churches; the schisms were related to biblical inerrancy and the World Council of Churches. Kim Chae-joon established a progressive theological school with active social participation, which developed minjung theology (Hanshin University). Chung Kyung-ok initiated the liberal theological school that has promoted Korean theologies of indigenization (Methodist Theological University).

All three received Western theological educations (Park, Princeton Seminary and Southern Baptist Seminary; Kim, Princeton seminary; Chung, Garrett seminary) and shared the task of trans-

---

22 Ryu Tong-sik, *The Veins of Korean Theologies: An Introduction to the History of Korean Theological Thought* (Korean) (Seoul, Korea: Chŏnmangsa 1982).

mitting their learning to Korea. Therefore, Ryu's book regrettably showed that the veins of Korean theology were essentially just American and Western theologies. Hence, in other places, I argued that Korean indigenous theological thinkers like Ryu Yŏngmo must be included in the list of veins since they offer authentic indigenous resources for the formulation of *bona fide* Korean theologies.[23]

Second is to consider hermeneutics of retrieval and multiple textual hermeneutics. Ryu Yŏngmo's claim to regard East Asian Scriptures as the Old Testament was a warning against the cultural illiteracy of Korean Christians; it was also a rhetorical statement that Korean Christians should now confess Christian faith genuinely as Koreans, while acknowledging our cultural and religious traditions. Ryu called this approach *chesori*, a voice out from the gut (whole mind and body), not just from the brain (cognition). *Chesori* demands a radical contextual theology, namely, as seeking Christian wholeness by owning up to our own metaphors. This task involves in-depth hermeneutics of retrieval in and through multitextual hermeneutics or interpreting our multireligious scriptures and traditions with Western biblical and theological resources. It also entails hermeneutics of restoration of our own theological, cultural, religious, and spiritual resources, much of which unfortunately have been destroyed by anti-indigenous and hostile Western Christian missions and evangelism.

Third is applying the hermeneutics of suspicion. Because of the

---

23 See Kim Heup-Young, "The 50 Years of Korean Systematic Theology: A Cross-Cultural Reflection," in *The 50 Years of Theological Studies* (Korean), ed. Han'guk Munhwa Yŏn'guwŏn (Seoul, Korea: Hyean, 2003), 139-88.

West's negative effects on Korean theology, the hermeneutics of suspicion must be an integral part of an effort to unearth and restore a theology with Korean-ness. Western Christianity itself is a translated and altered religion; correspondingly, Chinese Buddhism is an "altered Buddhism." Chinese Buddhism was introduced through the Daoian conceptual framework and was significantly shaped by Daoism. Similarly, Western Christianity was translated and altered in and through Greek philosophy to develop in the form of *logos* theology. Hence, Western theology is not universal but only contextually legitimate for the West. Therefore, Korean theology and biblical hermeneutics must decontextualize Western theology and hermeneutics from the Western context by employing hermeneutics of critique and suspicion. The hermeneutics of suspicion is a significant discovery of twentieth-century theology, as David Tracy stated, "There is no innocent interpretation, no unambiguous tradition, no history-less, subject-less interpreter, no abstract, general situation, no method to guarantee certainty."[24] After this process, Korean Christians can recontextualize with a good understanding of our contexts (contextual literacy) in support of the hermeneutics of retrieval and restoration. Modern biblical scholarship has various developed tools that can be an essential in this rehabilitation and reconstruction of Korean biblical hermeneutics and theology.

---

24 For the hermeneutics of suspicion, see David Tracy, "Theological Method," in *Christian Theology: An Introduction to Its Traditions and Tasks*, ed. Peter C. Hodgson and Robert H. King (Minneapolis, MN: Fortress Press, 1994), 36.

## Further Thoughts

By the adoption of *do* as theological root-metaphor and hermeneutical principle, theo-dao and *do* biblical hermeneutics can move
beyond the limits of Western dualistic theologies (theo-logos and
theo-praxis) and analytical-historical hermeneutics to produce
more biblical interpretations through Korean/East Asian thoughts.
To construct a solid biblical hermeneutic of *do*, first of all, theologians
must improve our contextual and textual literacy with adequate hermeneutics of suspicion. Then, we can develop constructive Korean
Biblical hermeneutics of retrieval and restoration in the application
of multiple textual hermeneutics by reading the Bible with our indigenous multireligious scriptures. For this, valuable insights can be
found from creative Korean Christian thinkers, such as Ryu Yŏngmo
and his intratextual hermeneutic, Lee Jung Young and his *yin-yang*
hermeneutic of Change, and even a modified form of Pyŏn Ch'an-lin's
*do* hermeneutic.

Furthermore, Koreans have an excellent language (*Han'gŭl*) for
the interpretation of the Bible. Note how Ryu Yŏngmo employed
Hangul to express an intention of biblical terms. For example,
*mal-ssum* (말-씀), the Korean translation of the Greek logos (Jn. 1:1),
is more biblically relevant than its English term, the Word, or even
the Greek logos itself. The Korean term implies both the word (*mal*)
and the deed (*ssum*) like *do* (道). Similarly, Korean has a unique naming of the Triune God (하나님 *hananim*) which means both one and
many at the same time, a translation hardly found in other languages.
However, there has been a tendency (anti-indigenous taboo) to emphasize differentiation rather than to utilize such excellences of

*Han'gŭl* for translating and interpreting the Bible. Although the more homologous term to *ruach* in the Old Testament and *pneuma* in the New Testament would be *ki* (氣 *qi* in Pinyin), a unique East Asian term connoting the wholeness of breathing, wind, and spirit, Korean Bible translations avoided it and instead used *yŏng* (靈); this may have been to make a clear distinction and emphasize the spiritual dimension.

Another example would be a Korean translation of John 12:24. It includes *miral* (밀알), which is a translation from an altered English translation ("a grain of wheat") from the original Greek (*kokkos tou sitou*), which means more likely "a seed of grain." Ryu Yŏngmo changed it to "*ssial*" (씨알) which means literally "a seed of grain" that would be both biblically and contextually (where the main food is not wheat but rice) more appropriate. To read the Bible more appropriately and thoroughly as Koreans, Korean Christians should further retrieve, recover, and restore such excellences of *Han'gŭl* in translating and interpreting the Bible and doing theology, with the fullest freedom of "owning up to our own metaphors."

Although a Western, Bede Griffiths (1907-1993), a British Benedictine monk who lived many years in Indian ashrams, shared a prophetic insight:

> This may sound very paradoxical and unreal, but for centuries now the western world has been following the path of *yang*—of the masculine, active, aggressive, rational, scientific mind—and has brought the world near destruction. It is time now to recover the path of *yin*, of the feminine, passive, patient, intuitive and poetic mind. This is the path which the *Tao Te Ching* [*Do*] sets before us.[25]

This passage agrees with my thesis: the paradigm of *Yang* Christianity (Western theo-logos) has become problematic and is waning, and it is time to restore the paradigm of *Yin* Christianity (Eastern theo-dao), which is waxing. Finally, therefore, it is time now to read the Bible freely through our interpretative metaphors such as *do* for recovery and rehabilitation of harmony, peace, and the wholeness of the polarized and broken world.

---

25 Bede Griffiths, *Universal Wisdom: A Journey through the Sacred Wisdom of the World* (San Francisco: Harper San Francisco, 1994), 27.

CHAPTER TEN

# Theodaoian Epistemology
# in the Global Age of Decolonization

Abstract

In einer Zeit, in der die Entkolonialisierung des Wissens und die
Anerkennung verschiedener Epistemologien gefordert werden,
setzt Theodao (Theologie des Dao) einen kritischen Kontrapunkt
zu westlich-zentrierten intellektuellen Paradigmen. Ausgehend von
den tiefen Einsichten des Daoismus und des Konfuzianismus stellt
die Theodao-Epistemologie die vorherrschende monochromatische
Logik des westlichen Denkens in Frage, indem sie für eine ganzhei-
tliche Weltsicht plädiert, die die reichen und oft marginalisierten
Erzählungen indigener Wissenssysteme integriert. Im Mittelpunkt
dieser Erkenntnistheorie stehen die Konzepte Do/Dao (der Weg),
Ki/Qi (metakosmische Energie) und T'aegŭk/Taiji (das Große
Endgültige) und ihr dynamisches Zusammenspiel von Yin und
Yang, die zusammen ein Verständnis des Kosmos als komplexe, mi-
teinander verbundene Einheit fördern. In diesem Beitrag wird un-
tersucht, wie diese Elemente die Epistemizität - die systematische
Auslöschung nicht-westlicher Wissensformen - überwinden und

eine Theologie unterstützen, die Vielfalt und Widerstandsfähigkeit inmitten globaler Herausforderungen fördert. Die theodaoische Erkenntnistheorie verfolgt einen transformativen Ansatz für globales Wissen und strebt eine Zukunft an, in der verschiedene erkenntnistheoretische Traditionen nebeneinander bestehen und sich gegenseitig bereichern, um ein gerechteres und ganzheitlicheres Verständnis von Wahrheit zu erreichen.

## Introduction: Theological Colonialism in Korea and Theodao (Theology of Dao)

### Theological Colonialism and the Rise of Christianity in Korea

The contemporary Christian landscape in Korea, predominantly shaped by Western Protestant theology, exemplifies a profound case of theological colonialism. This theology, deeply rooted in European traditions and propagated through American missionary efforts, has profoundly influenced Korean seminaries, often sidelining indigenous religious and cultural contexts in favor of a more conservative Western theological framework. Interestingly, even as adherence to traditional theological doctrines wanes in the West, this influence not only persists but has intensified in Korea, particularly among Korean Neo-Calvinists, underscored by the establishment of institutions such as Abraham Kuyper's research centers.

The rise of Christianity in Korea post-1945, particularly the surge in evangelical fundamentalism, serves as a complex example of both adaptation to and resistance against external influences. This period, immediately following the liberation from Japanese colonial rule, saw an intensified affirmation of Western influences in Korea, partly driven by geopolitical shifts during the Cold War. Western hegemony was not merely a continuation of cultural imposition but evolved into a nuanced form of ideological exchange where Korean society adapted Western religious forms to its own ends.

Evangelical fundamentalism, often perceived as a bastion of conservative Western values, played a paradoxical role in Korean society. On one hand, it represented an adoption of Western religious hegemony, reinforcing a new form of cultural dominance after Japanese colonialism. On the other hand, it provided the tools for spiritual and cultural resistance. Korean evangelical movements utilized the structures and fervor of fundamentalism not only to forge a distinct Korean Christian identity but also as a framework to resist the residual influences of Japan's oppressive colonial policies. The vigor with which Korean Christianity adopted these elements highlighted a deliberate act of reclamation - transforming an imported faith into a potent symbol of national resilience and autonomy.

### Epistemicide and Identity Formation Post-Colonization

This complex interplay between acceptance and resistance is pivotal in understanding the role of Christianity in shaping Korea's post-colonial epistemology. The enthusiastic embrace of evangelical Christianity was, paradoxically, both an act of submission to and an act of defiance against different forms of hegemony. As such, the Christianization of Korea post-1945 is emblematic of broader epistemic shifts that occurred in response to the nation's historical experiences of colonization and liberation.

The identity formation through Christianization after Japanese colonization, therefore, plays a critical role in the discourse on *epistemicide*.[1] It illustrates how imported religious ideologies were appropriated to reconstruct a national identity, often at the cost of sidelining Korea's indigenous epistemological traditions. This resulted in a form of epistemicide, where the pre-existing pluralistic intellectual traditions were suppressed under the overwhelming influence of a monotheistic worldview. Understanding this dynamic provides essential insights into the broader narrative of Theodaoian epistemology, which seeks to heal these wounds by reintegrating and revaluing the indigenous and marginalized knowledge systems of Korea. This epistemology advocates for a return to a more holistic, interconnected worldview, recognizing and rectifying the historical and ongoing impacts of epistemic suppression.

For example, this form of epistemicide led to the systematic dismantling of key components of Korean spiritual and intellectual life, such as 'Do/Dao' (the Way)[2], 'ki/qi' (metacosmic energy),[3] and

---

1 See Boaventura de Sousa Santos, *Epistemologies of the South. Justice Against Epistemicide* (New York, 2014).

2 As the widely used root-metaphor in all classical East Asian religions, including Confucianism, Daoism, and Buddhism, the Way ('do' in Korean, 'dao' [tao] in Chinese) is a very inclusive term with various meanings. For example, "[D]ao is a way, a path, a road, and by common metaphorical extension, it becomes in ancient China the right way of life, the way of governing, the ideal way of human existence, the way of the cosmos, the generative-normative way (pattern, path, course) of existence as such," Herbert Fingarette, *Confucius. The Secular as Sacred* (New York, 1972), 19.

3 Ki/qi ('ki' in Korean, 'qi' [ch'i] in Chinese) is a term similar to 'pneuma' and can be translated variously as energy, vital force, breath, or wind.

'T'aegŭk/Tàijí' (the Great Ultimate). Today, over a century of epistemically oppressive education within Korean seminaries has culminated in a generation of Christian leaders who, while often disconnected from their rich traditional intellectual heritage, ironically regard this theological dominance as a form of spiritual renaissance.

## Theodao: Reintegrating Indigenous Knowledge Systems

This paper proposes a radical rethinking of Korean theology through the lens of Theodao (Theology of Dao) - an approach that centralizes the core East Asian concept of Do/Dao. Theodao aims to reintegrate essential Korean and East Asian religious cultures and theological resources into contemporary theological discourse, thereby restoring a nuanced and comprehensive understanding of these rich traditions. This initiative is introduced with enthusiasm, leveraging the platform provided by this esteemed journal.

For German-speaking readers less familiar with the multi-religious context of East Asia, particularly Korea, this paper will delve into the "Ugŭmch'i phenomenon," as articulated by a notable Catholic resistance poet during Korea's military dictatorship era. This exploration will highlight Theodao's transformative potential in fostering a distinctly Korean epistemology — K-epistemology — responsive to the demands of our global age.

## 1. The Ugŭmch'i Phenomenon: A Parable for Theodaoian Epistemology

*Natural Resilience and Ki/Qi*

The phenomenon of small fish swimming upstream in a polluted South Korean stream during rainfall provides a vivid metaphor for resilience and defiance against adverse conditions. This natural event is interpreted as a profound testament to nature's capacity for resistance and renewal, first observed by Chi-ha Kim (1944-2022), a notable resistance poet during South Korea's military dictatorship era.[4] After enduring prolonged imprisonment for his political beliefs, Chi-ha Kim settled in a small city in South Korea, where he witnessed the transformative effect of rainfall on a local, polluted stream. The sight of small fish ascending against the formidable current inspired a significant shift in his philosophical outlook, connecting this natural resilience to the concept of ki/qi. In East Asian thought, ki/qi, often translated as "energy" or "breath", encompasses both material and immaterial aspects of life and is understood to embody the dual qualities of yin (receptive) and yang (active), continuously interacting to shape the cosmos.[5]

---

4 See Chi-ha Kim, *Saengmyŏng [Life]* (Seoul, 1992); also: Heup Young Kim, *A Theology of Dao* (Maryknoll, 2017).

5 Ki/qi is interpreted to have two forms of movement: yin (negative or female) and yang (positive or male), which form a unity of complementary opposites such as the Great Ultimate (T'aegŭk in Korean, Tài jí [T'ai-chi] in Chinese).

## *Historical Resonance: The Ugŭmch'i Battle*

Chi-ha's reflection on the resilience of the fish brought to mind the historic Ugŭmch'i Battle during the Donghak Peasant (followers of Eastern Learning) Uprising in December 1894, where the minjung - oppressed and marginalized peasants - confronted formidable Korean and Japanese allied forces.[6] This historic event is interpreted within Theodaoian epistemology as an embodiment of cosmic harmony and resilience, mirroring the natural world's patterns. Such historical and natural phenomena illustrate the Theodaoian principle that understanding and aligning with cosmic forces can empower even the most marginalized communities to challenge oppressive structures.

This narrative transcends a mere historical recount, introducing *Ecodao* — a Theodaoian ecological theology that underscores the importance of living in harmony with the natural world.[7] This eco-theology calls for an engagement with the environment informed by the wisdom of ki/qi, advocating for a dynamic resilience that sustains and rejuvenates life. This ecological interpretation of Dao prompts reevaluating our interactions with the environment, suggesting that a deeper understanding of ki/qi can foster more sustainable and harmonious ecological practices.[8]

---

6 Minjung in Korean literally means 'the multitude of people', but in Minjung theology, the term is closely related to the oppressed, exploited, and marginalized groups. Minjung Theology was heavily influenced by Chi-ha Kim's earlier thoughts.

7 See Heup Young Kim, "Ecodao. An Ecological Theology of Dao," in eds. Laura Hobgood, Whitney Bauman, *The Bloomsbury Handbook of Religion and Nature: The Elements* (London, 2018), 99-108.

## *Epistemicide and Reawakening Indigenous Knowledge*

Chi-ha poignantly reflects on the impacts of Western and Japanese colonialism on Korean epistemology, which he characterizes as an epistemicide—the systematic erasure and suppression of indigenous Korean and broader East Asian epistemological frameworks. By connecting the ecological resilience observed in the natural world with the philosophical resilience of the Donghak peasants, Chi-ha advocates for the reawakening of suppressed knowledge systems. He terms this resurgence the "Ugŭmch'i phenomenon," representing a broader, cosmic movement towards reclaiming and revitalizing the oppressed spiritual and epistemic energies of the minjung — the common people of Korea. Chi-ha poetically described:

> The collective spiritual ki/qi of the self-conscious minjung is a great cosmic movement to be united with the primordial spiritual ki/qi of history, i. e., the yin-yang movement of ki/qi, against the demonic currents of history that poured down against them. I will call this the Ugŭmch'i Phenomenon.

> Ah, Ah. The spiritual ki/qi of our minjung, the vitalization and spiritualization, with the climax of 1894, has been displaced, alienated, rooted out, oppressed, disgraced, divided, imprisoned, neglected, destroyed,

---

8 See Kim, *Theology*, 104-114; also: Heup Young Kim, "Theodao. Integrating Ecological Consciousness in Daoism, Confucianism, and Christian Theology," in ed. John Hart, *The Wiley Blackwell Companion to Religion and Ecology* (Oxford, 2017), 204-22.

and enslaved — therefore, has been slaughtered until now — by the wrong foreign ideas of the West or Japan. Even now, the flags of death are waving in the street. Only few people are searching around for the true subjectivity of minjung.[9]

The Ugŭmch'i Phenomenon serves as a compelling parable within Theodaoian epistemology, symbolizing the potential for both ecological and theological renewal through alignment with fundamental cosmic energies. This exploration underscores the urgent need to revisit and integrate traditional Korean and East Asian epistemological insights to address and transform contemporary theological, ecological, and philosophical discourses.

## 2. Ki/Qi Epistemology: Unveiling the Subversive Wisdom of Nature

### The Rain-Cleansed Stream and Ecological Renewal

These observations of the rain-cleansed stream and the ascending fish not only challenge the prevailing technocratic and industrialized worldviews but also serve as foundational elements in Theodao. Integrating Daoian and Neo-Confucian wisdom, Theodao with ki/qi epistemology offers rich pathways for both ecological and spiritual renewal, promoting a deeper connection with the natural world and fostering a holistic approach to contemporary environ-

---

9 Kim, *Theology*, 23.

mental challenges.

## *Chi-ha's Paradigm Shift: From Han to Ki/Qi*

Chi-ha's parable marks a significant shift in his intellectual journey. His earlier work centered on the concept of *han*, a deep-seated collective psychosomatic experience of oppression and suffering.[10] He developed a hermeneutics of suspicion grounded in *han*, advocating for its transformation into a force for change — a perspective that shaped minjung theology.[11] However, the parable signifies a rediscovery of Daoian wisdom and a move toward a hermeneutics of retrieval rooted in ki/qi. This shift represents a departure from the dualistic framework of *han* toward the complementary, inclusive, and harmonious worldview of yin-yang. Chi-ha's enlightenment emerged from recognizing the source of the life-empowering force - the ki/qi that animated both the fish swimming upstream and the minjung in their resistance.

Ki/qi, often translated as "energy" or "breath," is akin to the concept of *pneuma* in Western traditions. It denotes the primordial life force that permeates all existence - a concept that resonates with

---

10 Han became well known by the use of Korean minjung theologians. Suh Nam-dong (1918-1984), a founder of minjung theology, defined han as "the suppressed, amassed and condensed experience of oppression caused by mischief or misfortune so that it forms a kind of 'lump' in one's spirit." Nam-dong Suh, "Towards a Theology of Han," in ed. the Christian Conference of Asia Commission on Theological Concerns, *Minjung Theology: People as the Subjects of History* (Maryknoll, 1981), 55-72, here: 68. Suh's theology of han was heavily influenced by Kim Chi Ha's earlier thought.

11 Hyun Kyung Chung, "Han-puri. Doing Theology from Korean Women's Perspective," *The Ecumenical Reviews* 40/1 (1988): 27-36.

notions of Gaia or *anima mundi* in other ecological and spiritual traditions. Ki/qi embodies a holistic and inclusive understanding of reality, recognizing the interconnectedness of all beings and the dynamic interplay of yin and yang energies.

## *Theodao and the Epistemological Shift*

This epistemological shift toward ki/qi extends beyond a linear historical perspective, embracing the vast horizon of Dao that encompasses both the cosmos and human experience. Chi-ha offered a Theodaoian interpretation of history, revealing ki/qi's flow as the underlying pulse of both individual lives and global events. He saw in the turbulent waters of the stream a microcosm of this dance, with the yin and yang currents pushing and pulling in perpetual harmony.

In this journey of rediscovery, Chi-ha's parable becomes a powerful metaphor — a guide for embracing the subversive dance of change and thriving in the ever-changing tapestry of existence.

Chi-ha beautifully captures the dynamic flow of ki/qi in his description of water: "The ki/qi of water moves in both directions of yin and yang. While the yang of water runs downward, the yin of water runs upward. While water flows downward, water flows upward at the same time."[12] This simultaneous existence of opposing yet complementary forces — the downstream current (representing the river's overall descent) and the countercurrent (symbolizing the fish battling upwards) becomes a metaphor for the flow of ki/qi

---

12 Kim, *Theology*, 20-21.

and its relationship to history.

Rejecting a purely linear view of history, Chi-ha emphasizes the simultaneous movement of ki/qi in "a converging-diverging movement of 'in and out' and 'quality and quantity.'" Like the fish defying the current, history is not merely a forward march; it is a rhythmic ebb and flow — a constant return to its origin. Chi-ha challenges the Western tendency to categorize and compartmentalize, urging us to embrace the paradoxical unity of progression and retrogression, convergence and divergence.

Chi-ha's innovative epistemology of ki/qi offers a refreshingly holistic perspective compared to Western dualistic and analytic approaches. He views ki/qi as the source and medium of primordial empowerment - not merely a concept to be dissected, but a pulsating life force that connects us to nature and to each other. This understanding resonates with the biblical concept of pneuma, breathing life into both the minjung's resistance and the fish's defiant ascent.

Chi-ha's parable and ki/qi epistemology pave the way for a revolutionary Theodao and Ecodao (Ecological Theology of Dao). These approaches, grounded in the wisdom of ki/qi, transcend the pitfalls of Western dualism and historicism. They offer a path toward addressing eco-socioeconomic injustices not through division and categorization, but by embracing the onto-cosmic dance of nature - the subversive resilience found in the "simultaneously converging-diverging movement" of the cosmos. This framework invites us to reimagine our relationship with nature, grounded in respect, interdependence, and a harmonious flow with the yin-yang currents of ki/qi.

Informed by the dynamic phenomenology of ki/qi, Theodao

broadens the East Asian anthropocosmic view to encompass a profound unity of Heaven (God), humanity, and Earth (cosmos) through the dynamic spirit of ki/qi. This ki/qi/pneumato-anthropocosmic epistemology resonates deeply with Neo-Confucian epistemology of cosmic organismic unity. Theodao further enriches it by positing a spiritual communion between humanity and the universe, orchestrated by the ever-flowing dance of ki/qi.[13]

This vision, drawing upon elements of yin-yang correlation, Yijing's cosmology, and Neo-Confucian worldview, holds immense potential for revitalizing theologies and religious traditions grappling with ecological and postmodern challenges. It offers a potent resource for healing, revitalizing, and preserving contemporary Christian theologies that have become fragmented in the face of these complexities.

The Ugŭmch'i phenomenon stands as a luminous testament to the transformative vision of ki/qi. It exemplifies how ki/qi fosters a profound symbiosis within the life network, exceeding the limitations of transactional *societas* or fellowship-based *communitas*. However, for Theodao to fully bloom, it must transcend the pitfalls of naive idealism and individualistic mysticism. Instead, it should embrace the rich tapestry of the eco-socio-cosmic narrative of exploited life and nature. This narrative urges us to articulate their stories within the intricate web of interconnectedness, where ki/qi's spiritual communion emerges as a potent salvific force, facilitating liberation and reconciliation.

The metaphorical tapestry of the Ugŭmch'i Phenomenon weaves

---

13 See Kim, *Theology*, 221-22.

together the narratives of resilient fishes battling the river's tumult and the valiant minjung defying overwhelming odds in the battle. This tapestry exemplifies the transformative power of aligning with the cosmic flow of ki/qi. It highlights the profound interconnectedness of all life forms and the potential for collective empowerment and healing. Moreover, it challenges existing theological and ecological paradigms, demanding a more inclusive and holistic understanding of the cosmos — one where exploitation and suffering are transformed into sources of strength and renewal.

In sum, the epistemology of ki/qi, as illuminated by its phenomenology, offers a revolutionary lens for understanding life's resilience in the face of adversity. It emphasizes a profound 'ki/qi-sociocosmic narrative', inspiring a transformative theology deeply connected with the unity of cosmic elements and the harmonious flow of life's energies.[14] This approach addresses eco-socioeconomic injustices and forges a path toward a more holistic and interconnected understanding of the universe. Ultimately, it leads toward healing, renewal, and a harmonious dance with the onto-cosmic pulse of ki/qi.

---

14 Kim, *Ecodao*, 104-5.

## 3. T'aegŭk/Tàijí (the Great Ultimate) Epistemology for Onto-cosmic Resilience and the Subversive Dance of Nature

### The Concept of T'aegŭk/Tàijí

The concept of T'aegŭk/Tàijí (the Great Ultimate) is a central tenet in Theodao that epitomizes the ultimate state of harmony and balance within the cosmos. More than mere survival, onto-cosmic resilience, as articulated within Theodaoian epistemology, represents an active and continuous adaptation of beings and systems within the dynamic web of existence. This resilience is pivotal for sustaining harmony amidst the perpetual flux of cosmic forces, embodying East Asian wisdom traditions that prioritize balance and fluidity in the processes of life.

### Dynamic Equilibrium of Yin and Yang

In the realms of Daoian and Neo-Confucian thought, T'aegŭk/Tàijí signifies the dynamic equilibrium of yin (receptive, feminine) and yang (active, masculine) energies. This philosophical stance transcends Western dualistic epistemology, which often pits binaries in opposition. T'aegŭk/Tàijí offers a holistic perspective, viewing opposites as complementary components within a cohesive whole. This framework encourages a reinterpretation of conflicts and dichotomies as opportunities for achieving deeper harmony and balance across various dimensions of existence.

Zhou Dunyi (1017-1073), a seminal Neo-Confucian thinker, of-

290 Theodao (Theology of Dao) II

fers a compelling elucidation of this concept in "An Explanation of the Diagram of the Great Ultimate." Zhou articulates the continuous interaction between yin and yang as the foundational dynamic of all existence:

> The Great Ultimate, through movement, generates yang. When its activity reaches its limit, it becomes tranquil. Through tranquility, the Great Ultimate generates yin. When tranquility reaches its limit, activity begins again. So, movement and tranquility alternate and become the root of each other, giving rise to the distinction of yin and yang, and the two modes are thus established.[15]

This description underscores the inherently cyclical nature of cosmic processes. Each phase births its counterpart, ensuring a perpetual state of transformation and balance — essential for the endurance and adaptation of systems over time.

### Onto-cosmic Resilience and the Ugŭmch'i Phenomenon

Drawing insights from both the Ugŭmch'i Phenomenon and T'aegŭk/Tàijí principles, this narrative transcends traditional environmentalism, suggesting a deeper, cosmic return to the origins of life and existence. These theological/philosophical voyages advocate for a reconnection with the foundational processes where life is in constant regeneration and renewal, driven by the harmonious interplay of yin and yang. Such a reorientation is transformative,

---

15 Wing-tsit Chan, trans., *A Source Book in Chinese Philosophy* (Princeton, 1963), 463.

fostering resilience and creativity at an onto-cosmic level.

Daodejing further mirrors these philosophical insights. Laozi describes the cosmic genesis through the interplay of the Dao:

> [D]ao produced the One. The One produced the two. The two produced the three. And the three produced the ten thousand things. The ten thousand things carry the yin and embrace the yang, and through the blending of the material force [ki/qi] they achieve harmony.[16]

This cascade of creation, orchestrated through the yin-yang dynamics facilitated by ki/qi, underscores the intrinsic resilience and creative potential inherent in the natural order. It reflects the resilience observed in both natural phenomena and human endeavors, emphasizing a state of dynamic equilibrium. This echoes the transformative power of the Ugŭmch'i Phenomenon, where the small fish defies the current and the minjung resists oppression, demonstrating the potential for resilience and renewal inherent in the cosmos itself.

By embracing the onto-cosmic dance of the Great Ultimate, we can move beyond dualistic thinking and embrace a more holistic understanding of resilience. Through the lens of Theodao, the Ugŭmch'i Phenomenon becomes a powerful metaphor for this transformative journey, reminding us that the path to healing and renewal lies in aligning ourselves with the harmonious flow of yin and yang within the intricate web of existence.

---

16 Chan, *Source*, 160-1.

*Philosophical and Theological Implications*

The epistemology of T'aegŭk/Tàijí extends beyond mere philosophical abstraction; it weaves a rich tapestry of kinship within the
cosmos. Neo-Confucian thinkers like Zhang Zai (1022-1077) and
Wang Yang-ming (1472-1529) articulated this interconnectedness,
offering an East Asian *inclusive humanism* in contrast to Western *exclusive humanism*. Zhang Zai's evocative lines from "The Western
Inscription" resonate with a profound ecological sentiment:

> Heaven is my father, and Earth is my mother, and even such a small
> creature as I find an intimate place in their midst. Therefore, that which
> fills the universe I regard as my body and that which directs the universe
> I consider as my nature. All people are my brothers and sisters, and
> all things are my companions.[17]

Wang Yang-ming further expanded this vision with 'the doctrine
of the Oneness of All Things.' He posits that the great human being
perceives Heaven, Earth, and all beings as one body - a cosmic
family.

> The great man regards Heaven, Earth, and the myriad things as one
> body. He regards the world as one family and the country as one person.
> As to those who make a cleavage between objects and distinguish be-
> tween the self and others, they are small men. That the great man can
> regard Heaven, Earth, and the myriad things as one body is not because

17 Chan, *Source*, 497.

he deliberately wants to do so, but because it is natural human nature of his mind that he does so.[18]

Intriguingly, the "Trinitarian key" in Pope Francis' encyclical *Laudato si'* finds echoes in this framework.[19] Chinese-American scholar Cheng Chung-ying proposed a Confucian-Christian interpretation of the Trinity, with God the Son as the ideal human, God the Father as the creative spirit of Heaven, and God the Holy Spirit as the receptive co-spirit of Earth. Cheng further suggested a synthesis:

If Heaven embodies the spirit of incessant creativity and the development of life and Earth the everlasting receptivity and consistence of love, then the human must embody their combination in a harmonious fusion and should apply both in appropriate measure in thought, emotion, and conduct. Heaven is a symbol of the cosmology of creativity and development; Earth is a symbol of an ecology of the combination of the two, this producing the ethics of integration and fulfillment of values. Hence, we see in the Confucian sage the trinity of Heaven, Earth, and human that embodies the unity of cosmology, ecology, and ethics.[20]

---

18 Chan Wing-tsit, trans., *Instructions for Practical Living and Other Neo-Confucian Writings* (New York, 1963), 272.

19 Pope Francis (Jorge Mario Bergoglio), *Laudato si' of the Holy Father on Care for Our Common Home* (Vatican, Encyclical Letter, 2017), 239.

20 Chung-ying Cheng, "The Trinity of Cosmology, Ecology, and Ethics in the Confucian Personhood," in eds. Mary Evelyn Tucker/John Berthrong, *Confucianism and Ecology. The Interrelation of Heaven, Earth, and Humans* (Cambridge, 1998), 211-36.

Chi-ha's parable of the resilient fish swimming upstream becomes a powerful embodiment of this onto-cosmic dance. It challenges us to move beyond anthropocentrism and embrace our interconnectedness with the cosmos. The Ugŭmch'i Phenomenon further showcases how collective action, aligned with the harmonious flow of ki/qi, can foster resilience and renewal within the interconnected web of life.

Embracing T'aegŭk/Tàijí principles invites us to transcend dualistic thinking, deepening our engagement with the world in ways that foster harmony and balance. The Ugŭmch'i Phenomenon serves as a metaphor for this potential alignment with the cosmic order, advocating for resilience through harmony and fostering a sustainable, balanced existence. This philosophical-theological approach not only enriches our understanding but also equips us to navigate the complexities of modern life with wisdom and equilibrium.

## 4. The Yin (Feminine) Epistemology of Dao and the Power of Subversive Return

### The Feminine Metaphors in Daodejing

In the Daodejing, Laozi presents a captivating depiction of Dao using evocative feminine metaphors, positioning Dao not merely as a passive entity but as the vibrant source of all creation. This portrayal of Dao as the 'mystical female' - the mother of all things, the root and ground of being - highlights its role as a dynamic and generative force. Through metaphors such as the uncarved block, which symbolizes original nature imbued with feminine qualities of receptivity and openness, Laozi elevates femininity beyond gender constraints, highlighting its essential, foundational, and generative qualities in the cosmic order. "The spirit of the valley never dies. It is called the mystical female. The gateway of the mystical female is called the root of Heaven and Earth." (*Daodejing* 6) Here, femininity is eternal, foundational, and generative, reminding us of our interconnectedness with the nurturing womb of nature.

## *Yin and the Principle of Return*

A. C. Graham's analysis of Laozi's texts reveals a preference for yin elements within the Daoian worldview, emphasizing aspects like emptiness, passivity, and wisdom. These qualities are not presented as weaknesses but as potent sources of strength and transformation, pointing to a philosophical approach that values balance and integration rather than domination or conflict. This reevaluation of yin's power underscores a broader, more inclusive epistemology that challenges the often aggressive, yang-dominated paradigms of Western thought. However, it is not to diminish the yang, but rather to recognize the inherent power and balance embedded in their interplay. As Graham points out, "Lao Tzu's strategy is not to exclude the positive, but to show that its effectiveness ultimately depends on its conformity to the negative."[21]

---

21 A. C. Graham, *Disputers of the Tao. Philosophical Argument in Ancient China* (La Salle, 1989), 223.

The principle of return is a key theme in understanding resilience and renewal in East Asian thoughts, as illustrated by Daodejing's verses on achieving complete vacuity and maintaining quietude. This philosophy celebrates the cycle of emptiness to creation, where each end is a new beginning, symbolizing the eternal, regenerative nature of Dao. This concept is mirrored in the natural resilience shown by the ascending fish in the Ugŭmch'i Phenomenon, exemplifying how adversity can lead to a rejuvenating return to fundamental principles, a dynamic dance of yin and yang. Laozi captures the paradoxical potency of weakness and emptiness in verses like:

> Attain complete vacuity, maintain steadfast quietude. All things come into being, and I see thereby their return. All things flourish, but each one returns to its root. This return to its root means tranquility. It is called returning to its destiny. To return to destiny is called the eternal [Dao].[22]

Laozi's feminine vision of Dao and the principles of reversal and return offer a powerful framework for understanding onto-cosmic resilience and balance. By embracing the 'mystical female', valuing the yin path, and recognizing the transformative power of returning to our originality, we can navigate the challenges of our universe with renewed wisdom and a deepened respect for the subtle power of nature's cyclical rhythms. This subversive return becomes a journey of reclaiming wholeness, fostering harmony, and aligning ourselves with the flow of the Dao - the mother of all things.

---

22 Chan, *Source*, 147.

## Wu-wei and Feminine Power

Deep within the heart of the *Daodejing* lies the potent concept of wu-wei, often translated as "non-action action." This paradoxical term, beautifully described by Bede Griffiths (1907-1993), a Benedictine mystic, as "actionless activity," defies simplistic interpretation. It embodies a state of dynamic and creative passivity, a receptivity that pulsates with the essence of the feminine. Griffiths saw in wu-wei a crucial counterpoint to the dominant masculine tendencies within Western religion. He eloquently linked wu-wei to the feminine principle, emphasizing its powerful form of receptivity:

> This passivity is an active passivity, a receptivity which is dynamic and creative, from which all life and fruitfulness, all live and communion grow. The world today needs to recover this sense of feminine power, which is complementary to the masculine and without which man becomes dominating, sterile, and destructive.[23]

In wu-wei, emptiness ceases to be mere void and transforms into a potent space of possibility. Griffiths beautifully illustrates this Daoian passage through everyday examples:

> "We make pots of clay, but it is the empty space in them which makes them useful. We make a wheel with many spokes joined in a hub, but it is the empty space in the hub which makes the wheel go round. We

---

23 Bede Griffiths, *Universal Wisdom. A Journey Through the Sacred Wisdom of the World* (San Francisco, 1994), 27.

make houses of brick and wood, but it is the empty spaces in the doors
and windows that make them habitable."[24]

This echoes Laozi's own evocative imagery, where valleys, emptiness, and yielding become sources of power and transformation.
It reminds us that true strength lies not in forceful manipulation,
but in aligning oneself with the natural flow of the universe - a flow
orchestrated by the dynamic interplay of yin and yang.

### Embracing Yin for Onto-Cosmic Resilience

The *Daodejing*, through its nuanced portrayal of the feminine principle, offers invaluable insights for building onto-cosmic resilience
in the face of contemporary challenges. By embracing the power
of yin - the receptive, yielding, and often undervalued aspects of
existence - we can foster a more harmonious relationship with the
cosmos. This harmony becomes a cornerstone of resilience, allowing us to adapt, evolve, and thrive within the dynamic web of life.

Griffiths' call to recognize the feminine aspect of God resonates
deeply within this framework. Embracing the nurturing, life-giving,
and interconnected qualities often associated with the feminine can
lead to a more holistic understanding of the divine, and consequently,
a more sustainable and peaceful coexistence with all beings.

Wu-wei, with its emphasis on the feminine (yin) principle, transcends cultural and religious boundaries. It offers a powerful vision
for navigating the complexities of our world, reminding us that true

---

24 Ibid, 27.

strength lies in receptivity, interconnectedness, and a profound respect for the generative power of emptiness. By embracing the wisdom of the *Daodejing* and the transformative teachings of wu-wei, we can contribute to a future where onto-cosmic resilience flourishes, nurtured by the harmonious interplay of yin and yang, masculine and feminine, and nature and spirit. This vision aligns with the Theodaoian pursuit of a more inclusive, balanced, and harmonious world.

## Conclusion: Theodaoian Epistemology in the Global Age of Decolonization

### *What Theodaoian Epistemology Represents*

Theodaoian Epistemology, a neologism derived from 'Theology' and 'Da' (Theo-Dao), signifies a unique theological and ethical perspective that integrates traditional East Asian wisdom, particularly Daoian and Neo-Confucian insights, into a cohesive framework for understanding knowledge and existence. This epistemology challenges the prevailing Western-centric paradigms by advocating for a more holistic, interconnected, and fluid approach to understanding the universe. It emphasizes harmony, balance, and the continuous interplay of opposites, reflecting the fundamental wisdom of Dao that everything is interconnected and in constant flux.

*Core Intentions of Theodaoian Epistemology*

1. Holistic Integration: Theodaoian Epistemology seeks to transcend the binary oppositions common in Western thought,
promoting a more integrative view that encompasses both the
spiritual and material aspects of existence.
2. Respect for Plurality: It advocates for an epistemological pluralism that values diverse ways of knowing, including indigenous
and marginalized perspectives, thereby enriching global
knowledge systems.
3. Healing Epistemicide: This approach aims to recover and revitalize suppressed narratives and knowledge systems that have
been marginalized by dominant intellectual traditions, especially in contexts like Korea, where colonial and Western influences have historically overshadowed local epistemologies.

*Implications for Korean Theological Work and Beyond*

In Korea, Theodaoian Epistemology offers a framework for
re-engaging with and re-valuing traditional Korean religious and
philosophical insights, such as those from Confucianism, Buddhism,
and Shamanism, which have been underrepresented in the dominant Christian discourse. By integrating these elements, Theodao
seeks to heal the wounds of epistemicide within Korean society
and contribute to a more nuanced and comprehensive understanding of Korean identity and spirituality.

Globally, Theodaoian Epistemology serves as a model for how
localized religious and philosophical insights can contribute to

broader theological and ethical discussions. It challenges theologians, ethicists, and philosophers around the world to consider more inclusive and harmonious approaches that acknowledge and utilize the diversity of global epistemological traditions. This model fosters a deeper understanding and appreciation of how different knowledge systems can coexist and enrich each other, promoting a more resilient and adaptive global intellectual ecosystem.

In conclusion, Theodaoian Epistemology is not merely an academic construct but a call to action for embracing a more inclusive, holistic, and harmonious approach to theology, ethics, and philosophy. It invites scholars and practitioners alike to reconsider the foundations of knowledge and the ways in which we engage with the world, advocating for a future where diverse epistemologies are not only recognized but celebrated as essential components of the global quest for wisdom.

## PART IV

# Korean Cosmic Spirituality and K-Theology

# CHAPTER ELEVEN

# Introducing Dasŏk Ryu Yŏngmo's Korean Spiritual Disciplines and his Poem "Being a Christian"

## Abstract

This chapter is intended to provide an introduction to, and critical analysis of, the religious thought of Dasŏk Ryu Yŏngmo (1890-1981), one of the most innovative religious thinkers in Korea's modern history. His thought profoundly influenced a generation of thinkers both in Korea's Christian tradition and in Confucianism, Daoism, and Buddhism. It will argue that Dasŏk's thought, though currently unstudied and hardly known outside Korea, is an important form of inculturation of Christian thought in the Korean context, and with potential wider learning points for theological construction beyond this context. Dasŏk integrated indigenous resources from the Confucian, Daoist, and Buddhist traditions to contextualise Christianity to a multi-religious Korean context. The paper situates Dasŏk's spirituality and thought in broader discussions of religious pluralism and will attempt to answer the question of whether Dasŏk can be considered a pluralist. A further original contribution is the translation and commentary on one of Dasŏk's most important works, "Being A Christian."

## Introduction[1]

Dasŏk Ryu Yŏngmo (1890-1981) is one of the most innovative religious thinkers in Korea's modern history.[2] He was the teacher of many significant Korean religious leaders of the twentieth century. His most famous disciple was Ham Sŏk-hŏn (1901-1989), who also became a guru of Korean *minjung*(민중) or the people's theology and movement.[3] Dasŏk's religious thought profoundly in-

---

1 A note on romanisation: for Korean Romanisation, this article basically uses the McCune-Reischauer system. Chinese characters are also romanised according to Korean pronunciation, except for *dao* (道).

2 The pen name of Ryu Yŏngmo 柳永模 is Dasŏk 多夕, which literally means "so many nights." This name symbolically shows his Daoist inclination (namely, night rather than day, emptiness rather than substance, non-being rather than being, etc.). The most important primary source for the study of Dasŏk's thought is the photocopies of his diaries which he wrote from 1956 to 1975, but they are extremely challenging even for Korean scholars to comprehend due to his recondite writing style and innovative usage of Korean language: Ryu Yŏngmo, *Dasŏk-ilji* 多夕日誌 [The Diaries of Dasŏk], 4 vols (Seoul: Hongikje, 1990). Fortunately, his faithful student Kim Hŭng-ho published their complete commentaries that become a crucial aid for the study of *Dasŏk's* thought: Kim Hŭng-ho, *Dasok-ilji Gongbu* 다석일지공부 [The Study of Dasŏk's Diaries], 7 vols (Seoul: Sol, 2001). Another important primary resource is collections of shorthand records of his lectures: Ryu Yŏngmo, *Dasŏk-kangŭi* 다석강의 [Lectures of Dasŏk], ed. Society for Dasŏk Studies (Seoul: Hyŏnamsa, 2006).

3 See Ham Sŏk Hŏn, *Queen of Suffering: A Spiritual History of Korea*, trans. E. Sang Yu (London: Friends World Committee for Consultation, 1985). *Minjung* in Korean means the oppressed people. *Minjung* theology argued for the preferential option to the *minjung* and that they are real, authentic subjects of history in the reign of God and so of

fluenced significant intellectuals in Christianity and other religious traditions in Korea such as Confucianism, Daoism, and Buddhism. The primary purpose of this article is to introduce Dasŏk as an important, though often understudied, religious scholar in Korea, by focusing on his original understanding and interpretation of the Christian faith.[4] Most significantly, Dasŏk integrated indigenous resources from the Confucian, Daoist and Buddhist traditions to inculturate Christianity to a multi-religious Korean context. This paper will situate Dasŏk's spirituality and thought in broader discussions of religious pluralism and will attempt to answer the question of whether Dasŏk can be considered a pluralist. It will also provide an original translation of one of Dasŏk's most important works, "Being A Christian."

## 1. Opening Up a New Way of Spirituality

Dasŏk entered into the Christian faith as a Presbyterian at the age of fifteen (in 1905), though he later declared himself to be a Non-Orthodox Christian.[5] Dasŏk proved to be far ahead of his time

---

theology. For an introduction to *minjung* theology, see Kim Yong-Bock ed., *Minjung Theology: People as the Subjects of History* (Singapore: Commission on Theological Concern, Christian Conference of Asia, 1981).

4 Notably, this article may also be read alongside Heup Young Kim, "Dasŏk Ryu Yŏngmo's Korean Trans-Cosmic and Trans-Religious Spirituality: A Translation and Commentary on 'Spiritual Hiking'," *Interreligious Relations* 26 (2021).

5 With Christianity, his life and theological thoughts can be divided into four periods. In the first period (1905-1913), receiving new Western-style education, he faithfully studied, taught, and maintained a conventional form of Christianity. In the second period

amongst Korean Protestants, who were extremely loyal to what they had learnt from exclusivist Western missionaries and could not appreciate his provocative foresights which would, arguably, prepare Christians in the twenty-first century for a multi-religious world. Furthermore, even the so-called theologians of indigenisation in Korea had not recognised his thought as a vein of Korean Christian theology.

For example, in his well-known book, *The Veins of Korean Theology*, Yu Tong-sik summarised the history of Korean Christian theology in three figures: Pak Hyŏng-lyong (1897-1978, Evangelical Presbyterian), Kim Chae-jun (1901-1987, Ecumenical Presbyterian), and Chŏng Kyŏng-ok (1903-1945, Liberal Methodist).[6] Dasŏk is unfortunately excluded from this history. Pak Hyŏng-lyong founded the conservative, dogmatic school (presently, Chongshin University), loyal to Neo-Calvinism; Kim Chae-jun established a progressive theological school with active social participation, which later devel-

---

(1914-1939), after the tragic experience of his younger brother's death, he departed from the Protestant faith and explored in depth the East Asian philosophy of life to reach what he called "living day by day" (하루살이 *halu-sali*). In the third period (1939-1943), while focusing on the spirituality of the night and breathing (숨쉼 *sum-swim*), he developed the thought of *kaon-tchikki* (가온찍기 [see note 18]) and the theology of filial piety. In the fourth period (1943-1981), after the spiritual experience in the unity of heaven, earth, and humanity. He developed his mature religious thought, an attempt he summarized as "put the bone marrow of Western civilization into the bones of Eastern civilization (동양문명의 뼈에 서양 문명의 골수를 넣는다)." See Pak Chae-sun, *Dasŏk Yŏngmo: tongsŏ-sasang-ŭl aurŭn ch'angjojŏk saengmyŏng ch'ŏrhakcha* [The Creative Philosopher of Life who integrated the Eastern and the Western Thoughts] (Seoul: Hyŏnamsa, 2008), 40-83.

6 See Yu Tong-sik, *Han'guk Shinhag ŭi Kwangmaek: Han'guk Shinhak Sasangsa Sŏsŏl* (Seoul: Chŏnmangsa, 1982).

oped *minjung* theology (Hanshin University); while Chŏng Kyŏng-ok
initiated the liberal theological school which later promoted Korean
theologies of indigenisation (Methodist Theological University).[7]
However, all of them obtained their theological education from
American seminaries.[8] Hence, their primary tasks were to transmit
what they had learnt in the United States back to Korea and to translate them to the Korean context. Therefore, the book demonstrated
that the veins of Korean Christian theology are in fact merely Western
(and particularly North American) theologies. Hence, I argue that
genuine native Korean theologians like Dasŏk must be included
when talking about the development of Christianity in Korea as they
offer authentic indigenous resources to formulate, what may be
termed, *bona fide* Korean theologies.[9]

Indeed, Dasŏk was a precursor to intertextual interpretation,

---

7 Established in 1901 by North American Presbyterian missionaries, Chongshin University
has deep historical ties to conservative, evangelical Presbyterianism and belongs to the
Presbyterian Church in Korea (PCK). By the influence of Pak's fundamentalism, it pro-
voked schisms among Korean Presbyterian Churches, because of the issues of Biblical
interpretation and ecumenism (the World Council of Churches). Established in 1939 during the schism, Hanshin University, affiliated with the Presbyterian Church in the Republic
of Korea (PCROK), became one of the most progressive Protestant churches in Korea.
Meanwhile, Methodist Theological University is the first and main Methodist Seminary
in Korea, first established in 1907 by North American Methodist missionaries.

8 Pak, Princeton Theological Seminary and The Southern Baptist Theological Seminary;
Kim, also Princeton Theological Seminary; Chŏng, Garrett-Evangelical Theological
Seminary.

9 See Heup Young Kim, "Han'guk Chojikshinhak 50nyŏn: Kanmunhwajŏk Koch'al" [50
years of Korean Systematic Theology: a Cross-Cultural Approach] in *Sinhak Yŏn'gu 50
Yŏn* [50 Years of Theological Studies], ed. Ihwa Yŏja Taehakkyo Han'guk Munhwa Yŏn'
guwŏn (Seoul: Hyean, 2003), 139-188; also Heup Young Kim, *Doŭi Sinhak II* [Theology
of Dao II] (Seoul: Tongyŏn, 2013), 93-144.

multifaith hermeneutics, and comparative theology for the global age[10] Deeply embedded in East Asian scriptures, he developed an intriguing interpretation of Christianity in the light of East Asian thought. Put simply, he read the Christian Bible alongside indigenous resources such as Confucian, Daoist, and Buddhist scriptures. He made an interesting suggestion to "regard all the scriptures of East Asian religions as the Old Testament."[11] However, whether Dasŏk was a religious pluralist is still debatable. Theologians and scholars interested in Dasŏk hold three different positions on this subject. The first position regards Dasŏk as a pioneer of "religious pluralism" in Korea. Most of the members of the Dasŏk Society (Dasŏk Hak' hoe), a leading academic association of research on Dasŏk's teachings, support this position.[12] Those associated with the second posi-

---

10 Dasŏk said, "After Confucianism, Buddhism, and Christianity illuminate each other, they also know themselves better" (이렇게 유교, 불교, 기독교를 서로 비추어 보아야 서로서로 가 뭔가 좀 알 수 있게 된다), in Ryu Yŏngmo, *Dasŏk-ŏrok* 多夕語錄 [the Analects of Dasŏk]: Ssial-ŭi-maeari, ed. Park Young-ho (Seoul: Hongikje, 1993), 365. Most English translations of Dasŏk's original texts in this article are my own. I appreciate the assistance of Rev. David Sang-Jun Kim for translation.

11 Ibid, 82. Dasŏk partially supports the theory of preparation and fulfillment; he regarded Christianity as a New Testament that has completed the truth revealed in Asian religious scriptures, so to speak, East Asian Old Testaments. His cross-cultural Asian hermeneutics would be summarised in the following statement: "Putting the bone marrow of Western civilisation and culture into the backbones of Eastern civilisation and culture" (서양 문명 과 문화의 골수를 동쪽의 문명과 문화[의 척추]에다 집어넣을 수 있다[可西文髓東文骨]). See Ryu, *Dasŏk-kangŭi*, 310-12; Kim Hŭng-ho, *Dasok-ilji Gongbu* 2:176. For the fulfillment theory, see Paul Hedges, *Preparation and Fulfillment: A History and Study of Fulfilment Theology in Modern British Thought in the Indian Context* (Bern: Peter Lang, 2001).

12 The representative figures and their significant works for the first position are: Chŏng-yang-mo, *Nanŭn Dasŏk-ŭl Ilŏhke Bonta* [I see Dasŏk in This Way] (Seoul: Ture, 2009); Shim Il-sŏp, *Han'guk T'och'ak'wa Shinhak Hyŏngsŏngsa Non'gu* [A Study on the

tion are largely Dasŏk's followers who are inclined to believe that he founded a new Korean-style religion beyond Christianity in Korea's pluralistic religious environment. The leader of this group is Park Yŏng-ho, who served and followed Dasŏk as a student since his youth and became his only surviving disciple.[13] Meanwhile, the third position views Dasŏk as a religious and theological thinker who attempted to articulate and contextualise Jesus' teachings to the Korean context. Kim Hŭng-ho (1919-2012), a favorite disciple of Dasŏk during his lifetime, represents this third group.[14]

However, the first position, viewing him as a religious pluralist arguably construes him out of his own context by operating under the Western Christian missionary theological framework. It commits a fallacy of categorical imposition. Before the arrival of Christianity in Korea, the country had a long history of many different religions

---

Formation History of Korean Theology of Indigenisation] (Seoul: Kuk'akcharyowŏn, 1995); Yi Chŏng-pae, *Yu Yŏngmo-ŭi Kwiil-shinhak* [Yu Yŏng-mo's Theology of Returning to the Oneness] (Seoul: Miralbuksŭ, 2020). In English: Youn Jeong-Hyun, "The Existent Existing God: An East Asian Perspective with Specific Reference to the thought of Ryu Yŏngmo," Th.D. dissertation, University of Birmingham (Birmingham, United Kingdom, 2002); Yi Ki-sang, "Holiness and Spirituality: How to Communicate with God in the Age of Globalisation" in *Word and Spirit: Renewing Christology and Pneumatology*, eds. Anselm K. Min and Christoph Schwöbel (Berlin: Walter de Gruyter, 2014), 85-112.

13 Some significant books (commentaries) of Park Yŏng-ho are: *Ssial: Dasŏk Yu Yŏng-mo-ŭi Saengae-wa Sasang* [Seeds: Life and Work of Dasŏk Yu Yŏng-mo] (Seoul: Hongikje, 1985); *Dasŏk-ŏrok*, 1993; *Dasŏk Yu Yŏng-mo-ŭi Myŏngsanglok* [Meditations of Dasŏk Yu Yŏng-mo] (Seoul: Ture, 2000); *Dasŏk Yu Yŏng-mo Ŏlok* [Analects of Dasŏk Yu Yŏng-mo] (Seoul: Ture, 2002); *Dasŏk Machimak Kangŭi* [Last Lectures of Dasŏk] (Seoul: Gyoyangin, 2010).

14 For Kim Hŭng-ho, see note 2. Also, O Chŏng-suk, *Dasŏk Yu Yŏng-mo-ŭi Hankukchŏk Kitokkyo* [Korean Christianity according to Dasŏk Yu Yŏng-mo] (Seoul: Misŭba, 2005).

coexisting, including Confucianism, Daoism, Buddhism, and Shamanism. Religious pluralism is an alternative position that Western missionaries, theologians, and scholars, who previously had little or no encounter with other religious traditions other than Christianity, adopted when they discovered Asian religions and were shocked by their depth.[15] For Dasŏk, however, East Asian religions are not a matter of choice, but a historical and existential background already given to him. Secondly, although Park Yŏng-ho is knowledgeable and has produced many books about Dasŏk, his essay-style writings make it hard to do proper academic research. In many parts of his prolific writings, it is hard to distinguish the real author: whether it was Park or his teacher, Dasŏk. Moreover, Park suggests that the core of Dasŏk's spirituality is to liberate the spirit from the bondage of body, dividing the spirit-self (얼나 ŏl-na) from the body-self (몸나 mom-na). Although most scholars who regard Dasŏk as a pluralist subscribe to this view, this is an unfortunate misunderstanding of Dasŏk; instead, Dasŏk strongly advocated for "the spirituality of body and breath", a theme which we will discuss in this paper.[16] Thirdly, Kim Hŭng-ho also produced many works on Dasŏk, including a complete series of commentaries on the *Dasok-ilji* (*Dasok-ilji Gongbu*) which became a valuable resource for studying Dasŏk. However, his expositions seemingly overstress the Christian elements in Dasŏk's work.

---

15 See Heup Young Kim, *A Theology of Dao* (Maryknoll, NY: Orbis Books, 2017), 10-11.

16 See Heup Young Kim, *Kaon-tchikki: Dasŏk Yu Yŏngmo-ŭi Global Han'guk Shinhak Sŏsŏl* [Introduction to The Global Korean Theology of Dasŏk Yu Yŏngmo] (Seoul: Tongyŏn, 2013), 27, 42, 106-9, 216-19, 243-46, 397-400.

So far, research on Dasŏk have usually addressed partial subjects,[17] but few have systematically dealt with his religious thought as a whole. My volume *Kaon-tchikki: Dasŏk Yu Yŏngmo-ŭi Global Han'guk Shinhak Sŏsŏl* (*Introduction to The Global Korean Theology of Dasŏk Yu Yŏngmo-ŭi*) is the only work which analyses his thought and theology systematically.[18] Meanwhile, recent works on Dasŏk, particularly those from outside Korea, are largely based on secondary materials rather than recondite primary sources. However, for a holistic comprehension of Dasŏk's spirituality and thought, it is essential to decipher *Dasŏk-ilji*, which consists of his imaginative poems in classical

---

17 For example, see Kim Hŭng-ho and Yi Chŏng-pae, eds., *Tongyang Sasang-kwa Sinhak: Tongyang-chŏk Kitokkyo I-hae* [East Asian Thoughts and Theology: East Asian Understanding of Christianity] (Seoul: Sol, 2002).

18 Heup Young Kim, *Kaon-tchikki. Kaon-tchikki* 가온찍기 is a core concept of Dasŏk's thought. *Kaon* 가온 is composed of three old Korean characters, "ㄱ" (*kiŏk*), " ᆞ " (*arae a*) and "ㄴ" (*niŭn*). *Area a* (" ᆞ ") in old Korean can be both a ( ㅏ ) and o (ㅗ). (ㄱ + ᆞ = 가 *ka*; ᆞ +ㄴ = 온 *on*; therefore, 가온 *ka-on*). According to him, "ㄱ" signifies the heaven, "ㄴ" the earth, and " ᆞ " selfhood (humanity). Also, ka-on refers to center (가운데 *kaunde*), which, he said, is equivalent to the Chinese character *chung* (中). Hence, *kaon* means the center in the unity between the cosmos and selfhood (my anthropo-cosmic center), my real and true place (both existential and ontological). *Tchikki* literally means "to put a dot (myself)." Thus, *kaon-tchikki* connotes locating selfhood in its real anthropo-cosmic center (ontological and existential), which is the goal of and the true starting point for religion and spirituality.

This book also elaborates twelve central themes of Dasŏk's theological thoughts; (1) human self as the subjectivity (제소리 *Che-so-li*), (2) God as the One (하나 *Hana*), (3) Christ as the The anthropocosmic Center (가온 *Ka-on*), (4) philosophy of "living day by day" (하루살이 *halu-sali*), (5) transcendental method of correlation (무름-부름-푸름 *murŭm-purŭm-p'urŭm*), (6) theology of the body (몸 *mom*), (7) theology of the breath (숨 *sum*), (8) theology of the dao (theo-dao, 道), (9) paradoxical theology of being in non-being (없이 계심 *ŏpshi kyeshim*), (10) well-dying rather than well-being, (11) theology of Korean language (한글 *hangŭl*), and (12) "Our Nation as the Kingdom of God" (우리나라-하늘나라 *uli-nala hanŭl-nala*). See ibid, 31-50.

Chinese and Korean, with complex East Asian religious concepts. This task requires advanced knowledge of the Bible, Christian theology, and the scriptures and teachings of various East Asian religions including Confucianism, Daoism, and Buddhism, in addition to proficiencies in Korean (*hangul*) and traditional Chinese, interspersed in his writings. Hence, it is incredibly challenging to translate his religious thought into English or into other foreign languages.

Dasŏk's primary interest did not lie in religious epistemology, such as elucidating a theology of religious pluralism, but the constructive hermeneutics of his faith in and through the plurality of Korean traditional and indigenous religions. Kim Hŭng-ho argued that Dasŏk was first and foremost a Christian, a serious follower of Jesus Christ. Nevertheless, Dasŏk differed from other Korean Christians subjected to Western-style Christianity because he freely employed indigenous scriptures to understand the Christian Bible better and more appropriately in his multi-religious context. For longer than a millennium, East Asian religious scriptures and teachings have profoundly influenced and shaped and are deeply embedded in Korean (and East Asian) modes of life and thinking, much as the Bible is embedded in a Western context. By reading the Bible in and through interreligious dialogue with these indigenous scriptures, Dasŏk could conceive his new faith in Jesus Christ more clearly, intelligibly, and practically.[19]

---

19 For Dasŏk's Christology, see Heup Young Kim, "The Word made Flesh: A Korean Perspective on Ryu Young-mo's Christotao" in *One Gospel and Many Cultures: Case Studies and Reflections on Cross-Cultural Theology*, eds. Mercy Amba Oduyoye and Handrik M. Vroom (Amsterdam-New York, NY: Rodopi, 2003),129-48. This paper pointed out seven characteristics of his Christological thought: Jesus as the Filial Son

## 2. Life and Spirituality in "Being a Christian"

In this section, I will examine Dasŏk's unique view of the Christian faith as a Korean who is heavily influenced by Confucianism. Dasŏk sees no separation between spirituality and ordinary daily life, namely, between the sacred and the secular, much like how Herbert Fingarette famously summarised that the Confucian life is doing the "secular as sacred."[20] Simultaneously, as a Christian, Dasŏk regards spirituality as deeply embodied with prayer, which he does not distinguish from the totality of everyday life. He summarised his view of leading a Christian life and practicing Christian spirituality in a short Classical Chinese poem (漢詩 hansi) titled 'Being a Christian' (基督者 kitokcha). Dasŏk's pre-dawn prayer was proceeded by the recitation of verses from multiple scriptures of different religious traditions, and contemplation: a process he calls naal (나-알; knowing me). The prayer then concludes with him writing summary poems, a process he describes as alla (알-나; producing an egg).[21] It was through this process of naal-alla (나알-알나, self-awakening and egg-producing) that his literary gems of classical Chinese and Korean poems were born. I will proceed to unpack the meaning of each line of his poem, "Being A Christian," below.

---

(효자 hyoja; Confucian), the Rice (밥 bab; sacramental), the Flower (aesthetic), the Seed (씨알 ssiat; anthropological), the Spirit (pneumatological), the Dao (cosmic life; theodaoian), and the Being in Non-Being (apophatic). For a systematic theological review of Dasŏk's religious thought, see Kim, Kaon-tchikki.

20 Herbert Fingarette, Confucius: The Secular as Sacred (New York, NY: Harper & Row, 1972).

21 In this insight, Dasŏk played with the Korean word "al" whose pronunciation denotes a double meaning, both "knowing" and "egg."

Prayer is graciously and deeply breathing the original vital force.

The healthy beating of a pulse is the music of praise by the body [to God].

Every meal is the summit of a virtuous rite.

Wholehearted devotion with sincerity is the way to enter into the oracle.[22]

## Prayer is graciously and deeply breathing the original vital force (祈禱陪敦元氣息 kito paeton wŏn kisik)

Aligned with the teachings of the Korean church, Dasŏk identified Christians as "the people who pray," and prayer as the *breathing* of faith. For him, however, the reference to "taking a breath (숨 *sum*)" (氣息 *kisik*) does not merely end in symbolic and spiritual gesture but also includes the physical act of breathing. In the first line, he states that prayer is originally the act of breathing (元氣息 *wŏn kisik*). Besides, the Chinese characters in this phrase "*paeton*" (陪敦) denote to do so deeply, graciously, and respectfully. He explains:

As we are praying, we are taking a breath. When we do so, we breathe deeply, generously, and respectfully; the origin (元 *wŏn*) is breathing. Consequently, we should not say, 'we offer our prayer.' Instead, it is right to say, 'we offer our breath.'... The act of prayer is the act of offering the very thing we breathe, which we originally have received from God.[23]

---

22 "基督者. 祈禱陪敦元氣息. 讚美伴奏健脈搏. 嘗義極致日正食. 禰誠克明夜歸託." (Ryu, *Dasŏk-ilji*, 1956. 12. 8).

23 "우리가 기도를 하는데 숨을 쉬면 두텁게 후하게 그리고 정중하게 하는데 그 '원(元)'은 숨입니다. 그래서 기도드린다는 말은 안 됩니다. 호흡을 드린다는 말이 옳습니다. ⋯ 우리

This line also lends itself to another stimulating interpretation: prayer is to breathe the original vital force (元氣 *wŏnki*) deeply, generously, and respectfully. In other words, prayer is to breathe the root force of the Universe (the cosmic breathing) or the living natural force (浩然之氣 *hoyŏnchiki*) in communion with the Holy Spirit. This first line suggests the possible connection between Dasŏk and the breathing method of Korean Sŏndo (仙道), an inherited tradition of ascetic training in the mountains to become immortal (神仙 *sinsŏn*) through enhanced hypogastric breathing techniques (丹田呼吸 *tanchŏn hohŭp*), partially related to Korean Daoism.[24] Dasŏk's discipline clearly resembles Sŏndo, Dasŏk wasted no single act of breathing. In every moment of breathing, Dasŏk immersed himself deeply in meditation, contemplating God and reflecting on the meaning of being a Christian. Similar to the Jesus Prayer in Eastern Orthodox Christianity, Dasŏk received God (하나님 *Hananim*) as he breathes in, and offers his faith and reverence as he breathes out.[25]

---

가 숨쉬는 것, 곧 호흡하는 것을 바로 하느님에게서 받아서 하는 것이 기도입니다. 즉, 기도
는 우리의 '원기식'을 두텁게 해서 말하는 것입니다." Ryu, *Dasŏk-kangŭi*, 365-66.

24 For example, see Ko Kyŏngmin, *Yŏngsaeng-hanŭn Kil* [The Way for Immortality]
(Seoul: Chongno Ch'ulp'ansa, 1974). Ko Kyŏngmin (b. 1936, pen name: Ch'ŏngsan
青山) was the founder of Kuksŏndo (國仙道), literally the National Sŏndo, which con-
tributed to a revival of the Korean Sŏndo (especially, *tanchŏn hohŭp*) tradition. For
Ko and Kuksŏndo, see ibid.; also, Ko Kyŏngmin, *Kuksŏndo*, 3 vols (Seoul: Kuksŏndo
Publications,1993).

25 See Kim, *Kaon-tchikki*, 43-44, 239-56.

*The healthy beating of the pulse is the music of praise by the body(讚美伴奏健脈搏 ch'anmi panchu kŏn maekpak)*

For Dasŏk, hence, spirituality is not only psychological but also should be experienced in the most basic levels of human existence, biological and physical. Being alive means that one is breathing and that one's heart is beating. As in the previous line where he likens breathing as a prayer to God, he writes, in the next line, that the healthy beating of the heart is an inner musical accompaniment of doxological praise (讚美伴奏 *ch'anmi panchu*) to God:

> The pulse ought to be healthy. The healthy beating of the pulse (健脈搏 *kŏn maekpak*) is genuine praise. I am envious of no other things. For 'keeping the body healthy' (몸성히 *mom-sŏnghi*), 'relieving the mind-heart' (맘놓이 *mam-nohi*), and 'cultivating the selfhood' (바탈퇴히 *pat'al-t'oehi*) are to keep 'the healthy pulse-beating.' What else would it be if this is not genuine praise [to God]?[26]

Dasŏk explained his thinking about a Christian who lives an authentic life in this way: "The pulse leaps with vigour accompanying the orchestra of praise. Such pulsation is the blood of Christians. Is this not the image of a Christian, praying deeply, graciously, and respectably by offering the original breath and praising with the accompaniment of our healthy pulse."[27] The way of achieving a

---

26 "맥박은 건강해야 합니다. 맥박이 건강하게 뛰는 뚝딱뚝딱 하는 소리는 참찬미입니다. 다른 것을 부러워하지 않습니다. '몸성히 맘놓이 바탈퇴히'로 나가는 것이 '건맥박'으로 나가는 것입니다. 이것이 찬미가 아니고 무엇이겠습니까?" Ryu, *Dasŏk-kangŭi*, 366.

healthy pulse is none other than "keeping the body healthy" (*mom-sŏnghi*), "relieving the mind-heart" (*mam-nohi*), and "cultivating the selfhood" (*pat'al-t'oehi*).

This thought is not far away from traditional Christian spirituality. St. Paul in *Romans* had encouraged us to present our bodies "as a living sacrifice, holy and acceptable to God" and defined it as "spiritual worship" (Rom 12:1 NRSV). However, from the influence of Hellenistic dualism, many Christian spiritual traditions tend to idolise spiritual and cerebral aspects while neglecting the physical body (몸 *mom*) and the material. The rise of "theologies of the body" and "spiritualities of the body" is a legitimate attempt to supplement this shortcoming. Thus, Dasŏk's insight of "the healthy beating of the pulse as the music of praise by the body" along with "keeping the body healthy" is an in-depth resource for retrieving and developing a spiritual theology of the body that resonates with the current theological landscape.

*Every meal is the summit of a virtuous rite(嘗義極致日正食 sangŭi kŭkch'i il chŏngsik)*

In the third line, Dasŏk asserts that the attitude of reverence should also be applied when we gather around the table for a meal to sustain our health. Every meal should be regarded as the Christian Eucharist and the Confucian memorial rite (祭祀 *chesa*), essential

---

27 "맥박이 팔딱팔딱 찬미하며 반주합니다. 이렇게 뛰는 것이 그리스도인의 피입니다. 기도는 배돈하고 '원기식'을 드리며, 찬미에는 '건맥박'으로 반주하는 것이 그리스도인의 모습이 아닌가 합니다." Ibid.

for propriety (禮 *ye*) of filial piety. Dasŏk argues that worship does not occur only in the Church but also for every gathering to eat. He says:

> There is one phrase I ask [you] to remember. That "every meal as the summit of a virtuous rite" is the memorial rite and Eucharist. "The summit of a virtuous rite" (嘗義極致 *sangŭi kŭkch'i*) is to eat the meal with the spirit of love (愛食 *aesik*) and community (會食 *hoesik*). The Eucharist constitutes the origin of the memorial rite. However, there may yet lurk hypocrisy. We give thanks to God for what we are about to eat and drink; this ought not to be done only in the sanctuary. According to this very spirit, to live everyday life is "the summit of a virtuous rite". We could reach this summit only when we give an earnest expression to the spirit of "commemorating the memory of origins and ancestors" (報本追遠 *popon ch'uwŏn*) at every gathering for a meal.[28]

*Wholehearted devotion with sincerity is the way to enter into the oracle (禘誠克明夜歸託 ch'esŏng kŭkmyŏng ya kwit 'ak)*

In the last line of this poem, Dasŏk argues that wholehearted devotion with sincerity (禘誠克明 *ch'esŏng kŭkmyŏng*) is the prerequisite to know and to be in communion with God. Wholehearted devotion (禘 *ch'e*) refers to praying to God in such a manner as one

---

28 "이 한마디만큼은 기억해주십시오. '상의극치일정식'은 제사이고 성찬입니다. 애식과 회식의 정신으로 먹는 것이 상의극치인데, 성찬은 제사의 근본입니다. 그러나 여기에는 아직 가짜가 들어 있습니다. 먹고 마시는 것을 허락하여 주신 하느님께 감사를 드리는데, 예배당에서만 해서는 안 됩니다. 그 정신을 가지고 일상을 사는 것이 '상의극치'가 됩니다. 보본추원(報本追遠)의 정신을 매끼 식사 때마다 표시하여야 극치를 이룰 것입니다." Ibid, 329.

faithfully fulfils filial care (孝 *hyo*) towards the ancestors with sincerity
and humility.[29] Sincerity (誠 *sŏng*) here means an ontological fulfilment of the truth (참 *cham*). He says:

> Wholehearted devotion is the right way of prayer to approach God;
> evidently, it is substantiated by sincerity... The only way of fulfilling
> sincerity is to practise devotion. It should be done consistently and thor-
> oughly (克 *kŭk*). To pray in this way is how we can know God. As we
> always practise sincere devotion, we can enter the divine oracle, which
> is the night (夜 *ya*).[30] [In this way], the Word can enter the "truth" always.
> In this way, when we leave this world, we can enter with dignity. We
> enter the eternal "Night."[31](*획 구분)

Therefore, with this one line, Dasŏk suggests a perceptive East
Asian definition of a theology of prayer. For prayer is an effort to enter

---

29 Dasŏk continues to compare Christian spirituality to *chesa* (the memorial rite), which
is the core ritual of Korean family tradition. In traditional Korean families, *chesa* refers
to practising the propriety of filial piety for ancestors, a prime virtue of Confucianism.
Dasŏk therefore argues that Jesus is the filial son who completed the Word of God (see
Kim, "The Word made Flesh," 132-34). For the extended family/ancestors as the core
of Chinese and East Asian culture, society, and government, see Jordan Paper, *Chinese
Religion and Familialism: The Basis of Chinese Culture, Society, and Government*
(New York, NY: Bloomsbury, 2019).

30 Dasŏk views sunlight as a false light that hides far bigger cosmic realities in the darkness.
Thus, he believes that truth exists rather in the night, which is the reason why he used
the pen name which literally means "many nights" (多夕).

31 "하느님에 대한 추원(追遠)을 옳게 하는 것이 체(禘)요, 이에 바로 들어가가면 성(誠)입니다.
체성(禘誠)은 치성(致誠)입니다. 이 '체'를 밝혀야 '성'을 이룰 수 있습니다. 극은 늘 하자는
것입니다. 철저하게 '체성'을 하자는 것입니다. 이렇게 하여야 하느님을 알게 됩니다. 늘
'체성'을 밝히면 밤, 곧 신탁(神託)에 들어갑니다. 말씀이 늘 참에 들어갈 수 있습니다. 이래
야 우리가 세상을 떠날 때 떳떳하게 들어갈 수 있습니다. 영원한 밤에 들어갑니다." Ryu,
*Dasŏk-kangŭi*, 367.

into divine oracle (神託 *sint' ak*), to communicate with God, through sincere and thorough devotion (締誠克明, *ch'esŏng kŭkmyŏng*).

## 3. Three Basics for Spirituality

From the above poem, and in considering other works by Dasŏk, we can identify a central core of three key aspects within his spirituality. These come from, or are framed within, his Christian base, but are always infused within a Korean religious and contextual framework, which can also be seen as a grounding for them. They are: "keeping the body healthy" (몸성히 *mom-sŏnghi*); "relieving the mind-heart" (맘놓이 *mam-nohi*); and "cultivating the selfhood" (바탈 퇴히 *pat'al-t'oehi*).

### Keeping the Body Healthy (몸성히 mom-sŏnghi)

To enter into the true life and spirituality of a Christian, first of all, Dasŏk emphasises that we need the body to keep "the healthy pulse" (建脈搏, *jianpaibo*). He expresses it in Korean as "*mom-sŏnghi*". However, it does not imply an advocation of self-centered eugenics; on the contrary, for him as a Confucian and a Christian who pursues the *dao* of benevolence (仁 *in*) and love (*agape*), its aim is altruistic.[32]

---

32 The Chinese character of *in* 仁 (benevolence or co-humanity), the cardinal virtue of Confucianism, consists of two parts, meaning two (二 *i*) and human being (人 *in*), which entails the Confucian definition of ontological (original) humanity. Hence, the goal of self-cultivation, the primary project of Neo-Confucianism, is to achieve this original co-humanity or being-in-togetherness beginning from the concrete context to the uni-

He says: "If your body is healthy, you need to help those whose
body is unhealthy."[33]

## Relieving the Mind-Heart (맘놓이 mam-nohi)

Secondly, one ought to put down and relieve the mind-heart (맘
*mam*); that is to say, empty it.[34] Dasŏk refers to the putting-down
of the mind-heart as *mam-nohi* (맘놓이) and the relieving of the
mind-heart as *mam-bihi* (맘비히). *Mam-bihi* could be his East Asian
way of expressing a Christian spirituality of self-emptying (*kenosis*;
Phil 2:7). One ought to empty the mind-heart to be clean like a vacuum (眞空 *chin-kong*). He says: "We ought to empty our mind-heart.
Once there is a vacuum, then everything surges to rush in." We
should fill the vacuum by rolling the elements of truth, such as purity,
straightforwardness, and fidelity, that rush in (쳄말기 *ch'aem-mal-ki*).
This process of rolling (말기 *mal-ki*)[35] eventually leads to the body

---

versal extension, from self via family and society to the world (修身齊家治國平天下 *sus-
in-cheka-ch'ikuk-p'yŏngch'ŏnha*). For benevolence and agape, see Heup Young Kim,
"*Jen [Ren, In]* and Agape: Toward a Confucian Christology," *Asia Journal of Theology*
8:2 (1994): 335-64.

33 Ryu, *Dasŏk-kangŭi*, 56.

34 In Korean, mind (*mam* 맘) and body (*mom* 몸) are not mutually exclusive; rather, they
are inclusive as their characters are from the same origin (ㅁ + ㅁ + " · "). Since *mam*
(*maŭm* 마음 or 心 *sim*) connotes a psycho-somatic unity between the mind and the
body, it is translated as the mind-heart in this article. The "putting-down" of the
mind-heart refers to the process of freeing the mind-heart from the excessive occupation
of the brain by moving concentration down from the top (brain) to the bottom of the
body. It is regarded as a preparatory process of East Asian mind-heart cultivation.

35 The expression of "rolling" here indicates that his method resonates with that of hypogastric breathing (丹田呼吸 *tanchŏn-hohŭp*) which emphasises the rolling of the vital

achieving a state of cleaniness (맑기 *malk-ki*).[36] He explains: "Do not merely fill up with the rolling. When the body is empty in the state of wholeness (*mom-sŏnghi*), it will become clean and eternally ever cleaner. I do not mean in this life, but in the afterlife, beyond death."[37]

## Cultivating the Selfhood (바탈퇴히 pat'al-t'oehi)

Finally, the two stages of keeping and harmonising the healthy body (*mom-sŏnghi*) and relieving and emptying the mind-heart (mam-nohi) have the trajectory towards the process of cultivating and sanctifying the selfhood (*pat'al-t'oehi*). *Pat'al* (바탈) means the foundation of a person and one's individuality; that is, the selfhood. *T'oehi* (퇴히) is originally written with the consonant '*t'iŭt'* ("ㅌ") and the vowel "*arae a*". This Korean character simultaneously takes on the double meaning of "consuming by fire" (燃 *yŏn*) and "boarding to ride" (乘 *sŭng*).[38] As such, this refers to the perpetual process of consuming one's bad habits and renewing selfhood; in terms of Confucianism and Christian theology, the process of self-cultivation and sanctification, respectively. As he said: "There is only 'I.' There

---

forces (*ki* 氣) in the process of breathing. One can build up the true *ki* (眞氣 *chin-ki*) after fully emptying the mind-heart (空眞 *kongchin*).

36 Here, Dasŏk shows an example of his unique play on Korean words (*hangŭl-lori* 한글놀 이), based on the phonic and scriptural relatedness between *mal-ki* 말기 and *malk-ki* 맑기 (ㄹ+ㄱ becomes 리).

37 "'말기'만 채우지 말고 몸성히 비어 있으면 영원히 맑고 맑아집니다. 이승에서가 아니라 죽음을 넘어 저승에서 그러하다는 말입니다." Ryu, *Dasŏk-kangŭi*, 55.

38 See Ryu, *Dasŏk-kangŭi*, 174-76.

is no other way but to consume selfhood with fire so that I am born
again and again with new selfhood and ultimately take it off entirely.
Our life is to exert ourselves in bringing this new 'I' to be born again
by the will of God persistently."[39]

"Cultivating the selfhood" (*pat'al-t'oehi*) means to consume (然
*yŏn*) the selfhood by itself (自 *cha*). If the two Chinese characters
are combined, it becomes "*cha-yŏn*" (自然, nature).[40] Moreover,
Dasŏk interpreted that its first character (自) in Classical Chinese is
a hieroglyphic representation of "the inside of a nose."[41] Therefore,
it means that "the nose is on fire;" that is to say, to breathe through
the nose: "In our East Asian word, "*cha-yŏn*" means to consume with
fire... Breathing means that the fire is entering [our noses]. Thus,
it refers to the inside of the nose that is consumed by fire."[42] This
passage illustrates a clear correlation between Dasŏk and Korean
Sŏndo (仙道) again.

---

39 "'나'밖에 없습니다. 단지 내 바탈을 태워서 자꾸 새 바탈의 나를 낳는것밖에 없습니다.
　 종단에는 아주 벗어버리는 것입니다. 새로운 '나'를 하느님 뜻대로 자꾸 낳아가도록 노력하
　 는 것이 우리 인생입니다." Ibid, 206. This part shows that he is synthesising Confucian
　 self-cultivation with Christian sanctification. The subject of Confucian cultivation is my
　 selfhood, the body and the mind-heart (*sŭng*), and it also connotes the Christian process
　 of regeneration by the burning fire of the Holy Spirit (*yŏn*).

40 Although *cha-yŏn* also means "self-doing" in English, here, he interprets that its hiero-
　 glyphics have the following connotations.

41 Dasŏk was an excellent scholar in Korean (*Hangŭl*) and well-versed in classical Chinese
　 writings. While dealing with Confucian classics and Buddhist scriptures, he used
　 Chinese characters freely and expressed his thoughts in Chinese poems (as seen before).
　 Particularly, his interest devoted much effort to developing *Hangŭl* into a polysemous
　 language like Chinese.

42 "우리 동양 말로 '자연'은 불탄다는 말입니다. … 우리가 숨 쉬는 것은 불 타 들어가는 것입니
　 다. 그래서 코 속이 불탄다는 말입니다." Ryu, *Dasŏk-kangŭi*, 377.

There is a similarity between Dasŏk and Ko Kyŏngmin in method and theory that regards emptiness as the way to reach the truth (空-眞 kong-chin).[43] First of all, the process of mom-sŏnghi that aims at reaching the "true body" (참몸 ch'am-mom) corresponds to "adjusting the body" (調身 cho-sin) in Kuksŏndo, which is a process of harmonising the healthy body in order to embody the right body (正體 chŏng-ch'e) or the true body (眞體 chin-ch'e). Secondly, mam-nohi, which aims at the true mind-heart (참맘 ch'am-mam), is similar to "adjusting the mind-heart" (調心 cho-sim) in Kuksŏndo, which makes the mind-heart peaceful in order to realise the right mind-heart (正心 chŏng-sim) and the true mind-heart (眞心 chin-sim), the properly rectified mind-heart. Finally, pat'al-t'oehi that seeks to be sanctified into the true selfhood correlates to "adjusting the breath" (調息 cho-sik) in Kuksŏndo, which regulates the breathing evenly so that the right or the true breath (참숨 ch'am-sum; 正息 chŏng-sik, 眞息 chin-sik) is fulfilled. Thus, Dasŏk's three basics of spirituality, mom-sŏnghi, mam-nohi, and pat'al-t'oehi, are comparable to the three fundamentals of Kuksŏndo training: "adjusting the body" (調身 cho-sin), "adjusting the mind-heart" (調心 cho-sim), and "adjusting the breath" (調息 cho-sik), respectively.[44]

---

43 Ko Kyŏngmin, Kuksŏndo I (Seoul: Kuksŏndo Publications, 1993), iv.

44 Park Yŏng-ho and other scholars tended to ignore that Dasŏk-ilji, essential resources, is primarily a meditation diary in which Dasŏk recorded the enlightenment he acquired from the rigorous practice of psycho-somatic, apophatic contemplation with these methods, not to mention Sŏndo asceticism. See note 13; also, Kim, Kaon-tchikki, 251-256. The principle and prayer in Kim, "Dasŏk Ryu Yŏngmo's Korean" will make this point more evident.

## Conclusion

Herein, I have not attempted to give a full account of Dasŏk's
life, thinking, or spirituality, which would be the work of perhaps
several monographs with considerable translation of originals
needed. Rather, I have offered a contribution towards introducing
Dasŏk to the English-speaking academic world, with a particular
focus on how he relates to and contributes to thinking around questions of interreligious relations, dialogue, theology, and spirituality.
These elements, while often considered distinct within the literature, are integral to the way that Dasŏk, in a Korean context, makes
sense of his religious identity within a worldview where religious
borders are envisaged differently. As such, it makes a contribution
beyond that which already exists about how both religion, religious
identity, and religious plurality are considered within an East Asian,
or more specifically Korean context.[45] In particular, it also introduces an immensely creative and original thinker who has not
only been neglected within the Korean literature, for reasons noted,
but remains unknown beyond that context too. This paper opens
up the possibility, by exploring both an original translation of his

---

45 See, for example, on rethinking religious borders in East Asia from a theoretical per-
spective, Paul Hedges, "Multiple Religious Belonging after Religion: Theorising Strategic
Religious Participation in a Shared Religious Landscape as a Chinese Model," *Open
Theology* 3 (2017): 48-72, and for another Korean theologian's, Hyun Kyung Chung,
"Seeking the Religious Roots of Pluralism," *Journal of Ecumenical Studies* 34.3 (1997):
399-401. See also, Heup Young Kim, "Multiple Religious Belonging as Hospitality: A
Christian-Confucian Perspective," in *Many Yet One? Multiple Religious Belonging*, eds.
Peniel J. R, Rajkumar and Josepy P. Dayam (Geneva: World Council of Churches
Publication, 2016), 75-88.

work and noting the distinctive Korean context, for an indigenous Korean voice to contribute to wider theorising of issues around religious pluralism, intercultural theology, constructive theology, comparative theology, and religious diversity more broadly.

CHAPTER TWELVE

# Dasŏk Ryu Yŏngmo's Korean Trans-Cosmic and Trans-Religious Spirituality: A Translation and Commentary on "Spiritual Hiking"

## Abstract

This chapter provides an original translation and commentary on the prayer "Stroll (산보 *Sanbo*)" or "Spiritual Hiking (정신 하이킹)" by Dasŏk Ryu Yŏngmo (1890-1981). It places the prayer within his multi-religious Korean context and explores it to understand Dasŏk's spiritual principle of "*pint'ang-hante machhyŏ noli*," or "Playing Rituals in Harmony with the Emptiness Together." This paper has four main aims: to help stimulate Dasŏk scholarship in the English speaking world; to contribute to scholarship on contextual (Korean/East Asian) theology, global theology, theological inculturation, theology of religions, and comparative theology; to highlight Dasŏk's unique contribution to "religious pluralism;" and to provide an original translation and commentary on his work, making this not simply a basic survey of his ideas, but also a deep insight into his complex world of meaning.

## Introduction

In this paper[1], one of the most profound and important works of Dasŏk Ryu Yŏngmo (1890-1981) will be introduced. Little known and studied in Korea, Dasŏk is even less known within the English-speaking world. He is, arguably, one of the most innovative religious thinkers in Korea's modern history, and influenced a good number of important Korean religious leaders of the twentieth century. Amongst these, the most famous is Ham Sŏk-hŏn (1901-1989), who was influential in Korean *minjung* (민중), the people's theology and movement.[2] Importantly, here, we will explore exactly how Dasŏk integrated various resources from the Confucian, Daoist and Buddhist traditions to contextualise Christianity within a multi-religious Korea to create a more indigenous theological paradigm.

In particular, this paper will provide a translation of the prayer entitled "Stroll (산보 *Sanbo*)" or "Spiritual Hiking (정신 하이킹),"[3]

---

1 This paper is the second of two peer reviewed works introducing Dasŏk's work in English in the *Interreligious Relations* series. The former paper provides further background on Dasŏk as a thinker within the Korean context, see Heup Young Kim, "Introducing Dasŏk Ryu Yŏngmo's Korean Spiritual Disciplines and his Prayer 'Being a Christian'," *Interreligious Relations* 25 (2021). A note on romanisation: for Korean Romanisation, this article basically uses the McCune-Reischauer system. Chinese characters are also romanised according to Korean pronunciation, except for *dao* (道).

2 See Ham Sŏk Hŏn, *Queen of Suffering: A Spiritual History of Korea*, trans. E. Sang Yu (London: Friends World Committee for Consultation, 1985). *Minjung* in Korean means the oppressed people. *Minjung* theology argued for the preferential option to the *minjung* and that they are real, authentic subjects of history in the reign of God and so of theology. For an introduction to minjung theology, see Kim Yong-Bock ed., *Minjung Theology: People as the Subjects of History* (Singapore: Commission on Theological Concern, Christian Conference of Asia, 1981).

3 Ryu Yŏngmo, "Sanbo," *Chesori: Dasŏk Ryuyŏngmo Kangŭirok* [Lecture Book of Dasŏk

which is a profound working through of many themes and concepts
which blend Christianity into the Korean context. As such, through
this short text, much depth is unpacked in terms of how Dasŏk understood his spirituality, and how he integrated Korean indigenous
understandings into his faithful practice and theologising. Key in
understanding this, will be introducing what he saw as the spiritual
principle of "*pint'ang-hante machhyŏ noli*". This may be translated by
the phrase "Playing Rituals in Harmony with the Emptiness Together."
However, these words are packed with multiple meanings that play
upon various Korean, and wider East Asian, contexts and traditions,
as well as being related to Christian themes and concepts. Simply
seeing this wording does little to explain the meaning to an audience
unversed in Dasŏk's thought, while even many Korean speaking
scholars may not understand the depth of meaning because of the
way that each term is employed by him and how they combine to
create further meaning. Indeed, the same applies to the prayer and
its name of "Spiritual Hiking."

This paper, along with the previous study of Dasŏk's context,[4]
are intended to do several things. Firstly, to provide an initial starting
point for Dasŏk scholarship in the Western and Anglophone world.
Secondly, to contribute to wider scholarship on what are often
termed contextual theology, global theology, theological inculturation, theology of religions, and comparative theology with a distinct
contribution from the Korean context. Thirdly, to provide a study

---

Yŏngmo], ed. Kim Hŭng-ho (Seoul: Sol Ch'ulp'ansa, 2001), 122; also, in Ryu Yŏngmo,
*Dasŏk-ilji* 多夕日誌 [The Diaries of Dasŏk] (Seoul: Hongikje, 1990), 4:487.
4 Kim, "Introducing Dasŏk Ryu."

of Dasŏk's unique contribution to what may be termed "religious pluralism," and so to enrich an understanding of Christianity and wider discourses, specifically by providing original translations and commentaries. It is acknowledged that understanding Dasŏk's work is difficult, and, without a wider appreciation of Korea's religious heritage, what is provided here is only a glimpse of the meaning within his work, but as noted in the first point my aim is to give stepping stones towards making Dasŏk scholarship more widely known and available. This paper is offered, therefore, as an initial contribution, rather than as a definitive study or understanding of Dasŏk and his work, nevertheless, especially by giving original translations and commentary it is more than simply a cursory introduction, but proffers a deep insight into a complex world of meaning.

## 1. "Playing Rituals in Harmony with the Emptiness Together" (빈탕한데 맞혀놀이 *Pint'ang-Hante Machhyŏ Noli*)

For Dasŏk, the ultimate purpose of "living as a human being" (사람살이 *saramsari*) is "Playing Rituals in Harmony with the Emptiness Together" (*Pint'ang-Hante Machhyŏ Noli*), which he said is equivalent to *Kongyŏ Paehyang* (空與配享) in Chinese.[5] In Confucianism, *Paehyang* originally designated an act of veneration of Confucius together with

---

5 See Ryu Yŏngmo, *Dasŏk-kangŭi* 다석강의 [Lectures of Dasŏk], ed. the Society for Dasŏk Studies (Seoul: Hyŏnamsa, 2006), 464-67.

his ten disciples in Confucian worship (祭 *che*), which came to denote
"receiving a veneration together". Interpreting this as "living in harmony with each other,"[6] Dasŏk asserts that this phrase denotes "the
conclusion for humanity after I have seen life as the one born as
a human being."[7]

"*Pint'ang*" (빈탕) originally means a space or place (탕 *t'ang*) which
is empty (빈 *pin*). This word became a crucial term in Dasŏk's
thought, designating a great empty space, even referring to a reality
of Great Vacuity. He says: "The emptiness [虛空 *hŏkong*] can only
be called *pint'ang* ... There is nothing in this world that is as certain
as *pint'ang*. It is *kong-kong-hŏ-hŏ-tae-tae-sil* (空空虛虛大大實). It is said
that an empty emptiness is a great and greater reality." [8] Hence,
this term signifies both an empty space (空空虛虛 or 虛空) and the
Great Vacuity (虛虛大大 or 太虛), which also refers to sky or heaven.
In this way, Dasŏk tries to develop this particular Korean word to
be a polysemic conceptual term similar to Chinese characters,
broadly embracing Daoist, Confucian, and Buddhist concepts referring to emptiness, void, vacuity, nothingness, heaven, or cosmos
(空, 虛, 無, 天).[9]

This notion also involves Dasŏk's unique conception of the One
(하나 *hana*), the Ultimate Ontology.[10] He says:

---

6 "서로 짝이 맞아서 누리고 사는 것." Ibid, 464.

7 "이 사람이 인간으로 나서 본 인간에 대한 결론이라고 할 수 있습니다."bid, 4 158.

8 "허공도 빈탕이라고 할 수밖에 없습니다. … 이 세상에 빈탕같이 확실한 것은 없습니다. 공공허
허대대실입니다. 공(空)하고 또 공한 것이 크고 또 튼 실상이라 하였습니다." Ibid, 465.

9 Developing the Korean language (*hangŭl*) from a phonogram to an ideogram is a task
which Dasŏk paid special attention to. Likewise, he promoted *pint'ang* to have multiple
meanings, though this paper translates it simply as *emptiness* in English.

This person seems to have often thought that the emptiness (虛空) and the mind-heart are not two, but one ... the Absolute God or the mind-heart does not go back and forth. This person always feels that what is inside or what is outside is a perfect match. When looking at flowers, you usually only look at the flowers inside the flower frame, but not the empty space (literally, the face of *pint'ang*) outside the flower frame. You must also see the emptiness surrounding the flower. The colourless emptiness has been pleasant since long ago, but these days I feel it is even more pleasant. Anything you do without knowing the emptiness is false. Only the emptiness is true.[11]

---

10 For Dasŏk, also, theology (the doctrine of God) is closely interrelated with anthropology. The Korean name of God consists of three *hangŭl* characters, *Ha-Na-Nim* (하-나-님). Na in the middle denotes "I." The first character *Ha* can be the first character of *ha-na* (하나) meaning one and the interjection, "ha (하)!" Thus, *ha-na* means both "One" and "Oh, I!" *Nim* is an honorific suffix. Therefore, *Ha-Na-Nim* connotes both the Only One (하나님 *Hananim*) and the Venerable True I (하! 나님!). He said: "It is the 'One' as it is forever. Comes from the 'one' of eternity, will continue as it is toward the eternal 'One.' Going back to the 'One' eternal ... There is the Lord 'I', and trying to find the One." ("그대로 영원한 '하나'입니다. 영원한 하나에서 오고 그대로 영원한 하나를 향해 갑니다. 영원한 하나로 돌아갑니다. … 주초가 되는 '나'가 있어서 그 하나를 찾는 것입니다" (Ryu, *Dasŏk-kangŭi*, 304)). For this insight of "*hana*", see Heup Young Kim, *Kaon-tchikki: Dasŏk Ryu Yŏngmo-ŭi Global Han'guk Shinhak Sŏsŏl* [Introduction to The Global Korean Theology of Dasŏk Ryu Yŏngmo] (Seoul: Tongyŏn, 2013), 33-34, 89-94; for Dasŏk's anthropology, ibid, 115-36.

11 "이 사람은 허공과 마음이 둘이 아니라 하나라는 생각을 자주 한 것 같습니다. … 절대자 하느님이나 마음은 왔다갔다하는 것이 아닙니다. 안의 것이나 밖의 것이 완전히 일치하는 것을 이 사람은 항상 느낍니다. 꽃을 볼 때는 보통 꽃 테두리 안의 꽃만 바라보지 꽃 테두리 겉인 빈탕(虛空)의 얼굴은 보지 않습니다. 꽃을 둘러싼 허공도 보아주어야 합니다. 무색의 허공은 퍽 오래전부터 다정했지만, 요새 와서는 더욱 다정하게 느껴집니다. 허공을 모르고 하는 것은 모두가 거짓입니다. 허공만이 참입니다." Ryu, *Dasŏk-kangŭi*, 458-59. Furthermore, he identifies emptiness with God: "허공은 참이고 하느님입니다." Ryu, *Dasŏk-kangŭi*, 452-453. Combining this notion of God as emptiness (*pint'ang*) with the Daoian notion of nothingness or non-being (無 *mu*) and Neo-Confucian notion that

Although "*hante*" (한데) originally denotes outside (밖), Dasŏk expanded this meaning to the "maximum outness," which transcends the division between the inside and the outside to eventually become one "togetherness" which includes the inside (안팎 한테 *anp'ak hant'e*).[12] From this point of view, he equated "*hante*" to "*yŏ*" (與), which means "being together" (더불다), sharing, or participating (參與). He says: "From this vantage point, *pint'ang* means emptiness, *hante* which means the togetherness of the inside and the outside (안팎 한테 *anp'ak hant'e*) signifies togetherness."[13] He further equated "*machhyŏ*" (맞혀) to harmonising or "matching" to signify the continuous process of being weaved together. Finally, "*noli*" (놀이) refers to playing rituals saturated in an ecstatic engagement with the *pint'ang hante*. Thus, the "conclusion of life" for Dasŏk is:

---

"the Great Ultimate is the Non-Ultimate" (無極而太極 *mu-kŭk-i-t'ae-kŭk*), he develops an intriguing insight of "God as the *Being in Non-Being*" or "Non-Existent Existing God" (없이 계신 님 *ŏpsi kyeshin nim*), which is the pinnacle of his theology. Also, calling God "The Father, Being in Non-Being" ("없이 계신 아바." Ryu, *Dasŏk-ilji*, 1:607), he said, "God is the Being in Non-Being. Although God is not, God is: Although human beings are, they are not." ("한아님은 없이 계신 이다. 없으면서도 계신다. 사람이란 있으면 서도 없다." Park Yŏng-ho, ed., *Dasŏk-ŏrok: Ssial-ŭi-maeari* [Analects of Dasŏk: Echoes of Seeds] [Seoul: Hongikje, 1993], 371). For this notion of Being in Non-Being, see Heup Young Kim, "The Word made Flesh: A Korean Perspective on Ryu Yŏngmo's Christotao" in *One Gospel and Many Cultures: Case Studies and Reflections on Cross-Cultural Theology*, eds. Mercy Amba Oduyoye and Handrik M. Vroom (Amsterdam-New York, NY: Rodopi, 2003), 143-44; and Kim, *Kaon-tchikki*, 81-89. Also, Youn Jeong-Hyun, "The Non-Existent Existing God: An East Asian Perspective with Specific Reference to the thought of Ryu Yŏngmo," Th.D. dissertation, University of Birmingham (Birmingham, United Kingdom, 2002), esp. 124-196. For Dasŏk's understanding of God, see Kim, *Kaon-tchikki*, 81-100.

12 "'한데'는 밖이라는 말이긴 하나, 정말 '한데'라는 밖을 죄다 점령하면 안(內)과 밖(外)이 없어집니다. '한데'에는 안도 다 들어갑니다." Ryu, *Dasŏk-kangŭi*, 466.

13 "이렇게 보면 빈탕은 공(空), 안팎한테인 한데는 여(與) 가 될 수 있습니다." Ibid.

"Let us play rituals in harmony with the emptiness together".[14] Unfortunately, however, this creative and insightful apophatic spirituality and negative theology is still unpopular and even suspiciously rejected in Korean Protestantism, heavily influenced by Neo-Calvinist fundamentalism.

## 2. Spiritual Hiking: A Trans-Religious and Trans-Cosmic Prayer

Dasŏk's embodied spiritual principle of *"pint'ang-hante machhyŏ noli"* culminates in the prayer he has written entitled "Stroll (산보 *Sanbo)*" or "Spiritual Hiking (정신 하이킹)."[15] In this prayer, the profound concepts found in East Asian religions like Confucianism, Daoism, and Buddhism are integrated with one another. Therefore, it will be exceedingly difficult for those unfamiliar with these religions to understand it. Moreover, Dasŏk was playing here with his uniquely innovative adaptations of the Korean language (*hangul-noli*),[16] which will make the poetic prayer complex even for Koreans to understand. Thus, it is a tricky task to translate this short but dense prayer text into English; such a task crosses multiple religious, cultural, linguistic, conceptual, and metaphorical borders. This is probably the first ever attempt at translating Dasŏk's poetic prayer into English, thus this translation can by no means be considered com-

---

14 *"Pint'ang-hante-e match'u-ŏsŏ noli haja"*(빈탕한데에 맞추어서 놀이를 하자). Ibid, 467.

15 See footnote 3.

16 For an example of *hangŭl noli*, see Kim, *Kaon-tchikki*, 73-74.

plete (cf. "untranslatability"[17]). However, my aim here is to introduce Dasŏk's religious thought, via his prayer, to a global audience to establish his significance in the field of interreligious relations. It is hoped that this can serve as a foundation for deeper research and scholarship on this prayer in particular, or on Dasŏk more broadly. The prayer translates:[18]

> The Father (아버지 abŏji)[19] and the Only Begotten Son (한나신 아들
> han-nashin adŭl)[20] in the seat high, high, high, and higher than the mountain, even higher than mountains, higher than white snow, even higher

---

17 See Paul Ricoeur, *On Translation*, trans. Eileen Brennan (New York, NY: Routledge, 2006).

18 The original Korean text is as follows: "높고 높고 높고 산보다 높고 산들보다도 높고 흰 눈보다도 높고 삼만 오천육백만 리 해보다도 높고 백억 천조 해들이 돌고 도는 우리 하늘보다 높고 하늘을 휩싼 빈탕(虛空)보다도 높고 허공을 새겨낸 마음보다 높고 마음이 난 바탈(個性)보다 더 높은 자리에 아버지 한나신 아들 참거룩하신 얼이 끝없이 밑없이 그득 차이시고 고루 잠기시며 두루 옮기시사 얼얼이 절절이 사무쳐 움직이시는 얼김 맞아 마음 오래 열려 예여오른 김 큰김 굴려 코뚤리니 안으로 그득 산김이 사백조 살알을 꿰뚫고 모여 나린 뱃심 잘몬의 바탕 힘 바다보다 깊이 땅 아래로 깊이 은하계 아래로 깊이 한 알 알을 꿰어 뚫다. 이 긴김 깊이 코김 뱃심으로 잇대는 동안 얕은 낮에 불통이 튀고 좁은 속에 마음종 울리다 마니 싶으지 않은가, 우는 이는 좋음이 있나니 저회가 마음 싹임(消息)을 받을 것임이라. 우리 마음에 한 목숨은 목숨키기 깊이 느껴 높이 살음 잘몬의 피어 울리는 피도 이 때문 한 알 알의 부서져 내리는 빛도 이 때문 우리 안에 밝은 속알이 밝아 굴러 커지는 대로 우리 속은 넓어지며 우리 꺼풀은 얇아지니 바탈 타고난 마음 그대로 왼통 속알 굴려 깨쳐 솟아나와 오르리로다." Ryu, *Dasŏk-iljii*, 4:487; also, Kim Hŭng-ho, *Chesori*, 122.

19 Dasŏk called God the Father (*abŏji*) 아버지. For his understanding of the Trinity, see Kim, *Kaon-tchikki*, 101-14.

20 Dasŏk coined "*han-nashin adŭl*" (한나신 아들) as a Korean term to express Jesus as the Only Begotten Son (獨生子 *toksaengja*), which is a central notion for his Christology. For him, Jesus is first and foremost the Filial Son, as filial piety is a primary virtue of Confucianism. See Ryu, *Dasŏk-ilji*, 1:97-98, 108; also, Kim, *Kaon-tchikki*, 11-12, 111-12, 167-68. For his Christology (precisely, Christo-dao), see Kim, *Kaon-tchikki*, 136-93; also, Kim, "The Word made Flesh," 129-48.

than the sun three hundred million *li* (里)[21] away, higher than our sky a hundred million thousand trillion suns round and round above, even higher than the emptiness (*pint'ang*) surrounding the sky, higher than the mind-heart (*maŭm*) that carved out the emptiness, even more, higher than the selfhood (*pat' al*) born by the mind-heart!

Moreover, the truly Holy Spirit (참 거룩한 얼 *ch'am kŏruk'an ŏl*)[22] end-lessly and boundlessly fills, evenly submerges, and thoroughly moves to completely penetrate into my mind-heart! While the mind-heart is opened by receiving the spirit (얼김 *ŏl-kim*), the risen vapor (김 *kim*)[23] rolls through the nose, pierces through four hundred trillion cells (살알 *sal-al*), and gathers together to produce the original force in the lower abdomen (잘몬 *chalmon*).[24] It pierces deeper down the earth than the ocean and further down the galaxy by penetrating and threading the whole cells (알 *al*) as one.[25]

---

21 An East Asian unit to measure distance (1 *li* = about 0.4 km).

22 The phrase "*Ch'am kŏruk'an ŏl*" (참 거룩한 얼) is an expression of Dasŏk for the Holy Spirit. In Dasŏk's terminolgy, "*ŏl*" (얼) means both soul and spirit (靈 *yŏng*, 精神 *chŏng-sin*). While interpreting the word "*ŏl-tŏl-gyŏl*" (얼덜곌), he referred to "*ŏl*" (얼) as "going up" but "*tŏl*" (덜) to "falling-down". For this passage, he defined "*ŏl*" as denoting the Holy Spirit but "*tŏl*" the devil's spirit. see Ryu, *Chesori*, 123-24.

23 Although "*kim*" (김) originally means vapor, here it is equivalent to "*ki*" (氣; in Chinese *qi*), a key East Asian spiritual (also psycho-somatic) term, which can be translated in various ways, such as "vital force" or "meta-cosmic energy", while also meaning vapor. Hence, "*ŏl-kim*" is another of Dasŏk's neologism to express the Holy Spirit in pure Korean.

24 *Chalmon* is equivalent to the lower abdomen (丹田 *tanchŏn*) which is thought to be the central part of human energy circulation in Sŏndo's *ki* training (氣功 *kikong*).

25 It is intriguing to comprehend and translate this part. *Al* basically means eggs, but here this term seems to refer to both the cells (細胞 *se-p'o*) and the holes for ki-flow (氣穴 *ki-hyŏl*) in the human body. In this way, Dasŏk seemed to express "*hyŏn-pin-il-kyu* (玄牝一竅)", a highly advanced level of *Sŏndo Kikong* (仙道 氣功), where all cells and

When this long vapor passes deep through the nose and the abdomen, does not one feel the shallow face sparks and the narrow mind-heart rings? Those who weep will be blessed because they will receive good news. Because of this, in the mind-heart, we can live upward with the feeling of the depth of life, the blood growing up from the blossoming lower abdomen, and the brilliant light to the whole cells as one. Thus as much as the shining virtues (속알 sok-al) in us brightens to enlarge with rolling,[26] our insides will widen, and our skin becomes thin so that the mind-heart, as naturally born with the selfhood, will be awakened by rolling whole virtues to leap out and rise up.[27]

He meditated deeply, memorising and chanting it. He regarded it as his version of the Lord's prayer. As expressed in this prayer, Dasŏk identified himself as a cosmic person.[28] As implied by the name "Spiritual Hiking," it indicates a prayer integrated with the *modus operandi* of East Asian practices of contemplative breathing; piercing through the cosmos (namely, trans-cosmic) "to rise high and higher up to the throne of God and from there having received the Holy Spirit coming back down to this world and then again rais-

---

*ki* holes are opened so that meta-cosmic energy (*ki*) penetrates the whole body and spearheads everywhere as the one hole.

26 This phrase can mean cultivating virtues (德 *tŏk*) or practising inner Daoist alchemy (鍊丹 *yŏndan*), a top-level discipline of *Sŏndo Kikong*. Perhaps, *Dasŏk* would have intended both meanings.

27 Ryu, *Dasŏk-ilji*, 4:487.

28 Dasŏk said that he does not belong to any particular residence on the earth (無主 *muchu*), but the place of his life is the vast universe. Therefore, he confessed, his life is nothing but the prayer and cultivation to be united with the cosmos by the power of the Holy Spirit. See ibid, 4:611-612, see also Kim, "Introducing Dasŏk Ryu."

ing up by increasing my life in order that a flower blooms in the mind-heart."[29] Indeed, Dasŏk's understanding of prayer denotes spiritual cosmic hiking with the heaven as its stage. Therefore, I suggest adding the word heavenly (*hanŭl* 하늘) to the phrase *"pint'ang-hante machhyŏ noli"* (빈탕한데 맞혀 놀이) so to read *"pint'ang-hante machhyŏ hanŭl noli"* (빈탕한데 맞혀 하늘 놀이) (playing *heavenly* rituals in harmony with the emptiness together). Moreover, it provides a summary of Dasŏk's spiritual theology, together with the three basics of spirituality he argued for Christian life, namely, keeping the body healthy (*mom-sŏnghi*), relieving the mind-heart (*mam-nohi*), and cultivating selfhood (*pat'al-t'oehi*).[30] Here is Dasŏk's own interpretation of this prayer:

> First, imagine, starting from the mountain past the sun, the galaxy, the emptiness (*pint'ang hante*) surrounding the cosmos on the other side, the mind-heart residing in it, and the throne of God in the center of the mind-heart. Further, imagine the Holy Spirit that flows like a river from this throne. As it descends like dew, thus, it descends in the mind-heart. The Holy Spirit pierces into mouth, eyes, ears, heart, wisdom to fully penetrate through the four-hundred trillion living cells. Its energy gathers in the gut and becomes the force to move the cosmos. While penetrating the galaxy and the solar system, this force descends to make our faces spark and our mind-hearts ring the bell so that we feel deeply and think in order that our mind-hearts are emptied and

---

29 Ibid, 4:487.

30 For keeping the body healthy (*mom-sŏnghi*), relieving the mind-heart (*mam-nohi*), cultivating selfhood (*pat'al-t'oehi*), see Kim, "Introducing Dasŏk Ryu," 7-9.

brightened. When it happens, [furthermore] there will be an awakening
that will rear up our life and our soul. Therefore, we come to realise
that it is the core of life to feel deeply, live highly, think profoundly,
and practice honourably.[31]

It is noteworthy that this prayer, "the stroll in the cosmos" (hanŭl
sanbo) does not only end with "a spiritual cosmic hiking" (pint'ang-
hante machhyŏ nori), but there is also an intimate connection with
the cosmos in the body (mom). The internal and the external to the
body are micro-cosmos (microcosm) and the macro-cosmos
(macrocosm), which are inter-communicable through the vital force
and the Holy Spirit (ŏl-kim).[32] The "playing rituals (nori) in harmony
with the emptiness together" means this. It sounds very similar to
advanced practices of hypogastric breathing in the Sŏndo training,[33]

---

31 The original Korean text is as follows: "맨 처음에 산에서부터 시작하여 해를 거쳐서 은하계
저편 우주를 싸고 있는 빈탕한데 저편에 거기가 마음인데 그 마음 한복판에 하나님의 보좌
를 생각하고 그 보좌에서 생명의 강처럼 흘러내려오는 얼김을 생각해 본다. 그래서 이슬이
내리듯 내 마음에 내려 그 얼김으로 입이 뚫리고 코가 뚫리고 눈이 뚫리고 귀가 뚫리고
마음이 뚫리고 지혜가 뚫려서 사백조 살알 세포를 다 뚫고 그 기운이 배 밑에 모여 자연을
움직이는 힘이 되어 은하계를 뚫고 태양계를 뚫고 내리어 우리 얼굴에 불똥이 튀게 하고
우리 마음에 종을 울리게 하여 깊이 느끼고 깊이 생각하여 마음을 비게 하고 마음을 밝게
하면 우리 마음속에서 깨닫게 되는 것이 있으니, 그것이 우리의 목숨 키우고 우리의 생명을
키워가는 것이다. 그래서 깊이 느끼고 높이 살게 하는 것, 깊이 생각하고 고귀하게 실천하는
것 그것이 생명의 핵심임을 알게 된다." Ryu, "Sanbo," Chesori, 123.

32 East Asian religions in general regard the human body as a microcosm of the cosmos.
In the Sŏndo training, breathing is the way to develop the communion between the
body (a microcosmos) and the cosmos (macro-cosmos) in and through the movement
of ki (meta-cosmic energy).

33 Korean Sŏndo (仙道) is an inherited ascetic tradition to become the immortal (神仙
sinsŏn), that takes hypogastric breathing (丹田呼吸) as a crucial method, partially related
to Daoism. For example, see Ko Kyŏngmin, Yŏngsaeng-hanŭn Kil [The Way for

namely, the micro-cosmic (bodily) circulation (小周天 *sochuch'ŏn*) and the macro-cosmic circulation (大周天 *taechuch'ŏn*) of the vital force or meta-cosmic energy (氣 *ki*). Dasŏk wrote a poem after he first experienced the union of Heaven, Earth, and Humanity (天地人 合一 *ch'ŏn-chi-in hapil*) in 1943 at the lounge of Mt. Pukaksan in Seoul:

> Looking above, penetrate Heaven: Submerging, pierce under the Earth. Looking above, extend the Body to reach the Primordial Force of Heaven.
>
> Putting down the Mind-Heart, submerge, pierce, and arrive at the Axial Force of Earth.[34]

Likewise, it proposes a psycho-somatic exercise in a trans-cosmic nature to associate the bodily circulation and the cosmic circulations by breathing and meditating through the vital force's flow. Furthermore, this prayer suggests an illuminating *trans-religious* structure linking major East Asian spiritual traditions (Confucianism, Daoism, and Buddhism) with Christianity. This contemplative prayer can be summarised in six sequences as in the following diagram:[35]

---

Immortality] (Seoul: Chongno Ch'ulp'ansa, 1974); also, Ko Kyŏngmin, *Kuksŏndo*, 3 vols (Seoul: Kuksŏndo Publications, 1993); also Kim, "Introducing Dasŏk Ryu," 8-9.

34 He wrote about this experience in classical Chinese: "瞻徹天 潛透地 申身瞻徹極乾元氣! 沈心潛透止坤軸力." Pak Chae-sun, *Dasŏk Yŏngmo: tongsŏ-sasang-ŭl aurŭn ch'ang-jojŏk saengmyŏng ch'ŏrhakcha* [The Creative Philosopher of Life who integrated the Eastern and the Western Thoughts] (Seoul: Hyŏnamsa, 2008), 54, recited. English translation is mine.

35 These are the primary sequences concerning meditative objects. However, this contemplative prayer program uniquely formulated by Dasŏk does not have to be done precisely in this order. They can be modified in accordance with the ability and situation

## Figure 1: Summary of Dasŏk's prayer

| 1. Trans-cosmic | Mountains-Earth | Solar System-Galaxy | Macro-Cosmos |
|---|---|---|---|
| 2. Trans-religious (East Asian) | Emptiness(*pint'ang* 空) Daoism | Mind-Heart (*maŭm* 心) Buddhism | Selfhood (*pat' al* 性) Confucianism |
| 3. Trinity | God the Father | the Only Son (Jesus) | the Holy Spirit(*ŏl-kim*) Vital Force (*kim* 氣) |
| 4. Bodily (Inner) Circulation (小周天) | Circulate Vital Force (氣) through Breathing | Into Whole Body (Four Trillion Cells) | Fill up Lower Abdomen (*chalmon* 丹田) |
| 5. Cosmic (Outer) Circulation (大周天) | Ocean-Earth | Galaxy | Meta-Cosmos |
| 6. Awaken the Core of Life | Empty the mind-heart | Receive Good News | Expand Virtues (*sok-al* 德) |

This prayer presents five characteristics of Dasŏk's insights on spirituality. First of all, the spirituality Dasŏk conceived goes beyond the earth's narrow limits to the entire cosmos' vastness (macro-cosmos) to reach even further to the religious and spiritual dimensions. Hence, it is the *trans-cosmic spirituality* for a cosmic person.[36] Secondly, the spirituality of Dasŏk penetrates through three major East Asian spiritual traditions and, by embracing all of them, guides the practitioner into a new horizon of Christian spirituality, further sublimated but with unmistakably Korean and East Asian elements. As such,

---

of practitioners. For example: (1) Beginners can similarly practice them like an image training or an ordinary Christian prayer (by following the sequences of 1-3 and 6); (2) Those who can breathe through the lower abdomen (丹田呼吸) can raise their spiritual consciousness through the sequences of 1-3 to receive the *ki* (vital force) of life (the Holy Spirit) to activate inner circulation (4 and 6); (3) The advanced can accumulate the *ki* through the inner circulations to extend it outer. However, since this program primarily aims to awaken the Dao (Way) and its wholistic embodiment beyond intellectual and cognitive knowing, the personal help of a competent spiritual director or master is highly recommended.

36 In one of his lectures, he replied, "I live in the cosmos," when asking, "Where do I live?" (Ryu, *Dasŏk-kangŭi*, 292).

the emptiness (*pint'ang,* 空), the mind-heart (*maŭm,* 心), and the self-hood (*pat' al,* 性) could imply the spiritual dimensions of Daoism (Laozi), Buddhism (Buddha), and Confucianism (Confucius), respectively. Hence, it portrays a *trans-religious spirituality* that passes through these three East Asian religions and a way to communion with the Triune God.

Thirdly, it entails a solidly *Trinitarian spirituality.* Of course, this is related to the East Asian triadic cosmology consisting of Heaven, Earth, and Humanity (天地人 *ch'ŏn-chi-in*), a "the-anthropo-cosmic vision," which became the basic framework for his thought.[37] In this prayer, Dasŏk viewed the Holy Trinity - the God "the Father (*abŏji*)," "the Only Begotten Son (*han-nashin adŭl*)," and "the true Holy Spirit (*ch'am kŏruk' an ŏl*)" — as both the goal of his trans-cosmic and trans-religious spirituality and the origin of spiritual energy or vital force.[38] Fourthly, Dasŏk's spirituality is pneumato-centric (or *ki*-centric),[39] whose spirit works by breathing and through the flow of vital force or meta-cosmic energy (氣). It underscores the breathing discipline that embodies the Trinity's vital force in our body through the Holy Spirit's descent (a *spirituality of breathing*).[40] Finally,

---

37 The-anthropo-cosmic vision is a term to designate a fusion of horizons at the meeting between Christian theo-historical (salvation history) and Neo-Confucian anthropo-cosmic (天人合一) visions. For more, see Heup Young Kim, *A Theology of Dao* (Maryknoll, NY: Orbis Books, 2017), 43-48, 207-11.

38 For Dasŏk's understanding of the Trinity, see Kim, *Kaon-tchikki,* 101-114; also Heup Young Kim, "The Tao in Confucianism and Taoism: the Trinity in East Asian Perspective" in *The Cambridge Companion to the Trinity,* ed. Peter Phan (Cambridge: Cambridge University Press, 2011), 293-308.

39 *Pneuma* and *ki* are homologous terms, for both connote spirit, wind, and breath together.

what Dasŏk proposes is a *spirituality of the body*. The prayer of 'Spiritual Hiking' does not end as a psychological euphoria. 'Spiritual Hiking' illustrates the process of self-cultivation and sanctification through the transformation of our body (as mentioned above in relationship with Sŏndo). Indeed, the disciplines of *mom-sŏnghi*, *mam-no-hi*, and *pat'al-t'oehi* appear in physical changes and phenomenological signs. Therefore, this is not merely a simple spiritual prayer in association with the heaven (*hanŭl-noli*), but a contemplative prayer with physical embodiment (*hanŭl-mom-noli*) that results in inter-relationship and communion through the operation of the Holy Spirit or the meta-cosmic energy.[41]

These characteristics are related to the East Asian Spirituality of the Dao (道), as *dao* is an all-embracing concept for East Asian religions.[42] It also entails the spiritual context for the formulation of *theo-dao* (a theology of *dao*)[43] as a Korean/East Asian constructive

---

40 I call the theological paradigm with this insight "a theology of the breath" (숨신학 *sum sinhak*). See Kim, *Kaon-tchikki*, 239-56.

41 I call a theological paradigm with this insight "a theology of the body" (몸신학 *mom sinhak*). See ibid, 213-38.

42 For modern people, a holistic notion of the polysemic word *dao* is challenging to understand. Western people generally misunderstand that dao is only related to Daoism. However, other East Asian traditions widely use the term, such as the dao of Confucianism, the dao of Buddhism, and even the dao of Christianity. An excellent definition of dao in English: "Tao [*Dao*] is a Way, a path, a road, and by common metaphorical extension it becomes in ancient China the right Way of life, the Way of governing, the ideal Way of human existence, the Way of the Cosmos, the generative-normative Way (Pattern, path, course) of existence as such." See Herbert Fingarette, *Confucius: The Secular as Sacred* (New York, NY: Harper & Row, 1972), 19.

43 See Kim, *A Theology of Dao*, 14-33, 212-216. In Korean, see Heup Young Kim, *Do-ŭi Sinhak* (Seoul: Tasan Kŭlpang, 2000) and Heup Young Kim, *Do-ŭi Sinhak II* (Seoul: Tong-yŏn, 2012).

theology that adopts the *dao* as its root-metaphor instead of *logos* (theo-logy). Dasŏk's religious thoughts present a prototype of *theo-dao* (도의 신학 *do-ŭi sinhak*).[44] Theo-dao, with Dasŏk's spirituality as resources, can resolve two significant problems of the global Christian theology, still dominated by Western theologies. Firstly, a dilemma of global Christian theology is the split between *theo-logos* (classical theologies) and *theo-praxis* (liberationist theologies), owing to the inherited Greek dualism between theory (logos) and practice (praxis).[45] Since dao, a holistic East Asian notion, also implies the unity of knowledge and action (知行合一 *chihaeng hapil*), *theo-dao* can be an alternative paradigm of Christian theology that overcomes the prolonged dilemma of such severe theological division.[46]

Secondly, the ecological crisis. The starting point for Dasŏk's spi-

---

44 See Kim, *Kaon-tchikki*, 45-46, 395-97.

45 Liberation theologies (theo-praxis) originated in the unjust socio-economic situation in Latin America but expanded to deal with global classism, racism, sexism, etc. They represent the antithesis to dominant classical Western theologies (theo-logos). The former take praxis as their theological root-metaphor, focusing on orthopraxis (the right action) of God's reign and the preferential option for the poor (the central message of the Gospel), while the latter prioritises orthodoxy (the right doctrines) of the church. The division also represents the separation between the Global South and the Global North or the Third World and the First World. See Kim, *A Theology of Dao*, 14-33. For liberation theology, see Gustavo Gutiérrez, *A Theology of Liberation* (Maryknoll, NY: Orbis Books, 1988).

46 Since its Chinese character Dao (道) consists of two parts, head (首 *su*) and movement (辶 *ch'ak*), dao hieroglyphically means the unity of knowledge (head) and action (movement). For the unity of knowledge and action, see Heup Young Kim, *Wang Yang-ming and Karl Barth: A Confucian-Christian Dialogue* (Lanham, MD: University Press of America, 1996), 29-32, 71-74, 149-152. Whereas theo-logos searches orthodoxy (theory) and orthopraxis (practice) separately, theo-dao pursues the ortho-dao or ortho-ho-dos (the right way and wisdom of life) in the all-inclusive unity (dao) of theory and practice. See Kim, *A Theology of Dao*, 14-33.

rituality is *kaon-tchikki*, finding and locating one's true self in the ontological and existential unity.[47] It resonates with Martin Luther's notion of *Coram Deo*, a faith to find one's self in front of God. However, Luther's notion focuses on one's individual soul's relationship to God, neglecting the totality of one's existence with physical and cosmo-logical dimensions. Forgetting the body and earth, this anthro-pocentric spirituality in Western Christianity has been criticised as a theological cause for ecological exploitation. In contrast, *kaon-tchik-ki* takes the body, earth, and cosmos, as the very constituencies of its the-anthropo-cosmic spirituality. It is an ecological spirituality *par excellence*.[48]

47 *Kaon-tchikki* 가온찍기 is a core concept of Dasŏk's thought. *Kaon* 가온 is composed of three characters of old Korean, "ㄱ" (*kiŏk*), "ᆞ" (*arae a*) and "ㄴ" (*niŭn*). *Area a* ("ᆞ") in old Korean can be both *a* (ㅏ) and *o* (ㅗ). (ㄱ + ᆞ = 가 *ka*; ᆞ + ㄴ = 온 *on*; therefore, 가온 *ka-on*). According to him, "ㄱ" signifies the heaven, "ㄴ" the earth, and "ᆞ" selfhood (humanity). Also, ka-on refers to center (가운데 *kaunde*), equivalent to Chinese character *chung* (中). Hence, *kaon* means the center in the unity between the cosmos and selfhood (my anthropo-cosmic center), namely, my real and true place (both existential and onto-logical). *Tchikki* literally means "to put a dot (myself)". Thus, *kaon-tchikki* connotes locating selfhood in one's unique anthropo-cosmic center (ontological and existential), which is the goal of and the true starting point for religion and spirituality. See Kim, *Kaon-tchikki*.

48 See Heup Young Kim, "Eco-Dao: an Ecological Theology of Dao" in *The Bloomsbury Handbook of Religion and Nature: The Elements*, eds. Laura Hobgood and Whitney Bauman (London: Bloomsbury Academic, 2018), 99-108; also, Kim, *A Theology of Dao*, 204-222. The theanthropo-cosmic notion of eco-dao (instead of conceptual eco-logos) based on theo-dao is remarkably resonant with "*Laudato si'*: On the Care for Our Common Home," a recent ecological encyclical of Pope Francis (see "Eco-Dao," 105-8), available at: http://www.vatican.va/content/dam/francesco/pdf/encyclicals /documents/papa-francesco_20150524_enciclica-laudato-si_en.pdf.

## 3. Toward a New Horizon of Spirituality: Playing Heavenly Body Rituals in Harmony with the Emptiness Together (*Pint'ang-hante machhyŏ hanŭl-mom-noli*)

Even before the human species penetrated through the earth's atmosphere to reach space, Dasŏk Ryu Yŏngmo had learnt a spirituality of trans-cosmic scale and trans-religious depth to become "a cosmic spiritual person." His familiar climb up Mount Puk'an in Seoul was not merely a mountain climb. It was a spiritual discipline which he called a "stroll" or "spiritual hiking," where the cosmos is nestled, rolled, and breathed in his lower abdomen. To pray is not an anthropocentric demand for material blessings. For Dasŏk, on the contrary, to pray is to breathe and embody the meta-cosmic energy (*ki*) given to us by the triune God and to engage in the dance of harmony to the melody and rhythm of cosmic life movement, namely, "Playing Heavenly Body Rituals in Harmony with the Emptiness Together (*pint'ang-hante machhyŏ hanŭl-mom-noli*)." In an age where many cheap and superficial Christian spiritualities are prevalent in Korea and elsewhere, the spirituality conceived by Dasŏk shines brilliantly with its significance, like gold ore hidden in the murky water. These trans-cosmic and trans-religious spiritual insights of Dasŏk should not be a gift only for Korean or East Asian Christianity but for global Christianity. The significance of his insights lies in boldly realising Christian spirituality's holistic identity in Korea and East Asia's multi-religious and multi-spiritual context, where multi-religiosity is a reality rather than an abstract epistemological ideal as religious pluralism. Dasŏk's religious thoughts hold many clues for viable insights demanded by contemporary theology, religion, and spirituality in this global and cosmic age, with theo-*dao* as an example.[49]

## Conclusion

Dasŏk offers a horizon on the much-needed *spirituality of body and breath* to generations that need to cope with an age of Artificial Intelligence, Digital Revolution, Transhumanism (e.g., bio-hacking technologies for human enhancement), and Post-humanity, as we see today that a person is to be mechanised into a cyborg by an unprecedented advancement in science and technology.[50] For, in short, cyborg post-humans equipped with Artificial Intelligence will not have a human-like body and cannot breathe (cf. a sci-fi movie, *Matrix*).[51] However, this is a note on emerging trends and their sig-

---

49 See Kim, *A Theology of Dao.*

50 See Heup Young Kim, "Cyborg, Sage, and Saint: Transhumanism as Seen from an East Asian Theological Setting" in *Religion and Transhumanism: The Unknown Future of Human Enhancement,* eds. Calvin Mercer and Tracy J. Trothen (Santa Barbara, CA: Praeger, 2014), 97-114; also Heup Young Kim, "Confucian Religious Spirituality and Transhumanist Anthropology" in *Religious Transhumanism and Its Critics,* eds. Arvin Gouw, Brian Patrick Green, and Ted Peters (Lanham, MD: Lexington Books, 2022), 101-12.

51 The cosmic spirituality of body and breath is a significant aspect that modern Western thought and logos theology have neglected. The challenges of the ecological crisis, artificial intelligence, and transhumanism are issues related to the earth, the human body, and the spirituality and theology of the body. Furthermore, with Covid-19, nature is awakening us to the importance of breathing and the spirituality of breath. Thus, the cosmic spirituality needed in this age of the ecological crisis, artificial intelligence, and the pandemic (cf. Anthropocene) is the cosmic spirituality of body and breath. It is a

nificance, a subject matter beyond this paper's scope. Furthermore, many signs of difficult times are ahead, including the anthropogenic ecological crisis (climate change) and the coronavirus pandemic related to anthropocentric and kataphatic (or logo-phonic) spirituality. It is the time when we need Dasŏk's the-anthropo-cosmic and apophatic spirituality of "*pint'ang-hante machhyŏ hanŭl-noli*", which makes us breathe in the magnanimous cosmic-energy. Amid the darkness of the night, it may seem like a mere flicker of a very distant star on the other side of the galaxy. However, Dasŏk's spiritual disciplines of *mom-sŏnghi*, *mam-nohi*, and *pat'al-t'oehi* to learn and embody the true body, the true mind-heart, and the true selfhood are indeed preparing our body, mind-heart, and spirit, and so humanity can prepare for the challenging new age to come, by opening a new horizon (new heaven) of human spirituality, which is trans-religious and trans-cosmic.

spiritual core and basis of theo-*dao*, set in this world of *dao* and *ki* (meta-cosmic energy). For the theology and spirituality of body and breath, see Kim, *kaon-tchikki*, 197-256.

CHAPTER THIRTEEN

# Reviving Minjung Theology in the Technological Era:
## Kim Yong-bok's Seontopian Zoesophia in Dialogue with Theo-Dao

## Abstract

This chapter explores into Kim Yong-bok's final reflections on
Minjung Theology in dialogue with Theo-Dao, a theology of Dao.
Kim's groundbreaking assertion that Minjung Theology is a sociobiography of the minjung broadens the cosmological Zoegraphy
(the narrative of life) beyond historical constraints. It matures into
a sapiential Zoesophia (Wisdom of Life), envisioning a Seontopia
(East Asian Utopia). Minjung Theology prompts preparation for the
impending ultra-technological civilization, characterized by the
burgeoning evolution of artificial intelligence, marking a stride toward the future. Kim's profound insights into Seontopian Zoesophia
could serve as foundational pillars for the revival of Minjung
Theology in the Anthropocene era of technological civilization.
Furthermore, it extends an invitation to future theologians and
scholars of religion to perpetuate this line of inquiry.

## Introduction

My last interaction with Dr. Yong-bok Kim (1938-2022) occurred at the 5th CGU Global Symposium at Gyeongan Graduate University in Andong, Gyeongsangbuk-do, from June 28 to July 1, 2021.[1] The symposium centered on "Cosmic Spirituality in the Era of Artificial Intelligence and the COVID-19 Pandemic." Through his engrossing lectures and dialogues at the symposium, Yong-bok introduced the concept of "Seontopia" (in Korean, Seon-Gyeong [仙境]) - a notion that appeared novel within theological discussions.

Yong-bock's theological propositions underwent an expansive shift, incorporating cosmological aspects and layering indigenous Korean spiritualities over the socio-economic and historical bases of early minjung theology (predicated on the sociobiography of minjung).[2] For an extended period, I have criticized the constrictive hermeneutical confines of his early theology, proposing alternatives such as a "socio-cosmic biography of exploited life," a notion that cosmo-ecologically extends from the premise of "Theo-Dao" (a theology of Dao).[3] Over time, his historical perspective evolved from a socio-biographical viewpoint to a zoegraphical approach (narrative of life), and he started infusing theological insights into the conception of Seontopia (East Asian Utopia). Ultimately, we

---

1 For papers presented at the symposium, see Park Seong-Won, ed, *Cosmic Spirituality in the Era of Artificial Intelligence and the COVID-19 pandemic* (Gyeongsan: Life Wave, 2021)

2 See Yong-Bok Kim, "The Socio-biography of Minjung and Theology," in *Minjung and Korean Theology* (Seoul: Korea Theological Study Institute, 1982). Minjung generally means "the oppressed and alienated people in Korean.

3 See Heup Young Kim, *A Theology of Dao* (Maryknoll, NY: Orbis Books, 2017), 24-33.

concurred that the Dao (道) and Seon (仙), as opposed to the Logos, should serve as the fundamental metaphors underpinning our theological endeavors.

## Zoesophia

Yong-bok was an internationally recognized influencer in ecumenical theology, demonstrating an acute perceptiveness of global circumstances and an exceptional ability to interpret the zeitgeist. His passing is an incalculable loss, extending beyond the borders of Korea and Asia to resonate within the sphere of global theology. Despite his advanced age, he persistently sought to enhance his theological understandings, particularly in anticipation of the civilization-altering period precipitated by rapid technological developments, inclusive of the digital revolution and artificial intelligence, often termed the Fourth Industrial Revolution. Over two decades ago, he was at the forefront of discussions on transhumanism, the proposition that homo sapiens should evolve into posthumans, characterized by superintelligence and heightened capabilities, through the application of advanced scientific and technological tools.[4]

Fittingly, he transitioned from his initial focus on Minjung theology, grounded in the social biography of the minjung, towards a

---

4 For an East Asian theological analysis of transhumanism, see Heup Young Kim, "Cyborg, Sage, and Saint: Transhumanism as Seen from an East Asian Theological Setting," in *Religion and Transhumanism: The Unknown Future of Human Enhancement*, ed. Calvin Mercer and Tracy J. Trothen (Santa Barbara, CA: Praeger, 2014), 97-114.

Zoesophia (Wisdom of Life) predicated on a Zoegraphy (Life Biography). His presentation at the Andong Symposium elucidated his views on Zoesophia.[5] Notably, he posited "Zoesophia as the foundation for historical transformation towards a new civilization." He deliberately employed the term Zoesophia instead of Zoelogy, choosing the sapiential root-metaphor, Sophia, to challenge the dualistic Logos-based paradigm pervasive in Western theology. In this context, it becomes evident that both his Zoesophia and my Theo-Dao strive to disengage from the traditional theology of logos (theo-logos). Furthermore, Sophia encapsulates concepts closely aligned with the East Asian root-metaphor of Dao, rendering the comparative exploration and dialogue between Dao and Sophia an intriguing avenue for future research.[6]

Yong-Bock outlined the primary attribute of Zoesophia as "the cosmic web of life." In his words, "All living beings are creative subjects of life who are spiritual beings. All living beings sustain themselves as the web of life, in spiritual communion throughout the web. Zoegraphy, as part of Zoesophia, is a paradigmatic way to describe the history of life and its opposite: the Thanatography of the history of Zoecide."[7]

Yong-bok demonstrated a remarkable aptitude for creating novel theological terms. His theological reflection and written discourse appeared to initiate in English. I can empathize with this, having

---

5 See Yong-bok Kim, "A Creative Spiritual Convergence for Conviviality," in *Park, Cosmic Spirituality*, 45-54.

6 See Antoine Arjzakovsky, *Towards an Ecumenical Metaphysics, Vol 1: The Principles & Methods of Ecumenical Science* (New York, NY: Angelico Press, 2022), esp., 267-68.

7 Kim, "A Critical Convergence," 48.

also commenced my theological journey at the same American seminary. Writing first in English indicates the inception of theological thought in the same language - a possibility afforded by a sensitive awareness of global theological currents that extend beyond local circumstances. This approach facilitates the invention of novel theological terms that encapsulate and express our unique perspectives within our specific contexts. While a patriotic Korean theologian, Yong-bok possessed a remarkably broad global perspective that superseded most of his contemporaries. Consequently, he functioned as an inevitable boundary figure. Originating neologisms in English facilitated more accessible communication within English-speaking circles. However, translating these into Korean, a language embedded in a different cultural-linguistic context, presented a challenge. While the meaning of these English neologisms is relatively straightforward, a Korean translation that fully captures their essence remains an ongoing endeavor.

Therefore, an explication of Yong-bok's text, particularly his novel terminology, is required. For instance, 'Zoesophia' signifies a departure from Western Logos theology in at least two ways. Firstly, it delineates between wisdom (Sophia) and knowledge (Logos). Instead of Zoe-logy, which would be more conventional and associated with Logos, he opted for the compound term Zoe-Sophia, connoting wisdom, a concept more robustly developed in Eastern Orthodox theologies. This signifies a fundamental shift in the theological root-metaphor from Logos to Sophia, mirroring my own theological transition from Theo-logy to Theo-Dao. Secondly, it differentiates between life (Zoe) and death (Thanatos), suggesting that theology concerns itself with the narrative of life, not death. This insight segues into his other neologism, "Zoe-graphy" (the story of life), which will be discussed further.


## Zoegraphy

Yong-bock's divergence from conventional Western Logos theology was further evident in his distinction between Zoegraphy (history of life) and Thanatography (history of death). He posited that theology is not a Thanatology, associated with the Logos and potentially sliding into metaphysics, but a narrative of life with minjung as the subject of life opposing the life-annihilating forces of death. Zoegraphy constitutes a Zoesophic Minjung theology that broadens the sociobiography of minjung to encompass the cosmic dimensions of convivial life.

> Zoegraphy is the spiritual life story, from birth to death, the spiritual cycle of life, and the web of life of all living beings. The essential core of the living being is that it is the subject, which means the spiritual subject, and this subject lives in a spiritual communion of convivial life in the web of life. All religions and spiritual traditions understand this as the essence of all living beings.[8]

It is also notable that Yong-bok referred to the "sociobiography of Minjung", rather than the sociography. The term "sociobiography" already encompasses 'bios' (life), implicitly considering the body

---

8 Ibid, 49.

or living organism. Consequently, a more precise translation would be the "social life (body) story" of Minjung. The shift here is that, from the three Greek words for life featured in the New Testament — Bios, Psuche, and Zoe — he selected Zoe (Zoegraphy), considered more spiritual. Typically, Bios denotes the life of the physical body (Luke 8:14), Psuche signifies the life of the soul (Matthew 16:25), and Zoe represents divine life (John 1:14). The more fundamental, holistic, and ontological term "Zoe" is chosen to highlight the primary spiritual subjectivity and conviviality (symbiotic fellowship) of life. Consequently, it can be argued that his later theology sought the 'Dao of All Life', which promotes mutual benefit and shared circulation, as opposed to a dialectical dualism (modeled on an 'either-or' dichotomy) distinguishing between life and death or minjung and anti-Minjung. His ultimate focus was on conviviality and convergence, not anti-conviviality and divergence.

However, he never lost sight of the minjung's historical struggle for life, thematizing the biographies of life-preserving spiritual resistance movements (Zoegraphy) against life-destroying violence (Thanatography), and their historical convergence. He posited that within this convergence of life-preserving biographies (Zoegraphies), one must identify the hermeneutical foundation for a cosmic spirituality of life characterized by conviviality.

Spiritual resistance to the polity of violence against life, occurring throughout 5,000 years of history, can be the hermeneutical key to discerning the spirituality of convivial life in convergence. Spiritual religions emerged in human civilizations to counter despotic power regimes, and Karl Jaspers called the resultant changes civilizational mutations. Resistance of the peoples against imperial polities of old, as in the Egyptian despotic regime, the Babylonian empire, Greek empire, Persian empire, and Chinese despotic rules, provided a spiritual context for the reformation movement of Western Christianity in this matrix of historical civilization. In modern times, resistance movements of the colonized peoples in Africa, Asia and the Americas against the colonial powers have been fertile grounds for spiritual revitalization toward the liberated SangSeang [the original Korean word for conviviality] Web of Life. Resistance to the present globalized, neo-liberal economic and geopolitical power regime calls for cosmic convergence of spiritualities for ecumenical resistance against the regime.⁹

## Seontopia

Kim Yong-bok was not only a theologian but also a dedicated patriot with a profound love for his nation. He often counseled me, whenever I was tempted to venture abroad, that Korean theologians ought to remain in Korea, the true locus of their theology. He identified the utopia of Zoegraphy within the primitive life community of the Korean people, conceptualizing the spiritual life of the ancient tribal village as Seon-Gyeong(선경) or Seon-topia, yet another neologism.

The five thousand years of Zoegraphy (history of life: 생명의 역사) on the Korean peninsula and in East Asia can be a pivotal locus. We know

---

9 Ibid.

the story of the primitive communal villages of living beings in ancient times. This story is known to the people in and around the Korean peninsula about 5,000 years ago. In brief, I would like to call the spiritual life of ancient Korean tribal communities Seontopia. This is described in the saga of the Tangun [the legendary forefather of the Korean people] and related stories. Seontopia has evolved and converged with various spiritual experiences. [That is to say] the Sangsaeng web of life with its spiritual communion of life of all living beings (이화상생, 홍익인간, 태평천하). Modern historiography has neglected this dimension of spiritual communion and convergence in the framework of the web of life on Earth.[10]

This narrative signal the evolution of Yong-bok's theology from a resistant Minjung theology to a convivial Zoesophia, ultimately culminating in a "Theology of Seon." Here, his endeavors to transition from the Western theological paradigm to an authentically Korean and East Asian theological framework are more pronounced. Regrettably, he did not live to complete this shift, which remains an important task for future scholars. If Minjung theologians can understand and expand upon his attempts, it may facilitate their escape from the constraints of Western thought and ascend to a genuinely subjective thought of life (and Minjung) for us and the world.

Yong-bok investigated into Korean history, from the Three Kingdoms period (18 BC - 660 AD), to unearth the spiritual resistance narrative - a Zoegraphy of Seontopia. Firstly, he associated Seontopia with Pungryu (風流), "one classical spiritual event in the

---

10 Ibid, 49-50.

community of the people." He endeavored to formulate a Minjung theology of Pungryu in alignment with the concept of Seontopia. He facilitated a convergence, fusion, or union of Korean indigenization theology and Minjung theology narratives, which had been a troubling dichotomy in Korean theology.

This spiritual foundation had manifested in the Three Kingdoms period, though this was the time of royal regimes and their landed aristocratic classes. One classical spiritual event in the community of the people was a market festival called Pungryu. In the story of the three thousand palace women, we find the spiritual resistance against the brutal war caused by the military alliance between Shilla [57 BC - 935 AD] and Tang Dynasties [618-907 in China] for the unification of three kingdoms. Subsequently, the Maitreya Minjung Buddhist spirituality movement developed in the Honam province of Korea. This may have been a sequel to the convergence of the Nestorian Christian spirituality and Tang Buddhism in 6th century China.

An outstanding Minjung historiography of Samguk Yusa [Overlooked Historical Records of the Three Korean Kingdoms] is the Minjung spirituality described in the Saga of Tangun, which is a resistance story of Sentopia against 40-years-long Mongol military siege against the Koryeo Kingdom [918-1392].

This story has great importance in the history of spiritual convergence in Korea. In the early period of the Joseon Kingdom, the political economy took the form of a people centered economy, seeking to overcome the socio-economic violence of the ruling Yangban in the Koryeo Dynasty. Toward the end of the Joseon Dynasty [1392-1910], the people-centered economy and the Donghak Peasant Movement's economy (Donghak people-centered economy: 東學의 經世濟民) were the fruits of spiritual convergence in resistance to the socio-economic violence that was damaging the web of life.

During Japan's colonial domination over Korea, the Donghak legacy, the Confucian righteous "voluntary army" (義兵), the Donghak Movement, the Minjung Buddhist Movement, the Korean Christian Messianic Movement, and the liberal and social movement of the West all converged on the ground of the Seontopia legacy to declare a new vision of the web of life for a SangSaeng political economy, as expressed in the Declaration of the March 1st Independence Movement. This spiritual convergence laid the foundation for the liberated Korean peninsula.

However, the post-WW II situation, with the national division, the Korean War, and the global regimentation of the Cold War, did not allow the SangSaeng political economy of life to nurture the web of life and spiritual communion of life freshly. Nevertheless, despite the dire historical conditions after the Second World War, the Korean people in both the North and the South shared the same deep aspiration for a SangSaeng political economy in a reunified, peaceful East Asia.

This aspiration of the Korean people for the peninsula and East Asia provides an axial, pivotal point for historical transformation toward SangSaeng and a grand peace in East Asia. In this global context, let us deliberate on a creative spiritual convergence for Earth's web of life.[11]

To some extent, these ideas were expressed in his doctoral dissertation at Princeton Theological Seminary. As a student there, he often told me that he spent more time in the Oriental Studies courses

---

11 Ibid, 51-52.

and library at Princeton University than at the seminary. At that time, the seminary president was Dr. James I. McCord (1919-1990), a staunch global ecumenist. Yong-bok Kim was one of the "McCord kids" that McCord mentored for the globalization of ecumenism. Transitioning between Princeton Theological Seminary and Princeton University's Oriental Studies Library and seminars, he nurtured his theological subjectivity by studying Oriental Studies at the university, resolving his longing for his homeland while actively participating in global ecumenical theological discussions.

Yong-bok and the other Asian "McCord Kids" returned to their respective countries, collectively earning the nickname "the Asian Mafia," making significant contributions to the development of Asian theology and ecumenism. These include Kim Yong-bok of South Korea, Feliciano Carino, former secretary of the Asian Christian Council (CCA), K. C. Abraham of India, and Yeow Choo Lak of Singapore. The Congress of Asian Theologians (CATS) was founded in 1997 in Suwon under their leadership. CATS is a theological platform for all churches in Asia, including Roman Catholics, the only such continent-wide ecumenical organization globally.

However, the Zoegraphies listed above must be revisited and updated by new research on Korean history, especially ancient history. For example, Yong-bok recognized the history recorded in the Samguk Yusa as a Zoegraphy, interpreting it as the story of a Seontopian resistance to the Mongol Empire's invasion. While his intentions can be appreciated, it is essential to reconsider whether this aligns with the original purpose of his Minjung theology: to excavate the socio-biographies of Minjung, initially marginalized by vested interests. Some Korean archaeologists have criticized that

Il-yeon, the author of Samguk-yusa, mythologized the historical figure Tangun for political manipulation. By rediscovering the remains of the Yoha and Hongsan civilizations, ancient Korean history, including Gojoseon, becomes an intriguing field that warrants further study and updates by Korean theology, including Minjung theology.

## Grand Taegeuk Convergence of Spirituality in the Global Womb of Life

Kim Yong-bok proposed that we must extend the perspectives of SangSaeng Zoesophia and Zoegraphy beyond Korea and East Asia, to encompass the entire earth, in alignment with the spiritualities of the Pacific, Africa, and the indigenous communities of the Americas.

There has been the rich Indigenous spirituality of the web of life among the native community in American continents as well as in the islands of the Pacific Ocean, in Africa (Ubuntu ['being self through others']), and in the spiritualities of Asia. These spiritualities have been revitalized at times of historical crisis in their community life and their web of life. These legacies of spirituality have responded to the colonial regimes of the West and to the modern industrial capitalist economy by their revitalization to create new foundations for their web of life. These spiritual revitalizations in all the continents have laid catalytic foundations for new visions of the life of all living beings and their web of life. There are clear signs of these transformative revitalizations on all continents, from grassroots local communities to national and continental dimensions, in response to the critical signs of 21st global civilization, particularly the technocratization of the world economy.

The trans-continental black movement of spirituality beyond the national, continental, and global boundaries, challenging Western encroachment and global hegemony, is continuing its creative catalytic incubation of a new vision for the web of life for a convivial web of life. The movement led by Martin Luther King. Jr. in the 20th century has a pivotal point of this spiritual revitalization, affecting all black communities in the world, as well as all communities suffering the global hegemonic geopolitical war regime and war economy.

The spirituality of West Asia, Central Asia, South Asia and East Asia has been generating revitalizing at the bottom of all communities of life, deep in their web of life, from the time of colonization by the West, throughout the Cold War, and up to the present time of globalized economy and geopolitical hegemonic struggles by the world powers in the current post-Cold War age.

There is much to learn from the spiritual revitalization taking place in Native American communities, which have been the womb of wisdom about the "web of life" in the cosmos.

The convergence of spirituality in Asia is yet to come. However, there are strong historical connections among West Asia, South Asia, Central Asia, South East Asia, and East Asia, and there are signs of a creative ecumenical convergence of spirituality at this time of crisis of global civilization. Islamic spirituality, Buddhist spirituality, Hindu spirituality, and East Asian Confucian and Taoist spiritualities can all interact across religious and cultural boundaries in response to the West and Western technocratic civilization.[12]

Yong-bok sought to unearth the spirituality of Zoegraphy within the indigenous spiritualities of Asia, Africa, and the Americas. He suggested that this spirituality converges with the Black and Women's theological movements of the 20th century. To counteract the Western technocratic civilization, anticipated to grow more dominant in the 21st century, he called for a Grand Convergence, an ecumenical interaction with all global religions and spiritual traditions.

Yong-bok proposed a Korean title more advanced than the English one for this concept. The English title was "Grand Convergence of Spirituality in the Global Womb of Life". However, he changed the Korean title to "Convergence and Fusion in the Mode of Taegeuk in the Global Womb of Life" (생명의 세계 자궁에서 영성의 태극적 수렴과 융합). This modification introduces the cosmology and method-ology of Taegeuk's (太極 [Taiji], the Great Ultimate) to clarify his somewhat unclear concept of "convergence," alternatively used as convergence or fusion. This is a significant step from the perspective of Theo-dao (Theology of the Dao).[13] Finally, his Seontopian Zoesophia and my Theo-dao have found a more concrete "pivotal point" where they can converge and fuse. Unfortunately, his passing deprived us of a dialogue partner to develop this convergence further.

Contemporary astronomy continues to discover new things about Black Holes. Everything in the universe converges and fuses in these all-consuming black holes. Taegeuk is perhaps the closest image and metaphor to such a black hole. Taegeuk, while providing an accurate image of the black hole, also serves as the primary East

---

12 Kim, "A Critical Convergence," 52-53.

13 For theological applications of Taegeuk, see Kim, *A Theology of Dao*, 48-50, 61-64.

Asian metaphor for cosmogony. The diagram of Taegeuk (Taegeukdo) by Zhu Donyi (1017-1073), a fundamental Neo-Confucian, manifests its alignment with the Big Bang cosmology.[14] In terms of modern astronomical cosmology, the first phrase of Taegeukdo, "the Non-Ultimate is the Great Ultimate (無極而太極)", can be inferred to mean the creation of the universe (the Great Ultimate) by a Black Hole (the Non-Ultimate).

Taegeuk is divided into yin and yang, stillness and motion, principle (理 li) and vital force (氣 ki). However, it also serves to converge and fuse these opposites to create all things and birth life. Thus, the five elements of fire-water-wood-gold-earth (火水木金土), which are created, cycle through each other in opposition and symbiosis to birth life. The universe and life are generated and emerge through this Taegeuk movement of dialectical opposites (SangGeuk: gold > wood > earth > water > fire > gold) and cyclical conviviality (SanSsaeng: gold-water-wood-fire-earth-gold). The concept of Taegeuk can provide space for Minjung theology to develop further alongside (and not separate from) East Asian thought, beyond the Western dialectical and analytical framework of the dualistic paradigm. Kim Yong-bok's Seontopian Zoesophia already provides this.

---

14 For Taegeukdo, see Micael C. Kalton, *To Become a Sage: The Ten Diagrams of Sage Learning by Yi T'oegye* (New York: Columbia University Press, 1988), 37-42.

## Minjung Theology and Theogy of Dao: The Confluence of Two Stories

During the Minjung Theology for Life and Peace conference held in October 2022 in Jaeundo, Shinan, Jeollanam-do, I presented my argument for the historical intertwining of minjung theology and theology of Dao.[15] I asserted that minjung theology, distinct from Latin American liberation theologies, was originally established in alignment with early theodaoian thinkers. For the future development of minjung theology, I urged emerging theologians to deepen their understanding of their own religious cultures, citing notable collaborations like those between Suh Nam-dong and Kim Chi-ha, Ahn Byung-mu and Ryu Yŏngmo, and Kim Yong-bok and Theodao.

Suh Nam-dong (1918-1984), a pioneer of minjung theology, was greatly influenced by Kim Chi-ha's (1941-2022) innovative analysis of minjung's han, a term encapsulating the accumulated feelings of oppression and alienation. This deep connection means that Suh's theology must be examined alongside Chi-ha's original thoughts. As his ideas matured, Chi-ha shifted his focus from minjung to life, or 'Saengmyeong' (생명) in Korean. In his seminal work, "The Ugeumchi Phenomenon,"[16] Chi-ha argued that the minjung's Ugeumchi uprising was not just a manifestation of their han, but representation of a cosmic life movement embodied by Taegeuk.

---

15 See the sourcebook, "Speaking the Green Newspaper Name in Shinan," 2022. 10. 24-26, Ramada Hotel in Shinan, South Jeolla Province, 20.

16 See Kim Chi-ha, *Life* (Seoul: Sol Publishing House, 1992), 188-192. For English translation, see Heup Young Kim, *A Theology of Dao*, 18-23.

His ideas gradually formed a distinctive theodaoian perspective, though this shift was not universally accepted among minjung theologians. Despite the controversy, Chi-ha continued to expand on the hermeneutical understanding of the minjung's life movement, as exemplified in the Battle of Ugeumchi. He did so by incorporating principles of restoration and reversal found in the Daodejing and Yi Jing. In light of his ideas, I developed the 'hermeneutics of *ki*' (vital force) as a methodological framework for constructive Korean theology; for example, a Christology of Dao (Christo-dao) interpreting the crucifixion and resurrection of Jesus Christ as cosmic events of the Dao's reversal.[17]

Ahn Byung-mu (1922-1996), another crucial figure, is typically associated with Ham Seok-heon (1901-1989). However, this overlooks the substantial influence Ryu Yŏngmo (1890-1981), the shared mentor of Ahn and Ham, had on Ahn's thinking. Even Ham's central idea of "*ssial*" (seed) traces back to Ryu. As Ahn's last teaching assistant during his visit to the United States as a visiting professor at the Pacific School of Religion in 1989, I saw first-hand his struggle to shift his focus from minjung to '*min*' (민), the Korean word for 'people'. His association with Ryu's thoughts, including Ryu's devoted student Kim Heung-ho (1919-2012), should be considered in future studies of Ahn Byung-mu.

Lastly, I want to draw attention to the relationship between Kim Yong-bok and the theology of Dao. Starting with the sociobiography of minjung, Yong-bok's minjung theology evolved into Seontopian Zoesophia. This transformation highlights the paradigm shifts he

---

17 See ibid, 18-26.

han, but a representation of a cosmic life movement embodied by Taegeuk. navigated in response to global theological changes since the 20th century: from sociological considerations to an understanding of the global web of life, and from there to an engagement with world religions in a united response to the impending ultra-technological Western civilization. His cosmological expansion from minjung theology to Seontopian Zoesophia aligns with Theodao's attempt to narrate a 'Big History' that identifies signs of cosmic life movement within the "penumato-socio-cosmic trajectory," exposing through the "socio-cosmic biography of the exploited life."[18] After all, is not minjung theology intrinsically a quest for the Dao of Minjung?

## Great Convergence of Korean Theology for the Dao of Seontopia: Toward New Civilization of Green Life

Furthermore, Kim Yong-bok's conception of zoegraphy, Zoesophia, and Seontopia extends beyond the sociobiography of minjung. Likely aware of the potential for a dystopian future propelled by the uncontrolled growth of an ultra-techno-civilization, he envisioned threats posed by the intersection of transhumanism and capitalism. This perspective considers the path to post-human evolution through the merger with advanced technologies like artificial intelligence (AI), bypassing the essential process of self-cultivation

---

18 See Heup Young Kim, *A Theology of Dao*, 217-22.

or sanctification. He perceived the potential value of spiritual communities, such as the East Asian utopia of Muryeong-Dowon, as a counterbalance to the dystopia predicted by Western technological advancement.[19]

Prominent transhumanists like Yuval Noah Harari, author of best-sellers like *Homo Sapiens and Homo Deus*,[20] have taken the position that individuals not allied with AI might become a "useless people" who belong to a "useless class."[21] Harari, revered as a modern prophet at forums like the World Economic Forum, suggests that this marginalized group cannot resist AI-enhanced transhumans, thereby exerting significant influence on the global economy and politics.

Notable among these influencers is Elon Musk, the former richest man on the planet, who advocates for the fusion of human brains with AI through projects like Neuralink. Musk also contributed to the development of the ChatGPT large language AI model. The late physicist Stephen Hawking (1942-2018) also foresaw potential conflicts between ordinary humans and transhumans. Such transformations, largely driven by Big Tech magnates who have accrued massive wealth from the Fourth Industrial Revolution, are already in motion with the vision of 'longtermism.'[22]

---

19 In the last lecture at Hanil Jangshin University in 2021, Yong-bok hinted that Seontopia be translated as a utopia for Westerners who do not know East Asians' ideally dreaming place like Mureung-Dongwon (무릉도원).

20 See Yuval N. Harari, *Homo Sapiens: A Brief History of Humankind* (New York, NY: Harper, 2011) and *Homo Deus: A Brief History of Tomorrow* (New York, NY: Harper, 2016).

21 See https://www.nationalreview.com/corner/transhumanist-theorist-calls-the-ai-unenhanced-useless-people.

22 See https://www.salon.com/2022/08/20/understanding-longtermism-why-this-suddenly-influential-philosophy-is-so.

In the face of this impending era of eugenics and cybernetic totalitarianism brought on by transhumanism and longtermism, minjung theology may need to reinterpret and broaden its concept of minjung. According to the transhumanists, all unenhanced humans not aligned with AI and human-enhancement technologies, will become marginalized and vulnerable. The rise of techno-mammon marks the advent of these malicious ambitions. It is now a collective responsibility to prevent techno-mammon's destructive force against humanity and God's creation. We must prioritize protection for the "cybernetically vulnerable" in this age of AI and advanced technology, as advocated in the Sermon on the Mount.

A "new civilization of green life" aptly encapsulates Kim Yong-bok's idea of Seontopian Zoesophia. The preservation of global and universal ecology, life, and humanity is paramount to sustaining a life-nurturing utopia rather than a dystopia precipitated by Western technological civilization. As we navigate the so-called "Anthropocene," this becomes our shared destiny and kairos calling. Theologies across Korea, Asia, Africa, and the rest of the world must collaborate in finding a new Dao, a path to prevent the mechanization and destruction of God's creation by Western technological civilization and to create a Seontopia capable of preserving and restoring all ecosystems, humanity, and life. This is a divine call to action. We must unite in a monumental struggle for this vision of God's Kingdom, within the history of civilization and the broader context of Big History of Universes. Let us join the fight!

# Conclusion:
# Embracing Theodao in the Anthropocene

As we reach the culmination of "*Theodao (Theology of Dao) II: Advancing K-Theology in the Anthropocene*," it becomes evident that the integration of ecological wisdom, technological discernment, decolonized perspectives, and Korean cosmic spirituality forms a multifaceted tapestry uniquely suited to address the complexities of our time. This volume, composed of essays written after my retirement and before the advent of advanced AI language models like ChatGPT, represents a contemplative engagement with the critical concerns of the Anthropocene era, a period characterized by significant human impact on Earth's geology and ecosystems.

## Reimagining Theology in an Era of Global Challenges

Throughout the four thematic parts of this book, a consistent call emerges: to reimagine theology in a way that is responsive to the urgent global challenges we face—ecological degradation, rapid technological advancements, cultural hegemony, and the need for spiritual renewal.

— Part 1: Ecodao in an Age of Ecological Crisis underscores the imperative to restore harmony between humanity and the natural world. By integrating ecological consciousness from Confucianism, Daoism, and Christian theology, we introduced Ecodao—an ecological theology emphasizing interconnectedness, balance, and reverence for all life forms. This part challenges anthropocentric paradigms and advocates a shift toward a theanthropocosmic vision.

— Part 2: Technodao in an Age of Transhumanism and Artificial Intelligence explores emerging technologies' ethical and existential implications. Drawing upon East Asian wisdom traditions, we critically assessed the promises and perils of transhumanism and artificial intelligence, proposing Technodao as an ethical framework that promotes responsible innovation, human dignity, and moral discernment in the face of technological advancements.

— Part 3: Theodao in a Global Polyphonic Age of Decolonization addresses the necessity of decolonizing theology to embrace a multitude of voices and epistemologies. By advocating for a global, polyphonic approach, we sought to dismantle hegemonic structures, integrate indigenous knowledge systems, and foster interreligious dialogue. This part emphasizes the importance of acknowledging and valuing diverse cultural perspectives in constructing a more inclusive theological discourse.

— Part 4: Korean Cosmic Spirituality and K-Theology delves into the depths of Korean spiritual disciplines and theological thought. By exploring the works of thinkers like Dasŏk Ryu Yŏngmo and Kim Yong-bok, we uncovered a trans-cosmic and trans-religious spirituality that offers profound insights for contemporary faith practice. This part highlights the richness of Korean theology (K-Theology) and its potential contributions to global theological conversations.

## Theodao as a Transformative Framework

Emerging from this exploration, *Theodao* stands as a dynamic and transformative framework capable of addressing the multifaceted challenges of our age. It bridges Eastern and Western thought, integrating diverse disciplines and promoting ethical reflection and action.

- — Integrating Wisdom Traditions: Theodao invites us to draw upon the collective wisdom of Confucianism, Daoism, and Christian theology, fostering a holistic understanding of humanity's place within the cosmos.
- — Promoting Ethical Technology: It guides us in navigating the ethical complexities of AI and transhumanism, encouraging technologies that enhance human flourishing without compromising moral and spiritual values.
- — Embracing Decolonization and Inclusivity: Theodao emphasizes the importance of decolonizing theological discourse, integrating marginalized voices, and recognizing the validity of diverse epistemologies.
- — Cultivating Spiritual Depth: It allows us to deepen our personal and communal spiritual practices by embracing the richness of Korean cosmic spirituality and the insights of K-Theology.

## Reflecting on Temporal Context

The temporal context of these essays—crafted before the widespread influence of AI language models—adds a unique dimension to this work. Rooted in human scholarship and contemplative practice, the perspectives offered provide a reflective contrast to the emerging reliance on artificial intelligence in thought and communication. This positioning underscores the enduring value of human insight and the necessity of continuous theological reflection in an age of rapid technological change.

## Moving Forward: An Invitation to Dialogue and Action

As we look toward the future, the insights gleaned from "*Theodao II*" offer guidance and hope. *Theodao* challenges us to:

— Engage in Interdisciplinary Dialogue: Embrace conversations across disciplines and cultures to address complex global issues collaboratively.

— Practice Ecological Stewardship: Actively participate in restoring and preserving the natural environment through informed, compassionate action.

— Critically Assess Technological Impact: Evaluate the ethical implications of technological advancements, ensuring they align with human dignity and the common good.

— Foster Inclusive Communities: Promote theological and societal frameworks that value diversity, equity, and the inclusion of all voices.

This collection represents not an endpoint but a continuation of a journey—a journey toward a theology that is dynamic, integrative, and responsive to the evolving needs of our world. It is an invitation to scholars, practitioners, and readers alike to join in the ongoing exploration and application of Theodao.

By integrating ecological consciousness, technological ethics, decolonized perspectives, and spiritual depth, "*Theodao II*" seeks to contribute meaningfully to a theology attuned to the rhythms of the Earth, the complexities of technology, and the rich tapestry of global cultures. May this work inspire thoughtful reflection, meaningful dialogue, and purposeful action as we collectively navigate the challenges and possibilities of the Anthropocene.

Seoul, November 3, 2024
Heup Young KIM

# Theodao in Critical Making —Retrieved

# The Sciences and the Religions:
## Some Preliminary East Asian Reflections on Christian Theology of Nature

The rise of science in the nineteenth century induced a revision in Christian theology—what has sometimes been called the second Reformation. Some may think that Canon Warren exaggerates, but at least he calls attention to the seriousness of the new challenge, when he says that the impact of agnostic science will turn out to have been as child's play compared to the challenge to Christian theology of the faith of other men.[1]

This well-known passage of Wilfred Cantwell Smith, a forerunner of global or 'world theology', though exaggerated as he admitted, contains an undeniable truth about the value of non-Christian religions in relation to science that Christian theology should take seriously.[2] Nonetheless, Christian theologians participating in contemporary dialogue between science and *religion* do not seem to

---

1 Wilfred Cantwell Smith, "The Christian In a Religiously Plural World," *Christianity and Other Religions*, ed. by John Hick and Brian Hebblethwaite (Philadelphia: Fortress Press, 1980), 91.

2 See Wilfred Cantwell Smith, *Towards a World Theology: Faith and the Comparative History of Religion* (Maryknoll: Orbis, 1981).

listen to this prophetic warning of a wise person of the West as carefully as it deserves. Rather, most of them still seem to stick to the
'child's play', ignoring the irreversible reality of a 'religiously plural
world.' Science and religion dialogue still remains as a Western
phenomenon.

In what follows I would like to file a criticism of the agenda set
by the Center for Theology and the Natural Sciences. What CTNS
sees as a gulf to be bridged between science and religion is but a
narrow stream compared to the wide ocean that separates the my-
opia of Christian theology from the broad vision of a global theology
which sees the world's religions as a pluralism. For *Science* & Religion
to deal with the reality of pluralism among cultures and religions,
we need to advance to a dialogue between *The Sciences & The Religions*.

Instead of addressing Robert John Russell directly, in this chapter
I will engage his teacher, Ian G. Barbour. Even though Barbour identifies his own work in terms of an engagement between science
and religion; in fact, his domain is only science and Christian
theology. I will offer a critique of this unnecessarily narrow position.
Then I will offer a constructive substitute oriented around understanding nature through Chinese eyes, understanding Tao.

### The Myth of the Bridge

The child's play of the science-theology dialogue is vividly manifested in a popular metaphor of "building bridges between religion
and science."[3] This dramatic but romantic metaphor is not so much

---

3 W. Mark Richardson and Wesley J. Wildman, "General Introduction," *Religion and*

convincing, as it is awkward and mystifying to Koreans and East Asian people. For it was in fact science that attracted these people when Western missionaries came to East Asia to plant their churches in this strange world with complex histories of multiple East Asian religions. In this non-Christian world, Christianity was first welcomed because of the formidable power and impressive advantages of modern science that Euro-American missionaries brought with them. Because of this, East Asians are accustomed to viewing science as an inseparable part of Christianity. A number of missionaries explicitly utilized science as the means to indicate the superiority of Christian faith and Western civilization and accordingly the need for Christian conversion for true salvation and superior civilization, the intention of which was not innocent of Western imperialism. The most famous example was Matteo Ricci (1552-1610) who introduced "the emerging physical sciences" as "the foundation for the Christian faith and the revelation of Jesus Christ."[4] His translations of science classics such as *Euclid's Elements of Geometry* were intended as a tool for his Catholic mission in China.

To a people with this historical experience, it is not so much a description of reality as a quixotic myth that science and Christian theology are the two great worlds divided by a big ocean, desperately requiring bridges to connect them. On the contrary, they see them as two phenomena of the same world. In fact, they recognize

---

*Science: History, Method, Dialogue* (New York & London: Routledge, 1996), xi-xiii.

4 4 Scott W. Sunquist, ed., *A Dictionary of Asian Christianity* (Grand Rapids, William B. Eerdmans Publishing Co., 2001), 703, 703-5. Also see Jacques Gernet, *China and the Christian Impact: A Conflict of Culture*, trans. Janet Lloyd (Cambridge: Cambridge University Press, 1985), 20-22, 57-63.

the existence of a really great ocean separating their world (the East) and the Christian world (the West, more precisely the Occident). They do not find a great ocean between science and Christian theology, as some Western scholars romantically fantasize, but only some rivers.

Furthermore, they notice the preexistence of bridges across those rivers between these two children of Jerusalem and Athens. Hence, to their eyes, it would be not so much a matter of "creating" or "building" original bridges as of "rehabilitating" damaged bridges, "repairing" broken bridges, "renovating" old bridges, or "adding" fancy new bridges. From this vantage point, "creating bridges" is a misleading metaphor that does not fit the reality of global religious history and the contemporary geography of world religions. The bridge metaphor would be far more convincing and appropriate *when sciences meet non-Christian or, more broadly, non-monotheistic religions.* That is to say, *where sciences really meet religions!*

Ian G. Barbour is without doubt a great leader ("the doyen," "*the pioneer,*" or "the dean") in the dialogue between religion and science, a most important theological movement in this century.[5] Many scholars in this movement praise him as a (or the most) significant "creator" or builder of bridges between science and theology, as evidenced in the CTNS *Festschrift* celebrating his 50 years in this field.[6]

---

5 John Polkinghorne and Robert J. Russell, "Acclaims," in Ian G. Barbour, *When Science Meets Religion: Enemies, Strangers, or Partners?* (San Franscisco: HarperSanFranscisco, 2000), abbr. WSMR; idem, *Nature, Human Nature, and God* (Minneapolis: Fortress Press, 2002), backcover.

6 Robert John Russell, ed. *40 Years in Science and Religion: Ian G. Barbour and his Legacy* (Ashgate, 2004); see idem, "Ian Barbour's Methodological Breakthrough: Creating the 'Bridge' between Science and Religion."

Although Barbour was born and spent his childhood in Beijing, to my East Asian mind, his thought, a prototype of science and religion discourse, still preserves some remnants of the myth of bridges. In this chapter, as I admire his contributions greatly, I will juxtapose some important themes from an East Asian perspective that Western studies in religion and science, represented by Barbour's theology of nature, have missed, neglected, and insufficiently dealt with.

### Christian Theology vs. the World's Religions

Barbour's works are valuable first and foremost as a seminal interdisciplinary study between natural sciences and *Christian theology*. His 'classic" typology, "four views of science and religion," is an analysis of the relationship between science and theology exclusively in the Christian context, as its central arguments are in the defense of traditional Christian theism and in the division between natural theology and the theology of nature.[7] Hence, the title of his celebrated book *When Science Meets Religion* is a misnomer (likewise, his work *Religion and Science*). It should have been titled *When Science Meets Christian Theology or When Science Meets Theology* (likewise, *Theology and Science*). This unfortunate misnomer is *religiously* offensive and 'politically incorrect' from the vantage point of the geography of world religions as well as of the political econo-

---

7 For a summary of the typology, see Ian G. Barbour, *Religion and Science: Historical and Contemporary Issues*, (San Franscisco: HarperSanFranscisco, 1997), abbr. RNS, 7-38; also WSMR: 1-38. "Conflict," the basis of his typology, virtually denotes 'incompatibility' "with any form of theism" (WSMR: 2). For the division between natural theology and the theology of nature, see RNS: 98-105; WSMR: 27-38.

my of language in the twenty-first century. With this phraseology, Barbour could not avoid criticism that he views science and religion dialogue as a Western Christian project.

*Conflict* is the first model and a major underlying theme of Barbour's typology, which shows that his thought is culturally influenced. Whereas the history of the religiously homogeneous West (Occident) is filled with bloody religious wars and conflicts, such religious warfare is ironically uncommon in the history of religiously plural East Asia. In this world of *harmony*, exemplified by the yin-yang relationship, there was no serious conflict between science and religion.[8] In fact, *conflict* is a more Western concept based on Greek *dialectical* dualism.[9] In this world of *jen* (*or ren, being-in-togetherness*), the habit of the negative golden rule (Do not do to others what you do not want them to do to you!) is more appreciated, as "epistemological modesty" and "*ethical humility*" are crucial virtues to treat others as 'guests' or 'friends' to bring harmony in the world. The habit of the positive golden rule (*Love others in your own ways!*), preferred in the Christian West, is carefully avoided, because it could cause the opposite attitudes of "epistemological immodesty" and "*ethical hubris*," prone to treating others as "strangers" or "enemies" in a conflict-complex (*Enemies, Strangers, or Partners*).[10] These erroneous attitudes had been a root-cause for the modern

---

8 See Kim Yung Sik, "Some Reflections on Science and Religion in Traditional China," *Journal of the Korean History of Science Society* 7:1 (Dec. 1985), 40-49.

9 Cf. Shu-hsien Liu and Robert E. Allinson, *Harmony and Strife: Contemporary Perspectives, East & West* (Hong Kong: The Chinese University Press, 1988).

10 See Robert E. Allinson, "The Ethics of Confucianism & Christianity: the Delicate Balance," *Ching Feng* 33:3 (1990): 158-75.

failure of the arrogant Western Christian mission in the East. Theologians in science and religion dialogue, including Barbour, seem to be not fully liberated from these habits of epistemological immodesty and ethical *hubris.*

As both religion and science are culturally dependent, "the relationship between science and religion is profoundly culture-dependent." Hence, Yong Sik Kim is right to continue to say, "Understanding the science-religion relationship in China cannot be achieved by checking the presence or absence of those religious concepts, practices, groups, and links that were relevant in the Western scientific development (*as if the relation that developed in the West could be the only kind of relation that religion can have with science*). Study of the relationship in China should examine different kinds of relationships that were meaningful in the context of Chinese science, religion, and society ."[11] Although China was his birthplace, Barbour does not seem to have discerned these 'different kinds of relationship' and the contemporary reality of religious pluralism in the post-Christian world beyond his "Western bias."[12] His "methodological breakthrough" also has a greater plausibility in the context of Christian theology.[13]

### Suspicion, Not Consonance

Methodological "consonance" between science and religion is

11 Y. Kim, "Some Reflections," 44. Italics are mine.

12 WSMR: 5-6. Cf. Christopher Southgate, et. al., *God, Humanity and the Cosmos* (Edinburgh: T & T Clark, 1999)], abbrv. GHC, 10-12.

13 Russell, "Ian Barbour's," 27.

nothing new to the people in East Asia. Thus, striving for consonance looks like a genetic consequence for the two children of the same parents, the Christian father and the Greek mother (or vice versa).[14] Metaphorically, they are family members in the same forest. Scholars in the science and religion dialogue seem to be reluctant to leave their old home in the forest to see the outer world with new vistas and challenges of 'other religions.' Remaining in the forest and claiming theirs as *the dialogue* of science and religion is a suspicious attitude, vulnerable to a disguised, high-tech, missiological, and political plot for evangelism and cultural imperialism for the perpetuation of the Christian and Western hegemony (cf. *the Clash of Civilizations*).[15]

In this regard, it is appropriate and necessary to employ a "hermeneutics of critique and suspicion," a theological method for contemporary Christian theology, on contemporary science and religion dialogue in order to overcome the "social optimism" and politico-cultural naiveté that it seems to hold (e.g., the bridge metaphor).[16]

An immediate and profound issue for carrying out a genuine science and *religion* dialogue is how to include the wisdom of the other world religions in the discussion, as suggested by some participants in the dialogue.[17] However, the question is whether there is *really*

---

14 Cf. GHC: 24-27.

15 See Samuel P. Huntington, *The Clash of Civilizations: Remaking of World Order* (New York: Touchstone, 1997).

16 For the hermeneutics of suspicion, see David Tracy, "Theological Method," *Christian Theology: An Introduction to Its Traditions and Tasks*, ed. Peter C. Hodgson and Robert H. King (Minneapolis: Fortress Press, 1994), 36; also idem, *Blessed Rage for Order: The New Pluralism in Theology* (Minneapolis: the Seabury Press, 1975), 104, 147, 210. For Barbour's social optimism, see GHC: 347-48.

17 See GHC: 13, 226-43, 394.

any space open for non-Christian religions or Christian theologies beyond the Western walls to be part of the dialogue, still conceived as domestic affairs within the same Western *forest* (The doyen is still doing that!).[18] For example, the yet-to-be prevailing debates on theism such as the existence of God, divine design, and natural theology are important but are *only* theological issues. In the interreligious or religiously plural context, it is unwise and presumptuous to continue those stereotypical issues of the missionary era as the governing themes of the dialogue between science and *religion*.

In "the third epoch" of World Christianity, Asian and African Christians now know that God has many names beyond traditionally Westernized Christian categories, concepts, narratives, metaphors, and symbols.[19] While criticizing the material or physical reductionism of science, ironically, Barbour also seems to commit a religious reductionism, a shrinking of the grand magnitude of global Christian theology for the third millennium into the scale of traditional theism in the modern West. He said, "Theism, in short, is not inherently in conflict with science, but it does conflict with a metaphysics of materialism."[20] But this is not so much a helpfully perceptive statement from the perspective of interreligious dialogue and global Christian theology. For materialism and theism refer to axiomatic presuppositions ("belief systems") for the natural sciences and

---

18 I am concerning a possibility for "the inherent dominative mode" or "an exercise of cultural strength." See Edward W. Said, *Orientalism* (New York: Vintage books, 1979), 28, 40.

19 See *Proceedings of the Congress of Asian Theologians (CATS), 25 May-1 June 1997, Suwon, Korea*, ed. Dhyanchand Carr and Philip Wickeri (Hong Kong: Continuation Committee of the Congress of Asian Theologians, 1997-1998).

20 RNS: 82.

Christian theology, as Barbour himself agrees.[21]

## Diversity Within Christian Theology

To me, an East Asian constructive theologian, Barbour's theology looks conservative with no hint of proper hermeneutics of suspicion; it is politically naïve and problematically old-fashioned. What is lacking in his thought, first of all, is the complex problematic of "knowledge and power;" borrowing his favorite idiom, 'a critical realism' of *power*.[22] David Tracy stated well, "There is no innocent interpretation, no unambiguous tradition, no history-less, subject-less interpreter, no abstract, general situation, no method to guarantee certainty."[23] Through Barbour, however, the old dogmatics seems to have returned again as a central player in the game of religion and science dialogue.

His theology consists in an intriguing synthesis of two contradictory traditions, Barthian neo-orthodoxy and Whiteheadian process philosophy. The former seems to constitute the theological side (faith) of his thought, while the latter the metaphysical side (science). The point of departure for his theology is his faith commitment in line with neo-orthodox doctrines: "As I see it, neo-orthodoxy rightly

---

21 Barbour seems to agree this point (See NHG: 5).

22 In fact, John Bowker argued, "the really persistent issue between religion [thology] and science is not so much about different kinds of knowledge claims, but rather one of power" (restated by J. Wentzel van Huysteen, GHC: xxii); see J. Bowker, *Is God A Virus? Genes, Culture and Religion* (London: SPCK, 1995), 116-17. For the problem of knowledge and power, see Said, *Orientalism*, 15, 24, 36, etc.

23 Tracy, "Theological Method," 36.

stresses the centrality of Christ and the prominence of scripture in the Christian tradition."[24] But Barbour usually concludes his thought in line with process theology, as he finds it "helpful" in his "attempt to integrate scientific and religious concepts."[25] These two sides are always in tension in his thought and reveal a self-contradictory aspect of his theology.

An example of what I mean is found in his distinction between natural theology and the theology of nature. For a process theologian would not need such a distinction of a *metaphysical* natural theology and a constructive theology of nature. His theology of nature seems to begin in accordance with the classic definition of theology, *fides quaerens intellectum* (a faith-seeking-understanding). However, tensions occur when he reduces the *intellectum* into process metaphysics. At this juncture, the pendulum of his thought swings to the opposite direction, the process side. A neo-orthodox theologian whose aim is to overcome the Neo-Calvinist's fallacy of propositional reductionism with respect to the Word-event of God would dislike metaphysics. Moreover, it is noteworthy that a more profound dimension of *intellectum* in the contemporary development of Christian theology is not so much in the field of metaphysics (a theory) as in hermeneutics (an interpretation).

Further, Barbour engages in an apologetics in defense of traditional theism, an attitude also seemingly self-contradictory to the neo-orthodox propensity in his theology of nature (not a metaphysical theism but a faith proclamation!).[26] As already noted by

---

24 WSMR: 22; also see WSMR: 101, 160; NHG: 3.

25 NHG: 6. See also RNS: 303-32, 293-304; WSMR: 174-80; NHG, esp. 101-18.

Paul Tillich, the argument for the doctrine of a 'personal God' is not so helpful and effective in this age of ecological crisis when the anthropomorphic and anthropocentric nature of Christianity is under serious attack from many sides.[27] Barbour classifies Ralph Burhoe's evolutionary naturalism as a conflict model, because he thinks "Burhoe's views of the impersonal system of nature seems to conflict with the Christian understanding of a loving, personal God who transcends nature."[28] This somewhat odd statement clearly shows Barbour's conservative Christian prejudices toward the personal God and the natural-supernatural dualism. If his process theism of nature (a theological integration of science) is a model of integration (methodologically), why cannot Burhoe's evolutionary naturalism of religion (a scientific integration of theology) be so but should be regarded as a conflict model? In this classification, Barbour's typology does not seem to be so much a descriptive analysis, but rather a dogmatic judgment of his theological position.

His tireless endeavors in finding things in science "not incompatible with some forms of theism" are neither fertile nor so encouraging.[29] In danger of the categorical superimposition and the "fallacy of displaced concreteness," this sort of apologetic attitude hinders a genuine dialogue (A. Whitehead).[30] Moreover, theology does not

---

26 As much as he criticizes design arguments as deistic (perhaps from a neo-orthodox perspective), he needs to explain why his process theology is not so much deistic (or metaphysical) from a similarly coherent perspective (see WSMR: 114).

27 RNS: 81.

28 WSMR: 158; also see 157-59.

29 RNS: 80.

30 Alfred N. Whitehead, *Science and the Modern World* (New York: Macmillan, 1967).

need to defend its theistic faith against science or to beg science for an endorsement. God does not need to earn the proofs of his existence from the natural sciences!

Furthermore, postmodern, feminist, ecological, third-world, Latin-American liberation, Asian, and African theologies have fervently criticized the patriarchal, modern, rational, white, male, first world privatization and reductionism of Christian theology. With Christian theology moving into the third millennium, a macro "paradigm change" is in progress.[31] The aged dogmatics such as neo-orthodoxy and the first-world systematic theologies are under suspicion and revision, while "winds of the Spirit" are in favor of "constructive theology."[32] Moreover, no contemporary and future Christian theologies can ignore Asian and African theologies with "the rise of new Christianity" where "the myth of Western Christianity" is completely wrecked and Euro-American Christianity no longer occupies the center but becomes only a *minority* of global Christianity.[33]

31 For example, see Hans Küng, *Theology for the Third Millennium: An Ecumenical View*, trans. Peter Heinegg (New York: Doubleday, 1988); idem and David Tracy, *Paradigm Change in Theology: A Symposium for the Future*, t. Margaret Köhl (New York: Crossroad, 1989).

32 For example, see Peter C. Hodgson, *Winds of the Spirit: A Constructive Christian Theology* (Louisiville: Westminster John Knox Press, 1994).

33 Philip Jenkins, *The Next Christendom: The Coming of Global Christianity* (Oxford: Oxford University Press, 2002), esp., 79-105.

## Interreligious Dialogue as a Central Theme of Global Christian Theology

Most significantly, Barbour does not pay proper attention to the inter-religious dimension of contemporary Christian theology. However, he perpetuates the term "religion" in the place of Christianity or theology.[34] Religious pluralism has spread even more speedily, broadly, and seriously than Smith predicted. Interreligious encounters are a global phenomenon and local affairs at the heart of Western Christianity. In major Western cities such as London, Paris, Amsterdam, New York, Los Angeles, Chicago, and San Francisco, anyone can witness Buddhist Zen centers and people practicing T'ai-chi (Taiji), Taoism, and Confucianism (e.g., Boston Confucianism).[35] In this religiously plural situation, whatever name it has, whether interreligious dialogue, interfaith dialogue, comparative theology, or the theology of religion, it is a significant feature of contemporary Christian theology that one cannot ignore. Tracy was correct in recognizing that "dialogue among religions is no longer a luxury but a theological necessity."[36] More directly, "It is dialogue or die."[37]

---

34 Numerous places in his writings, he also identified 'theological' or 'Christian' as 'religious' (e.g., "religious experience," "religious community," " traditional religious doctrines," WSMR: 114, 113). It is offensive to the readers outside of Christian and Western traditions.

35 See Robert Cummings Neville, *Boston Confucianism: Portable Tradition in the Late-Modern World* (Albany: State University of New York Press, 2000). Diana L. Eck, *A new religious America: how a "Christian country" has now become the world's most religiously diverse nation* (San Francisco: HarperSanFrancisco, 2001).

36 David Tracy, *Dialogue With The Other: The Inter-religious Dialogue* (Louvain: Peeters Press, 1990), 95; also, idem, "Introduction," 58.

37 Diana L. Eck, *Encountering God: A Spiritual Journey from Bozeman to Banras* (Boston:

In fact, religion and science dialogue can learn much from the experiences of interreligious dialogue and the wisdom of East Asian religions. As I have suggested elsewhere, a successful dialogue for theologians can constitute two methodological stages, namely, "a descriptive-comparative stage" (interreligious dialogue) and "a normative-constructive stage" (theology of religion).[38] In the light of Barbour's typology, these two stages can be called simply 'dialogue' and 'integration.' Unlike an opaque distinction in the typology, however, dialogue and integration here refer to two different hermeneutical moments. In this first stage, one should take 'an attitude of reverence' to respect views and presuppositions that the other partners presumably hold (i.e., an epistemological modesty).[39] One should be careful of one's innate proclivity to superimpose one's categorical schema on others (Be descriptive, not prescriptive!). Otherwise, one cannot promote genuine dialogue but falls into a 'fallacy of misplaced concreteness.' A fruitful dialogue may compel one to have the courage to make an epoche, "faithful agnosticism," or a bracketing-off of one's own a priori axioms.[40]

In this stage of dialogue, such an apologetics for theistic persuasion as Barbour employs is not so much an effective strategy but a risky

---

Beacon Press, 1993), x.

38 Heup Young Kim, *Wang Yang-ming and Karl Barth: A Confucian-Christian Dialogue* (Lanham: University Press of America, 1996), esp., 139-41.

39 The attitude of reverence or respect, important for ecological concern, is a spiritual basis for Confucian (and Neo-Confucian) learning (esp., in the Korean Confucianism of Yi T'oe-gye [1501-70]). See Heup Young Kim, *Christ & the Tao* (Hong Kong: Christian Conference of Asia, 2003), 111-6.

40 See David Lochheed, *The Dialogical Imperative: A Christian Reflection on Interfaith Encounter* (Maryknoll: Orbis, 1988), esp., 40-5.

one, because it can lead to the suspicion that the purpose of the dialogue is *de facto* an extended version of Christian exclusivism or a crafty plot for mission and cultural imperialism. In this descriptive moment, a theologian should be self-critical and self-suspicious so as to overcome the missiological habits of epistemological immodesty and ethical hubris. In deep humility and even with courage to bracket off one's own theological agenda, as in the dialogue with the other religions, one should open one's heart to listen to the narratives that new discoveries of natural sciences expose about the mystery of God, humanity, and the cosmos as closely as possible.

In the second stage, however, a theologian has the complete freedom to do a constructive theology for oneself and one's own Christian communities. In this theological moment, Barbour's proposal for the 'theology of nature' is appropriate, but only with understanding that no theology is *creatio ex nihilo* and without limits. A theology is inevitably constructed on the basis of a theologian's limited religio-cultural experiences in one's particular social location, so that a theology so conceived inexorably carries over the prejudices and limitations of the theologian who constructs it.

### *Where Sciences Really Meet Religions?*

A comparison of two different traditions in terms of concepts, methodology, or metaphysics is beneficial for certain comparative studies, but also suspicious. For often it does not progress beyond an armchair scholar's mind game to search for a phenomenological parallel or proof texts of one's dogma and agenda in (or one's cultural strength or hegemony over) the other tradition (or culture). Particularly, the historical consequences of the latter by the Christian West have been devastating, as Orientalism and post-colonial criticisms have exposed noticeably.[41] Therefore, I am proposing to seek a more concrete locus for the dialogue between the partners from different religious traditions and scholarly paradigms elsewhere than such a metaphysical conceptuality.

In this twenty-first century, the era of science, theologians ought to accept the natural sciences as grand narratives for humanity as valuable as religious traditions. They need to regard an encounter between science and religion as a "fusion of hermeneutical horizons" (H. Gadamer).[42] In this encounter, theologians should make their utmost efforts, with 'an attitude of *respect* and epistemological modesty' to listen attentively to the voices and stories that contemporary sciences are revealing about the mystery of life, humanity, and the cosmos. In this moment of listening, scientific proofs for the existence of God, the divine design, or the purpose and the *telos* of the life system are not primary subject matters. After all, the goal of scientific narratives is also in the quest for the way of life to attain full humanity in a new techno-scientific situation. The actual meeting point between science and religion, therefore, is not so much in abstract metaphysics or a methodology of parallelism but in a hermeneutics (not just an epistemology) of the human person, the way of life, or more concretely, the ortho-praxis of humanization,

---

41 See Said, Orientalism; Bill Aschcroft, Gareth Griffiths, and Helen Tiffin, eds., *The Post-colonial Studies Reader* (London and New York: Routledge, 1995).

42 See Hans-Georg Gadamer, *Truth and Method*, 2nd ed., trans. Joel Weinsheimer and Donald G. Marshall (New York: Crossroad, 1989).

i.e., how to be fully human.

Here is the Confucian wisdom (not a speculative postulation for unverifiable supernatural knowledge but a pragmatic embodiment of practical wisdom for common humanity). In this regard, Hans Küng made a helpful correction. With the rejection of the generally accepted dipolar view (Middle Eastern and Indian religions), he argued for a tripolar view of world religions. The East Asian religions of Confucianism and Taoism should be regarded as "a third independent religious river system" of sapiential character, "equal in value" and in contrast to "the first great river system, of Semitic origin and prophetic character" (Judaism, Christianity, and Islam) and "the second great river system, of Indian origin and mystical character" (Hinduism, Buddhism, and others).[43]

Hence, Confucianism as a wisdom tradition does not situate its primary focus on theoretical speculation, though that is constitutive, too, on learning the "Tao" (Dao, the way in the unity of theory and praxis) of wisdom to attain full humanity.[44] The principal aim of Confucian investigation is not so much in the formulation of metaphysics or speculative theory, but in the enlightenment of the Tao toward the embodiment of the ortho-praxis of human life (right liv-

---

43 Hans Küng and Julia Ching, *Christianity and Chinese Religions*, trans. Peter Beyer (New York: Doubleday, 1989), xii-xiii.

44 As a widely used root-metaphor of all East Asian religions such as Confucianism, Taoism, and Buddhism, tao is a very inclusive term with various connotations. For an example of Confucian definition: "Tao is a Way, a path, a road, and by common metaphorical extension it becomes in ancient China the right Way of life, the Way of governing, the ideal Way of human existence, the Way of the Cosmos, the generative-normative Way (Pattern, path, course) of existence as such" (Herbert Fingarette, *Confucius—The Secular as Sacred* [New York: Harper & Row, 1972], 19).

ing). Confucianism argues that one can achieve the embodiment of the Tao through one's individually and collectively rigorous practice of self-cultivation in the 'concrete-universal' network of relationships under the direction of the Tao of wisdom.[45]

Sanctification is a doctrine of Christian theology homologically equivalent to this Confucian teaching of self-cultivation. Hence, I have argued that an ideal locus for the dialogue between Confucianism and Christianity is not metaphysics, psychology, or the philosophy of religion. However, they are essential, but a faith in radical humanization (more related to the orthopraxis or spirituality), namely, self-cultivation and sanctification.[46] Similarly, I am proposing that an ideal locus for the dialogue between science and religion is not so much in a metaphysical theory, a phenomenological parallelism, or technical knowledge, but in the common human quest for the Tao to cultivate and sanctify our scientific and religious knowledge to be a practical wisdom through mutual self-criticism and self-transformation.[47] Then, the issue of how to transform new scientific knowledge and technologies (data) into practical wisdom for the *Tao* of life in the "socio-cosmic" network of relationships in the unity of social and ecological concerns becomes a *koan* (an evocative point of departure) for science and religion dialogue.[48] That is to say, the *koan* for science and religion

---

45 See H. Kim, *Wang Yang-ming and Karl Barth*, 33-6, 171-4.

46 See H. Kim, *Wang Yang-ming and Karl Barth*, 139.

47 The Neo-Confucian teaching of *chi-hsing ho-i*, an attribute of the Tao, refutes the dualism of knowledge and practice, insisting on their ontological unity (see ibid, 29-32). Cf. Daniel Hardy, "The God who is with the world," *Science Meets Faith*, ed. Fraser Watts (Lodnon: SPCK, 1998), 136-37.

dialogue is how to make new discoveries of natural sciences into useful wisdom for humanity toward a new cosmic *humanity* in order to embody the Tao of life fully into the socio-cosmic web of the universe, transcending the uncontrollable greed of commercialism and unlimited selfish desires for convenience. Without a doubt, this koan refers to spirituality.

### *Some Preliminary Reflections from an East Asian Perspective*

The possibility of mutual self-transformation, self-cultivation, and sanctification is a constructive suggestion that East Asian inter-religious dialogue can advance dialogue between the sciences and religions. By learning and adding the insights of interreligious dia-logue and East Asian religions, science and religion dialogue could progress beyond its current confinement on the isolated Christian temporality (*when* science meets religion) toward the real, reli-giously plural globe (*where* sciences really meet religions). Hence, it is imperative for science and religion dialogue to include di-mensions and insights of interreligious dialogue in the discussion in order to *make genuine sciences and religions dialogues* in a real global sense (and so formulate a global Christian theology of nature or science). Here (*where sciences really meet religions*) are some of my pre-liminary reflections for future studies:

---

48 H. Kim, *Christ & the Tao*, 142-48. I proposed the tao paradigm of theology (*theo-tao*) and christology (*christo-tao*) in order to overcome the dualism in contemporary Christian theol-ogy between the logos model (*theo-logos*; in the context of religion and science dialogue, a metaphysical theology) and the praxis model (*theo-praxis; in this context, an ecological ethics*); see the chapters theotao and Christotao, ibid, 135-54, 155-82.

1. The primary locus for dialogue between the sciences and the religions should not be about theoretical metaphysics (knowledge) but about the *Tao* (way) of life (*wisdom*) in the common quest for a new cosmic humanity through mutual self-transformation, i.e., self-cultivation and sanctification. I have already elaborated on this theme.

2. The distinction between *inter-religious dialogue and intra*-religious dialogue is helpful for science and religion dialogue (R. Panikkar).[49] The prime purpose for dialogue is neither to do apologetics for one's hypothesis, theory, or system of thought, nor to proselytize dialogue partners, but for mutual learning and growth through self-criticism, cross-examination, and self-transformation.

3. The East Asian notions of *nothingness, vacuity, and emptiness* are worth serious consideration for the dialogue, as the reality of Non-Being becomes plausible in both the new physics and Christian theology.[50] The conception of God as the 'Absolute Nothingness' might be a theological strategy better and more profound than the notion of kenosis, an inevitable logical consequence of the conservative doctrines of a personal God and divine omnipotence to solve the problem of theodicy (i.e., from Non-Being to Being vs. from Being to Non-Being). When criticizing scientific materialism, theologians in the dialogue do not seem to be free from the deep-seated habits of essential-

---

49 See R. Panikkar, *The Intrareligious Dialogue* (New York and Ramsey: Paulist Press, 1978).

50 Though simplistic, Fritjof Capra is helpful in this regard. See his *The Tao of Physics: An Exploration of the Parallels Between Modern Physics and Eastern Mysticism*, 2nd ed. (Boulder: Shambhala, 1983), esp., 208-23.

ism and substantialism, a plausible cause for materialism. Process theology's theme of 'becoming' seems to be not a good option either because its basis is unavoidably associated with a metaphysical dualism ('the dipolar God') of being ('entity'). A contemplation of nothingness would yield a better alternative to overcome this fundamental dilemma of the modern, Western mode of theological thinking (cf. the apophatic tradition of Christian spirituality and the negative theology of via negativa).[51]

4. The traditional Christian notion of linear time and the supremacy of time, still operative in the theology and science dialogue (i.e., *when science meets religion*), should be scrutinized in the light of new physics and East Asian religious thoughts that underscore *the significance of space*. The logic of causality in Western thought, still prevailing in the dialogue, should be re-evaluated by the possibility of "*synchronicity*," a conceptual foundation of East Asian thought, *I-Ching*.[52]

5. The traditional Christian (or Greek) understanding of 'nature', customary in the dialogue, is problematic, because it cannot avoid

---

51 See Heup Young Kim, "The Word Made Flesh: A Korean Perspective on Ryu Yŏngmo's Christotao," *One Gospel—Many Cultures: Case Studies and Reflection on Cross-Cultural Theology*, ed. Mercy Amba Oduyoye and Hendrik M. Vroom (Amsterdam: Rodopi, 2003), 129-48, esp., 143-44; also, H. Kim, *Christ & the Tao*, 155-82, esp., 167-72. Cf. GHC: 43.

52 "Synchronicity takes the coincidence of events in space and time as meaning something more than mere chance, namely, a peculiar interdependence of objective events among themselves as well as the subjective (psychic) states of the observer or observers" (C. G. Jung, "Foreword," *The I Ching or Book of Changes*, trans. Richard Wilhelm, 3rd ed. [Princeton: Princeton University Press, 1967]), xxiv; also see xxi-xxix.

the pejorative connotation inherited by the hierarchical dualism between the supernatural and the natural. The notion of kenosis (self-empting to be natural) is a helpful, but not sufficient alternative, because it still holds the vestiges of dualism and definitional ambiguity. Hence, it is worth taking into consideration the profound Taoist insights of nature and *wu-wei* (cf. "let it be itself").[53] In Chinese characters, nature means "*self-so*," "spontaneity" or "naturalness," i.e., "the effective modality of the system that informs the actions of the agents that compose it."[54] In other words, *nature* in East Asian thought is the primary "self-so" (natural) manifestation of the Tao. Natural science in Chinese denotes "self-so" science, at least in the lexicography, so that it does not refer to mere knowledge but wisdom. In the Bible, nature as God's creation is "good," and the denial of its goodness as "self-so" was in fact a fallacy of Gnosticism. With an enhanced clarification of the ambiguous English term 'nature', Barbour's project for the "theology of nature" would make more sense.

---

53 WSMR: 113. Cf. GHC: 233-5; Jürgen Moltmann, *God in Creation*, trans. M. Kohl (London: SCM Press, 1985), 87-8; also, idem, *Science and Wisdom*, trans. M. Kohl (London: SCM, 2003), Ch. XII. Unfortunately, Moltmann also misunderstood the Tao because of his seemingly excessive positivism of 'hope', certainly based on the Western bias of the linear time (see ibid, 189).

54 Michael C. Kalton, "Asian Religious Tradition and Natural Science: Potentials, Present and Future," unpublished paper, the CTNS Korea Religion & Science Workshop, Seoul, January 18-22, 2002.

# Embracing and Embodying God's Hospitality Today in Asia

*Introduction*

Confucius said in the beginning of the *Analects*:

> Is it not a pleasure, having learned something, to try it out at due intervals?
> Is it not a joy to have friends come from afar?
> Is it not gentlemanly (a way of profound person) not to take offence when others fail to appreciate your abilities? (*The Analects* 1)[1]

These famous statements fittingly express this great event of the 7th Congress of Asian Theologians. The Congress of Asian Theologians (CATS) is established precisely to give Christian scholars and theologians in Asia the opportunity to enjoy these pleasures. Today, we have friends who have come from afar, from the East, the West, and the South. We are going to celebrate the pleasures of learning something together, trying it out at due intervals. With this genuine joy as a Confucian-Christian host, I express my deepest welcome to you, friends from four corners. Furthermore, the theme of this congress is hospitality.

---

1 Cf. D. C. Lau, *Confucius The Analects* (Penguin Books, 1979), 59.

When I was requested by the continuing committee to give this talk, I was puzzled as to whether I am the right person to do this. I was afraid that I would violate the attitude of a profound person dictated in the statements as the third condition, by pushing our dear friends to appreciate my abilities. Furthermore, so far, I have not been so much hospitable as suspicious and critical of the so called "hospitality" of expansive Christianity. My preparation for this talk was not so enjoyable but rather painful. But it offered me an opportunity to recall and reassess my Christian journey from the beginning. And it radically challenged my theology, still under construction, which I call a theology of Tao.

Whatsoever mistakes have been made in historical practice, hospitality is by all means "the practice by which the church stands or falls." But does my theology of today well suit Christian hospitality in its original meaning? This question demanded my repentance and theological reviews. This morning, I will share some of them with you, hoping that it may serve as a case to evoke fruitful discussions for the congress. I begin with two episodes, critical moments for my theological journey, that awakened me but also made me wander through a long maze of hermeneutics of suspicion against Western theological traditions.

*Episode One: Mother's funeral: Triumphant Christian Evangelism?*

In the preface of my volume, *Christ and the Tao* (CCA), I wrote: The most dramatic incident happened at the funeral of my beloved mother. Using my status as the eldest son of my family, which is, in fact, a Confucian authority, I succeeded in performing her funeral in a Christian style instead of the traditional Confucian one. This act, of course, involved an evangelical motive to make use of this event as an opportunity to proclaim the Good News to these stubborn Confucian relatives, in accordance with the evangelical teaching of the charismatic Korean Church I attended in New York City. However, the result of this change was tragic. My relatives became outrageous and received this as an offensive act, my obvious betrayal of their impeccable tradition. After the funeral, my eldest uncle, the most respected person in my clan, privately summoned me and said with a mournful face: "I don't care what kind of faith you have. But never have I expected that you will be the one who breaks up our impeccable tradition for a thousand years like this!" This remark struck me like thunder and made me realize that there is something wrong in my understanding of the new faith in an either-or dualism. This was the moment I committed myself in the study of Christian theology. After all, my essays are some of my theological attempts to respond to this event.[2]

The church's attempt to make my mother's funeral an opportunity for evangelism by proclaiming Good News to a great number of my relatives brought about tragic results in my life, particularly in my relationship with my family and relatives. It became one of the chief reasons for me to become a theologian to study what was wrong with it. This is a case of instrumental use of hospitality that is not so benevolent. Aggressive Christians misled the innocent Christian faith of a new convert, ignorant of theology, and used

---

2 Heup Young Kim, *Christ and the Tao* (Hong Kong: Christian Conference of Asia), v-vi.

Christian hospitality as a means for triumphant evangelism and mission.

Since then, I have frequently felt that I am a stranger (or a boundary person) both in my native Confucian community and in my newly adopted Christian faith communities. The aggressive, sometimes too kind, but bothersome hospitality of charismatic Christians was a reason that motivated my conversion. However, since then, I have not experienced much genuine hospitality from churches and theological communities in my fatherland. They did not seem to welcome me truly, but were rather arrogant, exclusive, disrespectful of others (people, cultures, religions, etc.), and reluctant to give up the position and the power of being a host, which is a prerequisite for Christian hospitality. Even more rigorously than Korean Confucians, who generally hold a genealogy for longer than 1.5 millennia, they proudly show off their Christian privileges with a relatively very short period of Christian experiences (less than two centuries), such as three or four generations of Christianity.

*Episode Two: A Church in a Southern US Seminary:*
*Hermeneutics of Suspicion.*

My hermeneutics of suspicion against Western Christianity began in earnest with my experience as a freshman in a seminary in the Southern USA. At that time, I was a new convert, through a series of radical spiritual experiences and so full of religious enthusiasm, who had nothing but a strong faith in Jesus Christ. It happened on a Sunday morning just before Christmas when I was walking toward the beautiful chapel on campus to attend their magnificent worship service. The sound of elegant music came out from the inside of the building, and the white snow covered all over the surface of the church. It was a really lovely scene for a blessed white Christmas. People, all well-dressed and with happy faces, were marching toward the chapel.

All of a sudden, however, there appeared an unexpected vision in my eyes. I saw an entirely different scene from an otherwise joyful Lord's Day morning. Under the fine-looking church building, I saw a red fluid, recognizable as human blood! What was it? I asked. Immediately, I realized that it was the blood of Native Americans whom white Christian soldiers massacred and eliminated so that this traditionally Caucasian church could be established. The church looks majestic in appearance: it had a terrible underside history.

It was built on the bloody sacrifice of Native Americans who welcomed the migration of European Christians and showed extraordinary hospitality to welcome these strangers to settle in the new land. In return for the hospitality of the native hosts, these Christian guests not only brutally killed and expelled them but also confiscated their lands to become the self-claimed hosts of the so-called continent of the great "discovery" of the new world (?). Furthermore, these new hosts theologically and biblically justified their terribly inhuman activities. This is the real story behind the Thanksgiving Day which American missionaries taught us to celebrate as an essential Christian festival. What did they want us to celebrate for? White Christians' cunning betrayal of the innocent indigenous hospitalities of Native Americans? Or Triumphant Christianity's conquest of the land through genocidal massacres of the natives?

Furthermore, is this the only story of its kind in the history of Christian mission and evangelism? How about the Crusade in the

Middle East and the Mission in Latin America, South Africa, Asia, and so on? Do you know the notorious 3 Ms; namely, missionaries, militaries, and merchants? With the excuse of proclaiming good news, missionaries came to East Asia (Japan, China, and Korea), sailing on threatening warships with heavily armed militaries. When a native country was compulsorily opened, merchants followed to begin prosperous trades such as gold mining and slaves. Isn't it a real story of the 19th-century mission of Western churches in Asia? What can you, Christians, say about hospitality after knowing this factual story (the awakening of truth)? What do you mean by "Christian hospitality" in this post-Christian era?

Christian hospitality, therefore, demands, first of all, *metanoia*, genuine repentance. Repentance is a precondition for discussing hospitality. This is not only related to Western Christians but to all Christians, all followers of Jesus Christ. After this introduction, we can now discuss what hospitality means theologically today in Asia. This morning, I shared some insights on reconfiguring the notion of Christian hospitality.

*Hospitality*

is the foundation of Christian faith and an unconditional command of God. Henri Nouwen stated it well, "if there is any concept worth restoring to its original depth and evocative potential, it is the concept of hospitality."[3] Mathew 25:31-46 unmistakably de-

---

3 Henri Nouwen, *Reaching Out: The Three Movements of the Spiritual Life* (New York:

scribes an eschatological vision for the judgment of Jesus Christ in the metaphors of sheep and goat. Particularly, it contains an absolute decree for preferential care for the poor, the thirsty, strangers, the afflicted, the sick, the disabled, and those in prison. There is no excuse by which one can avoid this responsibility. In the Old Testament, stories such as Abraham's hospitality to strangers enabling Sarah, his barren wife, to produce a son (Isaac), imply God's commandment, "You should treat strangers as my angels and messengers" (see Gen. 18:1-33).[4] In the New Testament, Christ made it even stronger, "You should treat them as me" by saying "whatever you did for one of the least of those brothers of mine, you did for me" (Mt. 25:40). This context of the Christian notion of hospitality makes sense of a provocative claim of minjung theology that we should regard *minjung* (the oppressed and alienated people) as Christ.

Christian Pohl, the author of *Making Room: Recovering Hospitality as a Christian Tradition*, said, "Hospitality is not optional for Christians, nor is it limited to those who are specially gifted for it. It is, instead, a necessary practice in the community of faith."[5] A key Greek word

---

Image Books, 1975), 66.

4 Christian Pohl summarized, "the theological and moral foundations for Old Testament hospitality were tied closely to Israel's special relationship of dependence on and gratitude to God. Israel's obligation to care was nurtured by an emphasis on its own experience as an alien and by reflection on God's gracious character. The teachings of the Law, the warnings of punishment for disobedience, and the promise of blessing on obedience reinforced Israelite hospitality toward strangers, as did the individual hospitality stories: guests might be angels, messengers from God, bringing promise or provision." (Christian D. Pohl, *Making Room: Recovering Hospitality as a Christian Tradition* [Wm. B. Eerdmans Publishing Co., 1999], 29).

5 Ibid, 31.

for hospitality, *philoxenia,* is a composite term combining *phileo* (meaning love) and *xenos* (meaning stranger). Etymologically and practically, in the New Testament, hospitality means "Love strangers!" The notion of hospitality, therefore, is not "a minimal moral component" nor "a nice extra" for Christians nor something to do with the professional "hospitality industry."[6] "Hospitality is the lens through which we can read and understand much of the gospel, and a practice by which we can welcome Jesus himself."[7] It relativizes every Christian doctrine and articulation of metaphysical, ideological, and systematic thought. In terms of social location, strangers are more important theologically than others. The notion of Christian hospitality demands Christians to pay a preferential option to the poor, strangers, the alienated, the disabled, those in prison, and so on. In this cosmic age, this preferential care for strangers should be further extended to embrace and embody God's transcendent agapeic love toward the world, including human nature, other lives, and the ecosystem on the earth.

### Theological Anthropology

The notion of Christian hospitality restores the original doctrine of man (humanity), namely theological anthropology. The passage in Genesis 1:27 states that God created the human according to the image of God (*imago Dei*). Further, it says that God created human beings, not one but two at the same time. Thus, this passage does

---

6 Ibid, 4.

7 Ibid, 8.

not support the modern definition of the human person as an iso-lated being (ego) separated from others but "the man with the fel-low-man" (Adam and Eve).[8] Karl Barth argued that the prototype of humanity created in the image of God stands for a joyful *Mitmenschlichkeit*," i.e., co-humanity, fellow-humanity, being-in-en-counter, being-in-togetherness, or being-for-others. He said that "man is the cosmic being which exists absolutely for its fellows." The nature of humanity involves "freedom in the co-existence of man and man in which one may be, will be, the companion, asso-ciate, comrade, fellow, and helpmate of the other."

This definition of humanity as being-in-encounter and be-ing-in-togetherness renders a remarkable parallelism to the Confucian definition of humanity as *jen* (仁). *Jen*, the cardinal virtue of Confucianism, generally translated as benevolence, in Chinese character literally means two people. Confucian anthropology, which conceives humanity as co-humanity, amazingly converges with Christianity. Compare this with Barth's statement that "man is indestructibly as he is man with the fellow-man." The human per-son in Confucianism also does not mean "a self-fulfilled, individual ego in the modern sense, but a communal self or the togetherness of a self as 'a center of relationship.'"[9] In both Christian and Confucian traditions, being human originally does not refer to an individual set or persona of substances or essences but a being in interpersonal relationship.[10] The original theological anthropology

---

8 Kart Barth, *The Church Dogmatics* (CD), Vol. III/2, 323, 208, 276, 324.

9 Heup Young Kim, *Christ and the Tao* (Hong Kong: Christian Conference of Asia, 2003), 12.

10 For more on this, see Heup Young Kim, *Wang Yang-ming and Karl Barth: a*

is not based on substantialism and essentialism but on the relationship with God, fellow humans, and nature (in East Asian terms,
among Heaven, Earth, and Humanity (天地人); in other words, in
a theanthropocosmic relationship).

The Christian notion of hospitality maximizes this relational anthropology in action. It radically challenges us to deconstruct the
Western habits of substantial thinking of both classical logos theologies and modern praxis theologies.[11] Hospitality basically refers to
a practice in personal relationships, neither a propositional doctrine
for orthodoxy nor a systematic ideology for orthopraxis. The practice of hospitality is a necessary condition to enter into the real meaning of life in the faithful response to the invitation of the Triune God,
who graciously invites us to the real life of true humanity in and
through the sacrificial hospitality of Jesus Christ. The unconditional
decree of hospitality is, in fact, a blessing for us, by which Christ
taught us how to open the door and receive God's welcoming to
enter into the genuine (holy) life. Pohl confessed, "Over and over
again, I've come to see that in God's remarkable economy, as we
make room for hospitality, more room becomes available for us
for life, hope, and grace."[12] Hospitality, as universal benevolence
unconditionally executed in the imitation of the life act of Jesus,
is a sufficient condition for radical humanization, the realization of
true humanity as being in encounter, being in togetherness, and
being for others. As a radical humanization, hospitality refers to a

---

*Confucian-Christian Dialogue* (University Press of America, 1996), 86-90, 158-60.

11 For this discussion, see Kim, *Christ and the Tao*, 135-51.

12 Paul, xiii.

*process par excellence* of sanctification and self-cultivation. Furthermore, this universal benevolence does not have limits and boundaries, "embracing neighbors and strangers, friends and enemies ... the good and gentle, but also ... the evil and unthankful ... every soul God has made" (John Wesley).[13]

Inclusive Humanism: The Christian notion of hospitality radically challenges us to revise the exclusive humanism dominant in the modern West since Descartes' dualist rationalism. Instead, it endorses such inclusive humanism as traditionally supported by Confucianism.[14] Whereas exclusive humanism "exalts the human species, placing it in a position of mastery of and domination over the universe," inclusive humanism "stresses the coordinating powers of humanity as the very reason for its existence." Confucian scholar Cheng Chung-ying criticized the idea that "humanism in the modern West is nothing more than a secular will for power or a striving for domination, with rationalistic science at its disposal." "Humanism in this exclusive sense is a disguise for the individualistic entrepreneurship of modern man armed with science and technology as tools of conquer and devastation." In contrast, the inclusive humanism that is rooted in Confucianism "focuses on the human person as an agency of both self-transformation and transformation of reality at large. As

---

13 John Wesley, *Works of John Wesley, vol. 10: Letters, Essays, Dialogue, Addresses* (Baker House, 1978), 68; recited from ibid, 76.

14 See Cheng Chung-ying, "The Trinity of Cosmology, Ecology, and Ethics in the Confucian Personhood," in *Confucianism and Ecology: The Interrelation of Heaven, Earth, and Humans*, eds. Mary Evelyn Tucker and John Berthrong (Cambridge, MA: Harvard University Press, 1998), 213-15.

the self-transformation of a person is rooted in reality and the transformation of reality is rooted in the person, there is no dichotomy or bifurcation between the human and reality."[15]

This daring Confucian argument sounds far more relevant to the original Christian meanings of humanity (being-in-encounter and being-for-others) and hospitality (universal benevolence) than modern theological anthropologies based on exclusive humanism. Against the essentialist and exclusivist view of the human person, inclusive humanism stresses the "between-ness" or "among-ness" of the person. (The Chinese character for the human being 人間 connotes in-between-ness). In inclusive humanism, a person is not so much a static substance as a network of relationships in constant change (I).[16] Inclusive humanism based on the ontology of humanity as being-in-relationship or being-in-togetherness was splendidly expressed by a Confucian scholar in the 11th century, Chang Tsai.

> Heaven is my father and Earth is my mother, and even such a small creature as I finds an intimate place in their midst. Therefore, that which fills the universe I regard as my body and that which directs the universe I consider as my nature. All people are my brothers and sisters, and all things are my companions...[17]

---

15 Cheng Chung-ying, "The Trinity of Cosmology, Ecology, and Ethics in the Confucian Personhood," in *Confucianism and Ecology: The Interrelation of Heaven, Earth, and Humans*, eds. Mary Evelyn Tucker and John Berthrong (Cambridge, MA: Harvard University Press, 1998), 213-15.

16 This key Confucian/Taoist notion is presented in *I Ching*, one of the Five Confucian Classics. See Richard Wilhelm, tr., *The I Ching or Book of Changes*. 3rd ed. (Princeton University Press, 1967).

17 Chan Wing-tsit, *A Source Book in Chinese Philosophy* (Princeton: Princeton University Press, 1963), 497-98.

*Christology*

The Christian notion of hospitality reinforces Christology as the
foundation of theological anthropology. Jesus Christ, as the person-
ification *par excellence* of the *imago Dei*, is the supreme paradigm of
humanity as co-humanity or a being for others. The human being
is "modeled on the man Jesus and His being for others ... God created
him [man] in his own image in the fact that He did not create him
alone but in the connexion and fellowship ... God Himself is not
solitary ... [but the triune] God exists in relationship and fellowship"
(as the Father, the Son, and the Holy Spirit).[18] Hence, the paradigm
of humanity as being-in-togetherness is nothing other than a copy
or a mirror of the intratrinitarian life of the Triune God. Between
the being of God (as Creator) and the being of human (as creature),
"there is correspondence and similarity;" namely, "*analogia relationis*"
(i.e., an analogy of relation). This analogy of relation was completely
fulfilled in the humanity of Christ, the root paradigm of humanity.
In this fulfillment, Jesus was by no means an exclusive humanist,
but on the contrary, showed a most inclusive form of humanism.
Christ was the prototype of being-in-between-ness or among-ness
(or as the "connecting principle"); between man-to-God, man-to-man,
and man-to-nature.

Reconciliation in these relationships in which Jesus is in between-ness, among-ness, and the connecting principle has been
achieved by Christ's sacrificial acts, which is in fact divine hospitality.
The incarnation of Jesus and His crucifixion on the cross were the

---

18 Barth, CD, II/2:323f. 220,

practices *par excellence* of embracing and embodying God's hospitality. In a nutshell, the sacrificial life-act of Jesus Christ is God's salvific hospitality to the human race. In sum, hospitality is a practice of fulfilling the mission of being human as being-in-between and be-ing-for-others, imitating and following the great examples of hospi-tality Jesus presented us throughout his life.

As Jesus practiced it, hospitality demands a radical denial of one's desires and self-empting (the spirituality of kenosis) for the sake of others. It resonates with an attitude of respect and reverence (敬, gyeong in Korean or ching in Chinese) rather than an aggressive love (in one's own way). *Gyeong* stands at the heart of Korean Neo-Confucian thought culminated by Yi T'oegye (1501-1570). It entails not only epistemic humility but also profound sensitivity to the sufferings of others and things in nature. *Gyeong* signifies the state of human mind-and-heart ready to realize its ontological psy-chosomatic union with others and nature, to fulfill the thean-thropocosmic vision (the communion among the triad of Heaven, Earth, and humanity, 天地人). By attaining this state of mind, a person can possess an ability to hear the voices and feel the pain and suffer-ings of people and nature (the virtue of commiseration) and can exercise beneficence (*jen*) the attributes of which Confucianism calls Four Beginnings, namely, humanity, propriety, righteousness, and wisdom.[19]

---

19 Michael C. Kalton, *To Become a Sage: The Ten Diagrams on Sage Learning by Yi T'oegye* (New York: Columbia University Press, 1988), pp. 119-41.

## Trinity

The notion of hospitality is ultimately based on the immanent and the economic Trinity and their *perichoresis*. Hospitality is a triune welcome of humanity in the life of the Trinity (the immanent Trinity). The triune God sent their only son to embrace humanity, which is an economy of the Trinity. The Incarnation of Jesus Christ is an embodiment of the Triune hospitality for the world. The Crucifixion of the God-man Jesus was the climax of the drama of divine hospitality. The blessings and joy of the Resurrection indicate the gifts to be received by the person who condescends, crossing boundaries, limitations, differences, and idiosyncracies, to execute hospitality to others, including strangers. The *perichoresis* (the Father in the Son as well as the Son in the Father) notes the prototype of humanity as co-humanity, being-in-fellowship, being-in-togetherness, or being-in-between. Hospitality as an active participation in the process of radical humanization is an act of copying this Triune coinherence (*perichorsis*) on our existences.

Creation is a masterpiece of God's hospitality to beings in the universe. Through Jesus Christ, God opened the door to enable us to enter into the life of the Triune immanence. The Economic Trinity is a supreme act of divine hospitality welcoming humanity in the world. Our hospitality in response to this gracious Triune hospitality is in fact for us to open the gateway to the glorification of humanity beyond sanctification. The Trinity embodied divinity into humanity and embraced humanity in divinity in and through the theanthropocosmic drama of Jesus Christ, which is the mystery of salvation. And it is in fact the ultimate foundation and source of hospitality. As a Christian mission is ultimately the mission of God (*Missio Dei*), hospitality is finally not a human, ecclesiastical, not religious deed, but an infused reflection of God's love in us. "God is already working in the lives of the people who come and in the lives of those who welcome them."[20] Doing hospitality does in fact signify embracing and embodying God's hospitality, by participating in the magnificent, gracious cosmic drama of the Trinity. The living God becomes the dialogical and ontological partner of the human, which Barth called "God's sovereign togetherness with man."[21] God's deity, which already has "the character of humanity," "includes" our humanity.

## New Paradigm of Theology: a Theology of Tao (Theo-tao)

The notion of Christian hospitality corrects the defective habit of Western Christian thinking since its contextualization with Greek thought—substantialism, essentialism, and either-or dualism-- both on a doctrinal, metaphysical level and on an ideological, societal level. The fundamental issue is not about essences at all. In fact, there is nothing like an unbreakable building block, but rather, natural sciences continue to prove that the structure of the universe is instead basically relational, as in the relationship between protons and electrons. The foundation of the world does not consist in un-

---

20 Pohl, 187.

21 Karl Barth, *The Humanity of God*, trans. John Newton Thomas and Thomas Wieser (Atlanta: John Knox Press, 1960), 45.

changing substantial essences but in relationships. As we have seen already, humanity is particularly, and by definition, relational. The Christian notion of hospitality announces that relationship is more important than everything else. Thus, Christian theology should be relational so as to embrace and embody the altruistic and salvific partnership of Jesus and the gracious hospitality of the Triune God.

I may argue that the Christian notion of hospitality endorses that a theology of the Tao (Way) is a more proper theological option than classical, dogmatic logos-theologies and modern, liberationist praxis-theologies.[22] Both logos-theologies and praxis-theologies are basically formulated on a substantialist/essentialist and on either-or (either the logos or the praxis) thinking. The former is more doctrinal, while the latter is more ideological. In contrast, the tao refers to the unity of knowing and acting and transcends the dualism of logos and praxis. In terms of the end part of First Corinthian 13, if faith is for the logos-theology (a faith-seeking-understanding, focusing on orthodoxy, the right doctrine for the church) and if hope is for the praxis theology (a hope-seeking-practice on orthopraxis, the right action for the Kingdom of God), then love is for the tao theology (a love-seeking-tao, on orthotao, the right way of companionship). Certainly, hospitality is a matter to do with love rather than with faith and hope. "Our hospitality both reflects and participates in God's hospitality. It depends on a disposition of love because hospitality is simply love in action."[23]

The Christian notion of hospitality that is displeased with the in-

---

22 See Kim, *Christ and the Tao*, 124-76.
23 Pohl, 172.

humanness of institutional and professional treatment commends us to revisit the doctrine of a personal God. The Christian God in the Bible is not so much metaphysical (as often appeared in the logos theology), nor ideological (as in the praxis theology), as relational (interpersonal or inter-subjective) in the fullness of personal connection with the complexity of human emotion. God incarnated in Jesus Christ is not so much a sovereign, omnipotent, and apathetic host of divinity, but a fragile, vulnerable, and sensitive guest in humanity. God in Jesus Christ is a human person, a companion on the road with us, as common pilgrims, sojourners, and strangers. Thus, a relational theology of the Way (Tao) is a more proper paradigm for Asian theology! God in Jesus Christ is, after all, the hospitality of the Triune God toward us to enable us to return to the original humanity in harmony with the divinity and others. Hospitality is the tao (way) of humanization *par excellence*. Rather than doctrine or ideology, thus, the theology of the Tao focuses on the way of life together with a preferential option to the yin side of the universe, including strangers, minjung, and Dalit, which precisely means radical humanization. A letter from L'Arche stated that "a society, to be truly human, must be founded on welcome and respect for the weak and the downtrodden."[24]

### New Interpretation

The notion of hospitality, the cornerstone of the Christian faith,

---

24 Letters of L'Arche 88 (June 1996): 2; Jean Vanier, *An Ark for the Poor: The Story of L'Arche* (New York: Crossroad, 1995), 117.

needs a new interpretation-- a hermeneutics of reconstruction-- in this post-era of so-called post-colonialism, post-orientalism, and post-Christianity (post-Christendom). Not to mention, the genocidal exploitation of European Christians in both the North and South American Continents! After the experiences of the 19th century colonialism of Western Christianity, furthermore, we Asians are particularly suspicious of Christian hospitality in a positive and expansive manner. Before mentioning any type of hospitality, we would ask of the host a total *kenosis* of oneself (self-negation), full respect or reverence for guests, and a partnership among strangers, just as the Triune God did for us in and through the life of Jesus Christ. Jesus completely self-emptied himself until death, paid the fullest respect to the people washing their feet, and lived among the minjung, comforting and healing them to accomplish his mission of "embracing and embodying God's hospitality" for us. We, Asian disciples of Christ, need such an *imitatio Christi* today in Asia! That is to say, "Embracing and Embodying God's Hospitality Today in Asia," the theme of the 7th Congress of Asian Theologians.

Hospitality, an unconditional decree to be a Christian, needs a spirituality of emptiness or nothingness rather than that of substantial, essential, or metaphorical something; traditionally speaking, it should be *apophatic* rather than *kataphatic*, *via negativa* rather than *via positiva*. At this juncture, we should note side-effects of the golden rule, the core of Christian faith and Confucianism. The positive golden rule (Love others as yourself), favored in the Christian West, can be misread as "Love others *in your own ways!*" An American scholar studying East Asian thought, Robert E. Allinson, made the critique that the positive golden rule caused the attitudes of "epistemological immodesty" and "ethical *hubris*," and makes one prone to treating others as "strangers" or "enemies" in a conflict-complex (*Enemies, Strangers, or Partners*).[25] Greek dialectical dualism reinforced by an expansive nomadic ethos underlined these attitudes of the conflict and aggressive model.[26] These erroneous attitudes would be a root-cause for the modern failure of the arrogant Western Christian mission in Asia.

However, (East) Asia is rather the world of *harmony*, exemplified by the Great Ultimate in the *yin-yang* relationship. In the *yin-yang* interdependent, dialogical relationship, both *yin* and *yang* are always interchangeable and exist together. The relationship between a host and a guest would better be understood in this dynamic relation. As *yin* can become *yang* anytime, it is always possible for a host to turn into a guest, and vice versa. Their existential status may look different, but ontologically, however, they are the same partners among strangers. In this world of *jen* (being-in-togetherness), the habit of the negative golden rule (Do not do to others what you do not want them to do to you!) is more appreciated, as "epistemological modesty" and "ethical *humility*" are crucial virtues for treating others as 'guests' or 'friends' in an effort to bring harmony in the world. Christian hospitality in the mode of the positive golden rule (Love others in my own way!) could bring out maleficent side effects. Rather, an attitude of the negative golden rule (Love others in their own ways!) would be

---

25 See Robert E. Allinson, "The Ethics of Confucianism & Christianity: the Delicate Balance," *Ching Feng* 33:3 (1990): 158-75.

26 Cf. Shu-hsien Liu and Robert E. Allinson, *Harmony and Strife: Contemporary Perspectives, East & West* (Hong Kong: The Chinese University Press, 1988).

preferable in order to avoid epistemological immodesty and ethical *hubris*. As Christian Pohl said, "Humility is a crucial virtue for hospitality, and especially important in keeping hosts' power in check. Power is a complicated dimension of hospitality."[27] Yes! However, here in Asia, we need a more fundamental change of attitude. As Yale theologian Miroslav Volf said better, "the will to give ourselves to others and 'welcome' them, to readjust our identities to make space for them, is prior to any judgment about others, except that of identifying them in their humanity."[28]

God is the only unconditional host. The nucleus of the Christian story is that the sovereign host-God emptied Godself completely to become a vulnerable human-guest and a stranger in this world. The being becomes a non-being (the being in non-being) so that we non-beings can become the being (a non-being in being). This is a key to understanding the mystery of Jesus, *i.e.*, God's hospitality par *excellence*. The theme of Embracing and Embodying God's Hospitality Today in Asia would be ultimately summarized in the question, "What would Jesus do to strangers and others in Asia if he came in this age of migration, globalization and science today?" What would he do and how would he welcome immigrant workers, multi-cultural marriages, refugees, the disabled, prisoners, people in other religions, other beings on this susceptible planet, possible extraterritorial (ET) guests from outer space, beings which come into existence by manipulations of science and technology, and so

---

27 Pohl, 120.

28 Miroslav Volf, *Exclusion and Embrace: a Theological Exploration of Identity, Otherness, and Reconciliation* (Nashville: Abingdon Press, 1996), 29

on? In the Asian context, furthermore, the hospitality list should include not only those in the present and the future but also those in the past, particularly ancestors.

This week, we, Asian theologians, have gathered together in Seoul to discuss these important issues. The CATS is so far the only existing platform and theological space in the world where Asian theologians freely speak for themselves, collectively together, without feeling timid against yet dominant Western theological discourses. Although it is a meeting of a small number, I believe it will become a historically significant event for Christians and churches in both Asia and the rest of the world, particularly anticipating the 10th General Assembly of the World Council of Churches to be held in Busan next year.

Asia, called the home of world religions, is the most diversified continent culturally, religiously, ideologically, politically, and perhaps economically. It is the predicted place for the so-called "clash of civilizations." Perhaps, the Korean peninsula would be a pinnacle of such a clash or an encounter, in a nutshell, both between the West and the East and between the North and the South. The symbol of the Korean national flag, the Great Ultimate in the dialogical *yin-yang*, would metaphorically prophesy this time in history. The duality of *yin-yang* is not permanently fixed but always interchanging. It is not an "either-or," but a "both-and." It represents dynamic phenomena in temporality to create and compose the ultimate wholeness, by not denying their distinctions, particularities, and idiosyncrasies.

Finally, hospitality is based on "God's Great Yes!" for us to join the Kingdom of God. It is our response to God's invitation to the heavenly banquet, in terms of sacrament, Eucharist. Christian hospitality is to celebrate this grace by inviting and welcoming friends, colleagues, neighbors, aliens, sojourners, the afflicted, and the disabled in response to this divine blessing. We, Asian theologians, as yet strangers in Christian theology, need to continue a corporate endeavor to open our spaces to "sing our own songs" and "own up to our own metaphors." At the same time, we need to let fellow friends in Asia do the same thing as humble partners among strangers. Jesus, both a human stranger and the divine host, is the Christ who has established once and for all the ontological space for us to be fully human. The Congress of Asian Theologians is the space where we Asian theologians gather together to sing our own song and own up to our own metaphors. We, members of the CATS, are all partners among strangers. Today, we gathered here to satisfy the command of God to attain our fullness as humans. Now, let's begin our fascinating discussions. May God dearly bless you all, and may His hospitality abundantly prevail throughout the congress!

APPENDIX THREE

# Paul Tillich, Boston Confucianism, Theology of Religions: A Short Reflection from the Perspective of Theo-dao

I was kindly requested to make a presentation on Tillich and Confucianism on this panel of the North American Tillich Society at the 2019 Annual Meeting of the American Academy of Religion, but I refused. I am not a Tillich scholar and felt presumptuous to say about Tillich's theology in front of distinguished Tillich scholars, and I have distanced from Western theologies for decades to focus on the formulation of a Theology of Dao (Theo-dao) as an East Asian theologian. However, he continued to plead with Dr. Lawrence Whitney's paper.[1] With his agreement, thus, I take this opportunity to share some thoughts on Tillich, Boston Confucianism (Ruism), and recent American theologies of religions.

*Paul Tillich and Confucian-Christian Dialogue*

*Theo-Dao* I have been proposing is an East Asian/Korean contextual theology in and through Confucian-Christian dialogue.[2] It

---

1 Lawrence Whitney, "Confucianism and Tillich's Protestant Principle, presented at the American Acadmy of Religion, November 22, 2019, San Diego."

sees Western theologies still in inherited dualism, namely, *theo-logos* (classical theologies) and *theo-praxis* (liberation theologies). Adopting holistic dao (道) as the theological root-metaphor, *theo-dao* offers a new paradigm of global theology to move beyond this theological dualism of logos and praxis. Here dao, of course, does not just refer to Daoism but closer to Neo-Confucianism.

When writing the doctoral dissertation on Confucian-Christian dialogue between Wang Yang-ming and Karl Barth, I met both Julia Ching and Hans Küng immediately after their co-publication of *Christianity and Chinese Religions* (1989)[3] and asked their advice on my dissertation project. Both unanimously inquired why I wrote with Barth, who thought to be an impossible person to make an interreligious dialogue with other religions at that time but suggested Paul Tillich instead. Küng established a famous doctoral thesis that there is no need for the schism between Catholicism and Protestantism on the doctrine of justification if Barth's doctrine is understood correctly.[4] Similarly but beyond the Western Christian horizons, in the dissertation, I argued that there are remarkably thick resemblances between the Confucian (Wang) notion of Self-Cultivation and the Christian (Barth) doctrine of Sanctification.[5] Later, Küng sent me a note appreciating this work. It would be the first work

---

2 Heup Young Kim (Hŭb-yŏng Kim), *A Theology of Dao* (Maryknoll, New York: Orbis Books, 2017).

3 Hans Küng and Julia Ching, *Christianity and Chinese Religions* (New York: Doubleday, 1989).

4 Hans Küng, Justification: *The Doctrine of Karl Barth and a Catholic reflection* (Louisville, KY: Westminster John Knox Press, 2004).

5 Heup Young Kim (Hŭb-yŏng Kim), *Wang Yang-Ming and Karl Barth: A Confucian-Christian Dialogue* (Lanham, Md: University Press of America, 1996).

to make Barth in dialogue (or comparative theology) with non-Christian traditions, especially an East Asian tradition. Almost three decades afterward, American Reformed theologians, too, began to see Barth as a comparative theologian.[6]

Neo-Confucianism, at least Korean Neo-Confucianism, was a study of dao (道學) that takes propriety (禮) and reverence (敬) seriously. Consisting of two components meaning head (首) and action (辶), Chinese character dao (道) literary means 'the unity of knowing and acting' for whose doctrine Wang Yang-ming is famous. Karl Barth, likewise, insisted on the unity of theology and ethics, but Tillich rejected ethics tied with theology. This difference is perhaps due to their backgrounds between Calvinism and Lutheranism, which emphasize sanctification and justification respectably. In this sense, Barth's theology is closer to a study of dao (and theo-dao), while Tillich's theology is a more typical Western logos theology (theo-logos).

A fundamental question for Tillich from the perspective of theo-dao is whether he understood the real meaning of Dao? Whether his notion of ultimate concern can embrace the depth of Dao? Or whether Tillich, as a propagator of 'existential theology of being', perceived the theological significance of ultimate nothingness sufficiently (ST 1.2.1)? Although he dealt with non-being, it seems to be only with reservation or more likely in a negative or inferior antithesis (finitude or the estrangement between essence and existence) of being. In Daoism and Neo-Confucianism, however, nonbeing

---

6 Martha L. Moore-Keish and Christian T. Collins Winn, eds., *Karl Barth and Comparative Theology* (New York: Fordham University Press, 2019).

and being form one as *yin* and yang compose a *Taiji* (無極而太極). David Chai made a helpful comparative study between Tillich and Zhuangzi and concluded.

> Herein is where Zhuangzi's meontology surpasses Tillich's *ex nihilo* hybrid. Unlike Tillich, Zhuangzi does not "weaponize" nonbeing by turning it into the ultimate threat facing being; on the contrary, he takes nonbeing to be the root and mutual partner of being. In this way, the world is nourished, not harmed, by nonbeing, living freely and without despondency.[7]

Since Western theological ontology, like Tillich's, disregards non-being or regards it only as negative dialectics to being, it inevitably entails a conflict (not harmony) paradigm when the ontological necessity for change or becoming occurs. From this vantage point, Tillich's claim that the Protestant Principle is universal and eternal (as Whitney vindicated) can be viewed as a Tillichian way of justifying this ontological weakness, self-contradictory to his insistence that only being is ontological. It will be further elaborated later.

### Boston Confucianism

As a 28th-generation descendant of the Korean Confucian family, first of all, I have been suspicious of whether Boston Confucianism (Ruism) can be more than an intellectual Confucianism, though appreciating it as a vital movement for this age. Can one be a genuine

---

7 David Chai, *Philosophy East & West*, 69:2 (2019), 352.

Confucian only by reading and understanding Confucian scriptures and literature but without learning and practicing the complex and highly nuanced Neo-Confucian system of *li* (propriety) in which humility (not epistemological immodesty) and moral conduct (not ethical hubris) in everyday life are essential? The main issue of Neo-Confucianism that takes one's relationship with others (仁) most seriously is whether one treats other(s) through dignified propriety with sufficient reverence, which is more important than the level of knowledge one has. For this discernment, feeling through the mind-and-heart is more crucial than the cognitive depth of others' verbal expression or logic.

Further, as a Korean, I am worried that Boston Intellectual Confucianism will become a school that reproduces Confucian ideologies centered on China. First of all, it is wrong to identify Confucianism as a Chinese religion. Although Christianity originated in Palestine or Israel, we do not call it Palestinian or Israeli religion. Confucianism is not only a Chinese religion, just as Christianity or Buddhism is not only a Palestine or an Indian religion. Further, as Tu Wei-ming said, it is not China but Korea that was "undoubtedly the most thoroughly Confucianized" country and still is as the only predominantly Confucian society in the world today.[8] Hence, 'Confucianism as a Chinese religion' is a misnomer. Furthermore, this expression can be offensive to Koreans because it reminds Koreans of thorny memories of Sinocentric imperialism in the history of East Asia. Thus, it would be more appropriate to call Confucianism inclusively an East Asian religion or tradition rather than exclusively

---

8 Ibid.

Chinese. Moreover, although I understand the need for an alternate term for Confucianism, I am not so convinced with 'Ruism' because Ru is also according to the Chinese pronunciation (Romanization) of the character 儒, whereas its Korean pronunciation is different (*Ryu*).

## Protestant Principle and Confucianism

I may add two points to Lawrence's paper. First, as already mentioned, the Protestant Principle would be a logical result of Western theology's static ontology and dualism. Tillich did not seem to sufficiently liberate from the modern Western premise that historical development can only be achieved through hierarchical dialectics, where finite and infinite can never be harmonized (cf., *coincidentia oppositorum*). Neo-Confucianism with the ontology of the Ultimate Paradox of *Taiji* (Non-Ultimate is the Ultimate 無極而太極) does not regard the relationship between Being and Non-Being as hierarchical and confrontational but as relational like yin and yang in the Taiji (when yin reaches the extreme, it becomes yang and vice versa). The Protestant Principle is needed in Western Christianity because it does not have a robust ontology of change. If a change occurs, dialectical logic is required in order to cope with the change, such as the Protestant Principle. Tillich should have known this ontological flaw of Western Christian theology so that he argued that the Protestant Principle is more enduring than Protestantism. However, Confucianism defines being itself as being of change. It changes from non-being to being for cosmogony and from *yin* to *yang* for life-giving, and vice versa. *The Book of Changes* (易經) characterizes life (道) itself as a continuous change (一陰一陽謂之道) like breathing. It also defines life (易) as a reversal (逆) against the general trajectory of the force, as trees grow against gravity. Yes, there is something like the Protestant Principle in Confucianism. However, it is more ontological and constitutional than merely epistemological or antithetical.

Second, the debate between Mencius and Xunzi on human nature would be better compared in a broader picture of the relationship between Confucianism and Christianity, namely, in comparison with the parallel debate between Augustine and Pelagius. In the Christian theistic context, on the one hand, Augustine's main concern in dealing with human nature was theodicy. As a theologian, he needed to charge the reason for existing sin and evil to the human being in order to justify God as the good Creator. In the Confucian non-theistic context, on the other hand, Mencius needed to find the ontological foundation from which the human can overcome the evil in the world to enable to do good. For this reason, he argued that humanity as the Heavenly Endowment (天命之謂性) is ontologically good, which Wang Yang-ming further developed in terms of the innate knowledge of good (良知). In other words, while Pelagius and Mencius were right in the ontological sense (體), Augustine and Xunzi would be right in the practical sense (用). In the histories of both traditions, this parallel polar relationship exists *de facto*, composing a unity of opposites (like *Taiji* and *tǐyòng*) and continuously appears in their related themes. For example, between *li* (理) and *xin* (心) in Neo-Confucianism and between faith and deed in Christianity.

## Recent American Theologies of Religions

After Tillich, Western theologians have been participating in inter-religious dialogue with other religious traditions. From the standpoint of theo-dao, however, they still seem not to move much beyond Eurocentric worldviews. Even John Hick and Hans Küng, two famous pioneers of pluralism and inclusivism, also are not so much exceptional. Notably, it is evident in their rejecting dual or multiple religious belonging (or citizenship), perhaps based on their European mono-religious experiences with violent religious war phobia.[9] Recently, a genre called 'comparative theology' appeared and now seems to lead the American theology, followed by 'theology without walls' or 'transnational theology.'

However, it is doubtful how much different comparative theology can be from a new (twenty-first century) version of the Jesuit mis-siology of Matteo Ricci. 'Theology without walls' or 'trans-religious theology' look even weirder. It seems like American theologians are trying to cover up dreadful mistakes and misconduct that Western Christianity has committed in Asia under the name of the mission and evangelism of Good News. In East Asia, our plural religions, such as Confucianism, Buddhism, and Daoism, had been peacefully to-gether for millennia with no brutal religious wars and conflicts (and 'without walls') before Western Christianity came in. However, mis-sionaries from Western churches built confrontational walls against

---

9 See Heup Young Kim, "Multiple Religious Belonging as Hospitality: a Korean Confucian-Christian Perspective," in *Many yet One? : Multiple Religious Belonging*, eds. Reniel J. R. Rajkumar and Jopsh P. Dayam (Geneva: WCC Publications, 2016), 75-88.

our religions and cultures for the sake of their aggressive membership expansion. Then, their heirs are now saying, "Since we no longer need the walls, let us remove them!" What an irresponsible and sneaky position bypassing necessary repentances and compensations for their deplorable missiological and theological failures that have often been causing irreversible religious and cultural damages throughout Asian countries.

The Congress of Asian Theologians (CATS), the unique ecumenical platform representing Christian theologians and scholars in whole Asia, issued the following statement reviewing the Western mission in Asia.

This Congress aimed at consolidating and advancing the new paradigm of Christian life among the rich variety of religious traditions of Asia. We acknowledge that the Christian mission in Asia has been to a great extent a failure if measured by its own aims. The failure emerged from its unhelpful theology of religions and its missiology ... Christians now must humbly acknowledge that in these many ways God has always been savingly present in the continent. In its failure to acknowledge these facts, the Christian mission in Asia was arrogant and colonialist ...

The modern missionary era in Asia ... was, to a great extent, a dismal phase with hostile, aggressive, and even arrogant attitudes to the other faiths. The local cultures and religious traditions of Asia were often looked upon as inferior and to be replaced by Christianity and Western cultural traditions. The missionary praxis, in general, was one of converting and baptizing people of other religions and extending the churches at the cost of the social, cultural and religious values that constituted their inherent sense of dignity and identity.[10]

American (and Western) theologians and scholars should listen carefully to reflect on this honest message from the hearts of Asian theologians before attempting any theological engagements with Asian religions and cultures! Whatever forms of theologies originated from the West, whether comparative theology, theology without walls, or trans-religious theology, we hope that it should not be another "unhelpful theology of religions and its missiology" for Asia and other Continents. Do Not Spoil Our Metaphors!

---

10 Daniel S. Thiagarajah and A. Wati Longchar, eds., *Visioning New Life Together among Asian Resources: The Third Congress of Asian Theologians* (Hong Kong: CCA, 2002), 294-95.

# Glossary

## Additional Romanized Korean Terms

| Romanizations | Korean | English Translation/Definition |
|---|---|---|
| ban | 반 | reversal or opposition |
| Dasŏk | 다석 | pen name of Ryu Yŏngmo |
| han | 한 | unresolved grief or resentment; a central concept in Korean theology and culture |
| hanpuri | 한풀이 | resolving accumulated han; significant in Minjung theology |
| Kim Chi Ha | 김지하 | Catholic poet pivotal in Korean theology |
| Kim Yong-bok | 김용복 | seminal Minjung theologian (Seontopia) |
| Lǎozǐ | 노자 | founder of Daoian thought |
| minjung | 민중 | the masses or oppressed people; key to Minjung theology |
| Ryu Yŏngmo | 류영모 | renowned Korean religious thinker |
| Seontopia | 선경 | East Asian utopian concept |
| Theodao | 도의 신학 | Theology of Dao formulated by Heup Young Kim |
| Ugŭmchi | 우금치 | historical battle and Theodaoian metaphor for resilience and empowerment |
| Wang Yang-ming | 왕양명 | seminal Chinese Neo-Confucian thinker (liáng zhǐ) |
| Yijīng | 역경 | Canon of Changes |
| Yi Pyŏk | 이벽 | early Korean Catholic Confucian scholar |
| Yi T'oegye | 이퇴계 | pivotal Korean Neo-Confucian thinker |
| Zhang Zai | 장재 | seminal Chinese Neo-Confucian thinker (Trinitarian ecology) |
| Zhou Dunyi | 주돈이 | seminal Chinese Neo-Confucian thinker (Tài ji) |
| Zoesophia | 생명학 | wisdom of life |

# Glossary
## Romanized Confucian Terms

| Chinese Romanizations | Korean Romanizations | English Translation | Chinese Characters |
|---|---|---|---|
| ài<br>(ai) | ae<br>(애) | love | 愛<br>(爱) |
| chéng<br>(ch'eng) | sŏng<br>(성) | sincerity | 誠<br>(诚) |
| chéng yì<br>(ch'eng-i) | sŏng-ŭi<br>(성의) | the sincerity of the will | 誠意<br>(诚意) |
| dào<br>(tao) | do/to<br>(도) | the Way | 道 |
| Dào xīn<br>(Tao-hsin) | To-sim<br>(도심) | the mind of Tao | 道心 |
| dé<br>(te) | tŏk<br>(덕) | virtue | 德 |
| gé wù<br>(ko-wu) | kyŏk mul<br>(격물) | the investigation of things | 格物 |
| jìng<br>(ching) | kyŏng<br>(경) | reverence, piety, mind-fulness | 敬 |
| lǐ<br>(li) | I<br>(이) | principle | 理 |
| lǐ<br>(li) | rye<br>(례) | propriety | 禮<br>(礼) |
| liáng zhī<br>(liang-chih) | ryang-chi<br>(양지) | the innate knowledge of the good | 良知 |
| liáng xīn<br>(liang-hsin) | ryang-sim<br>(양심) | good conscience | 良心 |
| lì zhì<br>(li-chih) | ip chi<br>(입지) | the establishment of the will | 立志 |
| míng dé<br>(ming-te) | myŏng tŏk<br>(명덕) | the clear character, the illustrious virtue | 明德 |
| qì | ki | material force, vital energy | 氣 |

| | | | |
|---|---|---|---|
| (ch'i) | (기) | | (气) |
| qīn mín (ch'in-min) | ch'in min (친민) | loving people | 親民 (亲民) |
| qíng (ch'ing) | chŏng (정) | feeling | 情 |
| rén (jen) | in (인) | human being | 人 |
| rén (jen) | in (인) | benevolence, co-humanity | 仁 |
| rén xīn (jen-hsin) | in-sim (인심) | the human mind | 人心 |
| Shàng dì (Shang-ti) | Sang-je (상제) | the Lord on the High | 上帝 |
| shēn (shen) | sin (신) | body | 身 |
| shén (shen) | sin (신) | Spirit, God | 神 |
| shén qì (shen-ch'i) | sin-ki (신기) | vital energy, divine energy | 神氣 (神气) |
| shù (shu) | sŏ (서) | reciprocity | 恕 |
| Tài jí (T'ai-chi) | T'ae-gŭk (태극) | the Great Ultimate | 太極 (太极) |
| Tài xū (T'ai-hsu) | T'ae-sŏ (태허) | the Great Vacuity | 太虛 |
| tǐ (t'i) | ch'e (체) | substance | 體 (体) |
| Tiān lǐ (T'ien-li) | Ch'ŏn-ri (천리) | Heavenly Principle, Principle of Nature | 天理 |
| Tiān mìng (T'ien-ming) | Ch'ŏn-myŏng (천명) | Heavenly Endowment, the Mandate of Heaven | 天命 |
| Wàn wù yī tǐ (Wan-wu i-t'i) | Man mul il ch'e (만물일체) | the Oneness of All Things | 萬物一體 (万物一体) |
| Wú jí (Wu-chi) | Mu-gŭk (무극) | the Non-Ultimate | 無極 (无极) |
| wú wéi | mu-wi | non-action action | 無爲 |

| | | | |
|---|---|---|---|
| (wu-wei) | (무위) | | (无 为) |
| xīn (hsin) | sim (심) | mind-and-heart | 心 |
| xìn (hsin) | sin (신) | faithfulness | 信 |
| xīn jí lǐ (hsin chih li) | sim chŭk ri (심즉리) | the identity of mind-and-heart and principle | 心卽理 |
| xìng (hsing) | sŏng (성) | Nature, human nature | 性 |
| xìng jí lǐ (hsing chi li) | sŏng chŭk ri (성즉리) | the identity of nature and principle | 性卽理 |
| yáng (yang) | yang (양) | yang | 陽 (阳) |
| Yì (I) | Yŏk (역) | The Change | 易 |
| yì (i) | ŭi (의) | righteousness | 義 (义) |
| yī qì (i-ch'i) | il-ki (일기) | primordial energy | 一氣 (一气) |
| yīn (yin) | ŭm (음) | yin | 陰 (阴) |
| yòng (yung) | yong (용) | function | 用 |
| yuán hēng lì zhēn (yuan heng li chen) | wŏn hyŏng ri chŏng (원형리정) | origination, flourishing, benefitting, firmness | 元亨利貞 (元亨利贞) |
| zhèng xīn (cheng-hsin) | chŏng-sim (정심) | the rectification of the mind-and-heart | 正心 |
| zhī (chih) | chi (지) | knowledge | 知 |
| zhì (chih) | chi (지) | wisdom | 智 |
| zhì liáng zhī (chih liang-chih) | chi ryang-chi (치량지) | the extension of the innate knowledge of the good | 致良知 |
| zhōng (chung) | chung (중) | equilibrium | 中 |
| zhōng yōng (Chung-yung) | chung-yong (중용) | The Doctrine of Means | 中庸 |

# Bibliography

Allinson, Robert E. "The Ethics of Confucianism & Christianity: The Delicate Balance." *Ching Feng* 33, no. 3 (1990): 158-175.

Ames, R. T., and H. Rosemont Jr. *The Analects of Confucius: A Philosophical Translation*. New York: Ballantine Books, 1998.

Ames, Roger T., and David L. Hall. *Dao De Jing: A Philosophical Translation*. New York: Ballantine Books, 2003.

Anon. "Mind in Indian Buddhist Philosophy." Stanford Encyclopedia of Philosophy. Accessed at: https://plato.stanford.edu/entries/mind-indian-buddhism/.

Ariès, Philippe. *The Hour of Our Death*. Oxford: Oxford University Press, 1981.

Arndt, William F., and F. Wilbur Gingrich. *A Greek-English Lexicon of the New Testament and Other Early Christian Literature*. 2nd ed. Chicago: University of Chicago Press, 1979.

Ashcroft, Bill, Gareth Griffiths, and Helen Tiffin, eds. *The Post-Colonial Studies Reader*. London: Routledge, 1995.

Assuncao Guimaraes, Cinthya, and Rafael Linden. "Programmed Cell Death: Apoptosis and Alternative Death Styles." *European Journal of Biochemistry* 271 (2004): 1638-1650.

Barbour, Ian G. *Religion and Science: Historical and Contemporary Issues*. San Francisco: HarperSanFrancisco, 1997.

_____. *When Science Meets Religion: Enemies, Strangers, or Partners?* San Francisco: HarperSanFrancisco, 2000.

Barth, Karl. *Church Dogmatics III. 2*. Translated by Harold Knight et al. Edinburgh: T&T Clark, 1960.

_____. *The Humanity of God*. Translated by John Newton Thomas and Thomas Wieser. Atlanta: John Knox Press, 1960.

Bassett, Daniells S., and Michael S. Gazzaniga. "Understanding Complexity in the Human Brain." *Trends in Cognitive Sciences* 15, no. 4 (2011): 200-209.

Beasley-Murray, and George R. John. *Word Biblical Commentary*, Vol. 36. Waco, TX: Word Books, 1982.

Bedau, Mark. "Four Puzzles about Life." *Artificial Life* 4, no. 1 (1998): 125-139.

Berling, Judith A. *A Pilgrim in Chinese Culture: Negotiating Religious Diversity.* Maryknoll, NY: Orbis Books, 1997.

Berthrong, John. *All Under Heaven: Transforming Paradigms in Confucian-Christian Dialogue.* Albany, NY: State University of New York Press, 1994.

Boogerd, Fred C., et al. "Towards Philosophical Foundations of Systems Biology: Introduction." In *Systems Biology: Philosophical Foundations.* Edited by Fred C. Boogerd et al. Amsterdam: Elsevier, 2007.

Bostrom, Nick. *Superintelligence: Paths, Dangers, Strategies.* Oxford: Oxford University Press, 2014.

———. "A History of Transhumanist Thought." *Journal of Evolution and Technology* 14, no. 1 (2005): 1-25.

———. "The Fate of the Dragon Tyrant." *Journal of Medical Ethics* 31, no. 4 (2005): 273-277.

Bowker, John. *Is God a Virus? Genes, Culture and Religion.* London: SPCK, 1995.

Braidotti, Rosi. *The Posthuman.* Cambridge: Polity Press, 2013.

Brooks, Rodney. "The Relationship Between Matter and Life." *Nature* 409, no. 6822 (2001): 409-411.

Capra, Fritjof. *The Tao of Physics: An Exploration of the Parallels Between Modern Physics and Eastern Mysticism.* 5th ed. Boston: Shambhala, 2010.

_____. *The Web of Life: A New Scientific Understanding of Living Systems.* New York: Doubleday, 1996.

Chai, David. "Paul Tillich, Zhuangzi, and the Creative Role of Nonbeing." *Philosophy East & West* 69, no. 2 (2019): 352.

Chan, Wing-tsit. *A Source Book in Chinese Philosophy.* Princeton, NJ: Princeton University Press, 1963.

_____. *Instructions for Practical Living and Other Neo-Confucian Writings.* New York: Columbia University Press, 1963.

Cheng, Chung-ying. *New Dimensions of Confucian and Neo-Confucian Philosophy.* Albany, NY: State University of New York Press, 1991.

_____. "The Trinity of Cosmology, Ecology, and Ethics in the Confucian Personhood." In *Confucianism and Ecology: The Interrelation of Heaven, Earth, and Humans.* Edited by Mary Evelyn Tucker and John Berthrong. Cambridge, MA: Harvard University Press, 1998.

Ching, Julia. *Confucianism and Christianity: A Comparative Study.* Tokyo: Kodansha International, 1977.

Chouldechova, Alexandra and Aaron Roth. "A Snapshot of the Frontiers of Fairness in Machine Learning." *Communications of the ACM* 63, no. 5 (2020): 82-89. https://doi.org/10.1145/3376896.

Chuang Tzu. *The Complete Works of Chuang Tzu.* Translated by Burton Watson. New York: Columbia University Press, 1968.

Chung, David. *Syncretism: The Religious Context of Christian Beginnings in Korea.* Albany, NY: State University of New York Press, 2001.

Chung, Hyun Kyung. "Han-puri: Doing Theology from Korean Women's Perspective." *The Ecumenical Review* 40, no. 1 (1988): 27-36.

Chung, Jin-hong. "Our Traditional Understanding of Death and Today's Tasks." In *Sarmgwa Jukeumeui Inmunhak (Life and Death: A Study of Humanities).* Edited by Jae-gap Park. Seoul: Seoktap Publications, 2012.

Cobb, John B., Jr. *Beyond Dialogue: Towards a Mutual Transformation of Buddhism and Christianity.* Philadelphia, PA: Fortress Press, 1982.

Confucius. *The Analects.* Oxford: Oxford University Press, 2007.

Corallo, Angelo, Luigi Foschini, Francesco Frasca, et al. "Natural Language Processing for Mental Health and Suicide Risk Assessment: A Systematic Review." *JMIR Mental Health* 9, no. 2 (2021): e23980. https://doi.org/10.2196/23980.

Dastin, Jeffrey. "Facial Recognition Technology Moves into HR." *Reuters,* 2018. https://www.reuters.com/article/us-hirevue-facial-recognition-idUSKCN 1NK0J1.

De Bary, Wm. *Theodore. East Asian Civilizations: A Dialogue in Five Stages.* Cambridge, MA: Harvard University Press, 1989.

de Sousa Santos, Boaventura. *Epistemologies of the South: Justice Against Epistemicide.* New York: Routledge, 2014.

Dowd, Michael, and Connie Barlow. "A Scientific Honoring of Death." *Metanexus,* July 15, 2012. http://metanexus.net/blog/scientific-honoring-death.

Eck, Diana L. *A New Religious America: How a "Christian Country" Has Now Become the World's Most Religiously Diverse Nation.* San Francisco: Harper SanFrancisco, 2001.

_____. *Encountering God: A Spiritual Journey from Bozeman to Banaras.* Boston: Beacon Press, 1993.

Eidelson, Roy J. "Complex Adaptive Systems in the Behavioral and Social Sciences." *Review of General Psychology* 1, no. 1 (1997): 42-71.

European Commission. "Communication from the Commission to the European Parliament, the Council, the European Economic and Social Committee, and the Committee of the Regions: Building Trust in Human-Centric Artificial Intelligence." *Brussels* (April 8, 2019).

Fingarette, Herbert. *Confucius: The Secular as Sacred*. New York: Harper & Row, 1972.

Floridi, Luciano, and Josh Cowls. "A Unified Framework of Five Principles for AI in Society." *Harvard Data Science Review* 1, no. 1 (2019). https://doi.org/10.1162/99608f92.8cd550d1.

Francis, Pope. *Laudato si' of the Holy Father on Care for Our Common Home*. Encyclical Letter, May 24, 2015. Available at http://www.vatican.va/content/dam/francesco/pdf/encyclicals/documents/papa-francesco_20150524_enciclica-laudato-si_en.pdf.

Fukuyama, Francis. "The World's Most Dangerous Ideas: Transhumanism." *Foreign Policy* 144 (2009): 42-43.

Gadamer, Hans-Georg. *Truth and Method*. 2nd ed. Translated by Joel Weinsheimer and Donald G. Marshall. New York: Crossroad, 1989.

Gernet, Jacques. *China and the Christian Impact: A Conflict of Culture*. Translated by Janet Lloyd. Cambridge: Cambridge University Press, 1985.

Girardot, N. J. *Myth and Meaning in Early Taoism: The Theme of Chaos (Hun-tun)*. Berkeley: University of California Press, 1983.

Griffiths, Bede. *Universal Wisdom: A Journey Through the Sacred Wisdom of the World*. San Francisco: HarperCollins, 1994.

Gutiérrez, Gustavo. *A Theology of Liberation*. Maryknoll, NY: Orbis Books, 1988.

Gánti, Tibor. *The Principles of Life*. New York: Oxford University Press, 2003.

Ham Sŏk Hŏn. *Queen of Suffering: A Spiritual History of Korea*. Translated by E. Sang Yu. London: Friends World Committee for Consultation, 1985.

Harari, Yuval Noah. *Sapiens: A Brief History of Humankind*. New York: Harper, 2011.

———. *Homo Deus: A Brief History of Tomorrow*. New York: Harper, 2017.

Hayles, Katherine. *How We Became Posthuman: Virtual Bodies in Cybernetics,*

*Literature, and Informatics.* Chicago: University of Chicago Press, 1999.

Hedges, Paul. *Preparation and Fulfillment: A History and Study of Fulfillment Theology in Modern British Thought in the Indian Context.* Bern: Peter Lang, 2001.

_____. "Multiple Religious Belonging after Religion: Theorising Strategic Religious Participation in a Shared Religious Landscape as a Chinese Model." *Open Theology* 3 (2017): 48-72.

Herzfeld, Noreen. *Technology and Religion: Remaining Human in a Co-Created World.* Templeton Press, 2011.

Hick, John. *An Interpretation of Religion: Human Responses to the Transcendent.* New Haven, CT: Yale University Press, 1989.

Hodgson, Peter C. *Winds of the Spirit: A Constructive Christian Theology.* Louisville, KY: Westminster John Knox Press, 1994.

Hopko, Thomas. "Apophatic Theology and the Naming of God in Eastern Orthodox Tradition." In *Speaking the Christian God: The Holy Trinity and the Challenges of Feminism.* Edited by Alvin F. Kimel, Jr., 157. Leominster/Grand Rapids: Gracewing/Wm. B. Eerdmans, 1992.

Huntington, Samuel P. *The Clash of Civilizations: Remaking of World Order.* New York: Touchstone, 1997.

Jaeger, Luc. "A Biochemical Perspective on the Origin of Life and Death." In *The Role of Death in Life.* Edited by John Behr and Conor Cunningham, 28. Eugene, OR: Wipf and Stock Publisher, 2015.

Jenkins, Philip. *The Next Christendom: The Coming of Global Christianity.* Oxford: Oxford University Press, 2002.

Jensen, Lionel M. *Manufacturing Confucianism: Chinese Traditions and Universal Civilization.* Durham, NC: Duke University Press, 1998.

Jobin, Anna, Marcello Ienca, and Effy Vayena. "The Global Landscape of AI Ethics Guidelines." Nature Machine Intelligence 1, no. 9 (2019): 389-399.

https://doi.org/10.1038/s42256-019-0088-2.

Johnson, Elizabeth. "Losing and Founding Creation in the Christian Tradition." In *Christianity and Ecology: Seeking the Well-Being of Earth and Humans*. Edited by Dieter T. Hessel and Rosemary Radford Ruether. Cambridge, MA: Harvard University Press, 2000.

Jung Young Lee. *The Theology of Change: A Christian Concept of God in an Eastern Perspective*. Maryknoll, NY: Orbis Books, 1979.

Jung, C. G. "Foreword." In *The I Ching or Book of Changes*. Translated by Richard Wilhelm, 3rd ed. Princeton, NJ: Princeton University Press, 1967.

Kairouz, Peter, H. Brendan McMahan, Brendan Avent, et al. "Advances and Open Problems in Federated Learning." *arXiv*, 2021. https://arxiv.org/abs/1912. 04977.

Kalton, Michael C. Translated, edited, and with commentaries. *To Become a Sage: The Ten Diagrams on Sage Learning by Yi T'oegye*. New York: Columbia University Press, 1988.

_____. "Asian Religious Tradition and Natural Science: Potentials, Present and Future." Unpublished paper, the CTNS Korea Religion & Science Workshop, Seoul, January 18-22, 2002.

Kauffman, Stuart A. *Reinventing the Sacred: A New View of Science, Reason, and Religion*. New York: Basic Books, 2008.

Kaufman, Gordon. "Response to Elizabeth A. Johnson." In *Christianity and Ecology: Seeking the Well-Being of Earth and Humans*. Edited by Dieter T. Hessel and Rosemary Radford Ruether. Cambridge, MA: Harvard University Press, 2000.

Keirsey, David M. "Toward the Physics of 'Death.'" In *Unifying Themes in Complex Systems*. Edited by Yaneer Bar-Yam. Cambridge: Perseus Books, 2000.

Kim, Chi Ha. *Saengmyŏng [Life]*. Seoul: Sol, 1992.

Kim, Heup Young. *Wang Yang-ming and Karl Barth: A Confucian-Christian Dialogue.* Lanham, MD: University Press of America, 1996.

_____. *Christ and the Tao.* Hong Kong: Christian Conference of Asia, 2003.

_____. *A Theology of Dao.* Maryknoll, NY: Orbis Books, 2017.

_____. "AlphaGo's Victory over Korean Go-master Showcases Western vs. Neo-Confucian Values." *Sightings* (University of Chicago Divinity School Martin Marty Center), June 23, 2016. https://divinity.uchicago.edu/sightings/alphagos-victory-over-korean-go-master-showcases-western-vs-neo-confucian-values.

_____. "Cyborg, Sage, and Saint: Transhumanism as Seen from an East Asian Theological Setting." In *Religion and Transhumanism: The Unknown Future of Human Enhancement.* Edited by Calvin Mercer and Tracy J. Trothen. Santa Barbara, CA: Praeger, 2015.

_____. "The Tao in Confucianism and Taoism: The Trinity in East Asian Perspective." In *The Cambridge Companion to the Trinity.* Edited by Peter Phan. Cambridge: Cambridge University Press, 2011.

_____. "Perfecting Humanity in Confucianism and Transhumanism." In *Religious Transhumanism and Its Critics.* Edited by Arvin Gouw, Brian Patrick Green, and Ted Peters. Lanham, MD: Lexington Books, 2022.

Kim, Heung-ho. *Jesori.* Seoul: Pungman, 1985.

_____. "Ryu Yŏngmo's View of Christianity from the Asian Perspective." In *Dasŏk Ryu Yŏngmo.* Edited by Park Young-ho. Seoul: The Sungchun Institution, 1994.

Kim Yong-Bock, ed. *Minjung Theology: People as the Subjects of History.* Singapore: Commission on Theological Concern, Christian Conference of Asia, 1981.

_____. "Theology and the Social Biography of Minjung." *CTC Bulletin* 5, no. 3-6, no. 1 (1984~1985): 66-78.

Kirkwood, Thomas B. L., and Steven N. Austad. "Why Do We Age?" *Nature* 408 (2000): 233-238.

Ko Kyŏngmin. *Yŏngsaeng-hanŭn Kil [The Way for Immortality]*. Seoul: Chongno Ch'ulp'ansa, 1974.

_____. *Kuksŏndo*. 3 vols. Seoul: Kuksŏndo Publications, 1993.

Koch, Christof. "How the Computer Beat the Go Master." *Scientific American*, March 19, 2016. http://www.scientificamerican.com/article/how-the-computer-beat-the-go-master.

Kurzweil, Ray. *The Singularity Is Near: When Humans Transcend Biology*. New York: Viking Press, 2005.

Küng, Hans, and Julia Ching. *Christianity and Chinese Religions*. Translated by Peter Beyer. New York: Doubleday, 1989.

Küng, Hans. *Justification: The Doctrine of Karl Barth and a Catholic Reflection*. Louisville, KY: Westminster John Knox Press, 2004.

Lao Tzu. *Tao Te Ching*. Translated by D. C. Lau. Harmondsworth, UK: Penguin Books, 1963.

Latour, Bruno. *We Have Never Been Modern*. Cambridge, MA: Harvard University Press, 1993.

Lau, D. C. *Confucius: The Analects*. Harmondsworth, UK: Penguin Books, 1979.

Lee, Jung Young. *The Theology of Change: A Christian Concept of God in an Eastern Perspective*. Maryknoll, NY: Orbis Books, 1979.

_____. *The Trinity in Asian Perspective*. Nashville, TN: Abingdon Press, 1996.

Leopold, Aldo. *A Sand County Almanac*. New York: Oxford University Press, 1949.

Lewis, C. S. *The Abolition of Man: Or, Reflections on Education with Special Reference to the Teaching of English in the Upper Forms of Schools*. New York: Macmillan, 1947.

Liu, Shu-hsien, and Robert E. Allinson. *Harmony and Strife: Contemporary*

*Perspectives, East & West*. Hong Kong: The Chinese University Press, 1988.

Lo Ch'in-shun. *Knowledge Painfully Acquired. Translated by Irene Bloom*. New York: Columbia University Press, 1987.

Lochheed, David. *The Dialogical Imperative: A Christian Reflection on Interfaith Encounter*. Maryknoll, NY: Orbis Books, 1988.

_____. *Nonduality: A Study in Comparative Philosophy*. New Haven: Yale University Press, 1988.

Marconi, Simone. "How AI Is Transforming Environmental Conservation Efforts." *World Economic Forum*, 2021. https://www.weforum.org/agenda/2021/06/ai-environmental-conservation-biodiversity-climate.

Mercer, Calvin. "Whole Brain Emulation Requires Enhanced Theology, and a 'Handmaiden.'" *Theology and Science* 13, no. 2 (April 2015): 175-186.

Microsoft AI for Earth. "AI for Earth: Empowering People and Organizations to Solve Global Environmental Challenges." *Microsoft*, 2020. https://www.microsoft. com/en-us/ai/ai-for-earth.

Midgley, Mary. *Science as Salvation: A Modern Myth and Its Meaning*. London: Routledge, 1992.

Moltmann, Jürgen. *God in Creation*. Translated by M. Kohl. London: SCM Press, 1985.

_____. *The Way of Jesus Christ: Christology in Messianic Dimensions*. Translated by Margaret Kohl. San Francisco: HarperSanFrancisco, 1990.

_____. *Science and Wisdom*. Translated by M. Kohl. London: SCM, 2003.

Moore-Keish, Martha L., and Christian T. Collins Winn, eds. *Karl Barth and Comparative Theology*. New York: Fordham University Press, 2019.

Neville, Robert Cummings. *Boston Confucianism: Portable Tradition in the Late-Modern World*. Albany: State University of New York Press, 2000.

Niebuhr, H. Richard. *The Meaning of Revelation*. New York: Macmillan, 1962.

North American AI Research Group of the Dicastery for Culture and Education of the Holy See. *Encountering Artificial Intelligence: Ethical and Anthropological Investigations*. Pickwick Publications, 2024.

Nouwen, Henri J. M. *Reaching Out: The Three Movements of the Spiritual Life*. New York: Image Books, 1975.

O Chŏng-suk. *Dasŏk Yu Yŏng-mo-ŭi Hankukchŏk Kitokkyo [Korean Christianity According to Dasŏk Yu Yŏng-mo]*. Seoul: Misŭba, 2005.

Pak Chae-sun. *Dasŏk Yŏng-mo: Tongsŏ-sasang-ŭl aurŭn ch'angjojŏk saengmyŏng ch'ŏrhakcha [The Creative Philosopher of Life Who Integrated Eastern and Western Thoughts]*. Seoul: Hyŏnamsa, 2008.

Panikkar, Raymundo. *The Intrareligious Dialogue*. New York: Paulist Press, 1978.

_____. *The Cosmotheandric Experience: Emerging Religious Consciousness*. Maryknoll, NY: Orbis Books, 1993.

Paper, Jordan. *Chinese Religion and Familialism: The Basis of Chinese Culture, Society, and Government*. New York, NY: Bloomsbury, 2019.

Park, Yŏng-ho, ed. *Dasŏk-ŏrok: Ssial-ŭi-maeari [Analects of Dasŏk: Echoes of Seeds]*. Seoul: Hongikje, 1993.

_____. *Dasŏk Yu Yŏng-mo-ŭi Myŏngsanglok [Meditations of Dasŏk Yu Yŏng-mo]*. Seoul: Ture, 2000.

_____. *Dasŏk Yu Yŏng-mo Ŏlok [Analects of Dasŏk Yu Yŏng-mo]*. Seoul: Ture, 2002.

_____. *Dasŏk Machimak Kangŭi [Last Lectures of Dasŏk]*. Seoul: Gyoyangin, 2010.

Plumwood, Val. *Feminism and the Mastery of Nature*. London: Routledge, 1993.

Pohl, Christine D. *Making Room: Recovering Hospitality as a Christian Tradition*. Grand Rapids, MI: Wm. B. Eerdmans Publishing Co., 1999.

Pontifical Academy for Life. *Rome Call for AI Ethics*. Vatican City: Libreria Editrice

Vaticana, 2020.

Pope Francis. *Laudato si': On the Care for Our Common Home*. Vatican Press, 2015. Available at: http://www.vatican.va/content/francesco/en/en-cyclicals/do cuments/papa-francesco_20150524_enciclica-laudato-si.html.

Pyŏn, Ch'an-lin. *The Principles of the Bible*. 3 vols. Seoul, Korea: Han'guk Shinhak Yŏn'guso, 2019.

Ramchurn, Sarvapali D., Perukrishnen Vytelingum, Alex Rogers, and Nicholas R. Jennings. "Agent-Based Control for Decentralized Demand Side Management in the Smart Grid." In *Proceedings of the 18th International Conference on Autonomous Agents and Multiagent Systems*, 5-9, 2019. https://doi.org/10.5555/2600428.2600435.

Rasmussen, Steen, et al. "Transitions from Nonliving to Living Matter." *Science* 3 (2004): 963-965.

Ri, Jean Sang. *Confucius et Jésus Christ: La Première Théologie Chrétienne en Corée d'Après l'Oeuvre de Yi Piek Lettre Confucéen 1754-1786*. Paris: Éditions Beauchesne, 1979.

Richardson, W. Mark, and Wesley J. Wildman. "General Introduction." In *Religion and Science: History, Method, Dialogue*. New York and London: Routledge, 1996.

Ricoeur, Paul. *On Translation*. Translated by Eileen Brennan. New York, NY: Routledge, 2006.

Rodier, Francis, and Judith Campisi. "Four Faces of Cellular Senescence." *Journal of Cell Biology* 192 (2011): 547-556.

Ross, Casey, and Ike Swetlitz. "IBM's Watson Recommended 'Unsafe and Incorrect' Cancer Treatments Internal Documents Show." *STAT News*, 2017. https://www.statnews.com/2018/07/25/ibm-watson-recommended-unsafe-incorrect-treatments/.

Russell, Robert J. *40 Years in Science and Religion: Ian G. Barbour and His*

*Legacy.* Ashgate, 2004.

Ryu, Tong-sik. *The Veins of Korean Theologies: An Introduction to the History of Korean Theological Thought.* Seoul, Korea: Chŏnmangsa, 1982.

Ryu Yŏngmo. *Dasŏk-ilji [The Diaries of Dasŏk],* 4 vols. Seoul: Hongikje, 1990.

_____. *Dasŏk-ŏrok [The Analects of Dasŏk]: Ssial-ŭi-maeari.* Edited by Park Young-ho. Seoul: Hongikje, 1993.

_____. *Chesori: Dasŏk Ryuyŏngmo Kangŭirok [Lecture Book of Dasŏk Yŏng-mo].* Edited by Kim Hŭng-ho. Seoul: Sol Ch'ulp'ansa, 2001.

_____. *Dasŏk-kangŭi [Lectures of Dasŏk].* Edited by the Society for Dasŏk Studies. Seoul: Hyŏnamsa, 2006.

Said, Edward W. *Orientalism.* New York: Vintage Books, 1979.

Sandberg, Anders, and Nick Bostrom. *Whole Brain Emulation: A Road Map.* Oxford: Oxford University, 2008. http://www.fhi.ox.ac.uk/wp-content/uploads/ brain-emulation-roadmap-report1.pdf.

Sandel, Michael. *The Case Against Perfection: Ethics in the Age of Genetic Engineering.* Cambridge, MA: Harvard University Press, 2007.

Schultz, Michael B., and David A. Sinclair. "When Stem Cells Grow Old: Phenotypes and Mechanisms of Stem Cell Aging." *Development* 143 (2016): 3-14.

Shim, Il-sŏp. *Han'guk Toch'ak'wa Shinhak Hyŏngsŏngsa Non'gu [A Study on the Formation History of Korean Theology of Indigenisation].* Seoul: Kuk'akcharyowŏn, 1995.

Shukla, S. "Meet ElliQ: The Robot Companion for the Elderly." *TechRadar,* 2021. https://www.techradar.com/news/meet-elliq-the-robot-companion-for- the-elderly.

Singer, Wolf. "Understanding the Brain." *EMBO Reports* 8 (2007): 516-519.

Slingerland, Edward. *Effortless Action: Wu-wei as Conceptual Metaphor and Spiritual Ideal in Early China.* Oxford: Oxford University Press, 2007.

Southgate, Christopher, et al. *God, Humanity and the Cosmos*. Edinburgh: T
&  T Clark, 1999.

Suh, Nam-dong. *Minjung Theology: People as the Subjects of History*. Hong
Kong: Christian Conference of Asia, 1981.

_____. "Towards a Theology of Han." In *Minjung Theology: People as the
Subjects of History, edited by the Christian Conference of Asia
Commission on Theological Concerns*. Maryknoll, NY: Orbis Books,
1981.

Sunquist, Scott W., ed. *A Dictionary of Asian Christianity*. Grand Rapids, MI:
William B. Eerdmans Publishing Co., 2001.

Swimme, Brian, and Thomas Berry. *The Universe Story: From the Primordial
Flaring Forth to the Ecozoic Era A Celebration of the Unfolding of
Cosmos*. New York: HarperCollins Publishers, 1992.

Taddeo, Mariarosaria, and Luciano Floridi. "Regulate Artificial Intelligence to
Avert Cyber Arms Race." *Nature* 556, no. 7701 (2018): 296-298.
https://doi.org/ 10.1038/d41586-018-04602-6.

Thiagarajah, Daniel S., and A. Wati Longchar, eds. *Visioning New Life Together
among Asian Resources: The Third Congress of Asian Theologians*.
Hong Kong: CCA, 2002.

Thomas, M. M. *Risking Christ for Christ's Sake: Towards an Ecumenical
Theology of Pluralism*. Geneva: WCC Publications, 1987.

Tillich, Paul. *The Protestant Era*. Translated by James Luther Adams. Chicago:
The University of Chicago Press, 1948.

_____. *Systematic Theology*, Vol. 1. Chicago: The University of Chicago Press,
1973.

Torrance, T. F. *Calvin's Doctrine of Man*. London: Lutterworth Press, 1949.

Tracy, David. *Blessed Rage for Order: The New Pluralism in Theology*.
Minneapolis: The Seabury Press, 1975.

Trindade, Lucas S., et al. "A Novel Classification System for Evolutionary Aging Theories." *Frontiers in Genetics* 4 (2013): 1-8.

Tu Wei-ming. *Centrality and Commonality: An Essay on Confucian Religiousness*. Albany, NY: State University of New York Press, 1989.

_____. "The Continuity of Being: Chinese Visions of Nature." In *Nature in Asian Traditions of Thought: Essays in Environmental Philosophy*. Edited by J. Baird Callicott and Roger T. Ames. Albany: State University of New York Press, 1989.

_____. *Confucianism in a Historical Perspective*. Singapore: The Institute of East Asian Philosophies, 1989.

_____. *Humanity and Self-Cultivation: Essays in Confucian Thought*. Berkeley, CA: Asian Humanities Press, 1979.

_____. *Confucian Thought: Selfhood as Creative Transformation*. SUNY Press, 1979.

_____. "Beyond the Enlightenment Mentality." In *Confucianism and Ecology: The Interrelation of Heaven, Earth, and Humans, edited by Mary Evelyn Tucker and John Berthrong*, 4. Cambridge, MA: Harvard University Press, 1998.

_____. "A Confucian Perspective on Human Rights." In *The East Asian Challenge for Human Rights*. Edited by Joanne R. Bauer and Daniel A. Bell. Cambridge: Cambridge University Press, 1999.

Tucker, Mary Evelyn. "The Philosophy as an Ecological Cosmology." In *Confucianism and Ecology: The Interrelation of Heaven, Earth, and Humans*. Edited by Mary Evelyn Tucker and John Berthrong. Cambridge, MA: Harvard University Press, 1998.

Tucker, Mary Evelyn, and John Grim, eds. *Worldviews and Ecology: Religion, Philosophy, and the Environment*. Maryknoll, NY: Orbis Books, 1994.

_____. "Series Foreword." In *Christianity and Ecology: Seeking the Well-Being of Earth and Humans*. Edited by Dieter T. Hessel and Rosemary R. Ruether. Cambridge, MA: Harvard University Press, 2000.

Turkle, Sherry. *Alone Together: Why We Expect More from Technology and Less from Each Other*. New York: Basic Books, 2011.

Vaidyam, Anmol N., Hannah Wisniewski, John D. Halamka, et al. "Chatbots and Conversational Agents in Mental Health: A Review of the Psychiatric Landscape." *Canadian Journal of Psychiatry* 64, no. 6 (2019): 376-384. https://doi.org/10.1177/0706743718821012.

Van Norden, Bryan W. "Ren and Li in the Analects." *Philosophy East and West* 45, no. 3 (1995): 313-339.

Vanier, Jean. *An Ark for the Poor: The Story of L'Arche*. New York: Crossroad, 1995.

Vincent, James. "DeepMind's AI Can Spot Eye Disease as Well as the World's Top Doctors." *The Verge*, 2018. https://www.theverge.com/2018/8/13/17 683412/deepmind-ai-eye-disease-identification-deep-learning-london.

Volf, Miroslav. *Exclusion and Embrace: A Theological Exploration of Identity, Otherness, and Reconciliation*. Nashville: Abingdon Press, 1996.

Vada, Kazuyoshi, and Takanori Shibata. "Living with Seal Robots  Its Sociopsychological and Physiological Influences on the Elderly at a Care House." *IEEE Transactions on Robotics* 23, no. 5 (2007): 972-980. https://doi.org/10. 1109/TRO.2007.906261.

Wang, Robin R. *Yinyang: The Way of Heaven and Earth in Chinese Thought and Culture*. Cambridge: Cambridge University Press, 2012.

Waters, Brent. "Flesh Made Data: The Posthuman Project in Light of the Incarnation." In *Religion and Transhumanism: The Unknown Future of Human Enhancement*. Edited by Calvin Mercer and Tracy J. Trothen. Santa Barbara, CA: Praeger, 2015.

Watson, Burton, trans. *The Complete Works of Chuang Tzu*. New York &

London: Columbia University Press, 1968.

Weisbuch, Gerard. "The Complex Adaptive Systems Approach to Biology." *Evolution and Cognition* 5 (1999): 1-11.

Wesley, John. *Works of John Wesley.* Vol. 10: *Letters, Essays, Dialogue, Addresses.* Grand Rapids, MI: Baker House, 1978.

White, Lynn, Jr. "The Historical Roots of Our Ecological Crisis." *Science* 155 (1967): 1203-1207.

Whitehead, Alfred N. *Science and the Modern World.* New York: Macmillan, 1967.

Whitney, Lawrence. "Confucianism and Tillich's Protestant Principle." Paper presented at the American Academy of Religion, November 22, 2019, San Diego.

Wilfred Cantwell Smith. *The Faith of Other Men.* New York: New American Library, 1963.

Wilhelm, Hellmut. *Heaven, Earth, and Man in the Book of Changes.* Seattle: University of Washington Press, 1977.

Wilhelm, Richard. *The I Ching or Book of Changes.* Translated by Cary F. Baynes. 3rd ed. Princeton, NJ: Princeton University Press, 1967.

Wing-tsit Chan, trans. *A Source Book in Chinese Philosophy.* Princeton, NJ: Princeton University Press, 1963.

Winner, Langdon. *Autonomous Technology: Technics-out-of-Control as a Theme in Political Thought.* Cambridge, MA: MIT Press, 1977.

Yi Chŏng-pae. *Yu Yŏngmo-ŭi Kwiil-shinhak [Yu Yŏng-mo's Theology of Returning to the Oneness].* Seoul: Miralbuksŭ, 2020.

Yi Ki-sang. "Holiness and Spirituality: How to Communicate with God in the Age of Globalisation." In *Word and Spirit: Renewing Christology and Pneumatology.* Edited by Anselm K. Min and Christoph Schwöbel, 85-112. Berlin: Walter de Gruyter, 2014.

Youn Jeong-Hyun. "The Non-Existent Existing God: An East Asian Perspective with Specific Reference to the Thought of Ryu Yŏngmo." Th.D. dissertation, University of Birmingham, Birmingham, United Kingdom, 2002.

Young, Simon. *Designer Evolution: A Transhumanist Manifesto*. Amherst, NY: Prometheus Books, 2006.

Yu Tong-sik. *Han'guk Shinhag ŭi Kwangmaek: Han'guk Shinhak Sasangsa Sŏsŏl*. Seoul: Chŏnmangsa, 1982.

Zhu, Xi. *Reflections on Things at Hand: The Neo-Confucian Anthology*. New York: Columbia University Press, 1990.

# Index

# Dates and Places of Original Publications

## Part One: Ecodao in an Age of Ecological Crisis

1. Theodao: Integrating Ecological Consciousness in Daoism, Confucianism, and Christian Theology

   (2017) *In The Wiley Blackwell Companion to Religion and Ecology.* ed. John Hart. Oxford: Wiley Blackwell, 104-14.

2. Ecodao: An Ecological Theology of Dao

   (2018) In *The Bloomsbury Handbook of Religion and Nature: The Elements.* eds. Laura Hobgood and Whitney Bauman. London: Bloomsbury Academic, 99-108.

3. Creation and Dao: A Theodaoian Perspective

   (2024) In *T&T Clark Handbook to the Doctrine of Creation.* ed. Jason Goroncy. London: T&T Clark, 694-706.

## Part 2: Technodao in an Age of Transhumanism and Artificial Intelligence

4. Death and Immortality: Biological and East Asian Religious Reflections on Transhumanism

   (2017) *Madang: Journal of Contextual Theology*, Vol. 28, 3-29.

5. Advancing Humanity: Artificial Intelligence, Transhumanism, and Confucianism

   (2024) In *New Confucian Horizons: Essays in Honor of Tu Weiming.* eds. Young-chan Ro, Jonathan Keir, and Peter C. Phan. Lanham: Lexington Books, 231-50.

and His Poem 'Being a Christian'

(2021) Interreligious Relations, *Occasional Papers of The Studies in Inter-Religious Relations in Plural Societies Programme* 25 (July/Aug), 1-11.

12. Dasŏk Ryu Yŏngmo's Korean Trans-Cosmic and Trans-Religious Spirituality: A Translation and Commentary on 'Spiritual Hiking'

(2021) Interreligious Relations, *Occasional Papers of The Studies in Inter-Religious Relations in Plural Societies Programme* 26 (Spet/Oct), 1-11.

13. Reviving Minjung Theology in the Technological Era: Kim Yong-bok's Seontopian Zoesophia in Dialogue with Theodao

(2023) *Madang: Journal of Contextual Theology.* Vol. 39, 139-63.

## Appendix: Theodao in Critical Making — Retrieved

A1. The Sciences and the Religions: Some Preliminary East Asian Reflections on Christian Theology of Nature

(2006) In *God's Action in Nature's World: Essays in Honor of Robert John Russell.* eds. Ted Peters and Nathan Hallanger. Hampshire: Ashgate, 77-90.

A2. Embracing and Embodying God's Hospitality Today in Asia

(2012) *C. T. C. Bulletin.* Vol. 28, No. 1, 1-13.

A3. Paul Tillich, Boston Confucianism, Theology of Religions: A Short Reflection from the Perspective of Theodao

(2020) *North American Paul Tillich Society Bulletin.* Vol. 36, Nos. 3-4, 13-16.